Directions in Cognitive Anthropology

Directions in Cognitive Anthropology

Edited by Janet W. D. Dougherty

University of Illinois Press
Urbana and Chicago

Manufactured in the United States of America
1 2 3 4 5 C P 5 4 3 2 1

This book is printed on acid-free paper.

Library of Congress Cataloging in Publication Data

Main entry under title:

Directions in cognitive anthropology.

Bibliography: p.
Includes index.
1. Ethnopsychology — Addresses, essays, lectures.
2. Cognition and culture — Addresses, essays, lectures.
I. Dougherty, Janet W. D.
GN502.D57 1985 306 84-2494
ISBN 0-252-01133-3 (cloth; alk. paper)
ISBN 0-252-01194-5 (paper; alk. paper)

For Frank, Marion, Ruthe, and Mark

Acknowledgments

This volume has been designed to provide scholars and students with a collection of current research by cognitive anthropologists reflecting the contemporary breadth and underlying unity of the field. As editor, I have put current research in historical perspective and organized the studies within a framework that integrates common goals of the authors' diverse approaches. I would like to thank all the contributors to this volume: their enthusiasm for a collection of current research made the editorial work a pleasure, and their intellectual contributions made the organizational work a worthwhile challenge.

Studies in cognitive anthropology frequently entail detailed analyses of extensive bodies of data. It was the authors' hope in such cases that representative samples of this material be included with their interpretations. The current economics of publishing, however, work against this. Much of the data originally included with the articles have been omitted in the interests of brevity and, eventually, accessibility of the volume.

I would like to thank the University of Illinois Research Board for support of the research on the strategical organization of knowledge published herein as "Taskonomy: A Practical Approach to Knowledge Structures." It was also during the period of the board's support for this project that the organizational framework for *Directions in Cognitive Anthropology* emerged. I also wish to express my thanks to the staff of the Department of Anthropology for assistance in typing, and to Dave Minor and Gary Apfelstadt for preparation of figures and tabular material. I am grateful to William Belzner, Edward Bruner, Joseph Casagrande, Clark Cunningham, Norman Denzin, John Gatewood, Dan Hunt, Charles Keller, Willett Kempton, F. K. Lehman, Jim Stanlaw, Niel Weathers, and Norman Whitten for their comments on the introductory material. None of them, of course, is responsible for its final form. And to Paul Kay and O. Brent Berlin, who have been a source of inspiration, go my special thanks.

Contents

Directions in Cognitive Anthropology

Introduction

Janet W. D. Dougherty

This volume presents current research directions and underlying premises in the anthropological study of cognition. In 1957 Goodenough suggested that culture be cognitively defined as ". . . whatever it is one has to know or believe in order to operate in a manner acceptable to its members . . ." (1957:167). This definition of culture formed a basis for the new subfield, and the new conception directed anthropologists to investigate the unity underlying diverse phenomena traditionally subsumed under concepts of culture. Tylor, for example, characterized culture in 1871 as "that complex whole which includes knowledge, belief, art, law, morals, custom, and any other capabilities and habits acquired by man as a member of society" (1871:1). And in 1930 Boas included an even broader range of phenomena within culture: ". . . all the manifestations of social habits of a community, the reactions of the individual as affected by the habits of the group in which he lives, and the products of human activities as determined by these habits" (1930:79).

At the outset, then, cognitive anthropologists aimed to explicate underlying systems of knowledge that would account for culture defined as broadly as Tylor and Boas define it above. Some of the early assumptions of cognitive anthropology continue to be basic to the tradition and underlie the diverse perspectives published here. They are: (1) Culture is defined in terms of mental phenomena that must be taken into account in understanding human behavior. (2) These mental phenomena are complexly rational and amenable to rigorous methods of study that lead to replicable results. (3) Culture is learned and represented individually. (4) Culture is shared by individuals. (5) Culture is a symbolic system with clear parallels to language.[1]

This emphasis on cognition—mental phenomena that cannot be directly observed—was associated with a methodology designed to provide explanatory accounts of human behavior. The methods emphasized formal procedures of elicitation (Frake 1962, 1964a; Conklin 1962; Black 1963; Agar 1980a), discovery procedures designed to reveal the cultural core conceived of as abstract systems of conceptual order.[2] In line with a precedent established in the work of A. L. Kroeber (1952), adequate theory was to be built from a consideration of the accumulated findings of descriptive analyses of real systems (Goodenough 1956). The positivistic faith in empirical discovery procedures, characteristic of much social science of this era, molded the developing perspective of cognitive anthropology.

Formal methods in combination with a conception of culture as learned phenomena, both individual and shared, entailed an initial mandate for cognitive anthropologists working in the late 1950s and early 1960s to construct cognitive models of culture or cultural segments. These models were to be inferrable from observations of behavior and material artifacts. These conceptual models were to be constructed as falsifiable hypotheses evaluated on the basis of their predictive success[3] and their formal elegance (Goodenough 1957, Lounsbury 1956:171, Hammel 1965:1-8).

Of all the behaviors an anthropologist might observe, language was held to provide the most direct access to cognitive phenomena with respect to both content and form. First, language was held to encode conceptual categories and world view (see Whorf 1956). People name and talk about what is important to them, thus indicating through their speech the specific directions anthropological research should follow. The issue of a linguistic hold on conceptual thought, raised by Sapir and Whorf, became pivotal. In the substantive analysis of culture as cognition a balance was sought between the contributions of an arbitrary linguistic order and that of induction from universally constrained human experience (Spradley 1972:9-18, Goodenough 1981, Berlin and Kay 1969, Berlin 1972, Berlin, Breedlove, and Raven 1973, Hammel 1965:3).

Second, with regard to form, the patterns of cognitive structure were to be elucidated on analogy with the formal structure of language. Elements from the traditions of structural linguistics and transformational grammar were combined and eventually cohere in the classical perspective of cognitive anthropology (Chomsky 1957, 1965; Jakobson and Halle 1956; Sapir 1949; Bloomfield 1933; Pike 1943, 1964). Linguistics provided at least seven principles that influenced the early anthropological studies of cognition. They include:

(1) The principle that particular, emic, systems can be derived from

universal inventories of distinctive, etic, features, a principle Kroeber had articulated with respect to the analysis of kinship (Lounsbury 1956:168). Such a structure is characteristic of phonology. The human vocal apparatus can be universally characterized in terms of etic features of articulation that are selectively utilized and differentially combined to form the speech sounds, emic systems, specific to individual languages.

(2) The principle that a finite set of basic units can be combined to produce an infinite set of derived units. This is evident in the structure of phonology, where a limited number of sound units combine to produce a vast and theoretically infinite set of words, and in transformational grammar, where a finite set of rules is posited to account for an infinite set of utterances.

(3) The assumption that a principled account of a theoretically infinite set of types of behavior can be inferred on the basis of a partial sample of those behaviors. This is an insight of transformational grammar: that the production of infinitely many appropriate utterances by members of a given speech community can be generated by a finite system of rules and basic categories inferrable from samples of that speech behavior itself. That this is possible, Chomsky (1975) suggested, is a consequence of innate constraints on learning that limit the possible structures of knowing.

(4) The idealized speaker-hearer as an analytical construct. This is an individual constructed for purposes of analysis who is the idealized representative of an ideally homogeneous speech community, competent in the conventions and rules of his language (Chomsky 1972:28, 116) and free from errors in performance.

(5) Procedures for systematic elicitation (Bloomfield 1933, Sapir 1949, Frake 1964).

(6) The principle of complementary distribution. That is, a single unit of behavior may take alternate forms in contrasting contexts.

(7) The principle of analogy as the basis for creativity (Bloomfield 1933, Goodenough 1963:148).

These seven contributions from linguistics provided initial specifications for the modeling of cognitive phenomena. Such models, whatever else they might be, should minimally include basic categories and their fundamental interrelations as abstract structural representations of cultural knowledge, with, where appropriate, rules that operate on these basic categories to generate the contextually appropriate ranges of behavior. It was assumed that universal features of mind and human experience delimit the class of possible structures for cognitive representation. Cognitive anthropologists held that cultural knowledge was inferred directly from experience, that basic categories were built out of perceived similarities in percepts and categorically distinguished from one another on the basis of relatively few criteria or distinctive features (Spradley 1972:9-18, Goodenough 1981:63-68).[4] The combination of basic categories, their fundamental interrelations, and the rules for their use and interpretation largely constitute this conception of culture. Such structures should be discoverable by the careful anthropologist, whose task, like that of every member of a society, is to learn the culture.

The picture of the individual implicit in this perspective is as the learner of culture. If we can differentiate culture (an individual's knowledge) from Culture (an overall system abstracted from individual versions of culture pertaining to all activities within a society),[5] then a given individual learns and represents to himself during his lifetime some aspects of Culture. The older, the wiser, and the more experienced an individual is with the activities of a society, the more likely he or she is to approximate an idealized, omniscient member of that society. It is from working with such individuals that complete Cultural systems as Chomskian idealizations can be constructed (see Boster this volume). It is such individuals who play the cultural analogue of the ideal speaker-hearer.

The individual and Cultural systems so conceived are mutually dependent. The individual through experience and interaction comes to order the world conceptually, that is, to develop a representation of Culture. Simultaneously the individual comes to behave in a manner that is governed by this representation of the Cultural order.

From the perspective of classical cognitive anthropology as just outlined, research developed in several traditions: componential analysis and ethnographic semantics (Goodenough 1956, Lounsbury 1956, Frake 1964b, Hage 1972, the collected works edited by Hammel 1965 and Tyler 1969), culture grammar and cognitive mapping (Colby 1973, 1975; Agar 1974, 1980b; D'Andrade 1976; Goodenough 1969; Wallace 1965; Rice 1980; Gladwin 1970), decision making (Geoghegan 1969, 1970, 1971; Quinn 1975, 1978; Fjellman 1976; Keesing 1967; Monberg 1970; Gladwin 1971, 1975), ethnoscience (Berlin and Kay 1969, Berlin, Breedlove, and Raven 1973, Hunn 1976, Brown 1977, Bulmer 1967, Conklin 1955), multidimensional scaling (D'Andrade et al. 1972; White 1978, 1980), and semantic modeling (Kay and McDaniel 1978, Rosch et al. 1976, Rosch and Mervis 1975, Kempton 1978).[6]

This research has established a foundation for the current directions collected here. Firmly committed to the basic premises of cognitive anthropology, yet aware of limitations in the conceptions of both culture and the individual associated with the classical tradition, research is currently developing a clearer understanding of the cognitive bases of cultural knowledge.[7]

What is necessary in this new orientation is a concept of what is learned (Chomsky 1972:72), an enriched notion of cultural competence and cognitive representation that entails an account of how learning takes place. This focus on learning and cognitive representation must initially emphasize the individual. From this individual focus the cognitive anthropologist then builds an account of Cultural systems. This should develop largely by providing adequate accounts of universal constraints on cognitive processes, of the phenonema of variation, sharing, and consensus, and of the principles for patterning behavior, for creativity, and for emergent qualities of both cognitive structure and interaction.

These goals build upon the classical tradition of cognitive anthropology but, with the benefits of hindsight, allow current research to take new directions. Fundamental premises of early cognitive anthropology are being reconsidered for the following reasons. First, the analogy of the ideal speaker-hearer is inappropriate to cultural analysis. Linguistic performance (for the monolingual) is governed consistently by an integrated grammatical system. As a result the postulation of an individual perfectly competent to produce and interpret the grammatical constructions of his language may be a useful analytical device. Cultural knowledge is less neatly integrated (Geertz 1973a), for both the individual and the Cultural system. There does not appear to be one general set of rules that provides the structural (let alone semantic or symbolic) possibilities for behavior relevant to all activities of a society. Nor is there any reason to assume that the individual's representation of culture is a coherent system. At best, it may be useful to speak of an omniscient informant with respect to a given aspect of Culture (see Boster this volume). Yet even this requires caution as our concepts of culture and the individual are increasingly elaborated.

Second, taken alone, formal systems of interrelated categories and associated rules have failed to provide an adequate account of the principles governing behavior. We need now a breadth that goes beyond linguistically based abstractions as we begin to approach a more holistic understanding of cultural knowledge. To this end research is focusing more often on contextualized behavior and interpretation or on the integration of cognitive systems and human experience. The notion of a cultural grammar is giving way to contextualized organizations of knowledge. Language is still key in the study of cognition, but the models for representation are diverse. Prototypes of performance or interaction, images of desired or undesired conditions, metaphors, key events remembered, fictional exemplars, pet theories, aphorisms, proverbs, schemata, scripts, and favored strategies provide a wider scope for the representation of culture than did the classical formal models (Quinn this volume, Dougherty and Fernandez 1982). The prior emphasis on reference is giving way to a more inclusive approach that integrates form and function, denotation and connotation in a richer exploration of symbol and meaning. The contextualized representations now being explored by cognitive anthropologists crucially presuppose basic categories, their definitions and associated rules, but at the same time go beyond these abstractions in accounting for social interaction and understanding.

Third, the restriction of the study of meaning to structural analyses by extension from principles of phonological analysis is inadequate to account for the construction and use of systems of knowledge. Fourth, systematic procedures of frame elicitation reveal only a limited range of meaningful features and conceptual relations. Analyses must explore with more sensitivity the conceptual bases of culture. And finally, analogy has failed to provide a general account of processes of change in cultural knowledge or Cultural systems. One of the major insights of the Chomskian revolution in linguistics was the generative principle, which followed from the inadequacy of analogy to account for the systematic acquisition or creative use of language. Cognitive anthropologists are now reckoning with the parallel failure of analogy alone to adequately account for the acquisition or creative use of cultural knowledge.

The picture of the individual emerging from current perspectives in cognitive anthropology is simultaneously as a learner and creator of culture. An individual represents his understandings of experience as cultural knowledge in various forms and reapplies this knowledge as it is seen to be contextually appropriate.[8] Both representation and reapplication simultaneously reinforce experienced patterns and, largely through the processes of establishing relevance or appropriateness, contain the elements for cognitive reorganization and creativity in behavior and understanding.[9]

In this perspective "the self is both a product and an agent of semiotic communication and therefore social and public" (Singer 1980:189). At the same time Culture is individual. Culture (small "c") is created in individual's representations of the form and content of experience and Culture is created in the emergent processes of individual's interacting. It is in this latter sense that cognitive anthropologists are beginning to develop an understanding of Cultural systems as public, socially established symbolic systems (Geertz 1973b) rooted in the individual. In this new orientation for cognitive anthropology we are beginning to approach an understanding of the complexity of cultural phenomena from a cognitive perspective.

The authors of the papers in this volume come to their research tasks united in their emphases on the cognitive basis of cultural knowledge. They simultaneously focus on general principles of cognitive processes and particular accounts of Cultural phenomena. Articles in Section I focus on the nature of concept formation. Section II aggregates papers that focus on contexts for learning and reapplying cultural knowledge. Section III proposes new models to account for systems of cultural knowledge.[10]

NOTES

1. These premises are implicit (and sometimes explicit) in the early publications of cognitive anthropologists. My attention was drawn to this specific cluster of assumptions in two seminars given by Brent Berlin and Paul Kay in 1971 and 1972. I remain fully responsible for their characterization here.

2. Gregory Bateson (1979:38) argued recently that "the division of the perceived universe into parts and wholes is convenient and may be necessary, but no necessity determines how it shall be done." The cognitive anthropologists, anticipating Bateson, set out to discover just how such ordering was accomplished and what forms this order could take in particular cultures.

3. Models were required to predict ranges of appropriate behavior in particular contexts but not to predict specific acts (see Lehman this volume, Goodenough 1957).

4. Similar to the more current "differences that make a difference" (Bateson 1972:453).

5. See Goodenough (1981:111) for a more detailed discussion of different senses of the term *culture.*

6. John Gatewood included many of these references with a historical discussion in an earlier version of his paper for this volume.

7. Naomi Quinn and Dorothy Holland suggested this perspective for viewing current directions in cognitive anthropology.

8. See Dougherty and Fernandez (1982) for an extended discussion.

9. In some ways this is an extension of the notion of "cultural drift" attributed to Fred Eggan (1941:13), in discussions by Goodenough (1981), and also evident in the writings of Edward Sapir.

10. Critical review of drafts of this introduction by F. K. Lehman, Willett Kempton, Norman Whitten, and Charles Keller has clarified a number of issues. Inadequacies remaining are my own.

REFERENCES

Agar, Michael
1974 Talking about Doing: Lexicon and Event. *Language in Society* 3:83-89.
1980a *The Professional Stranger: An Informal Introduction to Ethnography.* New York: Academic Press.
1980b Stories, Background Knowledge and Themes: Problems in the Analysis of Life History Narrative. *American Ethnologist* 7:223-39.

Bateson, Gregory
1972 Form, Substance and Difference. In *Steps to an Ecology of Mind,* pp. 448-69. New York: Ballantine Books.
1979 *Mind and Nature: A Necessary Union.* New York: E. P. Dutton.

Berlin, Brent
1972 Speculations on the Growth of Ethnobotanical Nomenclature. *Language in Society* 1:51-86.

Berlin, Brent, Dennis Breedlove, and Peter Raven
1973 General Principles of Classification and Nomenclature in Folk Biology. *American Anthropologist* 75:214-42.

Berlin, Brent, and Paul Kay
1969 *Basic Color Terms: Their Universality and Evolution.* Berkeley: University of California Press.

Black, Mary
1963 On Formal Ethnographic Procedures. *American Anthropologist* 65:1347-51.

Bloomfield, Leonard
1933 *Language.* New York: Henry Holt.

Boas, Franz
1930 Anthropology. In *Encyclopedia of the Social Sciences* 2:73-110. New York.

Brown Cecil H.
1977 Folk Botanical Life Forms: Their Universality and Growth. *American Anthropologist* 79:317-42.

Bulmer, Ralph N. H.
1974 Folk Biology in the New Guinea Highlands. *Social Science Information* 13:9-28.

Chomsky, Noam
1957 *Syntactic Structures.* The Hague: Mouton.
1965 *Aspects of the Theory of Syntax.* Cambridge: M.I.T. Press.
1972 *Language and Mind.* New York: Harcourt Brace Jovanovich.
1975 *Reflections on Language.* New York: Pantheon Books.

Colby, Benjamin Nick
1973 A Partial Grammar of Eskimo Folk Tales. *American Anthropologist* 75:645-62.
1975 Culture Grammars. *Science* 187:913-19.

Conklin, Harold C.
1955 Hanunóo Color Categories. *Southwestern Journal of Anthropology* 11:339-44.
1962 Lexicographical Treatment of Folk Taxonomies. In F. W. Householder and S. Saporta, eds., *Problems in Lexicography.* Bloomington: Indiana University, Research Center in Anthropology, Folklore and Linguistics.
D'Andrade, Roy G.
1976 A Propositional Analysis of U.S. American Beliefs about Illness. In Keith H. Basso and Henry A. Selby, eds., *Meaning in Anthropology.* Albuquerque: University of New Mexcio Press.
D'Andrade, Roy G., et al.
1972 Categories of Disease in American English and Mexican Spanish. In A. Kimball Romney, Roger W. Shapard, and Sara Beth Nerlove, eds., *Multidimensional Scaling,* 2:9-54. New York: Seminar Press.
Dougherty, Janet W. D., and James W. Fernandez
1982 Afterword. Special Issue on Symbolism and Cognition II. *American Ethnologist* 9:820-32.
Eggan, Fred
1941 Some Aspects of Culture Change in the Northern Philippines. *American Anthropologist* 43:11-18.
Fjellman, Stephen
1976 Talking about Talking about Residence: An Akamba Case. *American Ethnologist* 3:671-82.
Frake, Charles O.
1962 The Ethnographic Study of Cognitive Systems. In *Anthropology and Human Behavior.* Washington, D.C.: Anthropological Society of Washington.
1964a Notes on Queries in Ethnography. In A. Kimball Romney and Roy G. D'Andrade, eds., *Transcultural Studies in Cognition.* American Anthropologist Special Publication, vol. 66, no. 3, pt. 2, pp. 132-46.
1964b Diagnosis of Disease among the Subanun of Mindanao. In Dell Hymes, ed., *Language in Culture and Society,* pp. 193-211. New York: Harper and Row.
Geertz, Clifford
1973a Person, Time and Conduct in Bali. In *The Interpretation of Cultures.* New York: Basic Books.
1973b Thick Description: Toward an Interpretive Theory of Culture. In *The Interpretation of Cultures.* New York: Basic Books.
Geoghegan, William
1969 Decision-making and Residence on Tagtabon Island. Working Paper no. 17. Berkeley: University of California, Language Behavior Research Laboratory.
1970 Residential Decision Making among the Eastern Samal. Paper pre-

sented at the Symposium on Mathematical Anthropology, 69th Annual Meeting of the AAA, San Diego.

1971 Information Processing Systems in Culture. In P. Kay, ed., *Explorations in Mathematical Anthropology*. Cambridge: M.I.T. Press.

Gladwin, Hugh

1971 Decision Making in the Cape Coast (Fante) Fishing and Fish Marketing Systems. Ph.D. dissertation, Stanford University.

1975 Looking for an Aggregate Additive Model in Data from a Hierarchical Decision Process. In Stuart Plattner, ed., *Formal Methods in Economic Anthropology*. Special Publication no. 4, pp. 159-96. Washington, D.C.: American Anthropological Association.

Gladwin, Thomas

1970 *East Is a Big Bird: Navigation and Logic on Puluwat Atoll*. Cambridge, Mass.: Harvard University Press.

Goodenough, Ward H.

1956 Componential Analysis and the Study of Meaning. *Language* 32:195-216.

1957 Cultural Anthropology and Linguistics. In Paul L. Garvin, ed., *Report of the Seventh Annual Round Table Meeting on Linguistics and Language Study*. Monograph Series on Languages and Linguistics, no. 9, pp. 167-73. Washington, D.C.: Georgetown University Press.

1963 *Cooperation in Change*. New York: Russell Sage Foundation.

1969 Rethinking 'Status' and 'Role': Toward a General Model of the Cultural Organization of Social Relationships. In Stephen Tyler, ed., *Cognitive Anthropology*. New York: Holt, Rinehart, and Winston.

1981 *Culture, Language and Society*. 2d ed. Menlo Park, Calif.: Benjamin Cummings Publishing Co.

Hage, Per

1972 Munchner Beer Categories. In James P. Spradley, ed., *Culture and Cognition: Rules, Maps and Plans*. San Francisco: Chandler Publishing Co.

Hammel, Eugene A.

1965 *Formal Semantic Analysis*. American Anthropologist Special Publication, vol. 67, no. 5, pt. 2.

Heidegger, Martin

1962 *Being and Time*. Trans. John Macquarrie and Edward Robinson. New York: Harper and Row.

Hunn, Eugene

1976 Toward a Perceptual Model of Folk Biological Classification. *American Ethnologist* 3:508-24.

Jakobson, Roman, and Morris Halle

1956 *Fundamentals of Language*. The Hague: Mouton.

Kay, Paul, and Chad McDaniel

1978 The Linguistic Significance of the Meaning of Basic Color Terms. *Language* 54:610-46.

Keesing, Roger
1967 Statistical Models and Decision Models of Social Structure: A Kwaio Case. *Ethnology* 4:1-6.
Kempton, Willett
1978 Category Grading and Taxonomic Relations: A Mug Is a Sort of a Cup. *American Ethnologist* 5:44-65.
Kroeber, A. L.
1952 *The Nature of Culture.* Chicago: University of Chicago Press.
Kroeber, A. L., and Clyde Kluckhohn
1963 *Culture: A Critical Review of Concepts and Definitions.* New York: Vintage Books.
Lounsbury, Floyd
1956 A Semantic Analysis of the Pawnee Kinship Usage. *Language* 32:158-94.
Mandelbaum, David G.
1949 Selected Writings of Edward Sapir. Berkeley and Los Angeles: University of California Press.
Monberg, Torben
1970 Determinants of Choice in Adoption and Fosterage on Bellona Island. *Ethnology* 9:99-136.
Pike, Kenneth
1943 *Phonetics: A Critical Analysis of Phonetic Theory and a Technique for the Practical Description of Sounds.* Ann Arbor: University of Michigan Press.
1964 Towards a Theory of the Structure of Human Behavior. In Dell Hymes, ed., *Language in Culture and Society.* New York: Harper and Row.
Quinn, Naomi
1975 Decision Models of Social Structure. *American Ethnologist* 2:119-47.
1978 Do Mfantse Fish Sellers Estimate Probabilities in Their Heads? *American Ethnologist* 5:206-27.
Rice, Elizabeth
1980 On Cultural Schemata. *American Ethnologist* 7:152-71.
Rosch, Eleanor, and Carolyn B. Mervis
1975 Family Resemblances: Studies in the Internal Structure of Categories. *Cognitive Psychology* 7:573-605.
Rosch, Eleanor, et al.
1976 Basic Categories in Natural Categories. *Cognitive Psychology* 8:382-439.
Singer, Milton
1980 Signs of the Self: An Exploration in Semiotic Anthropology. *American Anthropologist* 82:485-507.
Spradley, James, ed.
1972 *Culture and Cognition: Rules, Maps, and Plans.* San Francisco: Chandler Publishing Co.

Tyler, Stephen A.
1969 *Cognitive Anthropology.* New York: Holt, Rinehart and Winston.

Tylor, E. B.
1871 *Primitive Culture.* London: J. Murray.

Wallace, Anthony F. C.
1965 Driving to Work. In Melford E. Spiro, ed., *Context and Meaning in Cultural Anthropology.* New York: Free Press.

White, Geoffrey
1978 Ambiguity and Ambivalence in A'ara Personality Descriptors. *American Ethnologist* 5:34-60.
1980 Social Images and Social Change in a Melanesian Society. *American Ethnologist* 7:352-70.

Whorf, Benjamin Lee
1956 *Language, Thought and Reality: Selected Writings of Benjamin Lee Whorf.* J. Carroll, ed. Cambridge: M.I.T. Press. (Earlier eds. 1936, 1940, 1941, 1942.)

SECTION I

The Representation of Basic Categories

The articles in this section offer formally precise characterizations of cognition with a view toward the development of a theory capable of accounting for the full flexibility of people's use and understanding of words (Kronenfeld, Armstrong, and Wilmoth). In the lead article Lehman explores the premise that universal constraints in the structure of mind delimit the class of conceptual structures realized in concept definition and other organizations of cultural knowledge. Searching for a learning theory in Chomsky's (1975) sense, that is, an innate predisposition which would account for uniformities in formal aspects of cognition, Lehman is working toward the specification of a "set of analytical categories . . . that rise above service to the presuppositions of any given cultural order." The computation of proper sets and classes and their membership, he argues, is a universal feature of cognitive processing. At a suitable level of abstraction "fundamental universals of a theory of cognition, and therewith of culture, may be readily identified and both formally and empirically motivated."

The interest in universal principles of class definition is central to each of the articles included in this section. One issue repeatedly addressed centers on the utility of fuzzy sets versus proper classes or discrete sets for the modeling of cognition. Given any class defined by some complex of attributes, membership in that class must be either discrete or fuzzy. For example, consider the color category *red,* defined by a complex of values for hue, saturation, and brightness. If every perceived color is either categorically a member of the class *red* or categorically not a member of the class *red,* then the class is discrete. On the other hand, if colors can be a member of *red* to varying degrees, then *red* is a fuzzy set. In conformance with previous research (Brown and Lenneberg 1954, Kay and McDaniel 1978), Burgess, Kempton, and MacLaury show that for color categories some stimuli may be designated as better exemplars than others. They expand this observation with data from the classification of color in the Tarahumara language. In this language basic color categories are designated by bound morphemes obligatorily modified by adjectives of relative intensity. Thus, when Tarahumara speakers name a color, they must always say to what degree it is a member of its fuzzy set. Burgess, Kempton, and MacLaury conclude that fuzziness is demonstrably evident in the lexical semantics of color.

The remaining papers of this section suggest that "lexical semantics" is a complex notion involving at least two aspects which need to be distinguished. The first is category definition. The second is the assignment of category designations to phenomena. Werner, as well as Kronenfeld, Armstrong, and Wilmoth, argue that category definition is determinate (nonfuzzy), while the mapping of experience into categories may be problematic and, as a consequence, fuzzy.

Taking the view that category definition is nonfuzzy, Werner proposes that definitional criteria are not isolated lists of attributes but, rather, cohere in a "theory" of the concept being defined. Such a theory integrates varied criteria ranging from simple attributes like size or color to complex propositional knowledge of such information as function or manufacture. Kronenfeld, Armstrong, and Wilmoth (and Hunn, whose paper appears in the next section) argue similarly, emphasizing the importance of attributes of both form and function to concept definition. These authors (with Brown, Quinn, and Dougherty and Keller, whose papers appear in subsequent sections) emphasize that a definitional theory can be differentially highlighted, allowing for the selective use of particular criteria in situated instances of matching categories to experience.

The labeling of experience according to named conceptual classes is addressed by Kronenfeld, Armstrong, and Wilmoth, who argue that a name may be "extended" to referents beyond a category prototype (the perfect match of experience with a definitional theory; cf. Shutz on typification, 1971a, 1971b) by selective emphasis on definitional criteria. A concept label may be applied to a segment of experience on the basis of a subset of the concept's definitional criteria, such as the properties of function or the properties of form. Within this framework these authors account for prototypical, "extended," and metaphorical usage. Werner also explores the "extension" of category designations to experience. He constructs a model of naming based upon increasing abstraction. A category label is not restricted to prototypical phenomena fulfilling its most concrete, richest sense, but may be applied at increasing levels of abstraction by the successive omission of criterial attributes. These two perspectives differentially focus on complementary aspects of the same process. A category definition is seen by Kronenfeld, Armstrong, and Wilmoth as "extended" through selective emphasis on a principled subset of definitional criteria, while the same "extension" is seen by Werner as selective de-emphasis of a subset of definitional criteria.

The issue of change in conceptual representations is raised in this section in the papers by Burgess, Kempton, and MacLaury and Kronenfeld, Armstrong, and Wilmoth. These authors argue that experiential phenomena that do not fall centrally within an established class provide likely foci for new category prototypes. Burgess, Kempton, and MacLaury find empirical support for this in Tarahumara speakers' modifications of existing color categories.

The analyses presented in the papers in this section are directed toward the integration of linguistically based conceptual representation and associated nonlinguistic behavior. As Kronenfeld, Armstrong, and Wilmoth argue, the aim is to specify how it is that the representations of category definitions provide "enough referential connections to enable . . . [people] to know what they are talking about, while also being free enough from any referential lock to enable them constantly to use existing language categories to talk of novel entities or to focus on novel features of existing entities."

While language is central to these analyses, they transcend Whorfian relativity by establishing a balance between experience and fore-structure, given linguistically or otherwise (see Heidegger 1962). It is this balance that allows the authors to account simultaneously for the continual process of representation on the one hand and the emergence of novel understanding on the other.

REFERENCES

Brown, Roger, and Eric Lenneberg
1954 A Study in Language and Cognition. *Journal of Abnormal Social Psychology* 49:454-62.

Chomsky, Noam
1975 *Reflections on Language.* New York: Pantheon Books.

Heidegger, Martin
1962 *Being and Time.* Trans. John Macquarrie and Edward Robinson. New York: Harper and Row.

Kay, Paul, and Chad McDaniel
1978 The Linguistic Significance of the Meanings of Basic Color Terms. *Language* 54:610-46.

Shutz, Alfred
1971a Equality and the Meaning Structure of the Social World. In *Collected*

Papers II: Studies in Social Theory, pp. 226-74. The Hague: Martinus Nijhoff.

1971b Common Sense and Scientific Interpretation of Human Action. In *Collected Papers I: The Problem of Social Reality,* pp. 3-27. The Hague: Martinus Nijhoff.

1

Cognition and Computation: On Being Sufficiently Abstract

F. K. Lehman (U Chit Hlaing)

This paper is addressed to two related problems. The first is a leading question among anthropologists: whether there should be one anthropology or whether the idea of a single, more or less homogeneous body of scientific discussion in anthropology (to say nothing of an agreed upon theory) is an illusion of science peculiar to European civilization, in which anthropology had its origins. It asks what the appropriate categories of cultural analysis are that can be taken as transcending culturally particular presuppositions.

The second problem is one of abstract theory: what is the nature of human cognition? Cognition, in the sense used in Lehman (1978) and Wessing (1978), is relevant to anthropology. Whatever else culture may be, it involves ways of thinking and knowing.

It is often objected that anthropology is something of a colonial enterprise. We find Europeans or Americans studying the societies and cultures of all sorts of other peoples and analyzing them on the basis of assumptions about science, man, and reality itself that derive, as does the discipline, from Western civilization and its conditions. It is possible to suppose that the results of such work are weakened by an inescapable bias, and this supposition arises from within anthropology. Does not anthropology teach that ways of looking at the world are to be taken relativistically, that no one of them can be used as a standard of evaulation or comparison for the others?

This problem can be raised for any science or scholarly discipline, insofar as international practice in such fields has its roots in the Western tradition. However, the problem is supposedly more serious for anthropology because its subject of study is cultures themselves. Here the question may be asked, how can one preserve a sense of the internal ordering of a culture from the viewpoint of either some other culture or some possibly neutral assumptions and categories?[1]

Two considerations lead me to my position. First, can we study man-in-culture with anything approaching scientific objectivity? This textbook question seems to be founded, in part, upon the view that the kind of objectivity intended would necessarily lead us to be able to predict human behavior with acceptable, possibly statistically defined, accuracy. Moreover, leaving aside such questions as those about being able to determine with reasonable statistical accuracy what a society will do under specified circumstances, given knowledge of its cultural categories, rules, etc., it might be thought unsurprising that relatively few kinds of facts are so hard to observe about the kinds of things ethnographers are interested in that they have never before been noticed—though it is equally clear that innumerable such facts are waiting for a proper account.

Leaving aside whether prediction of the hitherto unknown is basic to science, the problem is complicated by the relationship between cognition and behavior. Our role as environmental information processors has often been overstated (cf. Lévi-Strauss 1972, Wessing 1978, citing Von Foerster). The brain takes in information about the state of its own peripheral receptors. From that a perceptual-cognitive construction is made of a state "out there." It is obvious from our very survival that such constructions are reasonably accurate representations. Nevertheless, if we consider all that goes into the interpretation and evaluation of any given state of affairs, there seems to be a great deal of room for creativity. Thus, given any arbitrarily chosen set of cultural categories, rules, and the like, and any external state of affairs at all, there is no particular reason to insist that the "same" situation, supposing it could be narrowly and objectively specified, would have to be responded to successively the same way. The cultural rules might well determine different perceptions/evaluations of it on successive occasions, even apart from the effects of previous experience. It may indeed be surprising on this view that such a large degree of stability exists in our perceptions, and this stability we owe, no doubt, to the mysterious faculty of memory (see Gatewood 1978). In situations having a fair element of novelty in them, such as what some society will do under the impact of some novel conditions of cultural contact, it is far from astonishing that we may be unable to predict at all satisfactorily no matter how well we know and understand a culture and no matter how well and completely we are able to specify the environmental "input."

Consider, now, a cultural or cognitive system that consists of sets of generative rules, on the order of certain kinds of formal grammars.

It is quite possible that responses in terms of such a system would be "determined" by that system in a new sense. The system might generate an infinite set of constructions. Assuming that this lets us avoid questions concerning the fact that actual behavior can often deviate from normative well-formedness, we would have a reasonable and well-defined sense in which (idealized) behavior is determined by the cultural rules. Determination, then, would refer to the sense in which the rules define precisely (recursively) the set of well-formed descriptions of behavior (*and* possibly its complement).[2] In such a case, given any particular external state of affairs, the rules are likely to allow for an indefinite amount of creativity or novelty of well-formed behavioral and/or interpretative response, just as a grammar of a language allows for indefinitely many sentences, say of arbitrary length, for describing a given concept or percept. And just as a grammar can tell us, in principle, what is a sentence of a language but cannot say anything about what one might say on any given occasion, similarly, cultural rules of the intended kind need have no way of specifying what responses will go with any given state of affairs, though they will certainly say what is not a possible response to this or any state of affairs. Surely, if this is right, then the absence of predictive power in the naïve sense has no negative bearing upon the scientific status of possible cultural theories.

In addition, two hypothetical individuals with, as nearly as one pleases, the same culture-cognitive apparatus need not respond in quite the same way to the same external circumstances. Thus (cf. Chomsky 1972) there will be plenty of scope for creativity at the individual level, particularly on the view that ideally culture (rules) "determines" (more exactly "governs") behavior. Such considerations effectively dispose of White's (1958) culturological argument that the individual, his thought and actions "determined" by his culture, can have no meaningful effect upon the course of history; that intuitions about individual choice in a given situation are equivalent to metaphysical ideas of free will.

Our problem is whether one can preserve a sense of the internal ordering of a culture from the point of view either of some other culture, taken as a standard of reference, or of some possible neutral assumptions and categories. A well-known definition of social anthropology, associated with the name of Evans-Pritchard, makes the task of anthropology one of translation. One thinks of the quip (see Needham 1975:365), "There is only one method, the comparative method, and that is impossible." Evans-Pritchard seems to have meant that the appearance of comparability across cultures is at best an artifact of the use of the language and categories of European culture

each child there should be, in principle, one man responsible in some sense or other, possibly a ritual sense, for the child's having come into being. Moreover, it was through this male that genealogical connections were to be reckoned for the child or by him.

What, then, is universal is that for each person, on account of his or her birth, there is exactly one woman and one man, understood as being in some relationship, physical, jural, or whatever, jointly reponsible, in whatever sense, for the existence of the child, and also such that, through each, genealogical reckoning is done by or on behalf of the child, in just the sense in which we understand the mechanism of genealogical reckoning. This is a cognitive, and specifically a computational, matter. Reckoning is precisely a computation, namely, the construction (see Lehman and Witz 1974) of an abstract space of positions in "relative product form," which we call Primary Genealogical Space. What I shall call the genealogical father, then, is not necessarily to be identified with the genitor, as has been customary in social anthropology from Radcliffe-Brown onward. Even with ourselves, a jural father may be legally responsible for bringing up a child, and for passing an estate on to that child, etc., yet not be the male through which the child's genealogical connection is reckoned.

It is not a good counter claim that adoption and the like disprove the genealogical basis of kinship. Even though an adoptive relative may be given the same jural recognition as any other in his category of relationship to me, it is clear that adoption is a formal social process everywhere understood as creating a new relationship analogical to a more basic one. Such a process, treated computationally, maps an individual into a class otherwise or previously occupied by some other individual and such that what we can call the initial occupant did not derive his membership from the operation of such a mapping rule.

Second, it is nowadays often claimed (cf. Schneider 1972) that kinship is not even universally about genealogy. This argument depends upon an overly concrete idea of what would have to be required by way of substantive evidence in order to preserve the genealogical hypothesis. In some societies, apparently, what anthropologists call kinship categories are primarily defined on the basis of criteria having to do with such things as sex, relative age, relative social status, spatial, interactional, and affective "nearness" to ego, and other such social criteria. Thus if one asks why such-and-such is called "X," one is likely to be told that it is for such social reasons, and it is only indifferently that the person so called will have any relevantly specifiable genealogical relationship to ego. The people of Nukuoro, a Polynesian outlier, described by Vern F. Carroll, are commonly cited as the case in point (but now see Goldsmith ms.).

It is admitted that in such cases one can elicit rules according to which these categories constitute precisely and uniquely the targets for many-to-one mappings from genealogical positions. This, however, is dismissed as merely a game that the ethnographer gets people to play, an artificial, Western ethnographer's game. This dismissal of evidence should not be accepted. First, it can hardly be an accident that the people know from the outset how to play this game and need no training in it. Genealogical relative product language comes naturally to speakers of all languages. More to the point, they know just the closed set of categories that are the proper targets for these mapping rules in their system, and they are just the jural categories that the ethnographer is telling us are the kinship categories of that society. The ethnographer and his informants readily agree in defining the existence and the boundaries of the domain in question, except for trivial details.

It may or may not be that the categories in question have their primary perceptual definition on sociological rather than genealogical bases. It may also be that this only seems to be so because (a) the sociological-behavioral expectations associated with the categories are so important that massive realignments of membership on other than primary genealogical grounds are common, in order that social relations line up with these expectations, and (b) for practical purposes the people in question find it unnecessary to speak about the genealogical part of the meaning among themselves. After all, in numerous instances conventional discourse rather than revealing underlying conceptions effectually masks or mystifies them (the Marxist notion of fetishism). Clearly, the situation described is all we need to support the genealogical hypothesis in properly abstract form. That is, the categories need not be defined in the first instance genealogically but need only constitute a closed set of unique targets for many-to-one mapping from genealogical space.

Looked at with sufficient abstractness of a kind I have labeled computational, an appropriate universal definition of the domain of kinship is readily forthcoming, and leads directly to an affirmative solution to the question whether there is anything properly called the content of kinship: the content, genealogical reckoning, is the behavioral reflex of the computation. Ultimately, we are sure that this is not far from correct because there is never much uncertainty about what categories are to be called kinship in any society, either between the ethnographer and his informants, once conventional language barriers are overcome, or among social anthropologists.

The way to arrive at appropriate conceptual universals of social and cultural domains and categories is through the kind of formal, abstract, relational (structural) methods I have called computational. For this we need to look not at the level of fact at which cultures are realized substantively but, rather, at the level of principles by means of which categories and categorical relations are constructed, computed, generated.

So far I have argued as follows: In spite of interesting and seductive claims to the contrary, nothing inherent in the facts of the cultural order has to be seen as making it immune to the ordinary canons of scientific theory and generality. If we are to apply these canons in a reasonable way, we must look to universally applicable sets of categories that, whatever the background out of which they may have been suggested as pre-theoretical hunches, are not *simply* reflections of culturally parochial assumptions. The only reasonable hope for accomplishing this task is to try to establish universals at a cognitive-constructional level. That this level of reality or of analysis sees structure not as a kind of template or fixed grid of oppositions but as a generative device, taken together with similar work in cognition (see Gatewood 1978 and references there) and artificial intelligence (cf. Waltz 1978, *passim*), suggests in many ways that this is the proper character of human cognitive capacities, in particular, the capacity to acquire culture.

> "*. . . the treatment of variables as analogous to names is natural if we regard the device of quantification as an idealization of coordination beyond listable domains, that is, to domains of infinite size or unknown membership. For finite domains of known size and known (nameable) membership, quantification can be reduced to coordination (conjunction or disjunction). . . .*"
>
> (Chomsky 1981:102)

It now remains to sketch a few instances of the sense in which abstract computation, in a precise and rigorous sense, can apply with interesting results to the analysis of the conceptual or cultural order. I shall take the position that among our culturally salient cognitive capacities are formal ones having to do with the partitioning of spaces, concrete or abstract, and that culturally particular systems of categories often are to be accounted for or described by means of more or less formal theories of sets, and set partitions, or quantifications over sets. I shall do this by looking at a few specific problems in the way culture and language—which speaks about the cultural-cognitive order—organize their conceptual apparatus.

This will involve a discussion of the formal logic of quantification in natural languages, which speaks directly to the point of the first section of the paper. It shows that our cognitive capacities include critically set-theoretical computational operations. If, indeed, these are crucially involved in our cognitive approach to sets and classes, then they are involved in categorization in general, since there is an obvious connection between sets or classes and categories that amounts virtually to identity (for classes as intensional predicates over variables of set membership, see McCawley 1968, Lehman 1975; for the relationship from the standpoint of modal-intensional logic, cf. Montague grammar, e.g., Partee 1976; for the related distinction in set theory between set and proper class, see Takeuti and Zaring 1971:3). It is necessary to suppose not that the cultural order is structured identically with language, only that both orders are functionally motivated by some general cognitive capacities (cf. Chomsky 1981:138).

Let me begin with a discussion of the problem of the mysterious referentiality of nonspecific noun phrases. I can conveniently limit myself to the facts of English.

1. I want a book.

This sentence is ambiguous: either I mean a certain, specific book (Ioup 1977) and I am asking you to guess which one, or, on the more usual reading, any one or more books will satisfy my requirements. In this latter sense *a book* is a nonspecific noun phrase.

Now, it is usual, on the standard view of formal logic, to say that nonspecific noun phrases are nonreferring expressions. That is, (1) does not mention a certain book as the object of the *open* sentence

1′. I want NP.

More technically, (1) does not specify a book that can be represented as x in the following:

1″. $\exists x$: $x \in \{\text{BOOK}\}$ & I want x or
$\exists x$: λx (I want x) $\in \{\text{BOOK}\}$.

Here x is understood as a variable, a specified object or entity; BOOK will stand for the class or set of all imaginable books. In the relationship between the x standing outside and that standing inside the parenthesis, the outer one "binds" the interior such that without that binding operation what is within the enclosed expression cannot be turned from an open sentence into a closed sentence or proposition. What the open sentence contains is the free variable *x*. This is due to the function of the sign ∃, which is called the existential quantifier and means that there exists a certain *x*, the rest being a statement about it. The sign ∈ means that *x* is a member of a specified class (see Quine 1951).

Existential quantification turns an open sentence, with one or more free variables, into a closed sentence, statement, or proposition, which can be said to have a truth value. By this, in turn, is meant that the conditions under which it is true can be pointed to in terms of a particular state of affairs involving particular entities corresponding to the bound variables. Roughly, the binding of the variables allows us to identify whether some entity does or does not satisfy the conditions of a statement. If I say, for example,

2. I saw a boy and he was walking his dog.

we postulate that a certain boy exists, and if we can find such a boy, and that boy is involved in my having seen him and in walking his dog, then the sentence is true. In the case of (1), on its usual reading, I have not claimed that any such book exists, and so nobody could tell when one book might, or another might not, be the book "referred to"—there is no referring in this sense. For approximately this reason we do not ordinarily speak about sentences like (1) as being true or false, save that the speaker could be lying about his intentions, while in (2) we can have a false statement just in case there is no such boy.

The logical quantifier binds variables in open sentences (propositional functions). Noun phrases thus bound are referring expressions in the logical systems under examination. Now a pronoun is ordinarily taken as anaphoric to its antecedent, but one ought then to suppose that there must be something in the antecedent to refer to. Clearly, however, this does not work in the light of

3. I want a book and *it* had better be a nice one.

"It" is a pronoun, taking reference from what is now a nonspecific antecedent, which supposedly does not, itself, refer (cf. remarks on 1). But how can a pronoun co-refer with an antecedent that is nonreferring?

The standard theories of logical quantification seem to provide no good way of solving this puzzle. There are also some other difficulties with these theories: they identify the notion of quantification with binding of variables, but, apart from the already problematical idea that binding means "fixing reference," the notion of binding is not altogether clear (see, e.g., Quine 1951:76-80).

Two further difficulties resolve themselves into one. In the first place it is odd that quantification should bear no obvious relationship with the idea of quantity or number. In the second place the ideas of reference and binding appear intuitively to be most readily explicated in the context of the theory of sets or classes, which is not generally done in the standard theory. That is, reference is easily and naturally thought of as a selection (a choice function) the result of which is a partition of a set as between the selected members and any others. For example, in (2) the "a" partitions the set of boys between a certain boy, whom I saw, and all the rest. If binding fixes the reference of a variable, it surely does so by partitioning sets of classes in this way, and the variable may be identified with the unbound and possibly arbitrarily ordered (so-called unordered) members or elements of the set (cf. McCawley 1968 on set variables and indices, and Lehman 1975, 1979b). But (cf. Quine 1951:237ff.) number, and thence also quantity, amount to much the same sort of thing.[3]

Very roughly, "five men" refers to all subsets of men of size five, and these subsets may in turn be defined, after Quine, by a sort of partition, such that the sixth and subsequent men are dropped from each arbitrary subset of men of arbitrary size or cardinality. Essentially, this is what is involved in the idea of cardinal number having regard to sets, the limiting case being the recursive placing of the (arbitrarily) ordered membership of a set in one-one correspondence with the set of natural numbers (0,1, . . .), which, when the members are exhausted—anywhere up to infinity—gives the cardinality of the set itself (its total size or number). Moreover, ordinal enumeration is also readily understood as a selection-partition. "The fifth man" takes its referential meaning from an operation that selects man number five from the ordered totality of men.

In this light I wish to re-examine the puzzle of nonspecific referentiality. Employing the rhetoric of algebraic methods, "a book" in (1) here means "the ith or jth book." That is, we think of choosing one or other arbitrary member of the set, where i and j are distinct but range disjointly between 1 and N, the cardinality of the set of books. i and j are not variables but ordinal indices attached to the members of the set in virtue of their recursive enumeration.

Omitting a number of technical details, the problem posed by the reference of nonspecific noun phrases, as in (3), now vanishes. Let the (existential) quantifier be defined as an operator that selects not variables directly, as in the standard theory of quantification, but rather numerical indices. It is now a choice function whose domain is the cardinality of some set. Now let "a book" of (1) be defined as

4. $\exists i, j$: disjoint over $1, \ldots, N$ (I want $x_{i \vee j} \in$ BOOK).

Here $\vee$ is Boolean disjunction—the *i*th and/or *j*th, roughly.

Obviously, the "it" of (1) takes its referentiality from the antecedent nonspecific noun phrase "a book," in the sense of taking the same disjoint index as the latter, which, moreover, is said to "refer" precisely in the sense of having a well-defined, even if not uniquely specified, referential index.

A number of advantageous consequences follow from thus attributing to human cognitive capacity and to the logic used in natural language (Lakoff 1971b) a specifically computational functioning. I shall show some of these consequences summarily, because if we are to claim that semantic and cultural categories and related basic cognitive processes crucially involve operations on sets in the nature of quantification in the intended sense, we must be able to show that this idea of quantification provides a proper account of well-known problems concerning quantifiers.

Consider

5. Many arrows didn't hit the target.

6. Not many arrows hit the target.

7. All the arrows didn't hit the target.

8. Not all the arrows hit the target.

The well-known problem of so-called negation-and-quantifier scope (e.g., Lakoff 1971a) involving (5) and (6) has the solution under the present proposals

9. $\exists i$: (a subset *i* of arrows, of cardinality "many," didn't hit the target).

10. $\neg\exists i$: (a subset of *i* arrows, of cardinality "many," hit the target).

Extending this argument to (7), with "all" as a cardinal number, it is not the case that the number of arrows that may have hit the target has cardinality N, since there can be only one subset equal in size to the set itself.

By yet a further extension, we can distinguish between cardinal and ordinal numbers. Consider the noun phrase "a man" as a specific though indefinite expression. On the view of quantification being put forward, we specify the existence of one particular index identifying exactly one variable (set member) bearing it, viz., the ordinally ith member of the set of men. Its singularity establishes its connection with the cardinal number "one." Thus it can be said:

11. Each man (in turn) came, up to but not including John.

but not, apparently,

11′. *Every man came, but not John.

The latter, of course, is not the same as

11″. Everyone except John came.

where what seems intended is all the members of a set or subset from which John is excluded, although one's intuitions on these matters are far from reliable.

How to represent this notationally?

12. $\exists i, j_1^N: i = j \ \& \ ((i = j) \supset (i = (j + 1)_2^N))$.

This is especially motivated by what is needed to distinguish "each" from "every," perhaps, where "each" in a nonexhaustive sense is roughly

12′. $\exists i, j_1^N: i = j \ \& \ ((i = j) \supset (i = (j + 1)_2^M))$
where M is a large number approaching N, with the properties of "many."

"Some" has a specific sense. Given

13. I saw *a* book / I saw *some* guy croak.

the quantifiers italicized represent, respectively, a particular ith member of the set of books and a particular *i*th member of the set of men. This amounts to the following formulae, alternatively:

14. $\exists i \in (1,2, \ldots, N)$ (letting $\exists$ reintroduce quantification-as-variable-binding)

or

14′. i: $1 \leq i \leq N$.

"Some" also has a nonspecific sense, as has "a." Thus

15. I want a book/some book or other.

refers to the arbitrary *i*th or *j*th book. Here i takes, disjointly, the values from 1 to N. A rough notation for this might well be (4), or perhaps equivalently,

16. i: $\exists\, i = 1 \vee 2 \vee 3 \vee \ldots \vee N$,

perhaps entailing

17. a (certain) book: it is either the first, the second, the third, . . . , the *n*th; guess which!

Still, (15) seems not strictly to preclude being satisfied with more than one book, and I can suspend any implicature of exclusiveness of disjunction,

15′. I want a book or so.

Then, even if exclusive disjunction is derived by implicature (see Pelletier 1977, Gazdar 1978) from universally underlying inclusive disjunction, it has to be possible to state the exclusive form in an explicit and coherent notational form, albeit not as an elementary formula (see also McCawley 1978), as

18. $k \in (\, (i \vee j)_1^N - (i \wedge j)\,)$,

equivalently

18′. k: $k = (i \vee j)_1^N$ & $k \neq (i \wedge j)$.

Then, without implicated exclusiveness,

18″. $k \in (i \vee j)$.

"Any" is also nonspecific, as we see in

19. Anyone who applies will be hired.

where the referent of "anyone" is possibly null. In

19′. $\left\{\begin{array}{l}\text{Anyone who}\\ \text{Whoever}\end{array}\right\}$ came was given a job.

there appears to be a presumption of non-null reference, though it is cancelable:

19″. Whoever showed up was given food, but I don't know whether anybody actually showed up or not.

20. [disjoint over $(1 - N)$ or over $(0 - N)$].

Thus the variables must be allowed to be sensitive perhaps to pragmatic considerations.

"Any" is, then

21. $k \in ((i \vee j)^{N}_{1 \vee 0} - (i \wedge j))$,

equivalently,

21′. k: $k = (i \vee j)^{N}_{1 \vee 0}$ & $k \neq (i \wedge j)$.

Thus, for instance, "any book" is to be taken as $x_{(i \vee j)} \in$ BOOK, = book$_{(i \vee j)}$.[4]

So, a nonspecific "some" refers to an ordinal disjunct anywhere between 1 and N; specific "some" is also a cardinal number and refers to the (possibly arbitrary) subset such that its cardinality lies between 1 and M, the cardinality of the whole set. Similarly "all" as a cardinal number (see Burton-Roberts 1976) does not refer to the whole set directly, but the intuition that underlies this idea may be captured by the foregoing proposals, though, somehow, "all" distributes over the individual members of the (unique) subset of full cardinality. Thus (3) means the same thing as "each man died," and it will not be supposed that somehow they died as a mass unit.[5]

Consider, finally, the expression "the best doctor" typical of referential opacity (Cole 1976). If I say "the best doctor is arrogant," I may know a man, "X," but not know that X is actually the best (or, on the generic reading, the best kind of) doctor, and may also not think X is arrogant. I have not made any assertion about X, yet the expression is certainly a referring expression. The present framework suggests the solution

> 22. *n*: the doctors in subset $_n$ are the most highly valued; the subsets are ordered according to this metric, and the cardinality of the power set of doctors is *N*. Subset $_n$ is of cardinality *M*, and the arbitrary *i*th doctor from 1 to *M* (cf. "each") is arrogant (where *n* is the ordinal corresponding to *N*).

The quantifier somehow distributes over the indices of the elements of this subset, but opaquely with respect to their individual identities in other classes, e.g., the set of named individuals of my acquaintance.

In the context of Quine's (1951) reduction of the universal quantifier to the double negative NOT NOT, it is interesting that in the present system the universal quantifier vanishes concomitantly with the fact that quantification comes to subsume the ordinary facts about quantity.

In the final section of this paper I turn to points relating either to extension of the quantificational methods of the earlier section, to questions of possible anthropological/linguistic matters outside of English and its cultural world, or to cognition generally.

Consider first an interesting fact about the Lushai (Mizo) language, a Tibeto-Burman language of the India-Burma border. Suppose I wish to ask

> 23. To whom does this park belong?

The noun phrase "this park" can be put in two ways:

> 24. hĕ pàak hīi.

> 25. hĕ mi-pàak hīi, where hĕ . . hīi = "this."

(24) and (25) mean quite different things and cannot be used interchangeably. (24) contrasts "this" park with other parks, but (25) compares one thing, which just happens to be a park and is conveniently referred to by means of that class-name, with the large and arbitrary set of things in general, using the prefix *mi-* ("thing") on the class-name *pàak* (park) or whatever.

I take this as indicating that speakers of natural languages have access, having regard to the language acquisition faculty, to some kind of knowledge of quantification of the kind outlined above. They are able to formulate a grammar according to which one regularly takes account of the way the intersection of sets with sets, or of sets with several different proper classes (roughly sets with particular intensional-predicate criteria of membership—here, whatever it means to be a park) eventuates in the partition of sets and classes. It further suggests that the set theory relevant for ordinary cognition may well be of the kind that distinguishes between sets and proper classes formally. There, sets are just collections of objects or variables; proper classes have intensional definitions; sets can be members of other sets or of proper classes; but proper classes cannot be included in either sets or other proper classes, though proper classes can be interrelated by sharing (parts of) sets as member (Takeuti and Zaring 1975:13). More especially, what I have said on referential opacity seems to require this kind of set theory for any possible solution (for another extension, see Lehman 1979a).

My final point has to do with the way the theory of fuzzy sets bears on the major thesis of this paper, and with the way one might, preserving this thesis about quantification and computation, handle the kinds of facts that appear to have motivated application of the theory of fuzzy sets by anthropologists and others interested in the logic of ordinary language. The question is whether membership of a conceptual, say a nominally labeled, category is determined by checking an object or entity for the presence of a fixed set of (lexically) defining features of class-predication, or whether it is determined by evaluating the degree to which an object or entity resembles a prototype, itself possibly describable in terms of a fixed set of semantic features of some kind. In the latter case, just if by "evaluating" we mean measuring or estimating *degrees* of resemblance to a prototype, membership is not necessarily closed; some things may be more members than other things, and hence we have the phenomenon of so-called fuzzy sets applying (see Schwartz 1978, Kay and McDaniel 1978, Coleman and Kay 1981, for recent anthropological applications; Kamp 1975, Waltz 1978, for recent linguistic applications). However, I shall argue that a theory of categories in which objects are taken as members relative to a class defined on a prototype does not necessarily amount to the theory that these categories are fuzzy sets.

Let me begin by stating that I am not claiming anything about the mathematical theory of fuzzy sets itself (Zadeh 1975), which is formally coherent. The question is whether it describes interesting cognitive categories of human culture and natural language.

This question is far from trivial. Since fuzzy sets are not sharply bounded, i.e., membership is not, for all objects, an all-or-none matter, they are not the sets of Set Theory, as Zadeh clearly points out. More particularly, fuzzy sets need have no particular cardinality and so will not be subject to quantification as developed in the present paper; without specifiable cardinality the sets will not be well ordered; the axiom of choice, or its equivalent, which in general makes set partition in the intended sense possible, will not be defined on fuzzy sets. It is therefore essential to the argument to be able to show that there are intuitively plausible solutions within classical set theory to the problems which it has recently been proposed are best handled by the theory of fuzzy sets. Moreover, if, as I have shown, there is empirical evidence favoring the proposed theory of quantification as fundamental to cognitive operations on cultural and lexical categories, this must also count as evidence favoring classical over fuzzy set theoretical accounts of these categories generally.

Consider color categories. It is known that for any basic color category in a given language, there is something we can call the focal spectral neighborhood of that color, e.g., focal red, focal orange, and the like. This is a small region, definable by some combination of the three dimensions of hue, saturation, and brightness, such that objects with colors matching that of the focal region have, as nearly as you please, the highest likelihood of being unambiguously and unhesitatingly said to have the color in question. An object with a color very near that of focal red will "always" be called red by test subjects, but the farther from focal red, the more uncertain subject responses will be. This need not mean that color categories are fuzzy sets (Kay and McDaniel 1978).

The rule is, roughly, the farther from focal red (to the "right"), the greater the likelihood of choosing the point's membership in the orange category as more salient for color naming. A certain amount of obvious experimental evidence favors this reanalysis. Let the category red have its "right" bound as near as you please to focal orange. This is experimentally determinable from data showing, say, that right of such a line subjects respond with the color-name orange, or at least "sort of orange" and the like, and never "red." Similarly, let the "left" bound of orange come close to focal red. Then the fuzzy character of the experimental data is seen as having to do simply with the fact that a color may be equally in the red and orange categories, in the sense of ordinary set membership. In what we may call the far "left" of focal red, as one approaches theoretically infra-red, there is no such classificatory uncertainty, even though the name "red" for objects with colors matching this region may be qualified as, say, "sort of" red. Naturally! We cannot perceptually "see" infra-red; we have, then, no color category name matching it, so that the points in the intended region of the visible spectrum, in the red neighborhood, are not simultaneously in the neighborhood of any competing color focus. This is how color relates to hue, to bands of wavelengths of light, or to the linearized spectrum, regardless of the fact that the prismatic spectrum is continuous, with red going over, at the "left," into the purple-blue region (of another copy of the spectrum, actually). In the latter case it is simply a fact that every color overlaps some other, both "left" and "right." Moreover, were we not to linearize the spectrum, or rather the three-dimensional color sphere, each color might overlap more than two others. The essential argument would not be affected.

A similar solution applies to the case of pairs of polar adjectives. Consider the pair "short" and "tall." It is well known that there is no way to define absolute boundaries between them. Some "tall" men are, nevertheless, shorter than others; furthermore, what is relatively tall for a man is relatively short for, say, a skyscraper—assuming we are using ordinary linear measure in all these cases. This is thought of, too, as some sort of fuzziness, but, again, a classical set-theoretic solution exists and feels intuitively right. "Short" is a category-set with a fixed lower bound, namely, approaching nullity, zero measure. "Tall," on the other hand, is a category-set with an arbitrarily large upper bound. Since there is no answer to such questions as "How short does a short man need to be to be called truly short?" it is clear that a critical area of indeterminacy exists between short and tall. But all this need mean is that these two categories—and all pairs of categories that relate to each other in this sort of way—overlap as fully as you please. The lower bound of "tall" is the lower bound of "short," and similarly for upper bounds.

The fuzzy phenomenon here has to do not with category membership but rather with saliency and reasonable criteria of relevance in choosing which of two equally "correct" categories makes the most sense in context. If relative to most men of one's experience a given man is shorter than the average, then he has more chance of my calling him short; the greater the divergence, the greater the chance in question. And once again there is direct evidence supporting this analysis.

We speak of height as a matter of tallness, not of shortness. Thus we ask not how short someone is, in the neutral instance of inquiring about his height and not supposing he has already been categorized as short, but how tall he is. Linear measure is unidirectional, not bidirectional like the value measures (good-bad): the direction of what one might call shortness approaches absence of measure, while the positive direction, the degree of non-null height, is what we are interested in. This goes along with the fact noted earlier that this measure has a fixed lower bound but an indefinitely great upper bound. None of this is captured in any obvious way by the theory of fuzzy sets. Lyons (1977:276, citing Sapir and Lehrer) notes the fixed lower and unfixed upper bounds of these pairs but, failing to notice the way the domains overlap, does not account for the asymmetry.

What follows from these considerations? First, it is necessary to distinguish clearly between rules for labeling objects and the question of what various classes the objects may be members of. In particular, there will often be rules for selecting which of these classes is (contextually) more salient. Now, we need to make such distinctions anyhow, because labels are not necessarily one—one with proper classes. For example, "red" is often used for a certain hair color, and yet this coppery color on other kinds of material would more commonly be thought of as nearer focal orange (cf. The epithet "carrot top" in such cases). This sort of thing may also be a preferable cognitive-universalist alternative to the more relativistic treatment by Conklin (1955) of his Hanunóo color naming data.

It is also necessary to notice that fuzzy set theory makes implicit predictions that are empirically false, whereas the proposed classical solutions do not make these false predictions. For instance, if color categories were indeed fuzzy sets, we should have to expect that, with some small but nonvanishing likelihood, points in the color sphere arbitrarily remote from, say, focal red would be considered seriously as being at least in some non-null degree "red." This, however, is both counter-intuitive and empirically wrong. The neighborhood of any given color focus is bounded at a limit by neighboring color foci.

Of course, there are many instances conforming to what Wittgenstein (1978) calls family resemblances among objects categorized and labeled the same, in which no single feature or set of features of an intensional definition need be shared by all the objects in question, although any two or more of the objects will share some intensional features in common (see also Needham 1975). However, the chain of overlapping intensional characterizations is always rule-bounded, never unlimited; concomitantly, the sets of objects that are candidates for possible inclusion in such (labeled) categories are also not arbitrarily open. In short, some resemblances count, and others do not. Whether some object *in fact* resembles a prototype to some degree or other is quite another question.

For instance (cf. Sperber 1974), "dog" might be defined, *inter alia*, as an animal, hence "live" by definition, having four legs, a tail, two eyes, and so on. Yet we can speak of a "dead dog," and one might arbitrarily mutilate a dog, live or dead. Whether one might then call it a dog would clearly depend upon how far one could seem to explain away its deviation from the prototype definition or, equivalently, how far one could plausibly argue that "something about it" could be taken as meeting the prototype definition inclusively. Is the dog hairless? Hairlessness is genetically recessive and phenotypical hairlessness has been specially bred in these dogs, say, for the pot.

Similarly, a "king" is one who, by some possible prototype definition, "rules" and who has subjects. Still, it is obvious that there can be quite nominal, symbolic instances of ruling or of its acknowledgment. There is no rule for deciding how many persons in a population have to acknowledge the rule for this man to be a genuine king rather than a pretender to the throne or someone with royal hallucinations. In addition, although to be a king requires that one has been formally installed, there is no rule as to what might plausibly be argued as being at least a token instance of such recruitment. This sort of thing is true for indefinitely many social roles.

Several conclusions follow. Taken at a suitable level of abstraction, say as closed Boolean conjunctions or disjunctions of features of some intensional characterization, class definitions seem to be, after all, all-or-none. The family of resemblances to a prototype definition of a class is strictly rule-governed, and the rule constitutes grounds for treating the intensional definition of the class as unitary.

However, there clearly need be no finitely decidable rule evaluating objects as to whether they meet such intensional definitions. There are only pragmatic canons of relative plausibility for arguing that something about the arbitrary object might be taken as matching it. Still, any number of objects exist for which nobody at all would find grounds for claiming that they meet the category definition. The prototype, of course, meets the definition arbitrarily well.

In that case I have to conclude that, indeed, prototype theory (*contra* Coleman and Kay 1981) is not identical with fuzzy set theory because a distinction has to be maintained between "fuzziness" in the intensional definition of a class, which necessarily leads to objects being extensionally "in" classes to varying degrees, and "fuzziness" in the canons of plausibility for evaluating objects relative to intensional definitions. In the latter instance, neither membership nor meeting the definition is a matter of degree on any given value of the metric for evaluating objects relative to intensions. This metric, although scalar, is bounded; indefinitely many objects simply won't qualify at all.

More accurately, there exists a series of scalar-valued functions, where the scalar values are between 0 and 1 (not qualifying, qualifying arbitrarily well), each function in the series assigning objects a binary value, as meeting or not meeting an intensional definition. For any given scalar value, functions with it and all higher values assign objects a positive value relative to an intension, and each lower-valued function assigns objects a negative value relative to the intension.

Finally, indefiniteness—that is, indefinitely many values between 0 and 1—in the evaluation of objects as meeting or not meeting an intensional definition is highly motivated. The number of conceptual categories is relatively small, as measured with rough approximation by the number of nouns and verbs naming classes of things, states, events, and so on in a language. The two kinds of things are never the same size exactly; there are always conceptual classes with no lexicalized names; but the two kinds of things are unlikely to be of different orders of magnitude. This can be seen from work on folk taxonomies and the like, where it is repeatedly shown that no taxonomy is arbitrarily deep, and hence no taxonomy contains very many, possibly unlabeled, nonterminal classes relative to its, necessarily labeled, terminal class. Similarly, one can argue for this point by observing that every nonlexicalized description of an "unlabeled" category is a finite string of words and morphemes, and therefore contains a finite string of lexical nouns and verbs and adjectives, i.e., of lexicalized names for classes.

Now, the possible perceivable differences among objects are orders of magnitude greater in number than the number of conceptual classes in any language or cultural system. Thus the systems of conceptual classes are bound to be beds of Procrustes, into which the objects, actual or imaginary in actual or possible worlds (von Wright 1971), have to be forced. It is surely owing to this inescapable economy of the lexicon and the cognitive process of categorization generally that whether objects meet or do not meet intensional class definitions is, and has to be, not finitely decidable.

I have argued that an approach to culture through cognition taken as abstract computation will take us a great way toward resolving the problem of the scientific character of anthropological theory and, therewith, the question whether there should be one or many anthropologies if we are to keep our discipline from being a colonial agency of Western civilization. I have gone on to show that the same computational approach to cognition, when formalized in terms of a certain theory of quantification, has direct promise for an exemplary class of substantive analytic problems having to do with the way human beings categorize their world, and with the differences between languages and between cultures in the way systems of categories are formed and used.

Finally, by way of considering the particular problem of fuzzy sets and related matters, I have brought the argument to the problematic of the scientific status of cultural theory, by showing that the cognitive bases of much of culture are far more amenable to empirically and formally rigorous treatment than is sometimes supposed, and that, at a suitable level of formal abstractness, fundamental universals of a theory of cognition and, therewith, of culture may be readily identified and both formally and empirically motivated.

NOTES

An earlier version of this paper was written for the conference on World Anthropology: Anthropology for the Future, held during the 10th International Congress of Anthropological and Ethnological Sciences in New Delhi, 15 Dec. 1978. It was also subsequently presented to the panel on Relations between Symbolic and Psychological Anthropology at the Annual Meeting of the American Anthropological Association in Cincinnati, 30 Nov. 1979. It is part of a continuing study of cognition and computation linking ethnographic and linguistic semantics, and the chief concern of this larger work is the idea that much of cognition has to do with the representation of reality in terms of abstract spaces, somewhat in the sense of Piaget, and algebraic operations upon these spaces. It is related to work (Lehman and Witz 1974, 1979) on the algebra of kinship category spaces, and also to work by Maran and his colleagues (Maran 1979) on the semantics of space, time, and grammatical aspect in Tibeto-Burman languages.

1. Reservations about the scientific status of anthropology are not exclusive to radical humanist scholars interested in seeing human affairs as not amenable to scientific treatment. For those who identify with prediction of (classes of) events within specified probabilities, such reservations are equally salient. Wiener (1948:191) says that social sciences fail, on this view, in not having sufficiently long or massive statistical runs of observations to determine sharply converging statistical results (see, now, Lehman 1977).

2. See Wall (1972). The theory of infinite recursive sets makes it pointless to assume that cultural-cognitive rules, specifying possible well-formed behavioral descriptions absolutely, could enable us, assuming optimal knowledge of external circumstances, to predict behavioral responses in the naïve sense. Moreover, if well-formedness rules at least govern actual performance, the argument holds even if such rules generate only recursively enumerable sets, where "govern" means that the rules are part of, but not necessarily coextensive with, the mechanism generating performance. Similarly with regard to the learnability of this class of rules, see, e.g., Chomsky (1981, ch. 1).

3. The traditional Fregean treatment of logical quantification as the unrestricted binding of variables is inadequate for handling other than so-

called universal and existential (logical) quantifiers, in particular for quantity (see McCawley 1978). On the limitations of unrestricted quantification even here, see McCawley (1971:8.2) and Barwise and Cooper (1981). Cushing (1976) argues that the Fregean treatment can be made to handle quantity. However, his logical-propositional (model-theoretic) treatment is purely extensional. The present work may be thought of as representing the intensional logic of quantification.

It is clear that Fregean quantification, as employed by certain linguists, presents a further difficulty. Chomsky (1980) treats relative pronouns and question words as logical quantifiers that bind "traces" standing in the places from which wh-words in English have been moved. Antecedents similarly bind their pronominal anaphors. In this way variable binding is taken to establish *co*-reference, making the variable have the same referent (index) as its antecedent. But if variable binding establishes *co*-reference, it cannot establish reference itself without circularity. The present work is an attempt to avoid this. The Fregean apparatus is reduced to the so-called existential quantifier, ∃, which is taken as partitioning sets of variables.

Sets are algebraic spaces; the elements of (enumerable) sets are always at least arbitrarily ordered, even so-called unordered sets, and only some order on the elements allows for the cardinality of a set, its size or enumerability, taking the elements one at a time and pairing them successively with the natural numbers. Moreover, for at least denumerably infinite sets, the axiom of choice would otherwise fail (Takeuti and Zaring 1971:87ff.). ∃ selects some integer, i, that is the cardinal index of a set variable (set element or member).

4. Bolinger (1977) and Geis (1979) rightly reject "some" and "any" as surface variants of a single entity depending upon explicit or implicit negation in the predicate within whose scope a noun phrase so quantified falls.

i. I want some/*any.
ii. I don't want any/*some.
iii. Do you want any/some?

Negative polarity contexts (Horn 1970, Ladusaw 1980) of course induce the interpretation "possibly null" on a nonspecific quantifier, hence require "any" as against "some." (iii) merely permits that presumption.

An obvious extension disposes of the problem of the relative scopes of negation and quantifiers. Consider

iv. John doesn't know everything.
v. John doesn't know anything.

In (iv) we mean not "for all things, John doesn't know them," but, rather, "it's not the case that, for all things, John knows them." In (v), however, we mean "for anything whatsoever," hence, for all things, "John doesn't know them," and it is often supposed in logical analysis that (iv) and (v) differ in that (iv) has a universal quantifier inside the scope of negation, while in

(v) the negation applies to all things, and the universal quantifier is said to bind all variables under negation, having wider scope than negation. This is usually given as

iv′. $\neg \forall x$: KNOW (John, x).
v′. $\forall x$: $\neg$ KNOW (John, x).

However, there are problems with this analysis if negation takes in its scope whole verb phrases, quantifiers on objects included. On the latter view, a simple paraphrase for (iv) and (v), with the quantifier inside the negation, is

iv″. It's not the case that John knows every/each thing.
v″. It's not the case that John knows even one thing.

By considering "each/every" and "all," and other aspects of the problem of the relative scopes of quantifiers and negation (sentences 5 through 8), it is easy to formalize (iv″) and (v″) directly. It needs only a slight modification of the treatment of "any," which, in the scope of negation, always has the interpretation "*even* the arbitrary one." I have argued (1979a) that "even" is a second-order quantifier, operating over pairs or *n*-tuples of set partitions. In the present instance we *expect* that John might know *one or more* things; we *assert* that he does not know any; and we replace an expected partition of the set of things relative to John's knowing with a different partition, the sense of "any" given, say, in (20) or (20′). It is possible, with "any" ranging disjointly from 1 to *N*, to eliminate the second-order quantifier "even" in negative contexts, so, no matter which item in the set of things is "picked out" by the quantification, it will be something John doesn't know. Alternatively, it is possible to simplify the treatment in (20)/(20′) by supposing "any" is cardinal rather than ordinal, in which case it selects the arbitrary (*i*th) singleton subset of the class referred to. It is advantageous for a theory of the relation between syntax and logical form to have the relative scopes of negation and quantifiers in logical form follow directly from their relative scopes in syntactic form, and the present proposals have this result.

The referentiality of nonexistent things like unicorns is different. A pragmatically influenced model-theoretic interpretation assigns the set of unicorns in this world cardinality 0, in some imaginary world some positive integer.

The proposed theory of quantification also solves problems about reference and definite descriptions (see Lyons 1977:181-88). It is possible to dispense with Russell's "iota," or definite description, operator. *The book that I sold* has a restrictive relative clause cross-classifying the set of books and picking out a unique book. The subset of that intersection is a singleton, a subset of unit cardinality. Hence definiteness is just a case of specificity, viz., $\exists\, i \in \{1\}_{ki}$ definite plurals are unique subsets of subsets in second-order power sets. This extends to two other cases in English. Inherent singulars are definite (take the article "the"), as in *the President of the United States;* presumably, at any given time, this category has only one member. Generics are optionally definite, as in *the beaver builds dams,* where the (nonproper) subset that is the set itself is unique—in the second-order power set; the subset of subsets of cardinality N is necessarily of cardinality 1.

As to nonspecificity and opacity, Lyons (1977:186) refers to a problem raised by Donnellan (1966). The expression "Smith's murderer"/"the murderer of Smith" is definite, but on one reading also equivalent to "whoever murdered Smith," which appears to be nonspecific. However, if definite, it cannot be nonspecific, there being exactly one such person who exists, although I may not know how to pick him out. The foregoing treatment of definiteness suggests the solution. There is some *i*th or *j*th member of the set of persons, and that nonspecific person is the unique element of the singleton subset of persons picked out by cross-classification by the class of "killers of Smith." In that case

vi. $\exists\, k{:}\ k = (i \vee j)_1^n \;\&\; k \in \{1\}_l \;\&\; x_k \in \{\text{MAN}\}$
$\&\; x_k\ (\text{KILLER OF SMITH})$.

The difference between this and

vii. $\exists\, i{:}\ i \in \{1,2,\ldots,n\} \;\&\; \text{MAN}_i\ (\text{KILLER OF SMITH})$

is the distinction between the referentially opaque and the referentially transparent readings (see Lyons 1977:192-93 for opacity, and my remarks under (14), above; see also Maida and Shapiro 1982).

5. For the distinction between cardinal and ordinal enumeration underlying prominent syntactic facts about nominal classifiers in Thai and Tibeto-Burman languages, see Lehman (1979b) and Wongbiasaj (in press). For other relevant discussions of quantification, reference, and specificity, see, e.g., Cole (1978), Langendoen (1978), McCawley (1977), Bach (1976), and Selkirk (1976).

REFERENCES

Bach, E.
1976 Comment on Chomsky (1976). In P. Culicover et al., ed., *Formal Syntax*, pp. 133-56. New York: Academic Press.

Barwise, J., and R. Cooper
1981 Generalized Quantifiers and Natural Language. *Linguistics and Philosophy* 4:159-220.

Bolinger, D.
1977 *Meaning and Form.* London: Longmans.

Burton-Roberts, N.
1976 On the Generic Indefinite Article. *Language* 52:427-48.

Chomsky, N.
1972 *Language and Mind.* 2d ed. New York: Harcourt, Brace, Jovanovich.
1980 On Binding. *Linguistic Inquiry* 11:1-46.
1981 *Lectures on Government and Binding.* Amsterdam: Foris.

Cole, P.
1976 Attributiveness and Referential Opacity. In *Proceedings of the 3rd Annual Conference of the Berkeley Linguistic Society,* pp. 117-23.
1978 On the Origins of Referential Opacity. In P. Cole, ed., *Pragmatics* [=Syntax and Semantics 9]. New York: Academic Press.

Coleman, L., and P. Kay
1981 Prototype Semantics. *Language* 57:26-43.

Conklin, H. C.
1955 Hanunóo Color Categories. *Southwestern Journal of Anthropology* 11:339-44.

Cushing, S.
1976 *The Formal Semantics of Quantification.* Bloomington: Indiana University Linguistics Club.

Donnellan, K.
1966 Reference and Descriptions. *Philosophical Review* 75:281-304. Reprinted in D. Steinberg and L. Jakobovits, eds., *Semantics*, pp. 100-114. Cambridge: Cambridge University Press, 1971.

Evans-Pritchard, E. E.
1952 *Social Anthropology.* Glencoe, Ill.: Free Press.

Gatewood, J. B.
1978 Fishing, Memory, and the Stability of Culture Complexes. Ph.D. dissertation, University of Illinois at Urbana-Champaign.

Gazdar, G.
1978 *Pragmatics: Implicature, Presupposition, and Logical Form.* New York: Academic Press.

Geis, M. L.
1979 Review of Bolinger (1977). *Language* 55:683-86.

Goldsmith, M.
1975 Rethinking Nukuoro Kinship. Term paper, Department of Anthropology, University of Illinois at Urbana-Champaign.

Horn, L. J.
1970 Ain't It Hard Anymore? Negative Polarities and Presuppositions. *Papers from the 19th Annual Regional Meeting of the Chicago Linguistic Circle.*

Ioup, G.
1977 Specificity and the Interpretation of Quantifiers. *Linguistics and Philosophy* 1:233-46.

Kamp, J. A. W.
1975 Two Theories about Adjectives. In E. L. Keenan, ed., *Formal Semantics of Natural Language,* pp. 123-55. Cambridge: Cambridge University Press.

Kay, P., and C. McDaniel
1978 The Linguistic Significance of the Meaning of Basic Color Terms. *Language* 54:610-46.

Kuhn, T.
1962 *The Structure of Scientific Revolutions.* Chicago: University of Chicago Press/Phoenix Books.

Ladusaw, W. A.
1980 *Polarity Sensitivity as Inherent Scope Relations.* Bloomington: Indiana University Linguistics Club.

Lakoff, G.
1971a On Generative Semantics. In D. Steinberg and L. Jakobovits, eds., *Semantics,* pp. 232-396. Cambridge: Cambridge University Press.
1971b Linguistics and Natural Logic. In D. Davidson and G. Harmon, eds., *Semantics of Natural Languages,* pp. 545-665. Dordrecht: D. Reidel.

Langendoen, D. T.
1978 The Logic of Reciprocity. *Linguistic Inquiry* 9:177-98.

Lehman, F. K.
1975 Wolfenden's non-Pronominal a-prefix in Tibeto-Burman. *Linguistics of the Tibeto-Burman Area* 2:19-44.
1977 On Falsification and Science Once Again. *Journal of the Steward Anthropological Society* 8:53-66.
1978 Symbols and the Computation of Meaning. In D. B. Shimkin et al., eds., *Anthropology for the Future.* Research Report no. 4, pp. 181-91. Urbana: Department of Anthropology, University of Illinois.
1979a On Quantifier Floating in Lushai and Burmese with Some Remarks on Thai. Paper presented to the 12th International Conference on Sino-Tibetan Languages and Linguistics, Paris. (To appear in a Festschrift for Paul K. Benedict, edited by G. Thurgood.)
1979b Aspects of a Formal Theory of Noun Classifiers. *Studies in Language* 3:153-80.

Lehman, F. K., and K. G. Witz
1974 Prolegomena to a Formal Theory of Kinship. In P. Ballonoff, ed., *Genealogical Mathematics,* pp. 111-34. The Hague: Mouton.
1979 A Formal Theory of Kinship: The Transformational Component. Report no. 11. Urbana: Committee on Culture and Cognition, University of Illinois.

Lévi-Strauss, C.
1972 Structuralism and Ecology. The Gildersleeve Lecture, Barnard College, Columbia University, New York City.

Lyons, J.
1977 *Semantics.* Vol. 1. Cambridge: Cambridge University Press.

Maida, A. S., and S. C. Shapiro
1982 Intensional Concepts in Propositional Semantic Networks. *Cognitive Science* 6:291-330.

Maran, L.
1979 Localization and Representational Structures in Jinghpaw: A View of the Epistemological and Semantic Foundations. Paper presented to Symposium on Tense and Aspect, University of California at Los Angeles, 4-6 May.

McCawley, J. D.
1968 Where Do Noun Phrases Come From? In R. Jacobs and P. Rosenbaum, eds., *Readings in English Transformational Grammar*, pp. 166-83. Waltham, Mass.: Ginn and Co.
1977 Lexicographical Notes on English Quantifiers. *Papers from the 13th Annual Regional Meeting of the Chicago Linguistic Society*, pp. 372-83.
1978 Logic and the Lexicon. In D. Farkas et al., eds., *Papers from the Parasession on the Lexicon*, pp. 261-77. Chicago: Chicago Linguistic Society.
1981 *Everything That Linguists Have Always Wanted to Know about Logic.* Chicago: University of Chicago Press.

Needham, R.
1975 Polythetic Classification: Convergence and Consequences. *Man* 10(n.s.):349-69.

Partee, B. H., ed.
1976 *Montague Grammar.* New York: Academic Press.

Pelletier, F. J.
1977 Or. *Theoretical Linguistics* 4:62-74.

Quine, W. Van O.
1951 *Mathematical Logic.* 2d ed., reprinted 1962. New York: Dover Press.

Schneider, D. M.
1972 What Is Kinship All About? In P. Reining, ed., *Kinship in the Morgan Centennial Year,* pp. 32-63. Washington, D.C.: Anthropological Society of Washington.

Schwartz, T.
1978 Implications of Grouping and Memory Retrieval Trajectories for Internal and Inter-Category Structure. Paper for the 77th Annual Meeting of the American Anthropological Association, Los Angeles.

Selkirk, E.
1976 Some Remarks on Noun Phrase Structure. In P. Culicover et al., eds., *Formal Syntax,* pp. 185-316. New York: Academic Press.

Sperber, D.
1974 *Rethinking Symbolism.* Cambridge: Cambridge University Press.

Takeuti, G., and W. M. Zaring
1977 *Introduction of Axiomatic Set Theory.* New York: Springer Verlag.

Von Wright, G. H.
1971 *Explanation and Understanding.* Ithaca, N.Y.: Cornell University Press.

Wall, R.
1972 *Mathematical Linguistics.* Englewood Cliffs, N.J.: Prentice-Hall.

Waltz, D. C.
1978 TINLAP—2: Theoretical Issues in Natural Language Processing

2. New York: Association for Computing Machinery and Association for Computational Linguistics.

Wessing, R.
1978 The Place of Symbols in Human Interaction. In D. B. Shimkin et al., eds., *Anthropology for the Future.* Research Report no. 4, pp. 171-80. Urbana: Department of Anthropology, University of Illinois.

White, L. A.
1958 *The Science of Culture.* New York: Grove Press.

Wiener, N.
1948 *Cybernetics.* New York: John Wiley & Sons; Paris: Herman & Cie.

Wittgenstein, L.
1978 *Philosophical Grammar.* Berkeley: University of California Press.

Wongbiasaj, S.
in press Quantifier Floating in Thai and the Notion of Cardinality/Ordinality. *Studies in the Linguistic Sciences.*

Zadeh, L. A.
1975 Calculus of Fuzzy Restrictions (appendix). In L. A. Zadeh et al., eds., *Fuzzy Sets and the Applications to Cognitive and Decision Processes,* pp. 1-40. New York: Academic Press.

2

Tarahumara Color Modifiers: Individual Variation and Evolutionary Change

Don Burgess, Willett Kempton, and Robert E. MacLaury

Anthropological understanding of color terminology has advanced tremendously in just over a decade. Berlin and Kay's seminal study (1969) explained cross-cultural regularity in color nomenclature through universal color foci, acquired in an evolutionary sequence. Rosch demonstrated that color categories (and many other categories) are structured as gradations from a central focus (Heider 1972, Rosch 1973). McDaniel explained the universality of color foci in terms of the human visual system (1972, 1974). Kay (1975) reviewed evidence linking synchronic variability to evolutionary change. More recently, Kay and McDaniel (1978) use fuzzy set theory to formally describe the graded structure of color categories at various evolutionary stages.

This paper uses Tarahumara color naming, including nonbasic modifiers, to address recent issues in color categorization. We compare traditional field methods with newly developed ones. Some of our methods rely on the unusual Tarahumara modifier system, while others can be used in any language. To relate category structure to color term evolution, we provide two examples of Tarahumara categories, each named with a single basic color term, which have internal gradations corresponding to separate categories in later evolutionary stages. Such correspondence between category structure and evolutionary change could not be elicited by traditional methods. This

An earlier version of this chapter appeared in *American Ethnologist* 10:133-49, 1983. It is reprinted by permission of the American Ethnological Society and the authors.

introduction proceeds with a summary of Kay and McDaniel (1978), upon which our work draws heavily, and then briefly outlines the remainder of the paper.

Kay and McDaniel propose that color categories are fuzzy sets. Unlike a discrete set, a fuzzy set can have members that vary in their degree of membership or exemplariness (Zadeh 1965). For example, the English category *blue* is considered a fuzzy set; given many blue colors, English speakers will judge some to be more blue than others.

Kay and McDaniel posit that neural responses to color are directly expressed in six categories: black, white, red, yellow, green, and blue, the "primary color categories." They then derive all other known basic color categories by fuzzy set operations on the primary color categories, producing "derived color categories" and "composite color categories." *Derived* categories are the intersection, or overlap, of two or more primaries. For example, English "orange" is derived from red and yellow. *Composite* categories are the union of two or more primaries. For example, many languages form a single category as a composite of green and blue.

Kay and McDaniel use their proposals to explain the evolution of color vocabularies as follows. The least developed color vocabularies have only two composite categories. New color categories are added as composites split into their constitutent primaries, until the color vocabulary contains only primaries. Finally, the derived color categories are added as intersections of the primaries.

Kay and McDaniel present a plausible argument, but they have not provided the lexical data that would tie fuzzy sets to the semantics of color words. The apparent fuzziness might not be semantic but, rather, could reside in perception, pragmatics, or metalinguistic operations that occur when an informant names colors. Kay and McDaniel cite such constructions as "blue-green," "sort of red," and "a good red" as evidence that color categories are fuzzy, not discrete, and Lakoff (1973) makes a similar argument for other categories (also see Kay 1982). But a more traditional approach to semantics, such as Weinreich's, would consider such constructions "meta-linguistic operators," which "function as instructions for the loose or strict interpretation of designata" (Weinreich 1966:163). From Weinreich's point of view, fuzzy set theory would be inappropriate: "the vagueness of different signs is not commensurable since vagueness is a pragmatic factor in denotation and hence beyond the province of semantics as the study of designation" (1966:179).

Since color reference is so closely tied to perception, and since Kay and McDaniel draw heavily on perceptual and neurophysiological data, we would like to determine with more certainty whether or not fuzziness is intrinsic to the semantics of color terms.

Preliminary data on Tarahumara led us to select it as an ideal language to test Kay and McDaniel's proposals. Tarahumara has a system of obligatory postposed modifiers that specify a color referent's exemplariness of a color category. Thus, since a minimal Tarahumara reference to color specifies degree of membership, we will argue that fuzziness is inextricably linked to the lexical semantics of color categories. An additional reason to use Tarahumara is that is possesses a composite color category (green-or-blue). This permits us to use the obligatory modifiers to examine the structure of composite color categories.

We will begin this paper by locating Tarahumara color categories along the color spectrum. We will then examine the red category in order to decipher the Tarahumara modifer system, and conclude that the modifiers are based on fuzzy set membership. The red category is additionally interesting for its internal structure. High-membership Tarahumara "red" corresponds to English red. But low-membership modifiers are not symmetrically arranged around the high-membership focus; rather, they are concentrated on the pink colors. This, and later evidence from the "green-or-blue" category, suggests that a large low-membership area of a category presages the future evolution of a new category in that low-membership area.

Once the modifier system is analyzed, we will describe Kay and McDaniel's hypothesized composite structure, together with two alternative hypotheses also described in the literature. We conclude that apparent variation in Tarahumara category structure is explained by shifts of modifier usage—and that category structure is nearly constant across informants. This structure differs slightly from Kay and McDaniel's hypothesized structure because, we propose, Tarahumara is in the process of acquiring separate terms for blue and green.

Procedures and Tarahumara Color Terms

Tarahumara is an Utoaztecan language of the Taracahitic branch spoken in Chihuahua State, Mexico. During field trips to Samachique, Huicochi, and Rocoroibo in 1978, 1979, and 1980, we interviewed nine Tarahumara speakers of the Central Dialect (informants 1-9) and six of the Western Dialect (informants 10-15). Most of these speakers had limited command of Spanish. Color naming was elicited with reference to 330 Munsell Color Standards, 1976 issue. Our equipment consisted of both 330 loose color stimuli and a small array of the same colors arranged in spectral order. The ordered array is smaller than that of Lenneberg and Roberts (1956) or Berlin and Kay (1969), but is arranged almost identically. Note that we use "colors" (as in "green colors" or "red colors") to refer to the stimuli; "colors" are distinguished from "color terms" and "color categories."

We elicited color naming in indirect sunlight, in privacy. Informants were asked to name each of the 330 colors presented one-by-one in a fixed random sequence. We recorded root morphemes and all modifiers. After naming was complete, we presented all colors simultaneously on the ordered array, and asked the informant to indicate the best example or focus of each color term.

Definitions of Roots

Tarahumara informants named most color stimuli with modified forms of six basic roots, which we gloss with the names of their foci: *rosá-* white, *čó-* black, *sitá-* or *sehtá-* red, *saró-* or *sa'waró-* yellow, *siyó-* green or blue, and *ulá-* yellow or brown. The terms extend over wider ranges than do the English terms with the same foci. Tarahumara and English color terms are compared in Figure 1. Each part of Figure 1 displays data elicited from a single informant, using identical lighting procedures. Each of the 330 letters represents a naming response;

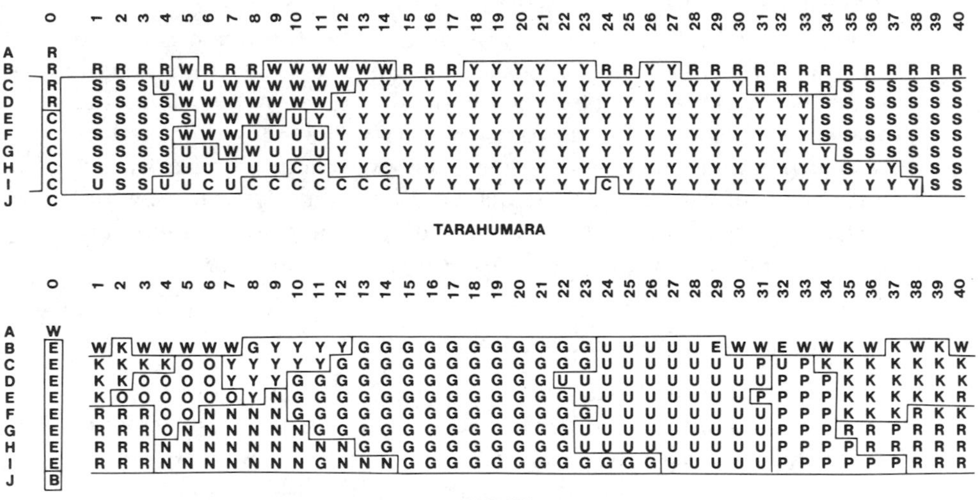

Figure 1. Tarahumara (upper) and English (lower) color naming. Key to the Tarahumara color roots: R = *rosá-*, C = *čó-*, S = *sitá-*, W = *sa'waró-*, Y = *siyó-*, U = *ulá-*. Key to the English basic color terms: W = *white*, B = *black*, R = *red*, Y = *yellow*, G = *green*, U = *blue*, N = *brown*, E = *grey*, O = *orange*, P = *purple*, K = *pink*.

the solid lines approximate category boundaries, and smooth out minor inconsistencies in the data.

We are primarily concerned with the two most frequently used Tarahumara color roots, *sitá-* and *siyó-*. We begin by using *sitá-* to analyze the modifier system. *Sitá-* is a primary category covering all of English *red* and *pink* and part of English *orange* and *purple.* With the modifier system understood, we will then turn our attention to *siyó-*. *Siyó-* includes both English *green* and English *blue;* such a "green-or-blue" color category is reported in diverse languages and is common in American languages. This color category has been called "grue" in the literature, and we adopt this name here.

Explanation of the Figures

Throughout this paper, lexical data will be presented in arrays of color like Figure 1. Although the 330 stimulus colors were presented in random sequence in the interview, in this paper they are arranged in an array like that of Lenneberg and Roberts (1956) or Berlin and Kay (1969); a color reproduction appears in Berlin and Kay (1969).[1] If the reader has such an array available, we recommend placing it in view while reading this article. Readers not familiar with the color array can easily follow this article by reference to Figure 1 and note 1.

This array arrangement is used for two types of figures, one showing data from single informants and the other aggregating data across informants. Individual figures, such as Figure 1, identify each naming response by a single informant. A key in the legend links the letter in the figure to the full word or phrase given by the informant. The second type of figure aggregates a single color name over all informants, as in Figure 2. Aggregate figures use darker, larger circles to represent higher proportions of informants using the name for the color stimulus. Blanks (no symbol drawn) indicate less than 20 percent of informants.

Sitá-, the Red-Focused Color Root

We first use aggregated figures to examine modifiers applied to the red-focused root, *sitá-*. This examination serves three purposes: to demonstrate that this color category is semantically fuzzy, to deduce the meanings of the modifiers, and to show a correspondence between the present internal structure of *sitá-* and the evolutionarily later split into red and pink. Conclusions about the modifier system derived from *sitá-* will later be used to infer the structure of the more complex *siyó-* category.

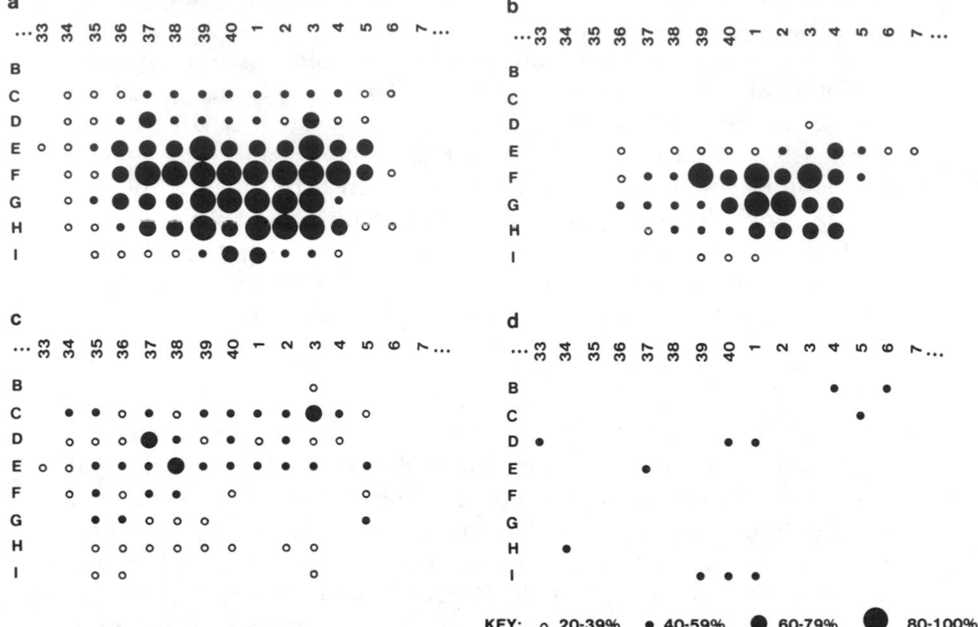

Figure 2. Aggregate data on *sitá-*, the red-focused category. (a) The root *sitá-*, combining all modifiers, aggregated from all 15 informants. (b) *Sitákame* (very red), aggregated from 9 informants. (c) *Sitáname* (somewhat red), aggregated from 9 informants. (d) *Sitánanti* (only slightly red), aggregated from 2 informants.

The normal arrangement of the color array splits the red colors, so *sitá-* did not appear as a single entity in Figure 1. In the four *sitá-* figures, 2a through 2d, we join column 40 to column 1 and truncate the irrelevant middle columns. This reorganization leaves *sitá-* undivided, making its structure more visible.

Figure 2a aggregates all uses of the root *sitá-*, regardless of modifier. There is a central area of high agreement, surrounded by progressively lesser agreement. The area of highest agreement also contains all the focal choices of *sitá-* given in the focal task. Figure 2a has a structure that indirectly suggests a fuzzy set: highest agreement in the center, declining gradually to low agreement on the periphery. To use this agreement data as evidence of a fuzzy set, we must assume that agreement among informants indirectly measures degree of membership for each informant. Although previous studies have considered agreement to be an indicator of membership (Labov 1973; Kempton 1978, 1981; McCloskey and Glucksburg 1978), we will use a more direct measure—explicit rankings by individual informants.

Tarahumara modifiers provide direct evidence for fuzziness of color categories. We examine first, in Figures 2b and 2c, the nine informants who contrast *sitákame* and *sitáname*. The postposed bound modifiers *-kame* and *-name* contrast clearly: *-kame* is used for the colors near the center of the category, and *-name* for colors outside the center. Figure 2d shows *-nanti*, a third modifier used by only two informants, which occurs on the outer periphery of the category.

The meanings of these modifiers can be inferred by their distribution on the color array. From the modifier distributions in Figures 2b through 2d, we infer that *sitákame* can be glossed "very red," *sitáname* can be glossed "somewhat red," and *sitánanti* can be glossed "only slightly red." The distributional analysis is consistent with an independent morphological analysis:

sitákame:	*sitá-*	*-ka*	*-ame*	
	"red"	augmentative	participle	
sitáname:	*sitá-*	*-na*	*-ame*	
	"red"	diminutive	participle	
sitánanti:	*sitá-*	*-na*	*-ame*	*-ti*
	"red"	diminutive	participle	"approximately"

Each of these modifiers is also used for other purposes in Tarahumara. Some informants combine these obligatory modifiers with the optional preposed modifiers *we* (much) and *pe* (little) to distinguish as many as four grades of membership. Burgess (1982) presents further grammatical background.

By the Berlin and Kay criteria (1969:6), *sitá-* would be a basic color term, but the modified forms would not because their meaning can be predicted from their constituent morphemes. Since postposed modifiers are obligatory, every Tarahumara color reference is necessarily graded. They cannot merely name a color *sitá-;* in order to name it, they must specify to what extent it is *sitá-*. We tried asking questions using unmodified *sitá-*, but such usage did not make sense to informants.[2] Thus the Tarahumara color system offers the most direct evidence to date for the Kay and McDaniel claim that *fuzziness must be considered part of the lexical semantics of color terms.* This finding lends further support to the claims of Fillmore (1975), Kay (1982), Kempton (1978), G. Lakoff (1973), Rosch (1973), and others that most lexical categories exhibit graded rather than absolute membership.

Internal structure of Tarahumara *sitá-* presages category boundaries in later-stage languages. Low-membership *sitáname* (Figure 2c, at 40 percent or more agreement) matches English *pink*, while high-membership *sitákame* (Figure 2b) corresponds to English *red*. Three

Tarahumara informants have a separate term for the pink area; these three restrict *sitá-* to the high-membership area of Figure 2b. This interinformant variation suggests change in progress. We will return to the inference that *sitá-* is splitting into red and pink after analysis of the structure of *siyó-*.

Structure of Composite Color Categories

In Kay and McDaniel's terms "composite color categories" include more than one primary color category. Tarahumara has just one composite color category: *siyó-*. To provide a basis for the analysis of *siyó-*, we compare the Kay and McDaniel hypothesis with two other hypotheses for the structure of composite categories. Some evidence in the literature supports each of the three hypothesized structures, so the Tarahumara data were intended to allow selection of one hypothesized structure as correct. The structures are illustrated in Figure 3. For simplicity, each graph of Figure 3 considers only one mid-brightness row of the color array; an inset shows what each category would look like on the whole color array, with brightness included.

For example, in Figure 3a, the curve for the fuzzy set *green* has zero membership for the brown colors, indicating that in English they

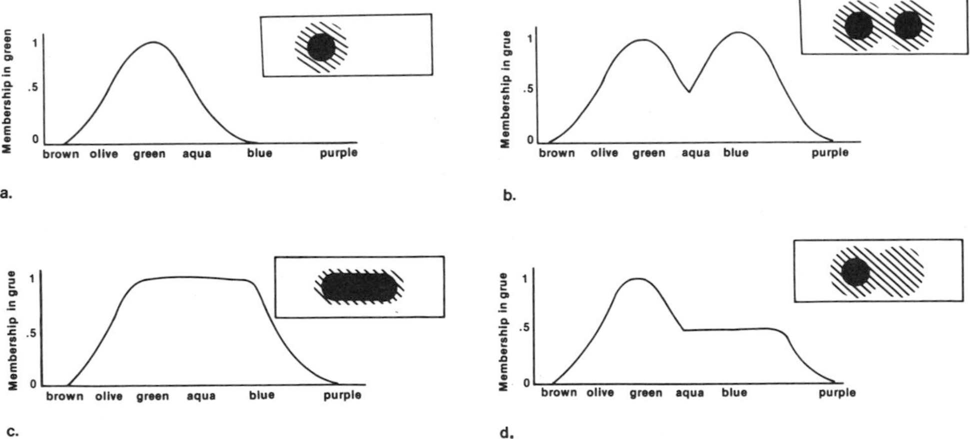

Figure 3. Hypothesized fuzzy sets graphs of hue against set membership. An inset in each graph shows how the category would appear on the color array, with solid black representing high membership. (a) English *green* represented as a fuzzy set. (b) Grue formed by union, as proposed by Kay and McDaniel. (c) Neutralization of the green-blue distinction. (d) Green-skewed grue, based primarily on green but including blues at lower membership.

are not the least bit *green*. The curve then moves up to 0.5 through the olive colors, indicating that they are somewhat *green*, reaches a maximum of 1.0 at the greenest colors, and then declines again through the aquas to zero at the bluest colors. A graph for the fuzzy set *blue* would be similar, but shifted to the right. Figures 3b, c and d illustrate the three hypothesized structures for composite color categories.

Union

Our first hypothesis is the fuzzy set union operation proposed by Kay and McDaniel (1978:629-31). For grue, Kay and McDaniel's union hypothesis can be summarized as follows: a color stimulus is grue to the extent that it is green in English *or* to the extent that it is blue in English, *whichever is greater.*

This hypothesis is illustrated in Figure 3b; the salient feature here is the dip between green and blue. The dip constitutes a claim that speakers will consider aqua colors to be less grue than the pure blues or the pure greens. The strongest evidence for this model has been focal choice data in languages with a grue category. Kay and McDaniel report that the "best examples" of grue are placed either on the green focus or on the blue focus, not between the two (1978:630).

In the Tarahumara data, the union hypothesis would be confirmed if the highest-membership modifier were used for pure green and pure blue, while a lower-membership modifier were used between green and blue as well as around the periphery of the grue category.

Neutralization

Our second hypothesis is that grue results from a neutralization of the lexical distinction between green and blue. Colors are less grue when they are removed from *both* green *and* blue toward other colors, but aqua, pure green, and pure blue are equally "most grue." This hypothesis is illustrated in Figure 3c.

This hypothesis is implicit in the descriptive linguistic literature prior to Berlin and Kay, and in discussions of neutralization and marking (Greenberg 1966). Some evidence for a neutralized or an aqua-focused grue has been presented by MacLaury, McMillen, and McMillen (1979), who found that three out of ten Uspantec Mayan speakers placed the grue focus at aqua. Rosch's discussion of category structure—a single focus surrounded by other members ordered from better to poorer examples—would also suggest neutralization or aqua-focus over the double-peaked union (see Rosch 1973:112, Rosch and Mervis 1975:574).

In the Tarahumara data, the neutralization hypothesis would be confirmed if high-membership modifiers were distributed through greens, aquas, and blues.

Skewing

Our third hypothesis supposes that grue is based primarily on green but includes blues at lower membership. This hypothesis, the "skewed" grue, is illustrated in Figure 3d. Although Berlin and Kay (1969) did not describe color categories as fuzzy sets, we infer a skewed structure from their figures (1969:18-19) and their discussion of Tzeltal. When asked which colors were the best examples of grue, most Tzeltal indicated the greens (1969:32).

We skew toward green in our example in Figure 3d, but we intend to also allow a skewing toward blue. Grue seems to be skewed toward green in some languages and toward blue in others (first observed by Berlin and Berlin 1975:82-83), and speakers of a single language sometimes vary (for example, men in West Futuna predominantly focus grue in blue, women in green; Dougherty 1977:117).

Using Modifier Distribution to Test the Hypotheses

This section uses the modifier system of Tarahumara to test the three hypothesized structures of grue, first using aggregated data and then examining individuals.

Aggregated Siyó- Data

Figure 4a aggregates all uses of *siyó-*, regardless of modifiers. *Siyó-* covers a large area in the center of the color array, including the areas of English *green* and *blue*. Without the modifier data, our analysis would be complete with Figure 4a; we would conclude that *siyó-* means "green-or-blue." Figures 4b and 4c are aggregations of the modifiers *-kame* and *-name* for the six informants who applied them productively to *siyó-*. Figure 4d aggregates *-nanti* for the two informants who applied it productively.

These data do not allow a clear choice; they provide some evidence for each of the three hypotheses. The double-peaked union is supported by the lower membership in aqua. (Lower membership in aqua is indicated by fewer *-kame* and more *-name* and *-nanti* in the area from column 22 through column 25.) Neutralization is suggested by the preponderance of *-kame* throughout the central area of grue and *-name* and *-nanti* on the outer edges. Skewing toward green is suggested by more frequent *-kame* in green and more frequent *-name* in blue.

In short, the aggregated *siyó-* data are confusing. Rather than allowing a choice of one hypothesis, the data suggest a combination of all three hypotheses, with the unexpected addition that lighter colors are less *siyó-* than darker colors.

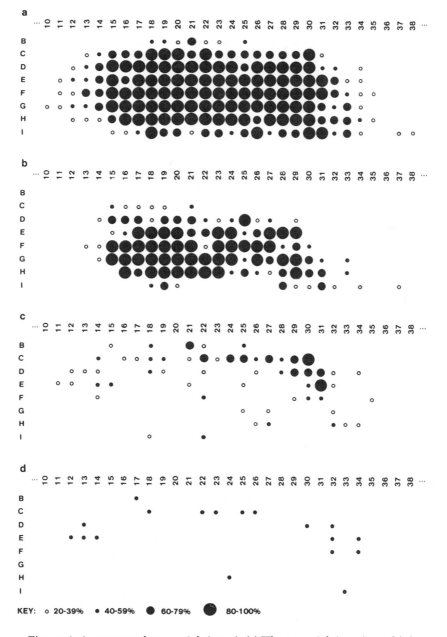

KEY: ○ 20-39% • 40-59% ● 60-79% ⬤ 80-100%

Figure 4. Aggregate data on *siyó-* (grue). (a) The root *siyó-* (grue) combining all modifiers, 15 informants. (b) *siyókame* (very grue), 6 informants. (c) *siyóname* (somewhat grue), 6 informants. (d) *siyónanti* (only slightly grue), used by only 2 informants.

Individuals Conforming to Each Hypothesis

Since the aggregated *siyó-* data were unclear, we examined data from each informant individually. Initially, each of the three hypotheses appeared to be supported by data from one or more informants, which accounts for the muddled aggregate data of Figure 4. This section presents data from three informants, each supporting one of three hypotheses. The following section will then explain this interinformant variation as due to differing modifier usage, while the structure of *siyó-* is constant across informants.

Among informants, different modifiers may be used to mean the same thing. For example, although we have illustrated only *-kame,* either *-kame* or *we* may be used for high membership. To improve readability of the following figures, we use a single symbol for high membership, regardless of which modifier the informant used to denote it. The actual modifier is given by a key in the figure caption. Unlike the previous aggregated figures, representing percentages, the following figures represent individual informants and thus use distinct symbols: "X" for the highest membership modifier, "-" for the second highest, ":" for the third, and, when four modifiers are distinguished, "." for the lowest membership.

Union is approximated by informant 7, in Figure 5. He has two clusters of maximum-membership *siyó-*, at the greenest and the bluest colors.

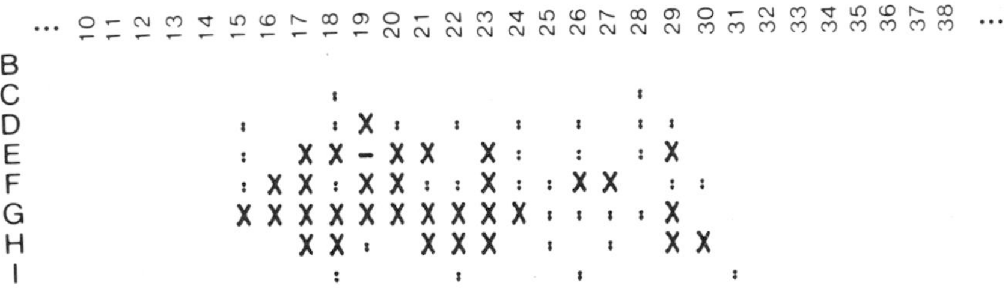

Figure 5. Informant 7, an imperfect example of a grue formed by union. Key: "X": *siyókame,* or *siyókame rosabókame;* "-": *pe siyókame;* ":": any *siyóname* construction.

Figure 6 is from informant 13, illustrating neutralization. This informant locates high-membership *siyó-* uniformly over the green, blue, and aqua colors.

Most informants skew *siyó-* slightly toward green, but combine the skewing with other patterns. For example, although Figures 5 and 6 are cited as evidence for union and neutralization, they partly support skewing, since both show more high-membership *siyó-* in green

	…	10	11	12	13	14	15	16	17	18	19	20	21	22	23	24	25	26	27	28	29	30	31	32	33	34	35	36	37	38	…
B								-		-			-	-			-														
C						-	X	X	-	X	-	-	X	-	-	-	-	-	-	-	-	-	-	-	-						
D						X	X	X	X	-	X	X	X	X	X	-	X	-	X	-	X	-	-	-	-	-					
E					-	-	-	X	X	X	X	X	X	X	X	X	X	X	X	X	X	-	-	-	-						
F					-	-	X	X	X	X	X	X	X	X	X	X	X	X	X	X	X	X	-	-	-						
G				X	-	X	X	X	X	X	X	X	X	X	X	X	X	X	X	X	X	X	X	-	X	-		X			
H					-	-	X	X	X	X	X	X	X	X	X	X	X	X	X	X	X	X	X	-	X	X	X				
I							-		X	-	X	X		-	-	X	-	-	-	X	X	-	X	X	-	X					

Figure 6. Informant 13, an example of grue neutralization. Key: "X": *siyókame;* "-": *siyóname.*

than in blue. The closest case to a pure skewed grue is in Figure 7, informant 6. Her *siyó-* is skewed because it has several high-membership modifiers near focal green but none in blue. (The two isolated high-membership modifiers in purple are either an error or some type of naming contrast with the color presented previously in the random sequence.)

	…	10	11	12	13	14	15	16	17	18	19	20	21	22	23	24	25	26	27	28	29	30	31	32	33	34	35	36	37	38	…
B																															
C					-	:	-	:	-	:	:	-		-	-			:													
D					:	-	-	-	X	-	-	-	-	-	:	-	:	-	-	:	-										
E				-	:	:	-	X	-	-	-	-	-	-	-	-	-	-	-	-	-	:									
F				-	-	:	-	-	X	-	X	-	X	-	:	.	-	-	-	-	-	-	-	.			:	X			
G				:		-	-	-	-	X	X	-	-	-	-	-	-	:	-	.	:	:	:		-						
H				:				-	:	:	-	-	:	-	-	-	-			:	-	:				X	:				
I									:	-		.	:	-	:		:	-				:									

Figure 7. Informant 6, an example of a grue skewed toward green. Key: "X": *we siyóname;* "-": *siyóname;* ":": *pe siyóname;* ".": all other *siyó-* forms.

Informant 4 provides an interesting case related to skewing. His *siyó-*, shown in Figure 8, covers green and part of the periphery of blue. He uses the term *rikásoami* (sky colored) for the 15 bluest colors, while the periphery of blue is named with the low-membership *pe siyó-*. (He did not vary the modifier on *rikásoami; rikásoami* is not shown

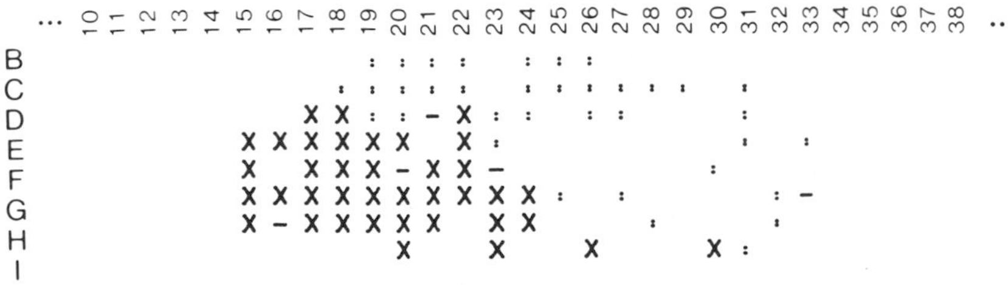

Figure 8. Informant 4, related to the skewed grue. A secondary color term is used for the bluest colors, while *siyó-* is used for all the greens and the peripheral blues. Key: "X": *we siyó-;* "-": *pe we siyó-;* ":": *pe siyó-* or *siyó-*.

in the *siyó-* data of Figure 8.) Of all informants, informant 4 provided the most color terms (15), including many secondary color terms. We believe the low-membership area of a skewed category to be fertile ground for emergence of a secondary color term. Thus we regard the encompassing *siyó-* structure of Figure 8 to be the likely aftermath of skewing toward green.

Expansion of -kame

We expected the structure of *siyó-* to determine the distribution of high-membership modifiers. Thus our initial interpretation of Figures 5 through 8 was that, since the modifier distributions varied among informants, the structure of the category varied also. We then noticed that informants vary not only in the distribution of high-membership modifiers but also in the number of times they use those modifiers. For example, the informant in Figure 6 uses *siyókame* for 96 colors, while the informant in Figure 5 uses it for only 32 colors. We think of this as expansion and restriction: some informants *expand* the use of *-kame* to many colors, while others *restrict* it to only a few colors. Pettigrew (1982) has shown that category expansion varies among individuals and seems related to personality or other individual characteristics. He observes that an individual will consistently expand (or restrict) across diverse categories. We argue below that the apparent *siyó-* variation is due to expansion of the high-membership modifier rather than to variation in color category structure.

Figure 9 illustrates the union curve, with two lines representing our hypothesized expansion and restriction. The top solid line represents an informant who restricts *-kame* to only the few highest-membership colors; those with membership above the line are *-kame* and those below are *-name*. In this case the aqua colors would be *-name*. The lower dotted line represents an informant who expands *-kame* to include both high and mid-membership. Here, with *-kame* expanded, the greens, blues, and aquas are all *-kame*, and the three hypothesized structures of grue are not distinguishable.

How could we determine whether the apparent neutralization cases are due to expansion of *-kame*? Figure 9 shows *-kame* expansion should include the aqua colors as well as the outer periphery of grue. By contrast, Figure 3c shows that true neutralization should include aqua but not the outer periphery of grue. In fact, the data of Figure 5 and 6 suggest *-kame* expansion, since the outer periphery is included.

We test for this possibility by measuring *-kame* expansion for each informant. A measure, *width,* is defined to be the number of columns from the leftmost to the rightmost use of *siyókame* (for related category measures, see Kempton 1981). Only the middle rows E, F, and G are

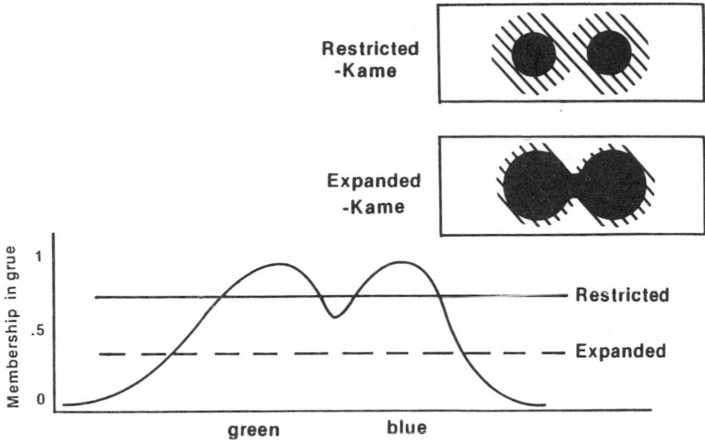

Figure 9. The hypothesized restricted (solid line) and expanded (dotted line) use of *-kame* to modify *siyó-*.

included because other rows introduce complicating effects of brightness.

All informants were classified according to which hypothesis their modifier distribution most closely matched. As indicated in Table 1, one informant exemplified skewing; two, union; and three, neutralization. Three informants were considered intermediate between union and neutralization because they used *-kame* for some but not all aqua colors (see Burgess, Kempton, and MacLaury 1983). Table 1 also includes the three informants who did not treat grue as a fuzzy set—those who used the same modifier with all *siyó-* references. The three informants not falling into any clear pattern are excluded.

The width measurements are summarized in Table 1 and correspond well to modifier distributions: the more an informant's modifier distribution appears to be an example of neutralization, the more his or her *-kame* is expanded. Thus *-kame* expansion is a plausible explanation for all the cases initially believed to be neutralization. It is logically possible that the *-kame*-expanding informants just happen to have a neutralization category structure, but we find no plausible justification for such a correspondence. We conclude that the apparent neutralization is an artifact of *-kame* expansion and discard the neutralization hypothesis, leaving evidence for both union and skewing.

The Structure of Siyó-

The one observed case of complete skewing, that of informant 6 shown in Figure 7, suggests that the true structure of Tarahumara

Table 1. Correspondence between modifier distribution and expanded use of *-kame* (or another high-membership modifier).

Modifier Distribution	Informant	Width of *-kame*	Average Width for Group
Skewed	6	2.7	2.7
Union	5	13.3	13.3
	7	13.3	
Intermediate (between Union and Neutralization)	15	15.0	15.4
	10	14.0	
	3	17.3	
Neutralization	11	17.7	17.6
	13	17.3	
	14	17.7	
Non-fuzzy set	1	24.7	22.0
	2	20.0	
	8	21.3	

grue is union with a slight skewing toward green. Our reasoning is as follows: if greens had higher membership in *siyó-* than blues, then the informant with the most restricted *-kame* would use *siyókame* for only the greenest greens. Figure 7 shows that informant 6 has such a pattern. In fact, informant 6 distinguishes three membership grades: *we siyóname* (high), *siyóname* (middle), and *pe siyóname* (low). He uses high membership for only the greenest colors, middle membership for the remainder of the greens and most of the blues, and low membership for the periphery of the greens and the blues, including a few aquas. This informant 6 has a grue with a high peak in green, a lower peak in blue, and a slight depression in aqua: union with some skewing toward green.

Besides the clear case of informant 6, aggregated modifier distributions also suggest that grue is structured as union with skewing toward green. That is, high-membership modifiers appear more frequently, but not exclusively, in green. The relevant data are summarized in Table 2. This table uses Kay and Kempton's (1984) experimentally determined division between green and blue—columns up through 22 are counted as green and from 24 to the right as blue. A color is counted in Table 2 if 60 percent or more of the informants apply the modified term to it (equivalent results are obtained with other cutoff percentages).

Table 2 shows that while *siyó-* is applied to equal numbers of greens (59) and blues (58), greens receive more high-membership modifiers

Table 2. Distribution of *siyó-* forms across green and blue colors. Color stimuli are counted if at least 60 percent of the informants named them with the linguistic form.

Siyó- Form	Membership	Green Colors	Blue Colors
Any *siyó-*	All	59	58
Siyókame	High	35	24
Siyóname	Low	2	9
We siyó-	High	12	1
Pe siyó-	Low	11	18

and blues receive more low-membership modifiers. From these data we conclude that *siyó-* is skewed toward green. This skewing would not have been visible if only the basic color term *siyó-* had been examined, since as we have shown the internal structure of *siyó-* is skewed, but the category boundary is not.

Change in Grue

Kay and McDaniel (1978:630) cite languages with both green and blue foci to argue for union in those languages. By parallel reasoning, we would expect a predominance of Tarahumara focal choices in green, since we have inferred a skewing toward green. However, green and blue were chosen equally. With only 13 focal choices, sampling error cannot be discounted, but we can advance a tentative explanation of these data, based on three bits of evidence:

1. In Tarahumara, grue is slightly skewed toward green but focal choices are equally divided between green and blue.

2. Grue focal choices are equally green and blue in some languages, predominantly green in others, and predominantly blue in still others (Berlin and Berlin 1975).

3. New color categories emerge from the large low-membership areas of highly skewed categories. (In the Tarahumara data this is seen in secondary terms for pink from the red-skewed *sitá-*, and informant 4's blue from the green-skewed *siyó-*.)

Our methodological interpretation of this evidence is that the focal task is not as sensitive to skewing as is modifier distribution. Our substantive interpretation is that grue has a union structure in some languages and a skewed structure in other languages, and that the latter languages are closer to evolving separate terms for green and blue.

This hypothesis is in contrast to Berlin and Berlin's suggestion that either green or blue has higher membership when a language initially acquires grue (1975:83). We propose that grue changes its structure through time, then divides into separate terms for green and blue. The proposed sequence is shown in Figure 10: first grue structured as union (10a), then slight skewing visible only by modifier distribution (10b), then greater skewing visible by both modifier distribution and focal choices (10c), and finally emergence of a new color term in the low-membership area (dotted line in 10c). Most Tarahumara informants are at 10b, while informant 4 is at 10c.

Figures 10a-c are picked as illustrative points along what is more likely a continuous change from equal green and blue through progressively greater skewing toward green. Although this sequence explains our Tarahumara data as well as the diversity of focal data in other grue languages, more complete diachronic and comparative data are needed.

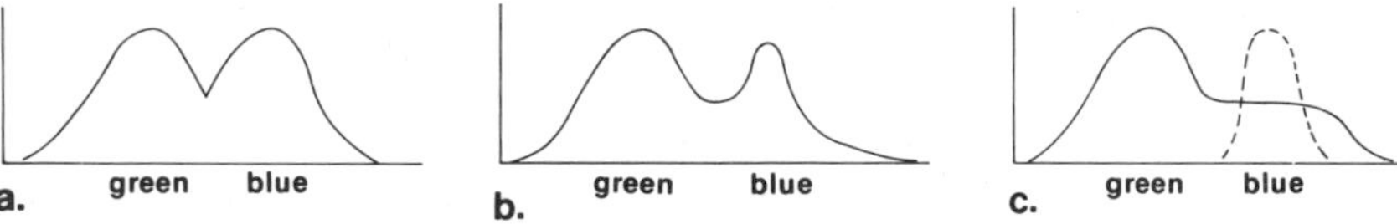

Figure 10. Transition of grue from (a) union through (b) partial skewing to (c) complete skewing. The dotted line in c indicates a secondary term for blue, most likely to appear after skewing.

Naming Data Compared with Mapping Data

To verify our tentative conclusions about Tarahumara grue, we performed two further tests. First, we re-elicited naming data to ascertain whether the same modifier distribution would appear on a second trial. Second, we employed a new elicitation technique, a mapping in steps.[3]

Re-elicitation of Naming Data

Lexical data were first elicited from informant 13 in October 1978, as shown previously in Figure 6. Throughout 1979 this informant was trained to assist in translation and linguistic research. In December 1979 we conducted a second interview with him.

This informant had expanded *-kame* in his first interview and thus was a case of apparent neutralization. In the second interview (not shown here), he restricted *-kame.* Since the second modifier distribution has less *-kame* in aqua than in either green or blue, it is most like union. His focal choices were greens in both interviews. We will interpret this difference between the first and second interviews after discussing the mapping data.

Mapping Elicitation

In all the figures of data from single individuals, we find a scattering due to inconsistent use of the modifiers. We attribute the problem to the random ordering of colors, and the fact that modifiers shift their meaning according to context. In this case the context is the immediately prior color in the randomized presentation sequence. We examined a few cases and found, for example, if an aqua color is presented after a red one, it will be called *siyókame,* but if presented after a green one it will be called *siyóname.* The random presentation order has been adopted in recent color research to eliminate other methodological problems, but for the fine distinctions necessary to distinguish modifiers, random order can introduce noise. We thus employed a mapping task, which both eliminates the random presentation order and provides a verification of modifier data.

In the mapping task we asked informant 13 to place a grain of rice on each color which he could name *siyókame.* He was shown the array of all colors (used in the focal task), so he was able to make choices while viewing all colors at once. He began by placing rice on the bluest colors, then placed rice on the greenest colors, and then paused as if finished. We recorded the mapping at his point of completion, which we call the first step, and then asked him to indicate more of the colors which he could call *siyókame.* When he again indicated he was finished, we recorded it as the second step and again asked him to go on. After his third step was completed, he commented that no more colors were *siyókame,* and that his fourth step must be called *siyóname.* Finally, when the fourth step was complete, he insisted that no remaining colors could be called *siyóname* or *siyókame.*

The mapping data are represented in Figure 11. The colors mapped in the first step are marked as 1; these are the greenest and bluest colors. The second step, marked as 2, lies in aqua and partially surrounds green. The third and fourth steps successively include more peripheral areas of grue. We conclude that these successive mapping steps represent successively lower membership in *siyó-*.

Correspondence between Naming and Mapping

The mapping task makes clear that informant 13's first and second naming tasks differ only in *-kame* expansion. In the first naming task he expanded *-kame* to almost all colors mapped in steps 1, 2, or 3 and to a few of those mapped in step 4. In the second naming task

	...	10	11	12	13	14	15	16	17	18	19	20	21	22	23	24	25	26	27	28	29	30	31	32	33	34	35	36	37	38	...
B									4	4	4	4	4	4																	
C							2	3	3	3	3	3	3	3	3	3	3	3	3	3	4	4									
D				4	4	2	2	2	2	3	3	3	3	3	4	4	4	4	4	4	4	4	4	4	4						
E			4	4	4	4	2	1	1	1	2	2	2	2	2	2	2	2	2	2	2	1	4	4	4						
F			4	4	4	4	2	1	1	1	1	1	1	2	2	2	2	1	1	1	1	1	4	4	4						
G			4	4	4	4	2	1	1	1	1	1	1	2	2	2	2	1	1	1	1	1	4	4	4						
H							2	2	1	1	1	1	1	2	2	2	2	2	1	1	1	1	1	4	4						
I										3	3	3											1	4	4	4					

Figure 11. Informant 13 mapped the category *siyó-* by placing rice grains on the color array. Key: 1, 2, 3: successive steps in mapping *siyókame;* 4: *siyóname.*

he restricted *-kame*, using it for colors mapped in step 1 and about half those mapped in step 2. That is why the first naming appeared to be neutralization and the second appeared to be union.

Since the first step of the mapping included green and blue but excluded aqua, it provides further evidence for union. Again, there is some skewing of the union: each of steps 1 through 3 included more greens than blues, while low-membership step 4 included more blues. Thus the mapping verifies our earlier findings based on modifiers.

The clear data of Figure 11 make the stepped mapping appear to be an ideal task. However, it is more difficult than simple naming, for both interviewer and informant. Berlin and Berlin (1975:note 5) discuss substantial problems with eliciting from an entire array of colors. When we tried mapping with other informants and a less experienced interviewer, informants indicated only colors corresponding to step 1. In short, the mapping task is a powerful and useful tool but requires careful elicitation.

Conclusions

Modifiers occur in every Tarahumara reference to color and distinguish two, three, or four grades of membership. These linguistic data strongly support Kay and McDaniel's attribution of fuzziness to the semantics of named color categories. We use the Tarahumara modifiers to ascertain the structure of the composite grue category. After adjusting for interinformant variation in modifier use, we find that Tarahumara grue is a union of blue and green, skewed toward green.

Why do we find a combination of union and skewing? We believe we have captured Tarahumara grue in the process of change: grue and other composite categories begin as balanced union, go through successively greater skewing, and split only after the skewing is extreme. In Tarahumara, secondary terms for pink and blue support this hypothesis of "skewing before splitting." From the present skewing toward green, we predict that in the future Tarahumara will borrow or coin a term for blue, and eventually will restrict the reference of *siyó-* to green.

We close with a proposal for future research directions. Berlin and Kay (1969) introduced two highly successful field methods to the study of color vocabularies: basic color term naming, which identifies the entire category, and focal choice, which identifies the single color most exemplary of the category. Kay and McDaniel (1978) revised the model of color category structure but did not provide corresponding field methods. Here, we have developed field methods that use color modifiers to explore internal category structure. We find that internal category structure changes before basic color terms change. In Tarahumara, analysis of modifiers was unavoidable because they occur in every linguistic reference to color. In other languages fieldworkers could elicit optional modifiers, and could use the method we demonstrate of mapping categories in graded steps. We advocate moving beyond basic color terms to color category structure, in order to understand the process by which category systems evolve from one stage to the next.

NOTES

We are grateful to Paul Kay for probing discussions as this paper developed—in conceptual contributions, we consider him a co-author. He, Brent Berlin, and Ann Millard provided extensive comments on preliminary drafts; they are, of course, not liable for errors in this revised version. We thank the Mexican branch of the Summer Institute of Linguistics for facilitating our fieldwork. Brent Berlin, Paul Kay, and William Merrifield provided equipment from the World Color Survey (NSF grant BNS 76-14153), a collaborative project of the University of California at Berkeley and the Summer Institute of Linguistics. The Experimental Semantics project (NSF grant BNS 78-15900) supported fieldwork by Burgess and Kempton and computer analysis by Kempton. Burgess worked also in collaboration with the World Color Survey, and MacLaury worked under a Fulbright-Hays fellowship.

1. The color array is arranged as follows. The leftmost column (labeled 0) represents achromatic colors. Each subsequent column (1-40) represents colors of constant hue, with dominant wavelength increasing from left to right. Each row contains colors of constant brightness; brightness decreases from top to bottom. Row A is pure white and row J pure black; thus they are placed only in the achromatic column 0.

The color array "wraps around" like a Mercator projection of the world. That is, apart from the neutral achromatic column 0, the colors on the leftmost edge (column 1) are perceptually adjacent to the colors on the rightmost edge (column 40). This explains why red and pink, in the English Figure 1, occur on both edges. Also like a Mercator projection, the points near the "poles" are expanded.

2. A double verb construction apparently can be used to neutralize the diminutive modifier. For example, *sitánaga ilí* (being red) can refer to all reds (Burgess 1982). However, informants never volunteered this construction when naming colors in interviews.

3. The stepped mapping task, developed by MacLaury (see MacLaury, McMillen, and McMillen 1979), improves upon Kempton's earlier techniques using grading phrases (1978, 1981).

REFERENCES

Berlin, Brent, and Elois Ann Berlin
1975 Aguaruna Color Categories. *American Ethnologist* 2:61-87.

Berlin, Brent, and Paul Kay
1969 *Basic Color Terms: Their Universality and Evolution.* Berkeley and Los Angeles: University of California Press.

Burgess, Don
1983 Western Tarahumara. To appear in Ronald W. Langacker, ed., *Studies in Uto-Aztecan Grammar,* vol. 4: *Southern Uto-Aztecan Grammatical Sketches.* Arlington: Summer Institute of Linguistics and University of Texas.

Burgess, Don, Willett Kempton, and Robert MacLaury
1983 Tarahumara Color Modifiers: Category Structure Presaging Evolutionary Change. *American Ethnologist* 10:133-49.

Dougherty, Janet W. D.
1977 Color Categorization in West Futunese: Variability and Change. In Ben G. Blount and Mary Sanches, eds., *Sociocultural Dimensions of Language Change,* pp. 103-18. New York: Academic Press.

Fillmore, Charles J.
1975 An Alternative to Checklist Theories of Meaning. *Proceedings,* 1st annual meeting, Berkeley Linguistics Society, pp. 121-31.

Greenberg, Joseph H.
1966 Language Universals. In *Current Trends in Linguistics,* vol. 3: *Theoretical Foundations,* ed. Thomas A. Sebeok, pp. 61-112. The Hague: Mouton.

Heider, Eleanor (= Eleanor Rosch)
1972 Probabilities, Sampling and Ethnographic Method: The Case of Dani Colour Names. *Man* 7(n.s.):448-66.

Kay, Paul
1975 Synchronic Variability and Diachronic Change in Basic Color Terms. *Language in Society* 4:257-70.

1982 Linguistic Competence and Folk Theories of Language: Two English Hedges. Paper presented at conference on Semantics, International Research and Exchanges Board, Budapest.

Kay, Paul, and Willett Kempton
1984 What Is the Sapir-Whorf Hypothesis? *American Anthropologist* 86:65-79.

Kay, Paul, and Chad K. McDaniel
1978 The Linguistic Significance of the Meanings of Basic Color Terms. *Language* 54:610-46.

Kempton, Willett
1978 Category Grading and Taxonomic Relations. *American Ethnologist* 5:44-65. Revised version in Ronald W. Casson, ed., *Language, Culture, and Cognition: Readings in Cognitive Anthropology.* New York: Macmillan, 1981.
1981 *The Folk Classification of Ceramics: A Study of Cognitive Prototypes.* New York: Academic Press.

Labov, William
1973 The Boundaries of Words and Their Meanings. In Joshua Fishman, ed., *New Ways of Analyzing Variation in English*, pp. 340-73. Washington, D.C.: Georgetown University Press.

Lakoff, George
1973 Hedges: A Study in Meaning Criteria and the Logic of Fuzzy Concepts. *Journal of Philosophical Logic* 2:458-508.

Lenneberg, Eric, and John Roberts
1956 The Language of Experience. Memoir no. 13 of *International Journal of American Linguistics.*

MacLaury, Robert E., Margot McMillen, and Stanley McMillen
1979 Uspantec Color Categories: An Experiment with Field Methods. Paper presented at the Annual Mayan Workshop IV, Palenque, Mexico.

McCloskey, Michael E., and Sam Glucksburg
1978 Natural Categories: Well Defined or Fuzzy Sets? *Memory & Cognition* 6:462-74.

McDaniel, Chad K.
1972 Hue Perception and Hue Naming. A.B. Honors thesis, Harvard College.
1974 Basic Color Terms: Their Neurophysiological Bases. Paper presented to American Anthropological Association, Mexico, D.F.

Pettigrew, Thomas F.
1982 Cognitive Style and Social Behavior: A Review of Category Width. In Ladd Wheeler, ed., *Review of Personality and Social Psychology,* 3:199-224. Beverly Hills, Calif.: Sage Press.

Rosch, Eleanor (= Eleanor Heider)
1973 On the Internal Structure of Perceptual and Semantic Categories. In T. M. Moore, ed., *Cognitive Development and the Acquisition of Language,* pp. 111-44. New York: Academic Press.

Rosch, Eleanor H., and Carolyn B. Mervis
1975 Family Resemblances: Studies in the Internal Structure of Categories. *Cognitive Psychology* 7:573-605.

Weinreich, Urial
1966 On the Semantic Structure of Language. In Joseph H. Greenberg, ed., *Universals of Language,* pp. 142-216. Cambridge: MIT Press.
Zadeh, Lotfi
1965 Fuzzy Sets. *Information and Control* 8:338-53.

3

Folk Knowledge without Fuzz

Oswald Werner

In this paper I try initially to demonstrate folk theories or models of the mind (i.e. intension) are, by necessity, deterministic (i.e. nonfuzzy).[1] However, the *application* of deterministic models of the world (in our heads) to the "real" world of actual objects (i.e. extension) *is* probabilistic (fuzzy?). In the second and following sections of this paper, I extend the Modification (Attribution) and Taxonomy, or MT, lexical/semantic field model (e.g. Werner and Topper 1976, Evens et al. 1980) to account for phenomena associated with various aspects of "fuzz."

I propose to make this extension through the use of a deterministic model using the lexical/semantic relations of Taxonomy and Modification (Attribution). First, I account for the problem of "cup" and "mug." Second, I discuss the problem of "willow trees" and "willow bushes." Third, I show how a deterministic model can be extended to deal with the problem of prototypical or "core" concepts. This is accomplished by looking at the acquisition of taxonomic structures developmentally. The key to the solution is the empirical fact that in low-context situations (e.g. in the use of citation forms) any phonological label (the phonetic aspect of a lexeme) is interpreted, by speakers and hearers alike, *always* as the most specific (lowest level) reference available in a folk taxonomy. For example, "man" in low-context situations is always interpreted as "human male," never as "human."

Probabilities and Hypotheses

In his article in the *Folk Classification Bulletin* (1978), Hunn postulates a membership function for objects in the "real" world. For example, for a cup this function could be assumed to be:

$$\text{i. } f(c) = (0.5,\ 0.3,\ 0.2).$$

If we assume that an "ideal" cup has the attributes

$$\text{ii. } c = (a,\ b,\ c),$$

then in the case of a certain cup X the membership function gives the degree to which each of the three attributes (criteria) are descriptive of the example:

$$\text{iii. } f(c)(x) = 0.5\ x(a) + 0.3\ x(b) + 0.2\ x(c).$$

I am assuming that Hunn means by (iii) that if I recognize features *a, b,* and *c,* I will necessarily be forced to say "This is a cup." He also seems to claim that there is a *smallest criterial set* of attributes that must be present, or I make my decision to call the object at hand a [cup] with a probability less than 1.

Hunn then discusses why fuzzy set theory is inadequate to express this state of affairs and proposes an as yet unexplored extension of fuzzy set theory. In the following discussion I would like to propose an alternate solution based on a radically intensional (for my use of the term see Lyons 1968:454) view that better accounts for the "facts." First, let me assume that "cupness" is not a closed but an open list of attributes. Which attributes are criterial depends on context, perspective, light conditions, etc., and perhaps the state of mind of the recognizer. Thus I restate (i) as

$$\text{iv. } c = (a,\ b,\ c,\ \ldots).$$

The attributes *a, b, c,* . . . may be simple (usually adjectives) or complex (phrases, paragraphs, even stories; e.g., in the definition of "cup" the description of the manufacturing process is a complex attribute). Thus simple criteria for "cupness" may be "small" (see below) or complex "used for drinking" (see also below), or very complex (how it is made). This implies that the concept (cup) is not *just* a bundle of attributes but a coherent theory of cuphood.

Second, we must answer the question concerning the status of these attributes or criteria in our theory. Though it may not be a universally accepted epistemological position, my assumption is that attributes are not primarily a part of the objects we encounter in everyday life but are "in my head." They are "theoretical" templates against which I check my experience in the "real" world.

Therefore, by applying my cup attributes to any object, I can, through a process of pattern matching, determine if the object at hand is a cup or not. That is, my "internal representation" (mental picture, eidetic image, and perhaps also "digital" attributes) of a cup or of "cupness" need not be fuzzy at all (see note 1). It is true that there are different people with different skills for identifying cups, but let us assume for now that I am an expert cup detector. With such expertise at hand, the only thing that appears to be fuzzy is the *application* of my nonfuzzy "template" for "cupness" to "real"-life *examples* of objects that may be "real" cups or masquerading as potential "cups." Thus, for each criterion $a, b, c, \ldots$ there exists a probability $D(a), D(b), D(c), \ldots$ that I will make the right choice, match, etc., on that attribute. If the probability for my recognition of a cup is $p(\text{cup})$, then

v. $$p(\text{cup}) = D(a) \times D(b) \times D(c) \times \ldots \times D(i) \ldots$$

Because of perspective, light conditions, my own state of mind, etc., I *cannot ever* in a "noisy" world see or recognize all possible attributes of an object. This applies equally to so-called "criterial" attributes.

In order to account for these facts, I redefine the functions $D(i)$, where $i = a, b, c, \ldots$, or $D(i)$ assumes the values of $D(a), D(b), D(c), \ldots$ respectively. This new set of $D(i)$ may assume three values: 0, 1, or $p(i)$. A given $D(i) = 1$ if I do not find the attribute but feel strongly on the basis of other evidence that I must hypothesize its presence. A given $D(i) = 0$ if an attribute is not recognizable and I feel strongly on the basis of other evidence that I must hypothesize its absence. As a recognizer I have actually four choices if one of the $D(i) = 0$.

First, I can accept this fact. That mcans that thc total probability for recognizing the cup also becomes zero and I conclude that the object at hand is not a cup but something else. However, all other *recognizable* attributes must support this conclusion.

Second, I may also find myself in a situation where I have no alternative name for the new object. If other evidence warrants, I may call it "almost a cup" or "cup-like," even though one or more prerequisites in my theory of full-blooded cuphood may be missing.

Third, I may revise my view on the basis of my theory of cuphood by assuming that the missing attribute is actually there, but that I cannot see it because of perspective (it may be on the wrong side), light conditions, my own mental state, etc. Following my theory of cuphood, I therefore set *all* hypothesized $D(i) = 1$. That is, I assume certainty, or the presence of not recognizable but purely hypothetical attributes.

Fourth, I may be forced to construct a more abstract theory eliminating one or more of the $D(i)$. This kind of a theoretical revision toward greater abstractness (reduction of attributes) will become relevant in the following sections. Thus

$$\text{vi. } D(i) = \begin{Bmatrix} 0 \\ 1 \\ p(i) \end{Bmatrix}$$

In other words, there is a probability for recognition but it is based only on the attributes that are *perceptually accessible.* All hidden attributes, if all evidence points to the acceptance of the theory of cuphood, must be assumed to have been identified with certainty (i.e. all such $D(i) = 1$), as part of my "cup" theory.

Formulas (vi) and (v) imply that if I want to be able to make a reasonably accurate choice of cups from among a set of objects that are competing for "cuphood," the probability of p(cup) must be close to 1. That assumption in turn implies that I must make very probable or accurate choices, matches, etc. on each of the recognizable attributes of a cup, or set the particular $D(i) = 1$, i.e., to hypothesize certainty. That is, each of the probabilities of matching the ith attribute of cup must also be very close to 1.

The interesting thing is how close to 1 they have to be. For example, let us assume an average probability for selecting the ith attribute correctly $p(i) = 0.8$. Being correct eight out of ten tries seems to be a relatively safe assumption. Given six attributes, the average probability for selecting a cup is only 0.26 or about one success in four tries. Only at probability levels of 0.99 or higher do we get a probability for correctly identifying a cup of 0.94 or larger, or about one mistake in seventeen tries. Perhaps this figure begins to approach everyday performance levels in the identification of objects. Note that the number of attributes may be crucial too: the fewer but the more certain my attributes, the better my final choice. Thus a correct hypothesis about the word (i.e. all $D(i) = 1$) seems to be the most crucial aspect for recognizing and classifying objects. It seems therefore very likely that "in our heads" we do not use probabilities for object recognition and classification at all.

Under given conditions of environmental "noise" it may be safer, quicker, etc., to take our theories about the world seriously and after a cursory stab at "reality testing" set all $D(i) = 1$. This would account—at least in part—for the fact that in daily life as in science "anomaly is detected with difficulty" (Kuhn 1962:52-76), or that sometimes on the basis of just one attribute (e.g. a lion's roar in the dark) we take appropriate action and survive.

This approach to object recognition through probability answers two additional questions of empirical fact. First, we rarely make category mistakes. Stating it another way, the "correct" assignment of a label to an object is a very highly probable event. Second, this picture of object recognition explains why category mistakes are highly distressing. Most of the time during everyday life we behave as expert taxonomists making assignments of labels with split-second accuracy (Polanyi 1958:80). Failure to correctly classify an item quickly is unusual and therefore upsetting.

Difficulty in classifying an item correctly implies, following formula (v), that the problem may often reside in *just one* of the attributes, that is, in cases where just one of the attributes affects our hypothesis for a highly probable assignment. This is, for example, the case with yuccas (*tsá'ászi'*) in Navajo. This "genus" has attributes which make assignment possible either to the flexible plants (*ch'il*) or to the cacti or thorny plants (*hosh*). Some Navajos assign yuccas one way because they are flexible, others another way because they have needles, and a third group "gives up" by attaching yuccas directly to plants as a fifth member of the contrast set which includes *ch'il* and *hosh* (Werner and Manning 1979:360).

Cup and Mug

The difficulties in distinguishing "cup" and "mug" are similarly dependent on hypothesized "cupness" and "mugness." In order to make my exposition somewhat more realistic I will consider more than visual criteria of "cupness" and "mugness" (e.g. Kempton 1978). To obtain acceptable and appropriate sets of attributes, I utilize dictionary definitions (as a substitute for folk definitions). For the sake of reliability I actually use three dictionaries as if they were three informants giving definitions. The dictionaries: the *American Heritage Dictionary* (AHD), the *Webster's Seventh Collegiate Dictionary* (W7CD), and *Webster's English Notebook Dictionary* (WEND) by Dennison. Using English, the reader will be able to judge the adequacy of the dictionaries *and* of my analysis. The definitions are given in full in the Appendix. These definitions and the composite definition which I construct are all in Aristotelian canonical form: "A is a B, which . . ." where after "which" follows a list of attributes (symbolized by ". . ."), both simple and complex. The lexical/semantic relation of the first part "A is a B" is taxonomic (T), the rest (after the "which") attributive

(M). The definitions of "cup" and "mug," following the dictionaries, are:

cup:	is a (kind of) container (T) is small (M) is open (M) has a flat bottom (M) has a handle (M) is used for drinking (M) has a rounded bowl (M)	*mug:*	is a (kind of) vessel (T) /is small/* (M) /is open/* (M) /has a flat bottom/* (M) has a handle or not (M) is used for drinking (M) is cylindrical (M) is made of metal or earthware (M)

(The starred items were not specifically mentioned in the definitions of "mugs" but are added on the basis of informant judgment, i.e. myself, to enhance consistency and comparability. I assume these attributes are not controversial and that their absence is simply due to the unsystematic nature of dictionary entries. The inclusion of these attributes makes the definitions more systematic and therefore more comparable.)

These definitions, especially by including the definitions of "vessel," "container," and "utensil," may be combined in the taxonomic structure represented by Taxonomy 1 (see Appendix for detailed definitions). The definitions are:

utensil: is a thing (T)
is used in a household (M)
is used domestically (M)
is used in a kitchen (especially) (M)

container: is a utensil* (T)
holds material (M)
holds something (M)
contains something (M)
is hollow (M)

vessel: is a container (T)
is for liquids (M)

*The assignment of "container" to "utensil" follows from WEND:43 if the definition is interpreted as a listing of "examples" or instances.

Several anomalies are not accounted for, by either the definitions or the diagram. According to W7CD "a mug . . . is a drinking cup" and "a cup is a bowl-shaped . . . vessel." Thus while in Taxonomy 1 "cup," "mug," and "bowl" are part of the same contrast set, the above two sentences suggest that "a mug is a cup" and perhaps "a cup is a

Taxonomy 1

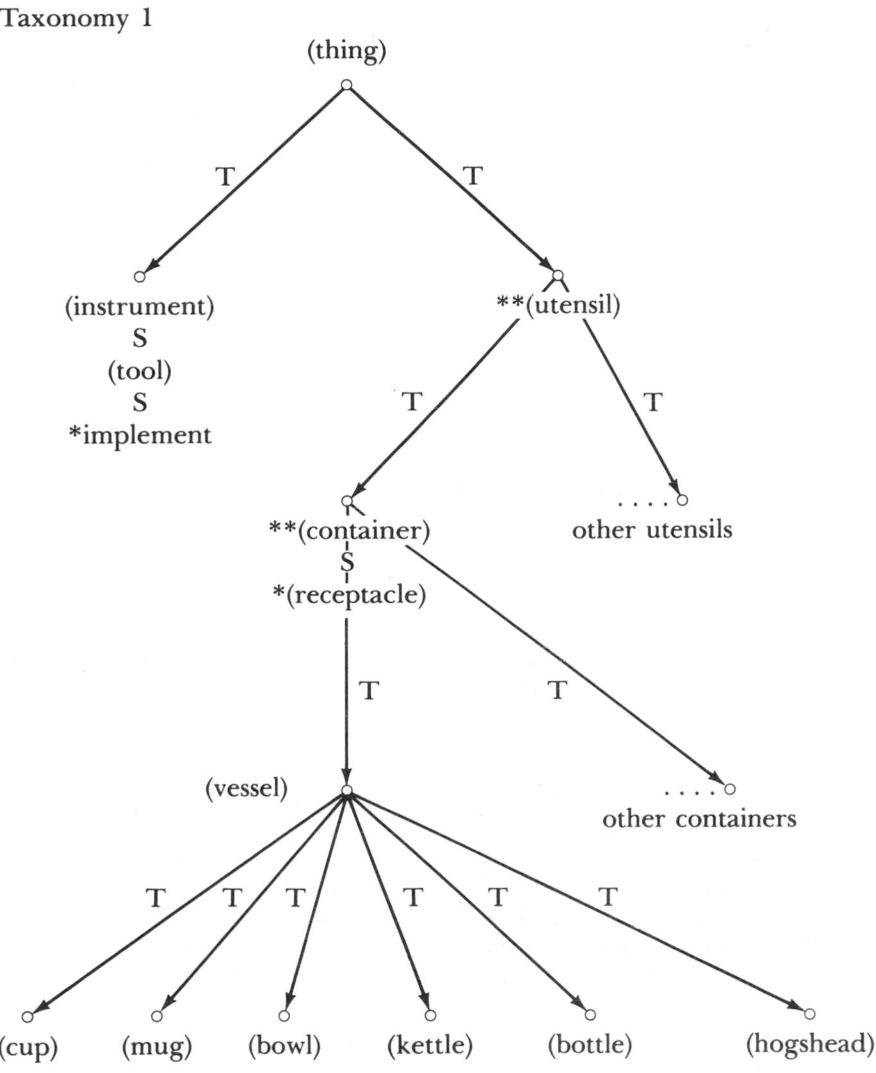

*S = synonymy or near synonymy, nontechnical usage here.
** Note that there are additional utensils that are not containers and containers that are not vessels. There may exist containers that are not utensils, though some definitely are. The former are of no concern here. Another possibility may be that the classes of "utensils" and "containers" intersect.

bowl." That is, there is a hierarchy descending from bowl to cup to mug. The status of a "bowl" as a "vessel" is confirmed by the dictionaries. Similary there seems to be no question about the status as "vessels" of either "cup" or "mug." Therefore the anomaly must exist between the relationship of "cup," "mug," and "bowl" to each other. How can we make sense of this interrelationship? Before going on to a concrete solution we need a prerequisite: Our formula (ii) is in fact not quite correct. The definition of "cup" demonstrates clearly that the "cupness" features attach to the "vessel" features. Therefore (ii) is better expressed as

$$\text{vii. cup} = (\text{vessel}) \cup (a, b, c, \ldots)$$

(∪ or union is roughly equivalent to M)

That is, all taxons inherit all attributes of their superordinate taxons.

With this in mind we can now compare the three definitions by adding to each entry all features that apply.

	*(cup)**	*(mug)**	*(bowl)**
1.	thing	thing	thing (taxonomic inheritance)
2.	utensil	utensil	utensil (taxonomic inheritance)
3.	container	container	container (taxonomic inheritance)
4.	vessel	vessel	vessel (taxonomic inheritance)
5.	small	small	small? (range: fist size)**
6.	open	open	open
7.	concave	concave	concave
8.	holds liquid	holds liquid	holds liquid
9.	flat-bottomed	flat-bottomed	flat-bottomed?
10.	cylindrical?	cylindrical	not cylindrical
11.	hemispherical?	not hemispherical	hemispherical
12.	wider than deep?	wider than deep?	wider than deep
13.	has handle	has handle?	has no handle

*Items in parentheses, as opposed to brackets, imply the concept of "cuphood" rather than the phonological noise associated with (cup), etc.

**The size range of bowls is greater than that of cups or mugs.

Items 1-8 are shared monothetic features: items 9-13 are nonshared polythetic features. A question mark implies that an item may or may not possess the feature. "Not" implies emphatic absence of the feature.

Lines 1 through 4 are all inherited attributes passed on through the taxonomic relationship. Lines 5 through 8 are also common to all three. Of these "hollowness" or "concaveness" is a characteristic of "container" and need not be mentioned again. The same applies to "holds liquid" as a characteristic of vessel. "Smallness" and "openness" are new. Given all the preceding superordinate attributes, "smallness" and "openness" are sufficient to define a *relatively abstract* category of "bowl," which I will call (bowl(0)). Up to this point we have only shared features of a monothetic classification. "Flat-bottomness" seems to be the only attribute of (cup(0)) in this system of attributes. Both more specific cups and more specific mugs possess it. A "bowl" is indeterminate on this attribute; it may or may not have a flat bottom. It is, however, always (?) hemispherical; a mug is always (?) cylindrical; and a cup may be either. A bowl is always wider than deep; a cup and a mug may be either (?). These are then cup(1) and mug(1) respectively. Additional levels can be added by making the distinction between cups and/or mugs with and without handles (no problem for mugs; for cups it applies, e.g. to sake cups). Thus in Taxonomy 2 we get a new version of the bottom part of Taxonomy 1.

To summarize: The abstract (bowl(0)) is a kind of (vessel). (Bowl(0)) is abstract enough to be superordinate to (bowl(1)) and (cup(0)). The

Taxonomy 2

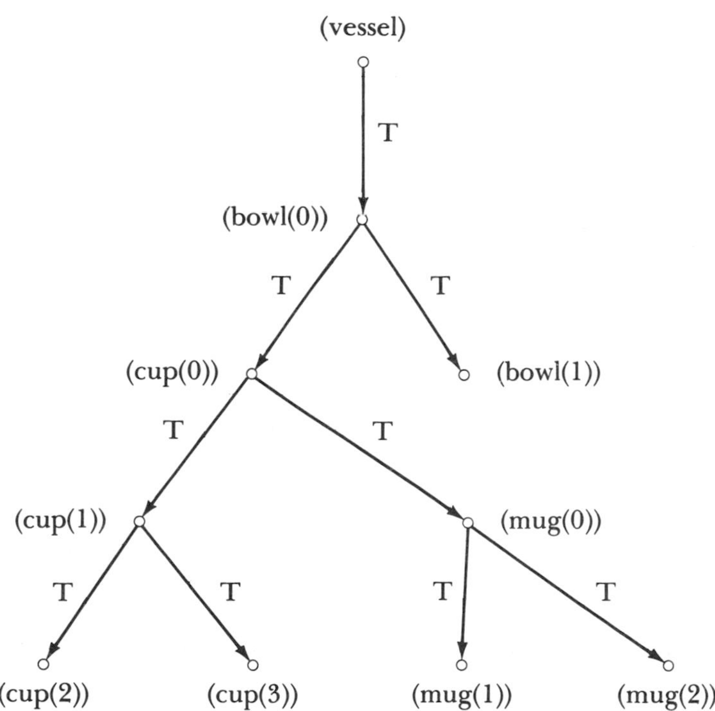

abstract character of (bowl(0)) is attested by the hedge "a cup is a bowl-shaped . . . vessel" (see next section). (Bowl(1)) has the attributes (shared by all subordinate concepts) of being small (ranging to considerably larger than a cup or mug) and open. (Bowl(1)) contrasts with (cup(0)) in that the former may or may not have a flat bottom, while the latter always has it, and possibly in the matter of size. (Cup(1)) and (mug(0)) contrast in the feature of shape: a mug is cylindrical while a cup may or may not be. On the lowest level (cup(2)) is relatively unusual because it does not have a handle (the sake cup), while (cup(3)) always has it. The same distinction of the absence and/or presence of a handle is assumed for (mug(1)) (no handle) and (mug(2)) (with handle).

The proliferation of labels surely looks bizarre at first. However, it may be well to remember that all node labels for concepts such as (cup (i)), for example, have the same phonological label (i.e. the "noise") [cup]. Luckily there is empirical evidence for the diversity of conceptual labels. We know from documented cases of multilevel labeling with identical labels (e.g. Werner and Manning 1979) that the more specific term is always the preferred choice (preferred interpretation or unmarked) in low-context situations, e.g. citation forms. Thus the most common "image" of a cup or a mug is with the handle, that is, (cup(3)) and (mug(2)). Contrasting a (cup(1)) with a (mug(0)) on the next level up, the cylindrical shape of the mug versus the bowl shape of the cup seems most salient. On the next level mug and cup, now united in (cup(0)), contrast with (bowl(1)). This model should be fairly easily testable via one or several clustering techniques now readily available.

Willow Trees and Willow Bushes

The theoretical notion of the taxonomic organization of human knowledge can be extended analogously to the problem of the classification of willows. The sources are again the three dictionaries (AHD, W7CD, WEND) treated as informants (see Appendix). The resulting taxonomy is represented by Taxonomy 3.

On the lowest level we have again the greatest degree of specificity. I assume that the tree form of a willow is the more common; therefore, the treelike (willow(2)) is the most common choice for the interpretation of "willow" in low-context situations. (Willow(0)) does not share the single trunk nor the multiple-trunk feature of tree or bush respectively—it may have both or neither. (Confirmation is based on the three dictionaries.) It is in this sense a more abstract "willow" than either a willow tree (willow(2)) or a willow bush (willow(1)). The

Taxonomy 3

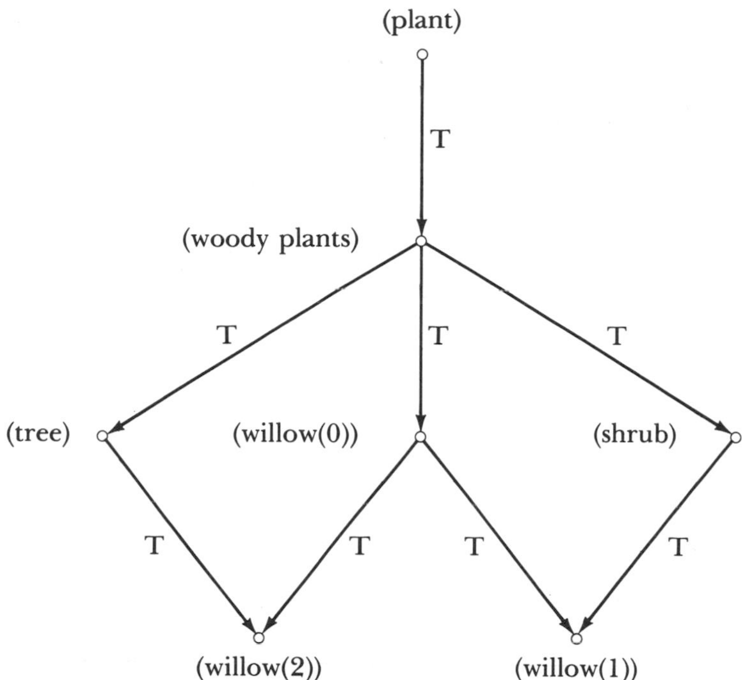

category of woody plants may or may not be a covert node in English, but it is not covert, for example, in Navajo, where *tsin* refers to both trees and bushes. Actually, it does not matter whether "woody plants" is covert or not because the three items "willow," "tree," and "shrub" are also connected directly to "plant." The transitivity of the taxonomic relation and the concomitant downward inheritance of features reduces or eliminates the need for all but explicitly labeled nodes.

Typicality

A final example deals with the problem of "fuzzy features" from the theoretical perspective of this paper. The problem as I see it is to account for the *most typical* core of a taxon. The existence of this core concept has received considerable attention in the recent literature.

My argument again proceeds from the notion that taxonomic hierarchies often display the same label (phonological form) on different levels of a taxonomy. I would like to warn the reader that I am knowingly oversimplifying because the process that I am going to describe is to some extent counter to the process by which some children learn the phonological form [mama]. They first apply it to all human beings (faces?), then to all females (or their faces?), and only in the final stage of development does the term become stabilized as referring to that female who has the special relation of mother to the child.[2]

The first part of the argument explaining "fuzzy reference" and "core concepts" relies on the fact that phonological labels are easily extended upward in a taxonomy, that is, upward on the scale of abstraction, or that greater abstraction always means a *reduction* of attributes or features. The fact that in the least context-sensitive situation the specific referent always comes to mind first implies that human concept acquisition starts, but by no means stops, there. Suppose we take the example of Smith, Shoben, and Rips (1974) that "robin" and "cardinal" are more prototypical birds than are (in descending order of prototypicality) chickens, ostriches, and penguins. The developmental steps leading to the "psychological reality" (including Lakoff's (1973) hedge for penguins: "Technically speaking, penguins are birds") could be imagined as follows. First, a child learns the term "birdie." The process must be similar to the "mama" example above (see note 2). Eventually "robins" and "cardinals" are recognized, distinguished, and related taxonomically to "birdie."

At some point in time, perhaps in grade school, we recognize that "birdie" is childish and replace it with "bird"—I would like to call this level (bird(*n*)). Gradually as we grow older we learn about other birds different from "robins" and "cardinals." Each time we learn about a new kind of bird we have to revise our notion of "birdness": each instance or at least many instances of birds we encounter force a revision of "birdness," and each revision is by necessity more abstract than the preceding one because we have to slough off attributes that previously were associated with our more primitive notions of "birdness."[3] In the process, spanning perhaps several years of intellectual growth and development, the taxonomy represented by Taxonomy 4 may result.

What is the empirical evidence for this taxonomy? First, the most typical class of "birds" is the label "bird" with the highest index, i.e. (bird(*n*)). That is, "citation forms" or forms elicited in a minimal context always refer to the most specific case: the superordinate label of "robin" and "cardinal." Chickens for city children are added later,[4] ostriches still later (eliminating the attribute of flight), penguins are perhaps last. By this time the attribute bundle of (bird(0)) is so small that hedges are employed as signs of our incredulity that we are still

Taxonomy 4

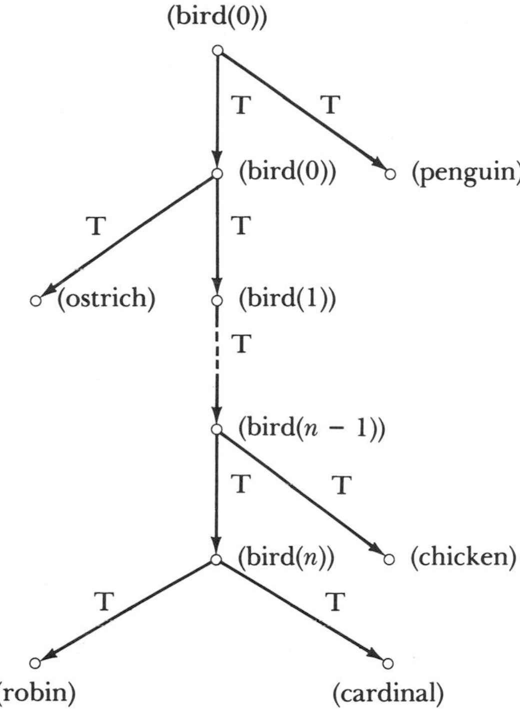

dealing with birds. Ornithologists have perhaps no qualms about penguins being birds. But as relatively untutored laypersons, "penguins" are surprising (or the comparison of (bird(n)) with (bird(0)) may be surprising). That the terms for "bird" form a continuum (from index 0 to index n) is also attested by the fact that we use superordinate labels continuously as pro-nouns. This is perhaps more often true in languages like English, which have an injunction against the repeated use of a label (especially in writing), than in languages without a literary tradition where such an injunction may not exist; however, I am not all that certain.

In a small zoo, for example, with one person in charge of all birds from robins to penguins, the director may ask an employee "Did you feed the birds yet?" and include them all. A turkey farmer's wife may ask the same question and it will be clear that she means only turkeys. If my wife asks that question of my son, it is a request for information whether he put out the suet for the cardinals, robins, or whatever small birds may come to visit the bird feeder in our back yard.

There is a final empirical question here: Is a robin/cardinal the prototypical bird for all speakers of English? I think the answer to this question is no. It would be interesting to study American populations (e.g., turkey farmers' children) where this is not the case.

Conclusions

The major argument of this paper is that "fuzzy" labeling decisions exist only at the interface between our knowledge, which I claim is deterministic and not fuzzy, and the "real" world, which is inherently fuzzy. That is, our knowledge of items in the "real" world is deterministic but our *application* of this knowledge to the real world is probabilistic, mitigated by our tendency to readily hypothesize features that in any particular instance may not be available to our perceptions. I tried to show that the cup/mug problem, the willow tree/willow bush problem, and the prototypicality of "birds" and similar classifications can be handled by a deterministic model—here the taxonomy and modification schema.

The schema does seem to proliferate labels and quasi labels. Seeing in this redundancy or elegance is in the eye of the beholder. I hope to show in a future paper that the difficulties encountered when trying to taxonomize abstract terms lie precisely in the fact that every term without a physical object referent in the "real" world is ambiguous on multiple levels, analogous to the multiple "cups," "mugs," "bowls," "willows," and "birds" of this paper.

Appendix

Definitions excerpted from the dictionaries: AHD: *American Heritage Dictionary;* W7CD: *Webster's Seventh Collegiate Dictionary*; WEND: *Webster's English Notebook Dictionary* by Dennison. Page number appears after colon.

CUP AHD:322—a small, open container, usually with a flat bottom and a handle for drinking. W7CD:203—an open bowl-shaped drinking vessel. WEND:11—rounded drinking bowl. MUG AHD:860—a cylindrical drinking vessel often with a handle. W7CD:556—usually metal or earthenware cylindrical drinking cup. WEND:25—drinking cup. BOWL AHD:157—a hemispherical vessel, wider than deep, for food and fluids. W7CD:100—a concave, usually hemispherical vessel used especially for holding liquids. WEND:5—round dish. DISH AHD:378—an open container, generally shallow and concave, for holding or serving food. W7CD:239—a more or less concave vessel from which food is served; any of various shallow, concave vessels. WEND:13—plate for food. VESSEL AHD:1425—a hollow utensil used as a container especially for liquids. W7CD:989—a hollow or concave utensil (as a hogshead, bottle, kettle, cup, or bowl) for holding something. WEND:44—container. CONTAINER AHD:278—a thing in which material is held or carried, receptacle. W7CD:180—one that contains, especially a receptacle or a flexible covering for shipment of goods. WEND:10—contain: to have within, hold, include. RECEPTACLE AHD:1088—something that holds or contains, a container. W7CD:714—one that receives or contains something, container. WEND:32—container. UTENSIL AHD:1411—(1) any instrument or container, especially one used domestically, as in a kitchen or on a farm; (2) any instrument or tool, implement. W7CD: 978—an instrument or vessel used in a household especially a kitchen. WEND:43—useful tool, container.

WILLOW AHD:1466—any of various deciduous trees or shrubs of the genus *Salix,* having unusually narrow leaves, flowers born in catkins, and strong lightweight wood. W7CD:1022—any of a genus (*Salix* of the family *Salicacae,* the willow family) of trees or shrubs bearing aments or apetalous flowers and including forms of value for wood, osiers, or tanbark and a few ornaments. WEND:45—slender tree. TREE AHD:1367—a usually tall woody plant, distinguished from a shrub by having comparatively greater height and characteristically, a single trunk rather than several stems. W7CD:943—a woody perennial plant having a single usually elongated main stem generally with few or no branches on its lower part. WEND:41—plant with wooden trunk, branches and many leaves. BUSH AHD:179—a low, branching woody plant, usually smaller than a tree, shrub. W7CD:113—a low densely branched shrub. WEND:6—shrub. SHRUB AHD:1200—a woody plant of relatively low height, distinguished from a tree by having several stems rather than a single trunk, a bush. W7CD:805—a low usually several-stemmed woody plant. WEND:36—small bush.

NOTES

I am indebted to grant MH 10940 from NIMH for partial support of this work. Several people have read drafts and offered advice. I wish to thank especially Ed Garrison, Christie Gladwin, Jim Boster, and Judy Abbott. Several of these friends and colleagues were dismayed at the apparent complexity of the model I propose here. However, I stubbornly stick to my conclusions. Thus any problems that remain are strictly my own.

1. My use of the adjective "deterministic" should be interpreted as referring to a model or theory that is fully determined, structurally complete, and without uncertainties at any one time in the life of a human being. How this deterministic folk knowledge is acquired and/or updated on the basis of experience is beyond the scope of this paper. The revision of our theoretical "templates" on the basis of experience *is* a serious problem in light of the fact that in folk theories as well as in scientific theories "anomaly" surfaces only with difficulty (Kuhn 1962).

2. Actually the two cases are not that different. (1) In the case of "mama" the child overgeneralizes; (2) in the case of "bird" it overspecifies. These two "strategies" of learning seem to be related to the fact that in the case of "mama" there are different labels available (i.e. [people], [lady], and the lowest level [mama]) to name different levels of the resulting taxonomy, whereas in the case of "bird" such labels are *not* available (i.e., there is only the label [bird], and [robin] on the lowest level.) The following diagram compares the two situations.

Stage of Development

	"mama"	"bird"
I.	○ (mama(0)) equivalent to all people	○ (birdie(0)) equivalent to all birds of certain size and appearance

II.

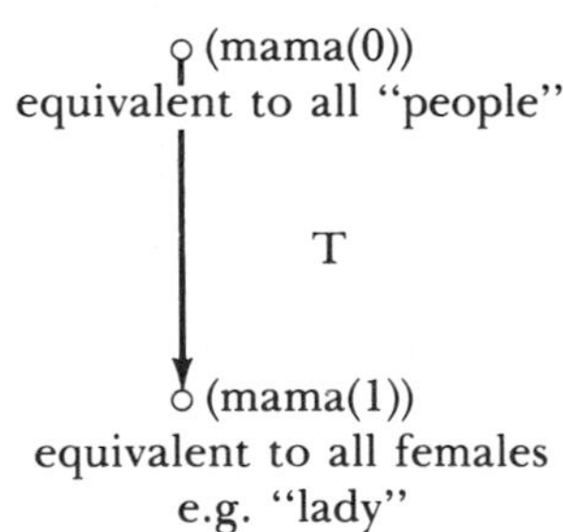

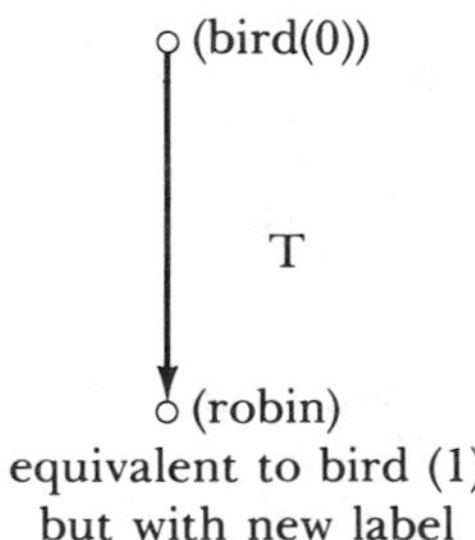

III.

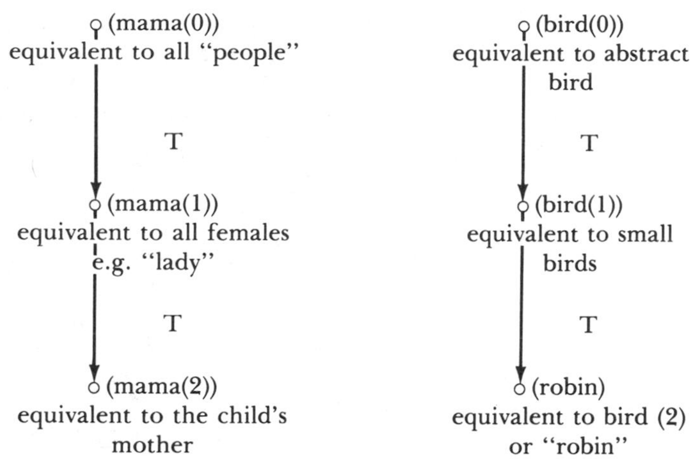

Juxtaposed here, the two approaches of learning seem to be much more similar than the differences would indicate.

3. A similar process of "elevation in rank" based on the conceptual development of plant nomenclatures is proposed by Dougherty (1979). Her data and generalizations are based upon fieldwork with children in Berkeley, Calif.

4. It is interesting that Navajo children have made a clear separation of store-bought, nonbirdlike chickens (*chigii*) and live chickens around the hogan (*na'ahoohaii*).

REFERENCES

Dennison Manufacturing Co.
N.d. *Webster's English Notebook Dictionary.*

Dougherty, J. W. D.
1979 Learning Names for Plants and Plants for Names. *Anthropological Linguistics* 20:298-315.

Evens, M. W., et al.
1980 *Lexical-Semantic Relations: A Comparative Survey.* Linguistic Research, Inc.

Hunn, E.
1978 Fuzzy Sets and Folk Biology. *Folk Classification Bulletin* 2.1:1-3.

Kempton, W.
1978 Category Grading and Taxonomic Relations: A Mug Is a Sort of a Cup. *American Ethnologist* 5:44-65.

Kuhn, T. S.
1962 *The Structure of Scientific Revolutions.* Chicago: University of Chicago Press.

Lakoff, G.
1973 Hedges: A Study in Meaning Criteria and the Logic of Fuzzy Concepts. *Journal of Philosophical Logic* 2:458-508.

Lyons, J.
1968 *Introduction to Theoretical Linguistics.* Cambridge: Cambridge University Press.

Merriam Co.
1969 *Webster's Seventh Collegiate Dictionary.*

Morrison, W., ed.
1969 *The American Heritage Dictionary of the English Language.* New York: American Heritage Publishing Co. and Houghton Mifflin.

Polanyi, M.
1958 *Personal Knowledge: Toward a Post-Critical Philosophy.* New York: Harper Torchbooks.

Smith, E. E., E. J. Shoben, and L. J. Rips
1974 Structure and Process in Semantic Memory: A Featural Model for Semantic Decisions. *Psychological Review* 81:214-41.

Werner, O., and A. Manning
1979 Tough Luck Ethnography versus God's Truth Ethnography in Ethnoscience: Some Thoughts on the Nature of Culture. In B. T. Grindal and D. M. Warren, eds., *Essays in Humanistic Anthropology: A Festschrift in Honor of David Bidney,* pp. 327-73. University Press of America.

Werner, O., and M. D. Topper
1976 On the Theoretical Unity of Ethnoscience Lexicography and Ethnoscience Ethnographies. In C. Rameh, ed., *Semantics and Application,* pp. 111-43. Washington, D.C.: Georgetown University Round Table in Languages and Linguistics.

4

Exploring the Internal Structure of Linguistic Categories: An Extensionist Semantic View

David B. Kronenfeld, James D. Armstrong, and Stan Wilmoth

A semantic theory that accounts only for the denotative meaning of terms, and that offers no insight into the connotative or metaphoric use of those same terms, is seriously lacking. A theory that has to treat "chair" (what we sit on) as being totally unrelated to the "chair" (the leader of our meeting) is obviously inadequate as a theory of our semantic competence. We want to suggest that we do not have to settle for necessarily inadequate theories and that the shape of a reasonable semantic theory is already beginning to emerge in work on extensionist semantics. In order to demonstrate this, we will show how traditional componential analysis (cf. Lounsbury 1964a, Goodenough 1956) can be treated as a special case of graded category membership analysis, which in turn can be treated as a special case of prototype/extension analysis (cf. Rosch 1973, Rosch et al. 1976, Coleman and Kay 1981). We then will show that there are semantic situations with which the first two kinds of analysis cannot deal, although the third can. Finally we will sketch the outlines of what a general semantic theory of word meaning that is based on prototypes and extension will look like; that sketch will include a discussion of kinds of extension.

Componential Analysis and Associated Problems

In a componential analysis, semantic space, or some particular region of it, is divided by a matrix of attributes or features into a set of clearly defined and sharply demarcated boxes. In such a representation of semantic space each region of meaning is defined by the intersection of relevant features such that each term or referent under consideration falls into one and only one box of the matrix (cf. Lounsbury 1969:21).

However, Berlin and Kay have shown, in the case of color terms, that contrasting terms label categories that are not sharply bounded but instead grade into one another. Similarly, in classroom experiments we have shown that some objects are clearly glasses and others clearly cups, while yet others will be called cups one time and glasses another time, depending on context. Examples such as these involving color terms and drinking containers suggest that the componential view is inadequate in at least one way; the boundaries between boxes cannot be volumeless planes but must be thick regions which can themselves contain the things (i.e. potential referents) that do not unambiguously belong to either of the two boxes that they separate.

Category Grading and Associated Problems

A semantic space with thick boundaries represents what is meant by a "category grading" or "fuzzy boundary" model. Since the thickness of the boundaries can vary from one region (or domain) to another, obviously the limiting case is one in which the boundaries are so thin as to become volumeless and so the componential model can be seen as a special case of the category grading model.

However, there remain some situations with which the category grading model (as described) is incapable of dealing. First of all, it does not entirely account for the structure that informants produce within the set of clear members of a category (cf. Lounsbury 1969:22). For instance, in Fanti father's brother is clearly and unambiguously a member of the kinterm category that may be glossed in English as "father," and belongs to no other kinterm category (see Kronenfeld 1973). However, father's brother is just as clearly, to Fanti speakers, not as good an exemplar of the FATHER category as is real father. Father's brother would seem clearly to lie inside the Fanti FATHER box (i.e. unambiguously inside the father category), and not in the thick border region around that box (where it would be if there were some ambiguity about its membership); yet it has a clearly derivative structured relationship to another, more prototypic exemplar of the FATHER category, real father.

A second limitation with category grading becomes apparent when one examines the relationship of verbal categories to their functional bases. The Fanti uncle category (see Kronenfeld 1973) includes mother's brother, mother's mother's sister's son, and mother's father's brother's son, among other relatives. Mother's brother is the relative, *par excellence,* from whom one expects to inherit. But only relatively rarely does any property last long enough (i.e. two generations after its original creator) for one to be able to inherit from one's mother's mother's sister's son; one can never inherit from one mother's father's brother's son *per se,* since that relative is not necessarily or normally a member of one's lineage or clan.

The essential functional basis of the uncle-nibling relationship in Fanti—i.e. the social fact that occasions the terminological categories—is (potential) inheritance (see Kronenfeld 1973), yet that functional basis, in the normal course of events, is only likely to be implemented with one kintype—the kernel, i.e. the prototype or core—out of the range of kintypes that make up the set of denotatively correct referents of the uncle term. That functional basis absolutely cannot occur with at least one another denotatively correct referent.

Any reasonable semantic theory should specify the referents of a term that participate in the essential semantic relations—i.e. functional bases—of the term and in the pragmatic relations that engender the category represented by the term. By any reasonable version of the category grading model, mother's brother, mother's mother's sister's son, and mother's father's brother's son in Fanti would all have to be clearly in the box within semantic space that defines the Fanti uncle term. And yet only a single kintype out of that larger set is in fact relevant to the essential semantic relations described above. This fact forces one to turn seriously to Lounsbury's assertion (1964a:1088) that even close-to-the-kernel denotatively correct referents of kinterms are best considered as metaphoric extensions of the kernel referents of such terms. That is, in the domain of kinship, at least, Lounsbury's assertion suggests the need for a different kind of semantic theory—one in which semantic space looks more like a constellation of stars than a matrix of boxes defined by distinctive features. In this space the stars are the small set of things that have their own special labels—that is, the referents to which the essential semantic relations of the relevant terms apply. Things falling elsewhere in the space are called by the label of the star in whose gravitational field they fall—that is, by the label to which they are closest or most similar in some relevant way.

A third kind of problem in the category grading model involves communicative function. In Fanti the contrast between the FATHER and UNCLE categories divides the class of nurturant, to-be-respected parental-generation males into those from whom one can inherit (the uncle category), and those from who one cannot inherit (the father category). The UNCLE category is a marked category (marked by one's potential inheritance of one's uncle's property) that contrasts with the unmarked FATHER category. Informants told DBK that one could call one's uncle "father" (as a sign of "respect") but not *vice versa*. The potential inheritance relationship is sharply limited to a particular genealogically defined subclass of kinsmen, while the nurturance and respect relations appropriate to FATHER apply to a greater or lesser degree to all appropriately aged men in the community. Thus the FATHER term is connotatively extended to non-kinsmen, while the UNCLE term is not. The use of either term implies a relationship of nurturance and respect, but the use of the UNCLE term carries the additional assertion of an inheritance relationship. Calling an uncle by the FATHER term, then, by downplaying the inheritance relationship, emphasizes the respect aspect. The relations between items (here, various kintypes) and attitudes (here, respect) that underlie such communicative functions do not in any way derive from the full ranges of the terminological categories. Empirically these relations focus on prototypic members of the categories but do not grade out according to category membership, as a grading model would imply.

We have laid out this information concerning the causal basis and communicative import of these two Fanti terms in order to examine the denotative semantics of the UNCLE term. More generally, we can see in Fanti kinship clear reasons for analytically separating definitions of prototypic or kernel members from definitions of mechanisms for extension. A single set of verbal labels can be shown to refer to a single set of kernel kintypes, but at the same time to be involved in three alternative patterns (or systems) of extension from the kernels (i.e. skewed, unskewed, and courtesy—see Kronenfeld 1973). Only the prototype/extension model of word meaning allows one to describe the separate extension patterns in a way that directly explains the relations among the patterns. The Fanti data on which these assertions are based and the reasoning by which the conclusions were reached are provided elsewhere (Kronenfeld 1973, 1975, 1980a, 1908b; also cf. Kronenfeld 1976).

The kinship version of the prototype/extension theory which we have just characterized derives from the work of Lounsbury, who has limited his own work to kinship terminologies. Generalizing out from kinship is hard, since the relative product mechanism by which semantic extension takes place in kinship seems (at least insofar as we are aware) to have no obvious parallel in any other domain. However, we do want to assert that a prototype/extension theory, incorporating heterogeneous means of extension, is the correct one on which to base a general theory of referential semantics. Even if the actual mechanisms of extension are different, the semantic considerations (which necessitate the choice of a prototype/extension theory for kinship) apply equally to many other domains as well (cf. Lounsbury 1969:21-22).

Prototype Extension View

In the prototype/extension theory, focal types—the stars in our model of semantic space—are defined in terms of attributes, features, or gestalten. Extension mechanisms may also be defined in terms of features. In the special case—in which there is only one pattern of extension—the prototype/extension theory reduces to the category grading theory, and thus any domain that can be covered by the category grading theory can also be covered by the prototype/extension one.

In general, in nonmetaphoric usage an item that does not have its own label is called by the label to whose focal member it is closest or most similar. In situations of actual use degree of similarity will not always be absolute but will be skewed by various kinds of context and by the cultural implications of the use of one versus another label. Many of the stars in our version of semantic space have, as it were, variable gravitational fields. For instance, a cuplike object will have to be much more similar to the focal cup to be referred to as "the cup" in a set of cuplike objects than it will to be referred to as "the cup" in a set of glasslike objects. A slightly sick American (with a single given set of symptoms) is likely to say "it's a cold" when he wants to go to a ball game and "it's the flu" when he wants *not* to go to work—even though "cold" and "flu" seem to be pretty clearly contrasting categories.

In our stellar model of semantic space, marking relations will give us something like subsidiary bodies, i.e. planets. For example, MUG is a category (as opposed to the CUP category) that has its own focal type and its own force field; at the same time the entire MUG category, including the focal type, lies within the CUP force field—i.e., almost any mug is a kind of "cup" (when CUP is opposed to GLASS).

An exploration of the domain of drinking vessels allows us to see how and why the relation among denotative definitions, functional relations, and derivational history is only apparent in connection with core referents of terms (as opposed to the full extended sets of referents). This special significance of core referents gives them a crucially different role in a prototype/extension theory than they have in a category grading (or fuzzy boundary) theory. The kind of imputation of primary semantic processes to the full extended range of term referents implied by the category grading view underlies both the "language-determines-thought" and the "language-simply-maps-thought" versions of theories about language/thought isomorphisms. The problems we find with category grading show why such isomorphism theories have never seemed satisfactory.

The prototype/extension view allows us to see how language can be the flexible tool it in fact appears to be. It allows us to see how language can be used to talk about things (as filtered and shaped by cognitive structures) in a reasonably precise way even in the absence of any simple language/thought isomorphism. Language has enough referential connections to enable users to know what they are talking about, but it is also free enough from any referential lock to enable them constantly to use existing language categories to talk about novel entities or to focus on novel features of existing entities.

Our experimental design was set up to compare our view with three alternative idealized views of language/thought relations. First, according to a strong "Whorfian" view, language determines perception. The structure of similarity relations among verbal categories should vary from one language community to the next, and there should be a simple direct relationship between people's verbal categories and their structuring of relations among the objects to which the words refer. Therefore, the structure of similarity relations among actual objects should differ from one language community to the next in a manner that parallels the differences among verbal category similarity structures. Second, according to a strongly "pragmatic" theory, language directly reflects the way objects are dealt with. A simple direct relationship should occur between structurings of sets of actual objects and the structurings of the verbal categories into which they fall. Therefore, verbal category similarity structures should be similar from one language community to the next. Third, according to the traditional version of the non-isomorphism position—a kind of "neo-Harrisian" view—people are expected to deal directly with actual objects on the basis of their functional characteristics (which in our drinking vessel domain are more or less uniform across languages). By such a view language would have no particular relationship to objective functional categorizations. In this case one should expect the structuring of similarity relations among actual objects to be similar across languages, but the structuring of similarity relations among verbal categories should differ from language to language. It follows that there should be no overall similarity from one language to the next in the assignment of objects to verbal categories.

The theory on which this paper is based uses the distinction between core and extended referents of labels to establish a *limited* isomorphism. In a domain such as the one under consideration, we expect similarity relations among verbal categories to parallel those that obtain among the actual objects. Therefore, such relations should be similar from one language to the next. However, like Wittgenstein, we recognize that a direct and simple categorical relationship between linguistic terms and their referents (of the kind that philosophers such as Russell looked for) does not obtain. We base the primary object-category link exclusively on core referents and allow a much freer and more flexible assignment of other (extended) referents to categories. Thus we expect significant differences among languages to show up in the assignment of (noncore) objects to categories.

Speakers of a language induce coreness for particular referents of a term[1] from a combination of factors, including the functions associated with the category, the relative facility with which alternative members of the category accomplish (or epitomize) the category's functions, the temporal priority of speakers' contact with alternative members, and the relative salience (perceptual and interactive) of alternative members. The set of core referents thus induced becomes the source of the various alternative bases along which extension takes place. Form attributes provide the basis for denotative extension from the core and are taken from descriptive characteristics of core members. Functional attributes of the category provide the basis for connotative extension of the category. Attributes can be either continuous (e.g. shape, volume, etc.) or discrete (e.g. presence of some particular material or appendage or some common use). Attributes of a given category can vary in their importance or salience relative to one another in two ways. First, they can vary according to paradigmatic context. For example, different attributes are used to distinguish a cup from a mug than are used to distinguish a cup from a glass. Second, attributes can vary according to the context of their use. For example, different attributes are used to select a "glass" from a set of glasslike objects than are used to select a "glass" from a set of cuplike objects. Some particular category may grade into another along some particular attribute, while a similar attribute might produce a discrete boundary between another pair of categories. For example, the transition from glass material to nonglass for a glass-shaped object moves one immediately out of the glass category, while the reverse transition for a cup-shaped object only moves one somewhat out from the prototype.

New categories emerge when noncore objects (in some verbal category) function importantly enough and frequently enough to acquire and maintain their own labels. The particular sound-images come into being as a result of any of a variety of mechanisms that are not relevant here. The objects in question then become the core referents of these new labels, and thus the core members of new verbal categories.

Denotatively "correct" extension of a category to noncore items is defined in terms of form attributes. Denotatively "correct" extended members of a category are items that fit the "definition" of the category in terms of form but differ noticeably from the specific form of the category's exemplars. An example might occur when the word "glass" is used for an unusually shaped (even if functionally appropriate) glass such as a goblet; a more extreme example might be the extension of the word "glass" to an object correct in form but inappropriate in function such as an Irish Coffee glass. Connotatively extended members of a category are items that function similary to the category's exemplars but differ from those exemplars along some significant form attribute(s), as for example a plastic cup referred to as a "glass."

Several kinds of structural ambiguity concerning category membership are possible. Taxonomic relations can include the situation in which the core item of one category is a denotatively extended member of another category (e.g., a MUG is a kind of CUP). Two taxonomically related categories can overlap so that a single item can be a denotatively extended member of both—or a connotatively extended member of both (as seen in the relationship of soup mugs to MUG and BOWL categories). More relevant to this paper is the situation in which an item (or a whole subcategory of items) is denotatively a member of one category while connotatively a member of another, as will be seen below for the case of plastic cup in English.

Drinking Vessel Data

Native speakers of Hebrew, English, and Japanese were interviewed about the labels they apply to a collection of objects generally referred to in English as drinking vessels.[2] The interviews were conducted in the language of the speaker for the Hebrew and English groups, and in English with the aid of an interpreter for the Japanese group. Twenty-three university students ranging in age from their early twenties to early forties served as the English-speaking informants. Ten native-born Israelis served as the Hebrew-speaking subjects. Twenty-one Japanese students were drawn from the ESL program at the University of California at Riverside. The Israelis ranged in age from 25 to 40 while the Japanese were all in their early twenties. Approximately the same number of females and males were interviewed.

Initially, the subjects were asked, in a general discursive way, to label each item in our collection of drinking vessels and to discuss the relations among the objects, their labels, and so forth. The set of objects comprised cups, mugs, and glasses varying in size, shape, material, and use. These interviews were intended to determine the range of terms applied to "drinking vessels" in the various languages, to explore the structure of the domain of the labels applied to these objects, and to identify core or prototypical objects in the set.

Subsequently, the informants sorted the collection of objects into groups based on inter-item similarity. After performing the sorting task the informants were asked to describe the attributes of the objects that determined inclusion in any given subgroup. The set of objects contained 35 items for Japanese- and English-speaking informants. Because the interviews in Hebrew were conducted in the field, a smaller subset of objects was used. With the help of two Israeli informants in the United States, this subset of 11 items had been chosen to provide a set of objects that included a comparable range of both core items and extended referents.

The next task in our research was to have the informants sort a set of words into groups based on the similarity inherent in the meaning of the words. The two sorting tasks are the basis for our MDS plots, which provide a means for comparing similarity relations among objects with similarity relations among verbal categories as well as for comparing each kind of relation across the languages.

The final task was to investigate the labeling of the objects. In this phase we asked our informants to classify the set of "drinking vessels" into groups based on the major category labels determined in the exploratory sessions (i.e. "cups" and "glasses" in English; "koppu," "kappu," and "gurasu" in Japanese; and "cosot" and "sefalim" in Hebrew). For example, the English-speaking informants were instructed to sort all of the items in the collection into one group of things called "glasses" and another group of things called "cups." The informants had the option of excluding items from membership in the specific categories mentioned for each language. No informant participated in more than one task during any given interviewing session.

Results of Research

The data from the object-sort task for speakers of each language were used to calculate pairwise similarity matrices that were then used for multidimensional scaling. The MDS plots show us how the different language communities structured the domain and provide us with a means of evaluating differences (see Figures 1-3) among them. We found a high degree of interlanguage-community similarity. The plots for each group of informants identify three clusters of objects: cups, glasses, and disposables (objects made of nontraditional material). The Japanese speakers have tighter clusters for each of the three subsets than have the English or Hebrew speakers. Both English and Hebrew speakers place the handled paper cup somewhere between the clusters of disposables and cups while the Japanese include this item with other paper cups. English speakers place the nondisposable plastic cup (called "tumbler" in the figures) between glasses and disposable cups. Calculating Pearson's R on the interpoint distances gives a rough measure of interplot congruence. Rs ranging from .81 to .89 indicate a high degree of congruence among the three plots.

Our preliminary interviews had suggested that there were important and interesting differences among the languages in their verbal segmentation of the domain. Subconsciously assuming language/thought isomorphism, we had naively expected the MDS analysis of object-object similarities to produce greater interlanguage-group differences than appear in Figures 1-3. But we found, as Kronenfeld had already found for Fanti kinship, that informants are perfectly capable of thinking about objects with only a minimum of interference from linguistic categories.

While conducting this research in Israel, the sharp differences between what is tapped by the sorting tasks and what is tapped by the object-label assignment task were driven home to Armstrong. His Israeli informants professed not to understand how there could be any differences between Americans and Israelis in the verbal classification of these items. In order to demonstrate to them the great variation between the linguistic categorizations of the two languages, he had an American partition the set of objects into "cups" and "glasses." Even though the prototypic "cup" in English was the same as the prototypic "sefel" in Hebrew (and the two terms were thus reasonable translation equivalents), nonprototypic items were classified quite differently. The American classified all things called "cup" in English together (paper cup, mug, plastic cup, tea cup, etc.), producing a group that made little sense to the Israelis. In contrast, Israelis classified a number of objects that in English are extended referents from CUP (paper cup, plastic cup, etc.) with the Hebrew equivalent of the English "glass." Some objects that are extended referents from the core "cup" in English turned out to be extended referents from the core "glass" (COS) in Hebrew.

By combining the data from our initial interviews with the data from the labeling task, we are able to describe the drinking vessel domains for each language. In English this domain is divided into two subgroups, one based on the core concept of cupness and the

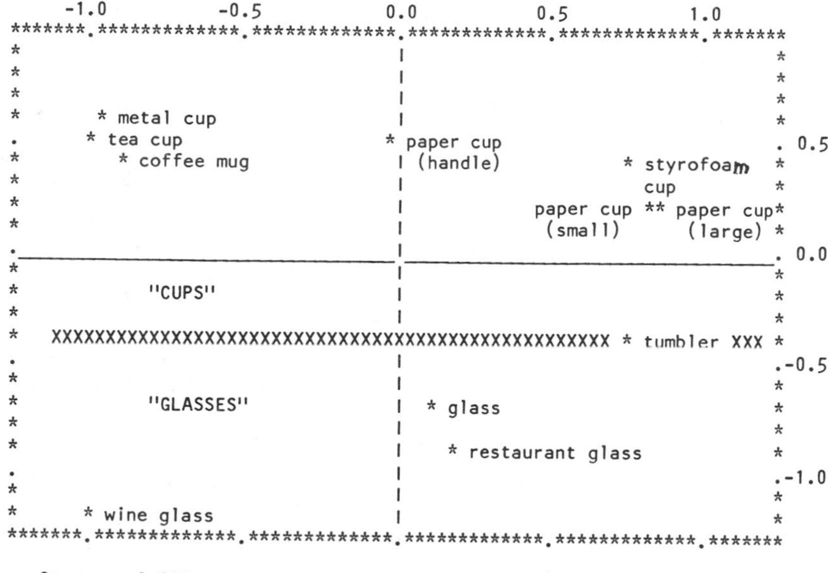

Figure 1. Two-Dimensional MDS Plot Object Sort by Americans

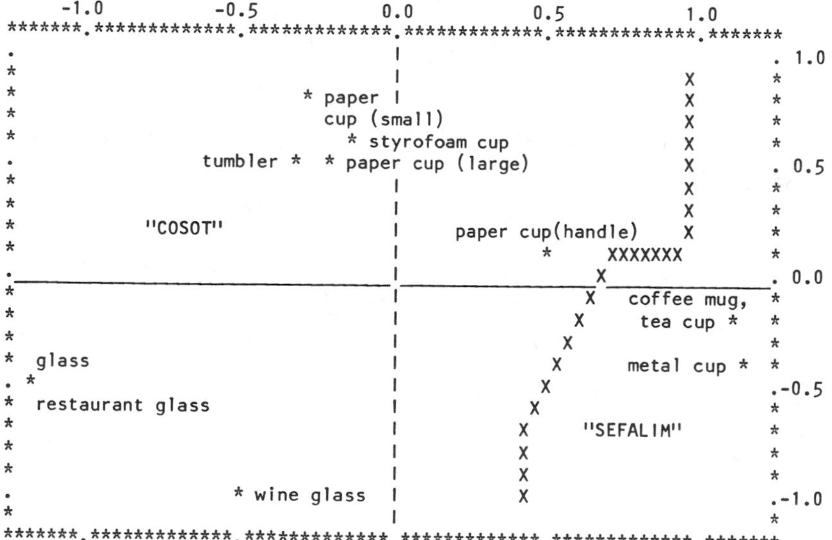

Figure 2. Two-Dimensional MDS Plot Object Sort by Israelis

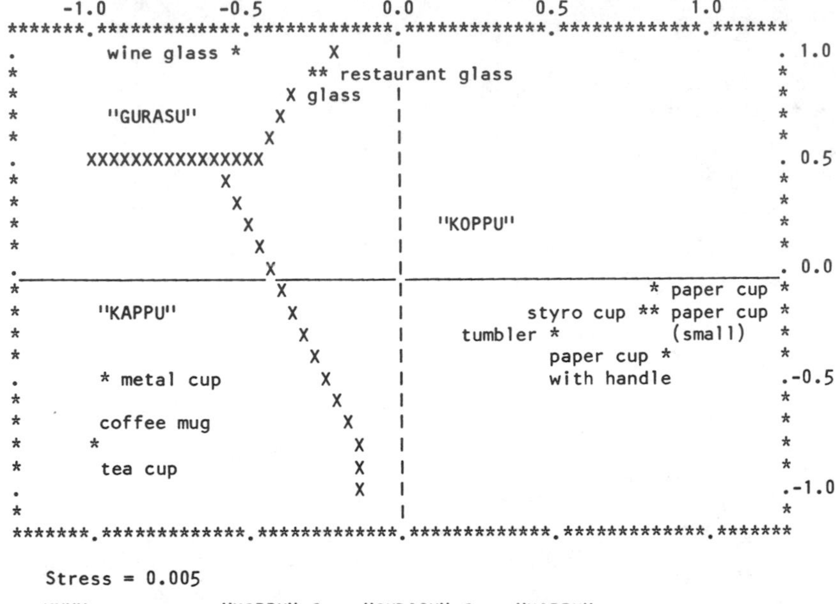

Figure 3. Two-Dimensional MDS Plot Object Sort by Japanese

other on the core concept of glassness. The concept of cupness predominantly involves a squat hemispherical shape, but includes opaque material and a handle, and typically implies use for hot drinks. The concept of glassness focuses on the material—glass—but also involves a tall cylindrical shape without a handle, and typically implies use for cold drinks.

In Hebrew the entire drinking vessel domain is referred to as "cosot." The item identified as the core "cos" by Israelis is the same item identified by English speakers as the core "glass." However, the salient attribute(s) determining coreness are not the same. Whereas the overriding determinant for glassness in English is material, in Hebrew it is cylindrical shape. The Israelis have a subgroup of COSOT called "sefalim," which are the equivalent of our "real" cups and mugs. In this case coreness is determined by the same attribute(s) in both languages, i.e. predominantly those form attributes that mark a particular function (e.g. a handle for insulation in the case of cups). As a mug is a kind of cup in English, a sefal is a kind of cos in Hebrew.

In Japanese the domain is segmented into three subgroups: KAPPU, GURASU and KOPPU. The core KAPPU is the same item as the core CUP for Americans and the core SEFEL for Israelis; it is defined by the same attributes as cups and sefalim, although the Japanese place more emphasis on the presence of handles than do speakers of the other languages. GURASU are noncylindrical, usually stemmed objects made of glass. The core GURASU is best exemplified by what we would call a "brandy snifter" in our collection of drinking vessels. The most salient attribute for this group is shape. KOPPU is the category of drinking vessels containing all the items made of nontraditional material; their most salient attribute is cylindrical shape. The Japanese identified a nondisposable plastic cup as the core item for this group.

By distinguishing core from extended referents and by distinguishing form from function attributes, our theory allows us to deal with some situations in which objects or subcategories have ambiguous membership in two categories but are not perceived as simply being on some gradient between the two categories. In so doing, it makes sense of certain common informant response that other theories (e.g. componential analysis or category grading) seem unable to handle. For instance, many Americans will say that a nondisposable plastic item shaped like a glass is "really" a "cup" even though it seems to them more like a "glass." For these people this item shares with the cup category the particular form-class attribute, namely nonglass, opaque material, that is essential in English to the distinction between cup and glass, even though this item is far removed from the core CUP. Hence it is denotatively an extended "cup." However, the object's function (for cold drinks), as well as several salient but noncriterial form attributes such as shape and durability, pull the object moderately close to the core "glass" (for which category both informant behavior and statements showed material to be the criterial attribute). This proximity to "glass," especially regarding function, accounts for the connotative extension of the glass term to the object and also for people's strong feelings that it ought to be a "glass."

Other American informants place the glasslike plastic object clearly in the GLASS category by reducing the special criteriality of material as opposed to shape or durability. Historically the movement seems to be in the direction of this shift in criteriality—we think in response to the strong functional pull of the glass category in conjunction with the relatively increased use of plastic glasslike objects. We suspect, once the drinking glass category is generally uncoupled from the material glass, the core referent of the category will rapidly shift to a plastic object, in response to the relative frequency with which people encounter the two.

In Japanese we found a similar example of structural ambiguity. Cylindrically shaped objects made of glass were called "koppu" by some informants and "gurasu" by others. These items possess the material that determines inclusion in the GURASU subset and the shape and function central to the KOPPU subset, and are therefore ambiguous. Slightly more than 50 percent of the Japanese informants labeled such items "koppu" and the remainder called them "gurasu." Another example of an ambiguous object (from Japanese) is the handled paper cup, which possesses attributes from both the KOPPU and KAPPU subgroupings. Slightly more than 50 percent of the informants classed this object with the KAPPU.[3]

Our theory indicates that a handled paper cup should be ambiguous for Israelis, since it possesses salient attributes from both the COSOT and SEFALIM subcategories. As with plastic cup in English, the form attributes of this object tend to push it in one direction (i.e. toward COS), while functional attributes tend to push it toward another (i.e. toward SEFEL). All the Israelis interviewed said this item was a kind of COS. Only one informant said that it might be called a SEFEL. The reason for the absence of ambiguity in this case reveals something more about the nature of function in our theory. Function is seen not simply to be a matter of the kind of use but also to involve experience, which depends on frequency of use. Paper drinking vessels have never been commonly used in Israel, and only recently have disposable plastic drinking vessels been introduced. In Hebrew there were no ambiguous items because the domain structure of the language and history combine to preclude this possibility.

Assessing Similarity

In the domains that we and others have experimented with so far, several different ways of assessing the similarity or contiguity on which extension is based have emerged. In denotative extensions of kinterms we and others have demonstrated the kind of relative product calculus that is represented by Lounsbury's rules and that is embedded in a Fanti speaker's assertion that someone is his father because that person is his father's brother. In the domain of color terms Berlin and Kay and others have shown that extension is based along values on the dimensions that structure the three-dimensional color solid, as represented physiologically in the opponent system. In the world of pens and pencils, similarity seems to be based on the number of discrete attributes shared (e.g. yellow wood versus other casing, and lead versus ink writing material). In the world of cups and glasses, similarity seems to be based on a mix of values along continuous attributes involved in shape (as Kempton 1981 has shown) and the presence or absence of certain discrete attributes involving materials and appendages. It is important to note that the similarity is relative and to a degree *ad hoc,* depending on the context of use, on the level of opposition, and on the nature of what is being communicated. In a sense it is a matter of using whatever works.

Form, Function, Contrast, and Metaphor

From what we have so far seen in a number of domains,[4] "denotatively correct usage" refers to use of a category label that is consistent with functionally relevant but external form features, while "connotative usage" refers to use that is consistent with the functional relationship on which the terminological isolation of the focal item is based but that is inconsistent with some aspect of the external form features. Operationally, it seems to us that what has traditionally been called "denotative usage" refers to usage for which informants will say, "yes, that *really* is a book," or "yes, he *really* is my uncle," while "connotative usage" occurs when informants say something like, "no, it's not really a book *exactly,* but its contents are like a book," or "no, he's not really my uncle, I just call him that out of respect and because I like him." Metaphoric usage is in no direct sense correct to informants, but does convey something about the broader meaning involved; "the thought is father to the deed" even if thoughts are too inanimate to have kin or to behave in a fatherly fashion.

In the kind of semantic theory that we are proposing, paradigmatic or "sense" relations among terms would be generated by relations among focal types, and would be defined in terms of the attributes or features by which those focal types contrast with one another. Considerations of paradigmatic consistency, conjunctivity, and the like would constitute the same kind of influence on category definition, and pressure toward the addition or deletion of categories, that they are felt to constitute in componential theories (cf. Nerlove and Romney 1967, Kronenfeld 1974), but these influences would apply directly only to the focal types. In effect, one would have a componential analysis that would often not cover a large part of the denotative range of the terms that it included. In our semantic space, such a curtailed componential analysis would apply only to the "stars" themselves, not to other objects caught in the stars' gravitational fields.

We began this paper by claiming that any reasonable semantic theory of reference should account for the broadest of metaphoric usage as well as for more narrow denotative or connotative usage. Every category has attributes and associations that are incidental to its denotation and that only thinly relate to its functional entailments. Such attributes and associations can be based on consequences of functional entailments or on incidental characteristics of salient exemplars. People are creative, and can seize on any such implied or "accidental" attributes or associations as a basis for metaphoric extension. As long as the relevant aspects of the source of the metaphor and of the target to which it is being applied are well enough understood pragmatically by speaker and hearer, and as long as there is sufficient context to allow them to deduce which aspects are at issue, people can understand the metaphor. People understand the reference, whether it is to be an object itself, to a use or quality of an object, or to some other connection of the object. Language itself provides speakers and hearers with one essential part of this necessary context via the paradigmatic or contrastive relations that words have with other words in their immediate domain (as well as via the normal syntagmatic associations of the words). These paradigmatic relations reflect functionally important distinctions of use as well as cognitively important distinctions of form. Thus, when Basso's Western Apache (1967) extend the word for a horse's eye to the headlight of a pickup truck, they are extending that word not in limbo but as part of a set that entails contrasts with the words for horse's leg, mouth, back, etc. These contrasts, which necessarily come automatically with the use of any word, help speakers to quickly isolate the relevant aspects of the object referred to, and thus to quickly identify that object. Even if there is more than one such contrast set to which a given word belongs, there are only a few such, and the focusing role of the paradigmatic contrast remains operative.

Similarly, people rely on such contrasts when they use a metaphor to make a statement about an object rather than to simply identify it. When speakers refer to a priest as "father," they are asserting that, as opposed to a brother, he is senior to them; that, as opposed to a mother, he is male; that, as opposed to an uncle, he is responsible for them, and they owe him obedience; and that, as opposed to a grandfather, he is proximate. Even if the usage is metaphoric, and thus the central feature that defines the domain (e.g. + kinsman—cf. Lounsbury 1969:25) is missing, the term's relationship to those with which it contrasts remains, and the semantic bases of those contrasts remain. Since the priest's gender and proximateness are presumably not at issue, seniority and obedience are the major assertions at issue in the metaphor.

Conclusion

We have seen that metaphoric extension is not intrinsically different from the more narrow or direct kinds of extension; only the kinds of attributes of the focal item on which the extension is based differ. An integrated semantic theory encompassing both direct and metaphoric usage can be built out of a prototype/extension view of folk categories.

NOTES

The research upon which this paper is based was supported in part by a research grant from the Dean of Humanities and Social Sciences at the University of California at Riverside and in part by an intramural grant to Kronenfeld from the Academic Senate of the University of California at Riverside. Additional support was provided to Armstrong by the Chancellor's Patent Fund and to both Armstrong and Wilmoth by nondissertation research grants from the Anthropology Department of the Unviersity of California at Riverside. We are most grateful for this support. We wish to thank Judy Z. Kronenfeld, Janet W. D. Dougherty, Willett Kempton, and Hiroshi Fukura for their many helpful comments on earlier drafts of this paper, as well as those who responded to the earlier papers on which this one is based (Kronenfeld 1978 and Armstrong et al. 1980).

1. Separate from the question of how a person learning a language induces the cores of already existent categories is the question of semantic category origins and the initial determination of focal items. We cannot treat these processes in any substantive manner in the present paper, but their role in our broader semantic theory necessitates a brief characterization here.

We consider that functional relations interact with the kinds of salience considerations that account for marking relations (such as initially encountered types, frequency of use, perceptual salience, and so forth) to produce focal items (and their attendant labels). This approach allows us to explore category prototypes and extensions within culturally variable domains, such as books and drinking vessels, that do not seem especially dependent on physical, physiological, social, or cognitive universals for their structuring. It also precludes the kind of circle that Rosch gets into (e.g. 1975:182,187; cf. Rosch and Mervis 1975:576, 598-99) when she defines category membership as being relative to prototypes while defining prototypes as best examples of categories. In the semantic theory that we are proposing, functional and interactive relations produce categories by causing (what will become) focal items to get labels. External form attributes of those focal items—physical attributes of size, type of construction, and so forth in the case of books—then become the normal basis on which the category is extended to nonfocal items.

Derivational histories or etymologies (both real and merely felt) are highly relevant to native speakers' senses of word meanings, and thus essential to any full theory of referential semantics. In our treatment of drinking vessels we are compelled to call upon diachronic considerations—even if in a relatively unexplicated way.

Throughout the paper for reasons of brevity and focus, we speak about the referents of words as if they were simply things. We agree with the suggestion of Gladwin (1974), Kay (1978:81), and others that verbal categories, or, rather, the features that define them, can often be based on cognitive schemas rather than on precise physically defined features of their referents, and intend our discussion to be taken in that light. Such notions as "functional relationship" and "functionally relevant, but external, form features" obviously refer to cognitive structures.

2. Our awareness of cups and glasses as an interesting domain for study probably derives from Kronenfeld's experiences in C. O. Frakes' classes in the mid-1960s. Other researchers have also used cups or cups and glasses for investigating category boundaries and category inclusion (cf. Labov 1973, Andersen 1974, Kempton 1978). Andersen's work with childhood development of "fuzzy" category boundaries is especially relevant and is generally consistent with our findings.

3. It might seem that nontraditional materials, rather than cylindrical shape, is the most salient attribute of KOPPU. However, most of our informants stated that most of those materials are not often encountered in Japan (e.g. "Hapo styro no koppe"). Hence we conclude that material is less functionally salient in this case than is shape.

There remain questions about indigenous Japanese drinking vessels (e.g. SAKI ZUKI and YOUNOMI CHAWAM). These items were usually initially grouped with KAPPU. However, all informants found this arrangement uncomfortable, resulting from the fact that the traditional items lacked handles. This lack pushed them away from KAPPU even though the presence of all other traditional form attributes pulled them toward the category. The more ritualized use of these items increased this feeling. Most informants felt that these items actually belonged to a separate and somewhat isolated category based on ritual use attributes. There appear to be differences between males and females in terms of their perceptions of these traditional items.

4. Some of the concerns at issue in the form/function (denotative/connotative) distinction can be more clearly explored in a brief consideration of some examples drawn from the domain of books and magazines. The distinction of concern here is that between extension from a focal sense that is based on function (characterized by attributes such as the relative permanence of book's contents versus the relatively ephemeral contents of a magazine) and extension from a focal sense that is based on form (characterized by attributes such as the nature of the binding). Form and function come together in focal books or magazines, but have to be separated into two different systems of semantic extension in order to account for people's inconsistencies in their classification of certain subtypes (such as ledgers or notebooks—cf. plastic cups), for judgments they make about ambiguous cases, and for reasons they adduce for these judgments.

REFERENCES

Andersen, Elaine S.
1974 Cups and Glasses: Learning That Boundaries Are Vague. *Journal of Child Language* 2:79-103.

Armstrong, James D., Stan Wilmoth, and David B. Kronenfeld
1980 Labelling Cups and Glasses in an Extensionist Semantic Theory. Paper presented at the 79th Annual Meeting of the American Anthropological Association, 6 Dec.

Basso, Keith H.
1967 Semantic Aspects of Linguistic Acculturation. *American Anthropologist* 69:971-77.

Berlin, Brent, and Paul Kay
1969 *Basic Color Terms: Their Universality and Evolution.* Berkeley: University of California Press.

Coleman, L., and P. Kay
1981 Prototype Semantics. *Language* 57:26-44.

Gladwin, Hugh
1974 Semantics, Schemata and Kinship. Revised version of paper presented at Mathematical Social Science Board conference on Formal Semantic Analysis of Kinsip, University of California at Riverside, Dec. 1972.

Goodenough, Ward H.
1956 Componential Analysis and the Study of Meaning. *Language* 32:195-216.

Kay, Paul
1978 Tahitian Words for Race and Class. *Publications de la Société des Océanistes* 39:81-91.

Kempton, Willett
1978 Category Grading and Taxonomic Relations: A Mug Is a Sort of a Cup. *American Ethnologist* 5:44-65.
1981 *The Folk Classification of Ceramics: A Study of Cognitive Prototypes.* New York: Academic Press.

Kronenfeld, David B.
1973 Fanti Kinship: The Structure of Terminology and Behavior. *American Anthropologist* 75:1577-95.
1974 Sibling Typology: Beyond Nerlove and Romney. *American Ethnologist* 1:489-506.
1975 Kroeber vs. Radcliffe-Brown on Kinship Behaviour: The Fanti Test Case. *Man* 10(n.s.):257-84.
1976 Computer Analysis of Skewed Kinship Terminologies. *Language* 52:891-918.
1978 Extensionist Semantics: The Basis of Similarity. Paper presented in the Symposium on Internal Category Structure at the 77th Annual Meeting of the American Anthropological Association, 16 Nov.
1980a A Formal Analysis of Fanti Kinship Terminology. *Anthropos* 75:586-608.
1980b Particularistic of Universalistic Analyses of Fanti Kin-Terminology: The Alternative Goals of Terminological Analysis. *Man* 15(n.s.):151-69.

Labov, William
1973 The Boundaries of Words and Their Meanings. In Charles-James Bailey and Roger W. Shuy, eds., *New Ways of Analyzing Variation in English.* Washington, D.C.: Georgetown University Press.
Lounsbury, Floyd G.
1964a The Structured Analysis of Kinship Semantics. In H. Lunt, ed., *Proceedings of the Ninth International Congress of Linguists.* The Hague: Mouton.
1964b A Formal Account of Crow- and Omaha-type Kinship Terminologies. In W. H. Goodenough, ed., *Explorations in Cultural Anthropology.* New York: McGraw-Hill.
1965 Another View of Trobriand Kinship Categories. In E. A. Hammel, ed., *Formal Semantic Analysis.* Washington, D.C.: American Anthropological Association.
1969 Language and Culture. In S. Hook, ed., *Language and Philosophy.* New York: New York University Press.
Nerlove, Sara Beth, and A. Kimball Romney
1967 Sibling Terminology and Cross-sex Behavior. *American Anthropologist* 69:179-87.
Rosch, Eleanor H.
1973 On the Internal Structure of Perceptual and Semantic Categories. In T. M. Moore, ed., *Cognitive Development and the Acquisition of Language.* New York: Academic Press.
Rosch, Eleanor H., and Carolyn B. Mervis
1975 Forty Resemblances: Studies in the Internal Structure of Categories. *Cognitive Psychology* 7:573-605.
Rosch, Eleanor H., et al.
1976 Basic Objects in Natural Categories. *Cognitive Psychology* 8:382-439.

SECTION II

Contexts for Learning and Reapplying Cultural Knowledge

With a view toward specifying the nature of cultural knowledge, the authors of the papers in this section examine patterns of consensus and variation. The primary emphasis on language evident in earlier papers in this volume is augmented in this section by a more comprehensive concern for cognitive phenomena in general. The authors come to argue separately for the centrality of the processes of acquiring and applying cultural knowledge in context for an understanding of the content and organization of that knowledge. People's use and understanding of cultural knowledge are rooted in the processes of interaction as constituted by individual understandings and situational relevance. In accounting for patterns of consensus and variation, these authors highlight the flexibility of social experience.

It was argued in the general introduction that cultural knowledge is acquired largely on the basis of social experience. In turn, an individual interprets this experience in light of previously acquired cultural knowledge. The focus around which social experience is made sensible is the interpretation of the purposes and goals of interaction (Goodenough 1981:81-82). It is, therefore, to purposeful analyses that the authors in this section turn. Each of these papers argues for the overriding notion of a project toward which action is directed such that the project provides an orientation for the selection and structuring of cultural knowledge (Heidegger 1962:99, Dougherty and Fernandez 1982).

The segmentation of the world is addressed by these authors in terms of an *a priori* template that is largely taken for granted. In any particular situation, however, the identification of experience in terms of cultural knowledge is an emergent process of hypothesis testing. Appropriate matches depend upon individual knowledge and previous experience (Boster, Gatewood), selective attention (Dougherty and Keller, and Werner's article in Section I), and situational relevance

(Stanlaw and Yoddumnern, and the papers in Section III by Randall, Quinn, Brown, and Agar and Hobbs). The individual, the ongoing activity, and the structure of the situation guide the conceptualization of experience.

This focus on categorization or identification as situationally governed hypothesis testing suggests that ambiguity is central to social experience. Ambiguities, which give rise to patterns of consensus and variation, result from the tension in any given situation between an obligation to already established cultural knowledge on the one hand, and to the possibilities for reconceptualization on the other (Dougherty and Keller, Stanlaw and Yoddumnern, Dougherty and Fernandez 1982).

Individual understanding and situated interaction are integrated in the learning process as well. Boster, Hunn, Gatewood, and Van Esterik argue that variations in the situations in which cultural knowledge is acquired have implications for the representation of that knowledge. Van Esterik contrasts possible structures for folk theories of design. She postulates that global or gestaltlike representations of designs are constructed by individuals as a consequence of interaction in diverse but interconnected contexts for learning. Such global folk theories contrast with representations of design that take the form of lists of isolated elements and rules for their combinations. The latter form of cultural knowledge, she argues, results when contexts for learning are relatively impoverished.

In a related vein, Gatewood argues that learning time is crucial to the form of represented understandings. He suggests that the development of conceptual schemata for the representation of complex activities such as salmon fishing involves an initial state in which a segmentation of discrete units, a "string of beads," is established. With time, a "string of beads" representation is gradually transformed into a more global understanding of the activity as a whole. This developmental analysis parallels Van Esterik's treatment of contrasting forms of folk theories of design. In each case crucial variables for the development of global representations are time and an associated diversity of experience.

Taking a somewhat different approach, Boster and Hunn explore the implications of cultural utility and individual interest for the degree to which particular aspects of cultural knowledge are elaborated. Again time and the diversity of relevant experience have significant implications for the cultural encoding of knowledge and for the nature of cognitive representation.

The question of the relationship of linguistic to nonlinguistic behavior arises in these articles as it is relevant to the acquisition and use of cultural knowledge. Gatewood argues, for example, that linguistically encoded cultural knowledge is largely public and consensual (Stromberg 1981, Fernandez 1965). Such overt representations guide an individual's construction of cultural knowledge and allow communication about personal understandings to occur. By contrast, Gatewood suggests that action is "cognitively organized by unlabeled and largely unreflected-upon categories of behavior that are not necessarily shared. . . ." While action can be segmented and labeled upon reflection, such capabilities are independent of the cognitive representation of the activities themselves. It is such ineffable organizations of experience that give content and meaning to consensual representations. The power of language to structure experience and the power of experience to give meaning to language are mutually constitutive of social process.

On the same question, Hunn argues that linguistic distinctions reflect culturally significant aspects of experience. Dougherty and Keller suggest that such linguistic distinctions often reflect knowledge that can be taken for granted in a broad range of situations, while in any particular context the relevant tasks serve to focus an individual's awareness on characteristics of the world independent of their significance for labeling experience. In each case the authors are arguing for the complementarity and mutual interdependence of language and nonlinguistic behavior in social experience.

REFERENCES

Dougherty, Janet W. D., and James W. Fernandez
1982 Afterword. Special Issue on Symbolism and Cognition II. *American Ethnologist* 9:820-32.

Fernandez, James W.
1965 Symbolic Consensus in Fang Reformative Cult. *American Anthropologist* 67:902-29.

Goodenough, Ward H.
1981 *Culture, Language and Society.* 2d ed. Menlo Park, Calif.: Benjamin Cummings Publishing Co.

Heidegger, Martin
1962 *Being and Time.* Trans. John Macquarrie and Edward Robinson. New York: Harper and Row.

Stromberg, Peter
1981 Consensus and Variation in the Interpretation of Religious Symbolism. *American Ethnologist* 8:544-59.

A. THE CREATION OF ORDER

The chapters herein illustrate multiple bases for the organization of concepts, going well beyond the traditional emphasis on form as an *a priori* and universal standard.

5

The Utilitarian Factor in Folk Biological Classification

Eugene Hunn

Lévi-Strauss opens *The Savage Mind* (1966) by asserting that "the universe is an object of thought at least as much as it is a means of satisfying needs" (p. 3). He reflects upon Handy and Pukui's characterization of native Hawaiian ethnobiology. They had noted that "every botanical, zoological or inorganic form that is known to have been named . . . , was *some thing* used . . . in some way" (Handy and Pukui 1953:127). Lévi-Strauss remarks that to characterize something as of no *use* is quite apart from it being of no *interest*, as "'use' concerns practical, and 'interest' theoretical, matters" (p. 2). Ethnoscientific investigations of folk biological classification have been favorably disposed to this point of view and have thus analyzed their subject matter as reflecting an intellectual or cognitive process of comprehending the world, a process motivated by "interest" first of all. This approach has been fruitful. It has generated theoretical models of perceptual, cognitive, and linguistic processes that underlie "natural categorization" (e.g. Hunn 1976; Kay 1971, 1975; Rosch 1978). However, the fact that cultural knowledge of the natural world might also be practically useful has been treated as beside the point, almost an embarrassment. Berlin, in a theoretical stocktaking addressed to an audience of biosystematists (1973), felt called upon to stress that "less than half of the named folk generic classes [i.e. basic core folk taxa] of plants in the folk botany of the Tzeltal . . . can be shown to have any cultural significance whatsoever" (p. 260).

We have been misled by Lévi-Strauss on this point. A careful examination of Berlin's own data discloses some explicit or likely prac-

An earlier version of this chapter appeared in *American Anthropologist* 84:830-47, 1982. It is reprinted by permission of the American Anthropological Association and the author.

tical relevance for nearly all of the Tzeltal folk botanical categories he has labeled "culturally insignificant" (Boster and McDaniel n.d.). Some are poisonous, others invasive weeds, others inedible "twins" closely resembling edible forms, others useful "just" as firewood, etc. (Berlin, Breedlove, and Raven 1974:277, 278, 291, 499, 500-501, 507-8, 512-13). Yet they are classed as "culturally insignificant."

These same Tzeltal Indians exhibit strong preferences for those parts of their zoological universe they consider worth bringing classificatory order to. For example, adult Lepidoptera (butterflies and moths)—the subject matter of a classificatory obsession of certain civilized folk—are of very little interest to the Tzeltal. Yet their larvae (caterpillars, cutworms, etc.) are carefully sorted into 16 terminal folk taxa in Tzeltal (Hunn 1977:280-85, 301-6). Some lepidopterous larvae are edible, others attack crops, and others acquire painful defensive ornamentation. The adults lack these characteristics. As a general rule, larval Lepidoptera are specialized for feeding, adults for mating: hence their contrasting cultural impact on the Tzeltal. There is, of course, ample morphological diversity visible to the human eye among both adult and larval Lepidoptera upon which to base a classificatory ordering. Yet for swidden farmers the larvae are noteworthy, the adults are not. The classificatory detail applied is clearly in large part a function of practically motivated interests in the Tzeltal case, but of a compulsion for intellectual order on the part of the civilized butterfly fancier.

We have unduly stressed the disinterested intellectualism of our informants, and as a consequence have taken for granted their practical wisdom. Pragmatism is no sin. Folk science is for the most part applied science, rarely truly theoretical (e.g. Jones and Konner 1976). To properly appreciate the achievements of folk science, we need to investigate its practical significance as assiduously as we have its formal order.

Folk Biological Classification as a General-Purpose System

Folk biological classification has been approached as if information about plants and animals were stored in people's heads in taxonomically organized domains (Berlin, Breedlove, and Raven 1973, Kay 1971; but cf. Hunn 1976, Randall 1976). In this well-known formulation of the general principles of folk biological classification, plant and animal domains consist of sets of plant and animal taxa arrayed at various taxonomic levels, with lower-level taxa related to higher-level taxa by set inclusion.

At the heart of these domains is the "generic partition" (Berlin

1973:262-63, Kay 1971:878-79), a basic set of taxa known to correspond closely with scientific taxa (Hunn 1975a). These core taxa are most frequently biologically natural groupings reflecting genetic discontinuities.

These taxa are also logically natural groupings, which is to say, they are general-purpose rather than special-purpose concepts. Berlin, Breedlove, and Raven (1966) defined this distinction: ". . . a system of classification is said to be general ('natural' in a logical sense [i.e. polythetic]) insofar as its members possess many attributes in common, and *special* ('artificial' in a biological sense [i.e. monothetic]) when it is based on a few attributes that are of special interest for a particular purpose" (p. 275). Sneath asserts that a general-purpose classification will have "high information content . . . [but] can never be perfect for all purposes," since "when we put together entities with the highest proportion of shared attributes, we debar ourselves from insisting that these entities share any one particular attribute. Thus a special classification is demonstrably the best one for the limited purpose for which it was constructed, a general one the best for a wide range of potential purposes" (quoted in Berlin, Breedlove, and Raven 1966:275).

Biotaxonomists now recognize that membership in a biological species cannot be predicated upon possession of a set of necessary and sufficient features. Biological taxa are polythetic, not monothetic. Members of a species rather exhibit a family resemblance consequent upon their participation in the species' gene pool. Thus biologically natural groupings will be defined by a high degree of shared resemblance rather than by some defining set of conditions (Simpson 1961:23-28). It is worth noting that this shared resemblance—a relation of similarity—is consequent to and expresses shared inheritance—a relation of contiguity (Simpson 1961:27).

Biologically natural groupings, whether in folk or in scientific taxonomies, being polythetic, will also be general-purpose concepts, useful in a variety of contexts. This necessity is apparent only if we recognize that there is structure in nature as well as in culture. Aristotle noted that in classifying nature it is best to "carve at the joints," in other words, to respect the structure inherent in the *pièce de résistance.* I have argued that human perception is programmed to recognize patterns of covariation among the variable dimensions by which perception of a set of objects is organized. Patterns will be more readily recognized if there is strong covariation among these perceptually relevant dimensions than if not. For example, species of pine trees will be readily recognized as distinct if differences between them in needle length correlate strongly with differences in number of needles, cone size and shape, growth form, and texture and odor of bark. They will be less readily distinguished otherwise. In the case of our recognition of patterns among living organisms, the facts of genetic transmission and natural selection all but guarantee that genetic discontinuities, which define species populations within a restricted ecological community, will be reflected in cultural classification via the application of panhuman perceptual algorithms.

This is no doubt also true for nonhuman animals. Vervet monkey alarm calls, for example, differentiate among leopards, martial eagles, baboons, and pythons as predators and elicit distinct evasive responses in wild monkeys (Seyfarth, Cheney, and Marler 1980). Lions are known to exhibit a variety of hunting strategies as a function of the prey species. If they did not, they would certainly be clumsy hunters. The genetic discontinuities which underlie natural classification are also expressed in consistent chemical and behavioral covariation among the individuals of a species which are highly relevant to interspecies interactions, including, of course, those to which human beings are party.

Our presumably innate propensity to "see" biologically natural categories allows our behavior to be flexible in a highly efficient manner. Biologically natural categories, defined genetically, will tend strongly to be categories useful for many human purposes. Species are not only *good to think* (cf. Tambiah 1969), they are *good to act upon,* since human actions appropriate to one member of such a category are very likely appropriate to any member of that category. We tend to respond to all individuals of a species in like manner. We either eat them or avoid them, use them to make bows or reject them for that purpose, apply them as treatment for boils or seek some other remedy, respect them as spiritually powerful or treat them matter-of-factly. Natural selection has facilitated that most problematic of adaptive tasks, extrapolating from the uniqueness of one's past experience to future encounters with reality. An apparent exception involves categorical uses that require further specification, such as "eating *green* apples may make you sick," or "harvest only the *largest males.*" However, such recipes for action nevertheless are predicated upon the prior recognition of an appropriate natural category. The qualification specifies a monothetic subset of the polythetic taxon, allowing a more effective adaptive response with mimimal added conceptual effort.

Selecting Natural Discontinuities for Cultural Recognition

The folk taxonomic model at this point may seem unassailable: a taxonomic hierarchy built on a core of naturally useful distinctions. Unfortunately, it is not so simple. First, there is the fact that the number of discontinuities in nature far exceeds the observed capacity of folk taxonomies. If every visible genetic discontinuity were culturally recognized, there would be room in memory for little else. No more than a small fraction of the potentially useful information about the environment is or could be processed and stored in human memory. For example, the Sahaptin Indians of the Columbia Plateau specifically name only some 200 of 2,000 or more species of vascular plants known to exist in the region they occupy. They name less than a half-dozen fungi of more than 1,000 species estimated locally, and name five kinds of bettles, though as many as 4,000 may occur in the region (Hatch 1953-71). As the Tenejapa Tzeltal will recognize insects at the species level if motivated to do so (Hunn 1977:259-74), such classificatory detail is within the capacity of the folk taxonomist.

This same information-processing limitation has led some biological taxonomists to conclude that modern science likewise will never achieve an exhaustive inventory of natural species, even with the aid of electronic data storage and retrieval. There are simply too many species and too little time, given that biologists are not solely concerned with naming. The alternative, for folk and academic scientist alike, is to impose a selective process based on utility (Raven, Berlin, and Breedlove 1971). For example, Sahaptin speakers, who depend heavily on fish as a staple food, recognize 60 percent of the native fish species nomenclaturally but only 25 percent of the native bird species (Hunn 1979). If we are to explain why a particular subset of the available natural discontinuities is selected for cultural recognition, we must model this selection process. This requires us to consider the practical consequences of knowing or not knowing some plant or animal.

The fact that only a fraction of the potential natural discontinuities may be recognized in a folk biological classification creates theoretical difficulties for the taxonomic model. What is to be done with all those unclassified entities? In some cases they are simply left out of the basic level of classification—there will be *empty regions* in taxonomic "space," regions where many or all tokens are recognized only in very general terms, for example, as some kind of "bird," but are not recognized as some *particular* kind, that is, in Berlin's terms, as a member of a folk generic taxon. The common Tenejapa Tzeltal response to a request for names for the many large and distinctive solitary wasps of their neighborhood provides another example (Hunn 1977:264, 270). Though extraordinarily adept at classifying social Hymenoptera, Tenejapanecos confess to ignorance of many common solitary species. If pressed for a name, they respond by noting only that the solitary wasp is "*kol pahaluk sok šuš*" 'about the same as a [social] wasp.' (Note that single quotes are used here and below to indicate a gloss of a native concept.) It is as if the informant had never *seen* the creature before (though not for lack of opportunity). This contrast between the detail of classification applied to social as opposed to solitary Hymenoptera may be due to the increased frequency and intensity of encounter between people and the social species of wasps, encounters with varied, but often highly significant, even painful, practical consequences (cf. Posey 1981).

The empty taxonomic space may also be labeled as a *residual category*, which is a convenient linguistic means to dismiss all organisms deemed not worth recognition on their own account. For example, the John Day Sahaptins of the Columbia Plateau of northwestern North America use the term *cik*^{w}*ácik*^{w}*a* 'dickey bird' for any smallish bird not otherwise named. Note that this label is *not* appropriate for otherwise similar species which have "proper" names, such as the chickadees, called *latítalwit,* an onomatopoetic rendering that also indicates the bird's role in myth as harbinger of the modern age. A great many species of herbaceous plants are similarly dismissed with the phrase *áwtya áy c'íc'k* 'just a grass' or *áwtya áy latít* 'just a flower.' However, useful 'grasses' and 'flowers,' recognized nomenclaturally as basic-level folk taxa, are excluded from the more inclusive categories *latít* and *c'íc'k.* Thus the boundaries of Sahaptin 'flower' and 'grass' are drawn with respect to practical concerns. For example, Sahaptin speakers ignore most taprooted species of the genus *Lomatium,* calling them 'just flowers,' while classifying tuberous-rooted lomatiums growing nearby with exemplary finesse. The former are of little use as carbohydrate resources; the latter produce a high energy return for the labor of harvest. The tuberous-rooted species are further classed as *x̣nít* 'edible plants which are dug' at a more inclusive taxonomic level (Hunn 1981, Hunn and French 1981).

Sahaptin is certainly not unique in this classificatory pattern. The Northern Paiute of the Great Basin use an extensive inventory of residual categories at various levels of inclusiveness (Fowler and Leland 1967). Though residual taxa in Northern Paiute may or may not include basic taxa as subdivisions, Fowler and Leland gloss the terms for these categories in precisely the form appropriate for Sahaptin, e.g. 'just flowers,' 'just grass,' 'just willows,' etc. (p. 390). The Cha-Cha of the Virgin Islands recognize a large, heterogeneous category of fish called *corail* on the basis of their "uselessness" for food and their "similar patterns of behavior" (Morrill 1967:408). Such categories are strongly reminiscent of folk English "weed."

The examples I have just described do not accord well with the "general principles of folk biological classification" enunciated by Berlin, Breedlove, and Raven (1973) or with the associated formal taxonomic model (Kay 1971). As noted above, that scheme requires a structure of sets of organisms related to one another by set inclusion and defines the generic partition as a set of mutually exclusive taxa that *jointly exhaust the domain.* These folk generic taxa are characterized by Berlin as highly salient psychologically, biologically natural polythetic, general-purpose groupings. Taxa that are superordinate or subordinate to the taxa of this generic partition are classified by Berlin into several obligatory folk taxonomic ranks, with *life-form* taxa immediately above and folk *specific* taxa immediately below the generic taxa.

As noted above, Sahaptin 'flower' and 'grass' are residual taxa, i.e. groupings of organisms that are alike only by virtue of having been passed over in the process of cultural recognition. They directly contrast with folk generic taxa in the context of naming, e.g., "that's not an X, that's just a flower." In fact, they typically substitute for generic names. However, they resemble life-form taxa in that they include a heterogeneous collection of biological species. But they are not life-form taxa by virtue of being "empty," to use Turner's apt phrase (1974:35), lacking folk generic subdivisions. Residual taxa lack the hallmark of taxa at the "generic core" of folk biological domains in that they are not *natural.* They are rather biologically artificial, monothetic, and special-purpose concepts. Their special purpose, apparently, is to collectively represent a nonresource. Thus we have taxa that are "neither fish nor fowl" within the presently dominant theory of folk biological classification, and we find that the folk generic taxa fail to fully partition the folk biological domains. Folk generic classification is highly selective, and the practical significance of the organisms classified is important to the selection process.

Two Competing Models of Folk Biological Classification

On closer inspection, we see that current folk biological theory is rent by a fundamental contradiction. There are two models of folk biological classification based on contrasting principles, each with a partial claim to represent reality. The *taxonomic hierarchy model* envisions folk biological domains as sets of taxa at various levels related by set inclusion. This model owes its form to a Linnean analogy and a set theoretic formulation (Gregg 1954, Kay 1971). Fundamental to it is the notion of *direct contrast,* derivative of the methodology of structural linguistics. A folk taxonomy of this type is generated by a series of queries of the form "What are the names of all the kinds of X in Y" (Metzger and Williams 1966:39). The alternate model, which I will call the *natural core model,* sees folk biological domains as composed of a general-purpose, polythetic core of taxa surrounded by special-purpose, monothetic concepts in peripheral positions. Since this natural core/artificial periphery distinction recognizes the purposiveness of human classification, the model is one of practically motivated reasoning.

Berlin's concept of taxonomic rank (1973:260, 1976:381-83) is an awkward compromise between the two, an attempt to fit the natural, polythetic core of a folk biological domain into the procrustean bed of a taxonomic hierarchy by interpreting this core as equivalent to a single taxonomic hierarchical rank, the generic partition. The fit is not adequate, as the examples discussed above should make clear. Artificial taxa creep into the generic "partition" as residuals. Nor can natural-core taxa be confined to Berlin's generic taxonomic rank, as such taxa may be found at taxonomic levels both superordinate and subordinate to his folk generic rank. I have demonstrated that both natural and artificial folk biological taxa may occur at Berlin's folk specific rank (Hunn 1977:53). Here I will show that the same is true of taxa at Berlin's life-form rank, a fact with serious theoretical consequences for the taxonomic hierarchy model of folk biological classification. If there is no necessary correlation between the taxonomic rank of a taxon and its status as natural or artificial, the notion of taxonomic rank is shown to be a purely formal distinction imposed by the analyst.

Problems at the Life-Form Rank

Brown (1977, 1979) and his colleagues have profitably directed our attention to folk biological taxa of life-form rank, defined by Berlin as "the broadest, most encompassing classification of organisms into groups that are apparently easily recognized on the basis of numerous gross morphological characteristics" (1973:261). In this definition Berlin explicitly includes life-form taxa within the natural core of a folk biological domain. In a later reassessment he revises this view, describing life forms as recognized on the basis of "a small number of morphological characteristics" (1976:385). Since "a small number" is neither many, i.e. polythetic, nor one, i.e. monothetic, the relationship between life forms and the polythetic generic core of the domain remains ambiguous. The status of life forms as polythetic or monothetic is the focus of the following critique.

First, it should be noted that the distinction between polythetic and monothetic concepts is not solely a question of the number of features relevant to the conceptual distinction. As a general rule, instances of polythetic concepts are *distinguished* by many features while monothetic concepts are *defined* in terms of one or a small set of criterial features (i.e. necessary and sufficient conditions for category membership). But, more essential, the monothetic concept is *imposed* on reality by logical fiat while the polythetic concept is *recognized* by virtue of a family resemblance shared by instances of the concept. I have elsewhere labeled these two types of taxa "deductive" and "inductive" respectively (Hunn 1976). Core folk biological taxa are polythetic for the reasons indicated above. Noncore taxa are often "hybrids" in which an organism is first recognized as a bird, fish, snake, or as an example of some core taxon, then classified, for example, as "large bird," "edible fish," "poisonous snake," or "large, blue butterfly," by the subsequent imposition of a criterial feature. Note that "large, blue butterfly" is no less monothetic for requiring the coincidence of two criterial features.

In addition to the number of relevant features, the pattern of variation with respect to the feature(s) is significant. In some cases features are absolute; for example, wings, legs, or flowers are either present or absent. In other cases features are relative; for example, size or woodiness is present to some *degree.* In the case of monothetic concepts the presence, absence, or degree of the criterial feature(s) tends not to correlate with patterns of covariation among other features descriptive of morphological variation within the domain. By contrast, polythetic concepts are bounded by natural discontinuities or "gaps" in the pattern of covariation among large numbers of features. In general, the more encompassing the biological taxon—as in the case of life forms—the less likely the taxon will be bounded by such a gap (Hunn 1977:50). It is also possible, though rarely the case, that a taxon is *both* polythetic and monothetic, if the presence or absence of the criterial feature(s) happens to match the natural gap. The life form 'bird' is an example. The presence of feathers is a criterial feature that marks the gap of correlated traits such as the presence of wings, two legs, hollow bones, a beak, egg-laying habit, and the capacity for flight that typify a bird's family resemblance.

Brown argues in a series of recent articles (especially 1977, 1979) that the naming of biological life forms exhibits a universal implicational sequence much like the naming of basic color terms (Berlin and Kay 1969, Kay and McDaniel 1978). According to Brown, the plant and animal domains initially lack named life forms. Terms are then added in a specific sequence. For plants, 'tree' is added first, then 'grass' or "grerb" (Brown's label for a taxon inclusive of 'grass' and 'herb'), then 'bush' and/or 'vine.' For animals, 'fish,' 'bird,' and 'snake' are named first, in any order. Only subsequently are terms for 'mammal' and/or "wug" (his label for a taxon inclusive of 'worm' and 'bug') introduced. Brown's analysis is restricted to these few allegedly universal concepts.

Brown's universalist-evolutionary arguments depend on the validity of a close analogy between the historical development of basic color term vocabulary and that of folk biological life forms. Just as Berlin and Kay's color term analysis rests upon the privileged position of *basic* color terms (1969:5-7), Brown's scheme requires that there exist a definitive set of life-form taxa in each folk biological domain characterized by consistent criteria of content and structure. Berlin has defined the structural prerequisites of life forms: they occur at level one of the taxonomic hierarchy, i.e. immediately below the unique beginner or source of the taxonomic tree, and include a plurality of folk generic taxa. Consistency of content is explicitly required by Brown's exclusion of taxa based on nonmorphological criteria, such as habitat and use, and of taxa defined in terms of the presence of plant parts, such as berries or flowers (Brown 1977:320, 1979:793).[1] Brown's insistence that life forms be based on "overall morphology" accords with Berlin's assertion that life forms are "recognized on the basis of . . . gross morphological characteristics" (Berlin 1973:261). I will show that these so-called universal life-form taxa represent no consistent type of concept, and that this restriction of life forms to concepts based on "overall morphology" is neither consistently applied nor theoretically justified.

First, there is a striking contrast within Brown's "universal" life-form set between 'bird,' 'fish,' 'snake,' and 'grass,' on the one hand, and "wug," 'mammal,' 'vine,' 'tree,' "grerb," 'herb,' and 'bush,' on the other. Members of the first group, if literally glossed, are biologically natural and thus polythetic core taxa that reflect dramatic natural discontinuities. The second group, however, includes a set of biologically arbitrary, monothetic, or residual taxa. For example, 'tree' life forms typically reflect large size and woodiness, two highly correlated but continuously varying morphological traits. Size and woodiness are relative characteristics. Thus 'trees' shade imperceptibly into 'bushes' and 'bushes' into 'herbs.' There is no perceptual (and, of course, no underlying phylogenetic) discontinuity motivating the recognition of 'tree.' How then are we to explain the near universal labeling of a concept inclusive of large woody vegetation (Brown 1977:324-26)?

Perhaps the answer lies in the universal practical value of 'trees' rather than in the perceptual salience of 'tree.' For example, Samal 'tree' (*kayu*) is more accurately glossed 'burnables' (Randall 1977:49). In a comparative study Witkowski, Brown, and Chase (1981) found the same term used for both 'wood' and 'tree' in 44 of 66 cases.

While this may be interpreted as polysemy in which the name for the concept 'tree' has been suggested by the name for the concept 'wood,' it is also likely that an aspect of the meaning of 'tree' in many languages is the organism's practical value as a source of burnable wood. Likewise, 'vines' may more faithfully reflect the utility of vinelike plants for bindings than the perception of any purely morphological discontinuity. 'Mammal' is biologically arbitrary for a different reason. This life form is inappropriately glossed in that what is usually found is a category of large animals not otherwise classified as to life form (a residual), or a category predicated on such biologically arbitrary features as four-footedness, as Brown himself recognizes (1979:793). Thus the life-form rank, like the folk generic and specific ranks, is divided by the fundamental contrast between natural and artificial taxa.

Furthermore, there is a noticeable instability in the apparently natural life forms. Such life forms often are manifest as simplified variants, monothetically defined, which broadly overlap the "natural" life form in denotative range. For example, the natural taxon 'bird,' which includes all and only those animals scientists place in the vertebrate class Aves, may or may not be the reference point of the folk life form 'bird.' Often the life form we gloss as 'bird' is, in fact, only 'quasi bird,' a monothetic taxon defined in terms of the capacity for flight or a preference for an aerial habitat. Examples include the Kalam life form *yakt,* which includes bats but excludes the flightless cassowary, a bird (Bulmer 1967, 1974). Northern Paiute *yozɨdɨ* includes bats, birds, and flying insects—the last named set apart internally from the subdivision *huziba'* 'bird' + 'bat' (Fowler and Leland 1967:386). Samal *manuk-manuk* also includes bats, birds, and flying insects (Randall 1976:49). Such quasi bird life forms are not "recognized on the basis of numerous [or even "a small number" of] gross morphological characters" (Berlin 1973:261) nor "on *the form of the whole animal*" (Brown 1979:793, emphasis in the original). Thus they reflect principles of classification inconsistent with those Berlin and Brown use to characterize the life-form rank.

Life forms are often residual with respect to practical significance. In Sahaptin, for example *c'íc'k* 'grass' includes all herbaceous plants that are not 'flowers,' unless they are otherwise named. Since all such named plants have recognized practical utility, the meaning of Sahaptin 'grass' includes the signification 'not useful.' Other examples include the very Tzeltal plant life forms that inspired Berlin's statement of general principles. Tzeltal 'grass' excludes three species of the genus *Lasiacis* (Graminae) while including two others of that genus.

Those excluded are considered culturally "significant" while those included in the 'grass' life form are considered culturally "unimportant" (Berlin, Breedlove, and Raven 1974:405, 424-29). The Tzeltal life forms 'vine' and 'herbaceous plant' also require such a special-purpose specification, much as does our folk English concept "weed."[2] This intrusion of practical considerations into the referential meaning of life forms is anomalous from the taxonomic perspective in that it divides species that exhibit strong morphological resemblances while uniting others that are morphologically dissimilar.

In sum, the delineation of a privileged set of heterogeneous folk biological taxa distinguished by their general morphological signification is shown to be a very problematical task. The best examples of such "life forms" are taxa that faithfully reflect natural discontinuities (exhibit clear "criteria clustering" in Brown's terminology [1979:806]). These are simply core taxa of exceptional heterogeneity, and their developmental priority (Brown 1979:801) is due to their perceptual salience, the same cognitive principle that underlies the recognition of folk generic taxa (Hunn 1976). Such taxa should not be "lumped" with monothetic "life forms," which appear to conform but rarely to the overall morphology criterion.

Furthermore, Brown arbitrarily restricts his analysis to a small set of folk biological concepts prejudged to be universal. It is with respect to this small set that the developmental progress of a language is evaluated. Consequently we are left in ignorance of the welter of utilitarian and ecologically defined suprageneric taxa most peoples rely on to organize their knowledge of the natural world. For example, Sahaptin is judged a very simple system because it is credited with but one reasonably unambiguous botanical life form, 'tree.' Yet Sahaptin conversation is full of reference to such general classes of plants as *x̣nít* 'food plants which are dug' and *tmaanít* 'food plants which are picked.' The utility of the plants in each of these categories depends upon morphological specializations of the included plants, underground starch storage organs in the case of most *x̣nít* and attractive fruit in the case of most *tmaanít,* just as 'tree' is notable for its burnable wood.

Brown has analyzed a shred from the larger and far more complex fabric of folk biological thought. His impressive body of comparative data is clearly patterned. However, the full significance of that pattern will remain obscure until we understand the interaction of core and peripheral classificatory principles. That task requires that we pay close attention to the practical context of folk biological knowledge systems.

Methodological Suggestions for Assessing the Practical Significance of Taxa

Previous studies of ethnobiology may be described as either pre-ethnoscientific or ethnoscientific (cf. Hays 1974:100-110). Pre-ethnoscientific ethnobiology was primarily concerned with the practical value of native distinctions. The typical ethnobiological account of this period is a list of scientific species known to the people of culture X, with a summary of native uses under each species heading. There is much useful data in these accounts relevant to a variety of theoretical issues; however, such studies lack intrinsic theoretical focus. They have generated no cross-cultural syntheses.

Ethnoscientific ethnobiology has focused on the task of defining the principles of folk biological classification and naming. The works of Berlin and Brown reviewed above represent this tradition of ethnobiological research. These authors have not entirely ignored the practical value ("cultural significance" in Berlin's terms) of folk biological knowledge. For example, Berlin et al. (1973) analyzed the correlation between "Cultural Significance and Lexical Retention in Tzeltal-Tzotzil Ethnobotany." Cultural significance was rated on a crude scale having four values, "cultivated," "protected," "wild but useful," and "culturally insignificant." Names for the more significant plants changed less rapidly. Brown has noted that "cultural significance" is an effective determinant of the content of life-form inventories. He explains the correlation between the stage of growth of a life-form inventory and a culture's societal complexity score by reference to the progressively reduced reliance in complex societies on detailed knowledge of specific plants and animals (Brown 1977:332, 1979:804-5), a connection first suggested by Berlin (1972; cf. Dougherty 1978).

What is striking in these ethnoscientific treatments of the practical significance of folk biological knowledge is their *ad hoc* quality. The methodological sophistication so productively employed to define referential meaning and formal structure in the folk biological domains is nowhere apparent when uses are considered. It is time we created a post-ethnoscientific ethnobiology, using the best ethnoscientific ethnography to record and analyze the practical value of ethnobiological knowledge.

The first task of post-ethnoscientific ethnobiology is to systematically describe the practical significance of each taxonomic distinction. Then, perhaps, we may learn to measure that significance. The range of questions we might address if we had a valid measure of the practical significance of taxa is impressive. For example, I have previously proposed that we measure the perceptual salience of a taxon and test the power of such a measure to predict the selection of natural discontinuities for nomenclatural recognition (1977:72-75). Berlin, Boster, and O'Neill (1981) have conducted such a test and found perceptual salience to be a highly significant predictor of nomenclatural recognition among Aguaruna Jivaroan bird classification. Yet they also found a large residual variance. The multiple r^2 of linguistic codability with perceptual salience + size was 0.32; thus 68 percent of the variance in codability remains unaccounted for by these two perceptual factors. How much of that residual might be accounted for by the relative practical significance of the birds in question? With such a measure we might evaluate predictions as to changes in the content of folk biological classifications on the basis of changes in patterns of resource use. Working backward, we could assess the significance of a class of resources, say, of roots, or fish, or game, on the basis of the nomenclatural elaboration within each class, having controlled for perceptual salience. This could provide a more precise basis for reconstructing defunct ecological patterns from folk biological knowledge still extant in the memories of the survivors of acculturation.

Yet measuring practical significance is easier said than done. Crude indexes, of course, have been applied with some success. For example, Jochim has offered a variety of ecological predictions for hunter-gatherers in an archaeological context based on a measure constructed of six factors: weight, density, aggregation size, mobility, fat content, and nonfood yields of prey species. These factors are rather arbitrarily combined in a single formula (1976:23). Foraging strategists attempt to predict utilitarian preferences using caloric yields as a standard (Smith 1979). Economists apply a monetary standard, though recognizing that "utility" is a nonlinear function of monetary value. Sociobiologists postulate inclusive fitness differentials as the measure of alternative cultural inventories (Cavalli-Sforza and Feldman 1973, Durham 1976). Closer to the present ethnobiological context is Lee's typology of !Kung San plant resources as primary, major, minor, supplementary, rare, and problematic (1979:169-70). Berlin's distinction among cultivated, protected, wild but useful, and culturally insignificant plants is of this type.

Though adequate for limited hypothesis testing, such schemes will be restricted in their relevance to particular domains, particular types of economy, or particular definitions of "practical significance." To transcend these limitations, I believe it is essential to specify practical significance from the native point of view. In the tradition of ethnoscience methodology we should first seek to understand the particular cultural system in its own terms, then seek to generalize. Hays has pursued this task of measuring the cultural significance of taxa from the native point of view as far as anyone to date (1974). He compiled a list of 269 uses cited by his Ndumba informants for plants and assigned each of 458 plant taxa to the appropriate indigenous use categories based on the judgments of a sample of informants. He recognized the problems raised by functional equivalence; that is, certain plants are uniquely appropriate for certain purposes while others may be but one of a large set of acceptable sources of material, as in the case of firewood. Hays was disappointed to find little apparent correlation between his utility measures and target variables such as nomenclatural agreement among informants. Nor did he find close agreement between his measures and Berlin's framework cited above for classifying the cultural utility of Tzeltal plant taxa (Hays 1974:196-201).

Hays's measures, though systematic and ambitious in scope, are not yet adequately descriptive of local use patterns. For example, he cites "tuber eaten" as one use with 85 functional equivalents. A comparison with Sahaptin is instructive. The Sahaptin taxon *x̣nít* 'edible plants which are dug' includes some 35 folk taxa. "Tuber eaten" is an appropriate functional gloss for all. However, no two such taxa are precisely alike with regard to how, when, and where they are used and who makes use of them. In fact, we may propose the working hypothesis that no two folk biological taxa, if their practical significance were adequately described, would be found to be precise functional equivalents. Our task, then, is to describe the practical context of folk biological knowledge in detail sufficient to discriminate each taxon from every other. Each taxon should be definable in terms of a unique *activity signature.*

Activity Signatures of Folk Biological Taxa: A Preliminary Sketch

To suggest the scope of information necessary to characterize an activity signature, let us examine more closely one highly salient Sahaptin "practical life form," *x̣nít,* introduced above. As already noted, this term subsumes some 35 core folk botanical taxa. The name is a verbal noun derivative of *x̣ní-* 'to dig plant foods.' Excluded are closely related plants that are not foods, e.g. *Lomatium gormanii* (for those who consider it inedible), or plants that are foods but not 'dug,' e.g. *L. nudicaule,* which has edible stems but roots that are not eaten. The category is meaningful in several important practical contexts. For example, *x̣nít* contrasts with *tmaanít* 'edible plants which are picked' in terms of the tools typically employed, i.e. digging sticks and soft-twined baskets for *x̣nít,* hands and coiled root or bark baskets for *tmaanít.* These two taxa together evoke the seasonal rhythm of the Sahaptin food quest, with *x̣ní-* an activity typical of spring, *tmaaní-* 'to pick plant foods' an activity of summer and fall. Each of these basic gathering activities involves a separate progressive upslope movement (Hunn and French 1981). Thanksgiving feasts ritually punctuate this seasonal round. Such feasts always incorporate the sacred foods: *núsux̣* 'salmon,' one or more kinds of *x̣nít,* one or more kinds of *tmaanít,* and *čúuš* 'water.' (The linguistic and ritual variant described here applies in particular to the Columbia River dialects of Sahaptin spoken from Rock Creek, Washington, to Umatilla, Oregon.)

Though the concept *x̣nít* is clearly instrumental in conceptually ordering the Sahaptin peoples' annual schedule of subsistence activities, it is insufficiently precise for most day-to-day contexts. It is a special-purpose concept of limited relevance. If one inquires, 'What are the women doing?' it would not be inappropriate to respond, 'They're root digging' (*pax̣níša*). Such an answer is far from adequate, however, as a "recipe for action." One may infer the need for digging sticks and twined baskets from that response, but one would not know where the women had gone or for how long, or what processing activities necessarily follow the 'digging,' unless, of course, one is already privy to the implicit knowledge of seasonal associations and personal histories sufficient to "read between the lines." For example, if the women have gone to Oregon and it is early May, they are almost certainly digging *x̣áwš* 'cous' (*Lomatium cous*). 'What are they digging?' provides a wealth of additional information by specifying the relevant core folk taxon. With each possible response comes a unique set of practical implications. It is this set of implications that constitutes an *activity signature.*

Likely responses to the query, 'What are you digging?' include: *pyax̣í* 'bitterroot,' *x̣áwš* 'cous,' *lúkš* '*Lomatium canbyi* in part,' *škúlkul* '*L. canbyi,* another part,' *max̣šní* '*L. farinosum* var. *hambleniae,*' *mámin* '*L. piperi,*' *púla* '*L. macrocarpum,*' *pank'ú* '*Tauschia hooveri,*' and *x̣máš* 'camas.' Within this set are plants harvested on 'lithosols' (*šám*) and others harvested in 'vernal meadows' (*táay*). Some are 'shallow' and easy to dig; others are 'deep,' such as *púla,* rarely sought today in part because of the labor required to dig it out. Some *x̣nít* are generally available (within appropriate habitat); others are available only in certain restricted regions or at certain sites: *x̣áwš* is an 'Oregon root,' *škúlkul* and *max̣šni* are 'Priest Rapids roots,' and *pank'ú* is a 'Yakima root.' Some, such as *max̣šní,* are dug only by children.

Lithosol species are available early to late spring depending primarily on elevation but also on exposure to sun and drying winds, the precise timing also a function of weather patterns, constantly monitored by the people. 'Maturity' of a species is dependent on factors that vary from species to species. For example, tuberous lomatiums (an unnamed and unrecognized category in Sahaptin) are typically preferred as the petals drop. Before that time they are often found to be too 'soft.' Shortly after the petals drop, the plant may be 'burned,' and the tops dry and blow away, effectively hiding the roots. 'Bitterroot' is preferred before the buds open, as subsequently the bitter 'bark' of the roots is difficult to peel and processing time increases to discouraging levels.

Processing strategy is perhaps the most salient dimension of variation differentiating these folk taxa. 'Camas' must be baked underground for from one to three days, which normally implies a complex, cooperative effort on the part of several women (and of men also, as quantities of firewood, rocks, etc., are required at the processing site). It has been shown that this processing significantly enhances the nutritional value of camas (Konlande and Robson 1972). Camas is less often harvested today in part, I suspect, because of the increasing difficulty of organizing the processing tasks. '*Tauschia hooveri*' is a great favorite—root-diggers traveling from three states to harvest a supply—in part because it is delicious raw, requiring no processing. The most subtle distinction (from the scientific botanist's perspective) drawn by Sahaptin speakers is that between *šḱúlkul* and *lúkš*. These terms label a partition of the botanical species *Lomatium canbyi.* The folk forms are identifiable on the basis of morphological cues, e.g. the texture of the leaves, the size and shape of the tuberous root, the color and 'oiliness' of the root in cross-section (cf. Washington n.d.). Yet both forms occur in the same habitat, mature at the same time, and are dug in the same way. There would seem insufficient practical motive to separate them (and their perceptual salience is vanishingly small!). Yet contemporary Yakima Indians not only emphatically distinguish them; they will travel 200 kilometers to dig *šḱúlkul*, while *lúkš* is found in abundance near their homes. A sharp distinction is drawn in terms of appropriate processing; that is, *lúkš* is dried or ground and mixed with *mámin* '*Lomatium piperi*' to form finger cakes. By contrast, the more oily *šḱúlkul* should be baked underground like camas. It is thus a very different *food* and contributes substantially to the Yakima's perception of culinary variety. Also highly significant are the sociopolitical associations. *šḱúlkul* is a 'Priest Rapids people's root.' One may speculate that its cultural value at Yakima may reflect the value of extended kinship ties, which constituted the sociopolitical foundation of the Plateau subsistence strategy (Marshall 1977).

I have sketched only the bare outline here of the relevance of folk biological distinctions for practical affairs. Such an account requires that folk biologists ask not just what the names for things are but also the who, what, when, why, and how that define their practical significance. This involves no radically new methodology. It simply requires that our ethnobiological queries be as systematic and exhaustive with regard to the behavioral relevance of terms as to their denotative meaning. Once we have learned to describe the activity signatures of folk taxa, we will be in a much better position to appreciate why one group of organisms is more highly differentiated than another, why one culture concentrates here, another there, within their respective floral and faunal "spaces." We will better understand what underlies taxonomic variation within a culture, and how changes in folk biological knowledge affect the environment (and vice versa). However, description is not an end in itself. It is a first step toward theoretical generalization. Our next step is to analyze the role of an activity signature in the larger cultural system. This requires that the analysis of folk biological classification be joined with an effort to characterize formally the routine action plans that link thought and action.

Activity Signatures and Routine Action Plans

One might define the activity signature of plant or animal X as the set of all culturally valid imperative sentences in which the noun X occurs as object. Such sentences may be seen as instructions to act, e.g. "bake camas in the underground oven for three days." One might compare taxon X with taxon Y by counting the number of such sentences in each activity signature, but this would surely be a poor way to measure the relative practical significance of taxa. All sentences of an activity signature are not equally significant. The task of evaluating the practical significance of recognizing taxon X leads us to assess the significance of a particular instruction to act within the larger strategy for living that defines a particular culture.

Two recent analyses of cultural plans suggest how this might be accomplished. Geoghegan's seminal though still unpublished analysis of Tagtabon residence choice shows the feasibility of such a program. His cultural model is composed of a sequence of assessments, e.g. age, marital status, viability of household, house ownership, economic means, that collectively determine in culturally appropriate terms the "proper" mode of residence for an individual. Though of modest scope, this model passes the behavioral test with high marks. It predicts with 98 percent accuracy the choice of residence mode of several hundred individuals in two populations of Philippine Samal (Geoghegan n.d.). His model is formally explicit, informed by cognitive psychological research, and faithful to the native rationale (Geoghegan 1973). The variety of residence choices is shown to follow from a single cultural rule. Geoghegan illustrates how changes in rule-generated behaviors in a community may result without changes in the rule itself. Such rules may "evolve" in response to environmental changes.

Randall has completed an ambitious analysis of Samal fishing (1977) that extends Geoghegan's approach to a human context as complex and fundamental as 'making a living.' Though Randall does not attempt an empirical verification of his model, he defines the hierarchical organization of over 300 explicit Samal instructions-to-act necessary to the conduct of nocturnal multihook scad fishing, the primary mode of production among the Linungan Samal. In Randall's analysis the relative significance of an instruction to act is a function of several considerations, including the number of alternative means to accomplish a particular element of the larger plan, the preference ranking of optional realizations of a subplan, and the hierarchical level of an instruction to act within the total plan. For example, an effective medicine that may cure a debilitating illness makes possible a large number and variety of essential activities otherwise impossible. Thus plans to sustain health are broadly ramifying. By contrast, instructions to harvest a rare and little-favored berry have but minor ramifications, under routine conditions.

Geoghegan and Randall show us how culture *works*, how ideas about the world may affect our choice of action in the world, and how a varied and changing world, via cultural assessments, generates behavioral choices well adapted to enviromental circumstances. The practical value of an element of folk biological knowledge is a function of its role in the cultural plan that generates adaptive behavior.

Conclusion

I have argued that ethnoscientific research in ethnobiology should be guided by the premise that cultural knowledge is adaptive. In pursuit of this objective, students of folk biological classification must systematicaly investigate the practical significance of folk biological knowledge. I argue that our theoretical accounting of folk biological classification is hampered by the contradictions between a taxonomic hierarchy model of folk biological classification and one based on the distinction between the natural core and artificial periphery of such classification systems. The latter model is predicated on the fundamental distinction between general-purpose and special-purpose concepts. From the perspective of the core-periphery model, taxonomic anomalies such as residual taxa and empty portions of the generic partition are resolved and the selective cultural recognition accorded taxa within the core is more fully explained.

Brown's hypothetical sequences for the naming of folk botanical and zoological life forms is questioned, since his scheme presumes that life forms—originally defined taxonomically—constitute a privileged set of concepts free of practical signification. I show that some life forms are natural taxa but most belong on the artificial periphery of a folk biological domain. Thus a set of morphologically "pure" life forms cannot be recognized universally as distinct from the variety of practically motivated categories by which core taxa are most often conceptually organized by folk systematists.

I then discuss the advantages of and obstacles to reliable measurement of the cultural utility of folk categories. As a proximate goal I outline a method for describing the *activity signatures* of folk taxa. Such a detailed description of a concept's practical relevance presumes a systematic, native-language characterization of cultural plans as recipes for action. This seems a most promising frontier of scientific anthropology, integrating cognitive, linguistic, ecological, and evolutionary theory to define a dynamic ethnoecology.

NOTES

My research on Sahaptin ethnobiology, which has informed much of this discussion, was made possible by grants from the National Science Foundation (BNS 76-16914), the Melville and Elizabeth Jacobs Research Fund (Whatcom Museum Foundation), and the Graduate School Research Fund (University of Washington). I benefited greatly from logistic support in the field from the Kamiakin Research Institute of the Yakima Indian Nation and from correspondence with B. Rigsby. I would especially like to thank my expert Sahaptin consultants, too numerous to single out here. James and Elsie Selam, Sara Quaempts, Elsie Pistolhead, and the late Don Umtuch testified in depth to the sophistication and scope of Native American knowledge of the natural environment in the Columbia Plateau. This paper was originally presented to the symposium Renewing the New Ethnography, organized by J. Dougherty, at the American Anthropological Association Annual Meetings, Washington, D.C., 2 Dec. 1980. This revision has profited from the critical evaluations of B. Berlin, C. Brown, R. Bulmer, J. Dougherty, R. Ellen, D. French, T. Hays, J. Howe, B. Meilleur, R. Randall, E. Smith, D. Spain, and N. Williams. If my treatment here of my mentor, B. Berlin, seems harsh, it is not for lack of appreciation of his contribution. More than anyone, Berlin has made of ethnobiology a challenging theoretical frontier.

1. Brown asserts that this consistency of life-form content is an empirical finding. However, the consistency is clearly *imposed* by his analysis.

2. Note the similarity of life-form taxa such as those just described, which are residual with respect to utility, and residual "generic" taxa such as Sahaptin *cik*ʷ*ácik*ʷ*a* 'dickey bird.' Brown and Chase, in a recent report of their Zapotec research (1981), in fact suggest that life forms may evolve from residual "generic" taxa such as those I have described above for Sahaptin.

REFERENCES

Berlin, Brent

1972 Speculations on the Growth of Ethnobotanical Nomenclature. *Journal of Language and Society* 1:63-98.

1973 Folk Systematics in Relation to Biological Classification and Nomenclature. *Annual Review of Ecology and Systematics* 4:259-71.

1976 The Concept of Rank in Ethnobiological Classification: Some Evidence from Aguaruna Folk Botany. *American Ethnologist* 3:381-99.

Berlin, Brent, Dennis E. Breedlove, and Peter H. Raven

1966 Folk Taxonomies and Biological Classification. *Science* 154:273-75.

1973 General Principles of Classification and Nomenclature in Folk Biology. *American Anthropologist* 75:214-42.

1974 *Principles of Tzeltal Plant Classification: An Introduction to the Botanical Ethnography of a Mayan-Speaking People of Highland Chiapas.* New York: Academic Press.

Berlin, Brent, James S. Boster, and John P. O'Neill

1981 The Perceptual Bases of Ethnobiological Classification: Evidence from Aguaruna Jívaro Ornithology. *Journal of Ethnobiology* 1:95-108.

Berlin, Brent, and Paul Kay

1969 *Basic Color Terms: Their Universality and Evolution.* Berkeley: University of California Press.

Berlin, Brent, et al.

1973 Cultural Significance and Lexical Retention in Tzeltal-Tzotzil Ethnobotany. In Monroe S. Edmonson, ed., *Meaning in Mayan Languages,* pp. 143-64. The Hague: Mouton.

Boster, James S., and Chad K. McDaniel

N.d. Untitled. Paper presented to the Conference on Anthropology, Psychology, and Cognitive Structures, University of California, Riverside, May 1979.

Brown, Cecil H.

1977 Folk Botanical Life-Forms: Their Universality and Growth. *American Anthropologist* 79:317-42.

1979 Folk Zoological Life-Forms: Their Universality and Growth. *American Anthropologist* 81:791-817.

Brown, Cecil H., and Paul K. Chase

1981 Animal Classification in Juchitan Zapotec. *Journal of Anthropological Research* 37:61-70.

Bulmer, Ralph N. H.
1967 Why Is the Cassowary Not a Bird? *Man* 2(n.s.):5-25.
1974 Folk Biology in the New Guinea Highlands. *Social Science Information* 13:9-28.
Cavalli-Sforza, L., and M. W. Feldman
1973 Models for Cultural Inheritance, I: Group Mean and Within Group Variation. *Journal of Theoretical Population Biology* 4:42-55.
Dougherty, Janet W. D.
1978 Salience and Relativity in Classification. *American Ethnologist* 5:66-80.
Durham, William H.
1976 The Adaptive Significance of Cultural Behavior. *Human Ecology* 4:89-121.
Fowler, Cathryn S., and Joy Leland
1967 Some Northern Paiute Native Categories. *Ethnology* 6:381-404.
Geoghegan, William H.
1973 *Natural Information Processing Rules: Formal Theory and Applications to Ethnography.* Monograph no. 3. Berkeley: Language-Behavior Research Laboratory, University of California.
N.d. Residential Decision-Making among the Eastern Samal (with Addendum on Refugee Population). MS. Department of Anthropology, University of California, Berkeley.
Gregg, John R.
1954 *The Language of Taxonomy: An Application of Symbolic Logic to the Study of Classificatory Systems.* New York: Columbia University Press.
Handy, E. S. C., and M. K. Pukui
1953 The Polynesian Family System in Ka-'u, Hawai'i'. *Journal of the Polynesian Society* 62:123-68.
Hatch, Melville H.
1953-71 *The Beetles of the Pacific Northwest.* 5 vols. Seattle: University of Washington Press.
Hays, Terence E.
1974 Mauna: Explorations in Ndumba Ethnobotany. Ph.D. dissertation, University of Washington, Seattle.
Hunn, Eugene S.
1975a A Measure of the Degree of Correspondence of Folk to Scientific Biological Classification. *American Ethnologist* 2:309-27.
1975b *Cognitive Processes in Folk Ornithology: The Identification of Gulls.* Working Paper no. 42. Berkeley: Language-Behavior Research Laboratory, University of California.
1976 Toward a Perceptual Model of Folk Biological Classification. *American Ethnologist* 3:508-24.
1977 *Tzeltal Folk Zoology: The Classification of Discontinuities in Nature.* New York: Academic Press.
1979 Sahaptin Fish Classification. *Northwest Anthropological Research Notes* 14:1-19.

1981 On the Relative Contribution of Men and Women to Subsistence among Hunter-Gatherers of the Columbia Plateau: A Comparison with *Ethnographic Atlas* Summaries. *Journal of Ethnobiology* 1:124-34.

Hunn, Eugene S., and David H. French

1981 *Lomatium:* A Key Resource for Columbia Plateau Native Subsistence. *Northwest Science* 55:87-94.

Jochim, M. A.

1976 *Hunter-Gatherer Subsistence and Settlement: A Predictive Model.* New York: Academic Press.

Jones, N. Blurton, and Melvin J. Konner

1976 !Kung Knowledge of Animal Behavior. In Richard B. Lee and Irven DeVore, eds., *Kalahari Hunter-Gatherers,* pp. 325-48. Cambridge, Mass.: Harvard University Press.

Kay, Paul

1971 Taxonomy and Semantic Contrast. *Language* 47:866-87.

1975 A Model-Theoretic Approach to Folk Taxonomy. *Social Science Information* 14:151-66.

Kay, Paul, and Chad K. McDaniel

1978 The Linguistic Significance of the Meanings of Basic Color Terms. *Language* 54:610-46.

Konlande, J. E., and J. R. K. Robson

1972 The Nutritive Value of Cooked Camas as Consumed by Flathead Indians. *Ecology of Food and Nutrition* 2:193-95.

Lee, Richard B.

1979 *The !Kung San: Men, Women, and Work in a Foraging Society.* London: Cambridge University Press.

Lévi-Strauss, Claude

1966 *The Savage Mind.* G. Weidenfeld and Nicholson Ltd. translation. Chicago: University of Chicago Press.

Marshall, Alan G.

1977 Nez Perce Social Groups: An Ecological Interpretation. Ph.D. dissertation, Washington State University, Pullman.

Metzger, Duane, and Gerald E. Williams

1966 Some Procedures and Results in the Study of Native Categories: Tzeltal Firewood. *American Anthropologist* 65:389-407.

Morrill, William T.

1967 Ethnoichthyology of the Cha-Cha. *Ethnology* 6:405-16.

Posey, Darrell

1981 Wasps, Warriors and Fearless Men: Ethnoentomology of the Kayapo Indians of Central Brazil. *Journal of Ethnobiology* 1:165-74.

Randall, Robert A.

1976 How Tall Is a Taxonomic Tree? Some Evidence for Dwarfism. *American Ethnologist* 3:543-53.

1977 Change and Variation in Samal Fishing: Making Plans to 'Make a Living' in the Southern Philippines. Ph.D. dissertation, University of California, Berkeley.

Raven, Peter H., Brent Berlin, and Dennis E. Breedlove
1971 The Origins of Taxonomy. *Science* 174:1210-13.
Rosch, Eleanor
1978 Principles of Categorization. In E. Rosch and Barbara B. Lloyd, eds., *Cognition and Categorization,* pp. 27-48. Hillsdale, N.J.: L. Erlbaum.
Seyfarth, R. M., D. L. Cheney, and P. Marler
1980 Monkey Responses to Three Different Alarm Calls: Evidence of Predator Classification and Semantic Communication. *Science* 210:801-3.
Simpson, George G.
1961 *Principles of Animal Classification.* New York: Columbia University Press.
Smith, Eric A.
1979 Human Adaptation and Energetic Efficiency. *Human Ecology* 7:53-74.
Tambiah, S. J.
1969 Animals Are Good to Think and Good to Prohibit. *Ethnology* 8:423-59.
Turner, Nancy J.
1974 Plant Taxonomic Systems and Ethnobotany of Three Contemporary Indian Groups of the Pacific Northwest (Haida, Bella Coola, and Lillooet). *Syesis* 7, Supplement no. 1.
Washington, Nat W.
N.d. Tsukulotsa (*Lomatium canbyi*): Key to Understanding Central Washington Nonriverine Archaeology. Paper presented to the 29th Annual Northwest Anthropological Conference, Ellensburg, Wash., 10 Apr. 1976.
Witkowski, Stanley R., Cecil H. Brown, and Paul K. Chase
1981 Where Do Tree Terms Come From? *Man* 16(n.s.):1-14.

6

Thai Spirits: A Problem in the Study of Folk Classification

James Stanlaw and Bencha Yoddumnern

How people see the world has been the perennial philosophical problem for thousands of years. Since the beginnings of scientific fieldwork, when it was discovered that exotic people may have an equally exotic view of the universe, ethnologists have realized that classifying and ordering knowledge is one of the most fundamental issues in anthropology. Cognitive anthropologists for the past two decades have tried to develop formal techniques to examine a key aspect of this problem—the relationship between labeled categories and conceptualization.

Work by Berlin (1972, 1974, 1976), Berlin, Breedlove, and Raven (1966, 1968, 1973, 1974), and others seems to indicate that, cross-culturally, some form of taxonomic hierarchy is basic to the ordering of the biological world. In addition, these researchers have proposed some general principles of nomenclature that could be used to describe how native speakers classify things in their natural environment. Several attempts have subsequently been made by other cognitive anthropologists to extend these principles to nonbiological folk classification (e.g. Hage 1972, Lindstrom 1975, Noah 1979, Spradley 1970, Spradley and Mann 1975, Spradley and McCurdy 1975:79-101). Among these are Brown et al. (1976), who identified these naming principles in the classification of American automobiles, Finnish winter vehicles, American tools, and Thai spirit-ghosts. They conclude that these "principles originally attributed solely to biological classification actually relate to more general aspects of human psychological unity" (1976:73).

In this paper we argue that the strict application of folk biological nomenclature principles to nonbiological data is inappropriate, or at best problematic. As a data base we will examine Thai ghosts or spirits (*phǐi*), one of the domains Brown et al. have already analyzed. Reservations about the significance of taxonomies in anthropological research have been raised by numerous scholars (e.g. Burling 1964, Dougherty 1978, Dougherty and Keller this volume, Keesing 1972). We believe, however, that taxonomies or other organizational schemes can be useful and enlightening—even if they do not always conform to strict nomenclature principles—as long as they do not become detached from their ethnographic context. The reasoning behind a taxonomy, such as the criteria for subgrouping, can give anthropologists insight and allow them to pose interesting questions relevant to the rationale of cognitive organization. To exemplify this point, we show that one way Thai spirits are conceptually ordered is by analogy to the Thai view of the world.

The *Phǐi*

Introduction

Life in a traditional Thai village (and even in contemporary urban settings) abounds with spirits, ghosts, and demons. In general, these ghosts or spirits are referred to as *phǐi*,[1] though this term, for reasons to be explained shortly, is ambiguous and may include nonspiritual beings and exclude essences with many ghostlike characteristics. Names of particular ghosts or spirits are usually preceded by this term to indicate their supernatural status: e.g., *fáa* = sky, *phǐi fáa* = spirit which lives in the sky; *pàa* = forest or jungle, *phǐi pàa* = forest ghost or demon. There are spirits which cause disease, seduce men, protect towns, or guard hidden treasure. Some *phǐi* are the restless ghosts of those who have suddenly died, while others are the spirits of ancestors who are still concerned about the living, and require attention and appeasement. The spirit personality is even thought by some anthropologists to mirror that of human beings in many ways (Potter 1977:115).

Definition of Phǐi

When a Thai person uses the word *phǐi*, he may be speaking of one of several things. Besides referring to a ghost or spirit wandering about, guarding a house, or haunting a piece of land, the term *phǐi* may also be applied to the soul (*winjaan*) of a dead person, as well as to his corpse (*phǐi khon raaw*) (Tambiah 1970:263). It can also be used to refer to a spirit that possesses a person or, in some dialects, to the person being possessed. Sometimes *phǐi* might mean a dreaded or epidemic disease, such as cholera or smallpox, or the germs that spread the disease. Textor (1960:185) mentions that the term *phǐi* may also refer to "corpse oil" or other material extracted or derived from a corpse used in aggressive magic. The literature seems to indicate that most of these meanings of *phǐi* share some association with death.[2]

The number of *phǐi* found in Thai society is difficult to judge. Anuman Rajadhon (1954) cites about 20 evil *phǐi* he believes to be common. Textor, in his 1960 summary of non-Buddhist supernatural objects in a central Thai village, found around 30 "true" ghosts, though if borderline cases are considered, the total would probably exceed 40. In their taxonomy of Thai spirit-ghosts, Brown et al. (1976) elicited around two dozen terms for spiritual beings that were not some kind of god (*theewadaa*). Among our informants we gathered around 40 salient terms (i.e. known to everyone), and about a half-dozen that were less salient. There is certainly much regional variation, perhaps even village variation as well.

Descriptions of the various *phǐi* are often vague and inconsistent (but this in no way seems to hamper their usefulness or importance). Generally, *phǐi* are more human, individualistic, and personal than other Thai supernatural objects and beings. They come close to being mere invisible humans, with all the corresponding fears and foibles. *Phǐi* normally do not make themselves visible except at night, in certain circumstances. Sometimes they are tall, long, and very thin and have no heads; they may have only a tiny mouth which never seems to allow them to consume sufficient nourishment. *Phǐi* may make loud, shrill sounds (something like "koi koi") to frighten humans (Anuman Rajadhon 1954:15). Generally *phǐi* seem to be sexless, and even ancestor spirits tend to lose their previous sexual identity. However, a few *phǐi* may be exclusively female, especially those associated with fruit-bearing plants and trees.

Becoming a Phǐi

Some *phǐi* are the result of the transformation of the human soul after death. However, it is not exactly clear how or why one becomes a *phǐi*.[3] According to Tambiah (1968:49), general Thai thanatology claims that one's fate depends on the balance of demerit (*bàab*) or merit (*bun*) at the end of one's lifetime. If someone's balance of merit is great enough, his *winjaan* (soul or spiritual essence, which leaves the body after death) will go to heaven; when his merit is exhausted, he will be reborn on earth. If he has acquired both merit and demerit, he will go to hell (*naróg*) until he has made restitution for all his accumulated demerit, after which he will go to heaven for a while to reap the benefits of his merit. He will then be reborn back on earth. Those who have led an excessively sinful life will be banished to hell, or must wander the earth as a *phĭi* for a long time before another rebirth is possible.

Particular *phĭi* may also be created by special situations. The stillborn fetus of a dead expectant mother may become a *phĭi kumaan thɔɔŋ*, 'golden boy ghost' (*kumaan* = boy, *thɔɔŋ* = gold). If appropriate steps are not taken in handling and burying her corpse, the mother herself may become a *phĭi taaj thɔ́ɔŋ klom*, 'ghost of a dead expectant mother' (*taaj* = to die, *thɔ́ɔŋ* = belly or stomach, *klom* = to be round). The ghosts of those who have died suddenly or violently are especially to be feared, perhaps because of their still-lingering attachment to the human world.

At least in the central Thai village investigated by Tambiah (1968, 1970) the *winjaan* (soul) of *any* person is thought to become a *phĭi* with dangerous powers soon after death. The corpse is also thought to attract other malevolent spirits. Great care must be taken during the funeral procession and cremation rites, as coffin bearers expose themselves to possible harm from the dead person's *phĭi*. Besides offering protection for the living, these rites are generally concerned with merit making for the deceased, separating the *winjaan* from the status of ghost to ancestor (Tambiah 1968:97, 1970:191).

Sometimes when respected parents or grandparents die, they become ancestor spirits, a group of *phĭi* that offers protection to their survivors. The belief in these *phĭi* allows for continued interaction with the deceased.[4] Ancestor *phĭi* are venerated, unlike most ghosts who are feared, yet these ancestor *phĭi* may take revenge for failure to treat them properly (see Potter 1977). Tambiah (1968:98, 1970:190) claims these ancestor spirits form a category, but there are no firm genealogical or individual remembrances of persons beyond the paternal generation.

Our informants were reluctant to say that the spirits of departed ancestors were, indeed, ghosts (*phĭi*), though certainly they were not considered to be deities (*theewadaa*). Rather, they were often described as a "felt presence" or a "feeling" that made itself known, particularly during times of need or trouble.

Besides *phĭi*, which are the transformation of human beings who have died either through appropriate natural causes or suddenly by accident or violence, some spirits seem to be more or less permanent and not derived from human *winjaan* (souls). Often these spirits will be thought of as guardians and might be associated with the local village, monastery, or other territory. Other miscellaneous permanent spirits may be found in nature in trees, mountains, forests, and rivers. Usually no human origin is involved with these *phĭi*, and many of them are malevolent or quite deadly. Being dangerous and capricious, these *phǐi* must be handled with extreme caution. For example, before entering the jungle or forest one must request permission from *phǐi pàa*, 'spirit of the forest' (*pàa* = forest, jungle) lest the trespasser become stricken with illness or face other hardships while traveling through his domain. One must also beware of the *phǐi* who confuse travelers, the *phǐi* of various supernatural animals, and a myriad of miscellaneous and minor *phǐi* of ponds, trees, or plants.

Other Properties of Phǐi

One the most outstanding characteristics of the *phǐi* is the vagueness and flexibility in the way in which they are conceptualized by Thais. Besides the ambiguities of origin and physical description, previously mentioned ancestral spirits, at least, form a kind of common "pool of the dead" (Tambiah 1970:314), and whenever affliction from these types of *phǐi* is diagnosed, no effort is made to determine *which* paternal or ancestral spirit is the agent. (The use of these vague definitions for daily problem solving will be discussed later.)

Textor (1960:226-29) claims that some ancestral ghosts, especially those of deceased grandparents or elderly parents, may possess their descendants living on earth. This is particularly common if someone had a close emotional relationship with the deceased. This possession is often manifested as frequent dreaming about the deceased or as an illness (presumably caused by insufficient ritual respect paid to the ancestor, or insufficient merit transferred for the benefit of the departed's soul).[5]

Tambiah (1970:321-26) makes a distinction between spirit *affliction,* resulting in relatively minor illnesses, and spirit *possession,* accompanied by "mental" disturbances such as inappropriate and prolonged crying or laughing, hiding the face, or frequent complaints about a lack of food or attention. A spirit affliction can be treated by divination (of the malevolent agent) and placation (such as paying some compensation to the *phǐi* to get them to cease their harmful actions or to ensure their continued protective function). Spirit possession requires the services of an exorcist who both identifies the spirit and purges it from the patient.

It has been noted by our informants as well as in the literature that women tend to be bothered more often by *phǐi* than men and are also more likely to actually see them. The reason for this is attributed to the women's "soft soul" or generally weaker and more sensitive personality. Textor (1960:205) believes the reasons women are more troubled by ghosts are (1) they fear the suffering of pregnancy and childbirth, and (2) retiring and passive personalities (which generally characterize Thai women) are the most likely to be possessed.

Tambiah (1970:320-21) concurs, and believes that spirit possession may be a hysterical reaction that climaxes at the time of impending childbirth.

Some Functions and Uses of Phǐi

Tambiah makes a distinction between village Buddhism and other village religious activity ("cults"). However, the "*phǐi* cult" (1968:114) is not just the remnants of an earlier, more pervasive animism upon which a Buddhist cosmological order and worldview has been imposed. Instead, as Van Esterik (1982) argues, *phǐi* and guardian spirits incorporate into a single Thai Buddhist conceptual order Hindu deities, various Buddhist figures, and the ghosts of nature and locality. *Phǐi* tend to accomplish this at the familiar, physical level, while *theewadaa* (venerated Thai gods) usually operate at the cosmological, metaphysical level.

Phǐi have important and significant roles in the totality of Thai religious behavior, even though there are marked distinctions between the Buddhist and the *phǐi* ritual (Tambiah 1968:41, 42, 50, 1970:263, 285). The various contrasts to Buddhism posed by the *phǐi* may be crucial in resolving some of the ultimate paradoxes Buddhism and merit making present for the average individual: How can a person rooted in this world adhere to religious practices devoted to its renunciation? Why do people make merit, often at taxing cost, with no certainty of payoff?

The *phǐi* also provide important tools to be manipulated, and strategies to be called upon, in the day-to-day living of villagers (and, to a somewhat lesser extent, city dwellers). Ghosts may be used to symbolize or anthropomorphize particular problems confronting someone. As Textor mentions (1960:199-200), ghosts provide a plausible explanation for why someone has caught no fish; it is difficult to provide contrary evidence after someone says a *phǐi* has eaten his catch. Likewise, gambling losses or a gambling addiction itself may be attributed to ignoring important spirits.

This situated significance of *phǐi* is especially evident with regard to one ghost cited by Textor (1960:368-76). The "whispering ghost" (*phraaj krasib*)[6] allows males to engage in divination without first having to become possessed by a spirit. As mentioned, the cultural expectation is that men, because of their stronger personalities, will not become possessed by ghosts as easily as women, and the *phraaj krasib* provides the desired divinatory information without the necessity of a man having to step out of his male role. Also, since the whispering ghost is inaudible to anyone else, what the ghost says to him cannot be disputed.

Another function of the *phǐi* may be to help reinforce the everyday cultural proscriptions and definitions of Thai society. The *phǐi câaw thîi* or *câaw thîi* (spirit of the place)[7] guarantees that someone's land is safe from both human and supernatural intruders. This guardianship enhances a person's awareness of the jurisdiction and property of others, and makes it less likely that he will trespass or infringe on someone else's land (Textor 1960:241).

Phǐi and *Theewadaa*

Besides the *phǐi*, Thai spiritual and religious life involves another category of supernatural beings, the *theewadaa* (deities, angels, or gods). The word *theewadaa* comes from the Pāli and Sanskrit term *deva* meaning "shining one" or "heavenly being" (Brandon 1970:94), and the *theewadaa* are thought to inhabit one of the six heavens of the sensual world. *Theewadaa* are thought by most Thais to be divine, fantastic beings quite different from either humans or *phǐi*. While *phǐi* may be capricious and vindictive, *theewadaa* are usually constant and moral. Their predictability is further reinforced by astrological causation (Textor 1960:188).

The relationships between *phǐi* and *theewadaa* have been diversely interpreted in the literature. Illustrative views are given in Anuman Rajadhon (1954, 1969, 1976), Kirsch (1977), Tambiah (1970), Textor (1960), and Van Esterik (1982). Some scholars (e.g. Van Esterik 1982) see Thai cosmology as consisting of a continuum of supernatural beings, starting with extremely evil *phǐi*, going through a series of relatively benevolent *phǐi* and minor *theewadaa*, and ending with the most venerated *theewadaa*. Others (e.g. Tambiah 1970:59-61, Textor 1960:188) see *phǐi* and *theewadaa* as separate kinds of supernatural beings. Our informants clearly made this distinction. For example, our informants said that when a person dies, he knows he might become a *phǐi* but he would never expect to become a *theewadaa*. Even asking if one could expect to become a *theewadaa* after death was thought to be humorous to some informants.

Taxonomies and *Phǐi*

Development of the Taxonomic Approach

In the late 1950s and early 1960s the formal problems and characteristics of folk taxonomies began to be investigated by anthropologists. One of the earliest detailed theoretical descriptions was given by Conklin (1962), who pointed out that one of the crucial goals of eliciting a folk taxonomy was to delineate significant sets of semantic units within particular domains.

Berlin, Breedlove, and Raven (1966, 1968, 1973) expanded upon this by examining the formal naming principles in several folk biological taxonomies. Berlin et al. hoped to find general regularities that would hold cross-culturally. Basically they claimed that all biological folk taxonomies have five levels of inclusion, and that the classificatory labels at the deeper levels of the taxonomy are morphologically more complex than the names for the more abstract categories (near the top). Several attempts have been made by anthropologists to extend these principles to nonbiological folk classifications, including Brown et al. in their analysis of Thai spirit-ghosts.

Problems with the Taxonomic Approach

The taxonomic method has been criticized by anthropologists of divergent philosophies (e.g. Keesing 1972, 1974, 1979; Quinn 1974; Harris 1975, 1979). Keesing (1972:306, 317) claims that taxonomic linguistics is primarily concerned with the study of elements rather than relational systems, a limited endeavor because people *live* in a world of relations rather than a world of taxa, propositions, or classes. Keesing also argues (1972:316) that cultural expectations and distinctions need not be directly labeled in language, and that taxonomies cannot account for metaphor, polysemy, or context. Burling (1964) criticized the taxonomic approach because he felt it glossed over problems of indeterminacy. The attempts by Brown et al. (1976) to provide a taxonomy of Thai spirit-ghosts seem particularly susceptible to such criticism (Van Esterik 1978, 1979, 1982).[8]

A New Approach to the Phǐi Taxonomy

We approached the understanding of Thai spirits with as few expectations and prejudices as possible. Not only did we try to remain culturally unbiased but we tried to impose no artificial structure on the data as a result of our elicitation procedures. The data we gathered emerged in open-ended interviews. We felt substitution frames commonly associated with cognitive anthropology were too confining, almost forcing a term to belong to some category of an already presumed structure. We chose to rely on more natural definitions and classifications (cf. Boehm 1980), and were interested in the rationale *behind the ordering* of terms as much as the ordering itself. An attempt was made to maintain the ethnographic context by having informants explain their notions of how spirits operate, recount the experiences of those people they have known who had encounters with ghosts, or mention any famous incidents involving ghosts that happened in their area.

Informants were asked informally to group spirits that somehow seemed to belong together. The basis might have been origin, location, habits, physical appearance, or any other criteria or property of *phǐi* that felt comfortable to an informant. After an informant gave some indication that several ghosts might be linked, we solicited information about their "taxonomic" status. Indications of linkage included (1) sequential responses (e.g. several *phǐi* being mentioned in the same sentence or train of thought); (2) direct attributions (e.g. an unprompted informant stating that one ghost was "kind of" another); (3) various assertions, stated or implied, of resemblances or differences among ghosts regarding location, jurisdiction, power, ritual, etc.

As groupings implicitly emerged, informants were explicitly asked if it was sensible to think of these spirits as being associated together in any way. If so, we asked for possible names for this group, and for any other spirits that the informant might want to place in this category. An attempt was then made to see if any higher-order groups could be built using combinations of these smaller ones. Similar questions and checks were asked at each of these subsequent steps.

Not all our informants agreed on every specific detail. Spirits that were not recognizable to all our informants were not used in our organizational scheme. The final typology, based on data from all the informants and presented in Figure 1, is an average consensus model and represents an interrelationship of spirits presumably equally acceptable to everyone (but is probably exactly right for no single informant).

As mentioned previously, after informants indicated their reluctance to place *phǐi* and *theewadaa* in the same category, we concentrated on eliciting information about ghosts and spirits. The "domain" of the typology, then, is subsumed under the term *phǐi,* as seen in Figure 1. This organizational scheme is less elegant than the way corresponding terms are handled in Brown et al.'s (1976:79) taxonomy of Thai "spirit-ghosts."

One reason for the inelegance is synonymy. Several *phǐi* have the same or similar name (e.g. *phǐi pàa, câaw pàa; phǐi pùujâa, phǐi banphaburud*). For example, *phǐi pàa* and *câaw pàa* can both mean "spirit of the jungle or forest" and may sometimes be used interchangeably by some informants. The choice of terms might depend on the informant's location (*câaw pàa* being the *guardian* of a local jungle, *phǐi pàa* being the *ghost* of a forest in unfamiliar territory), or on the informant's perception of a spirit's jurisdiction. That is, a *câaw pàa*

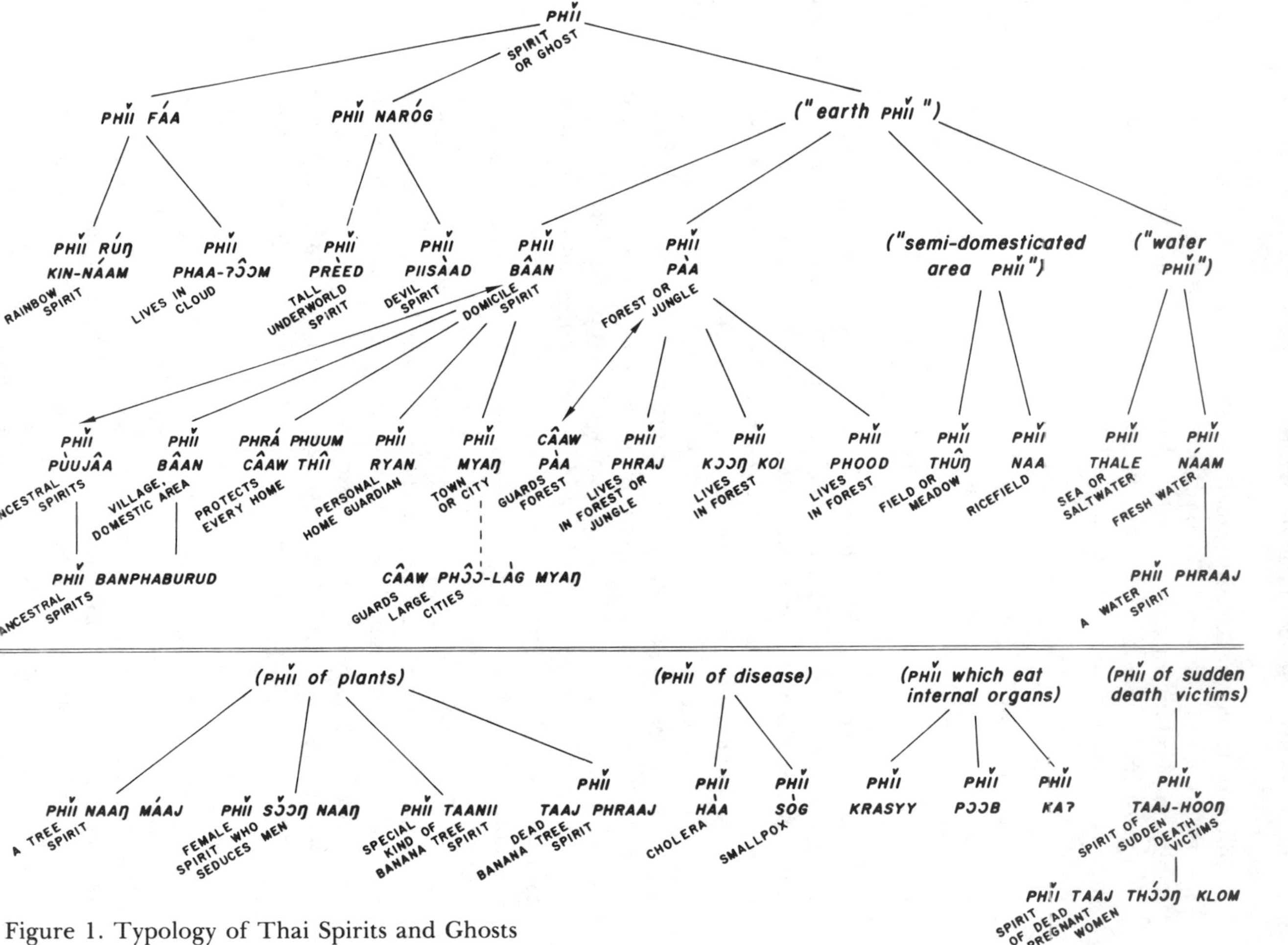

Figure 1. Typology of Thai Spirits and Ghosts

could be thought of as a spirit found in the deep jungle *(pàa chád),* while *phǐi pàa* might be found only in less dense forests. Some informants feel there is little difference between the two terms and are rather indeterminant in their usage. Others see *phǐi pàa* as a more general category used to refer to all supernatural beings inhabiting the jungle, including, among others, the *câaw pàa.* Some of these informants were reluctant to simply include *câaw pàa* with other forest-dwelling ghosts because of its special nature: a *câaw* is an elevated, presumably benevolent, spirit, while the personalities of the other *phǐi* are at best capricious or unknown (cf. Hunn 1975, 1976; Berlin, Breedlove, and Raven 1974).

We encounter problems of cross-referencing (Lehman 1974:xi) in the terms *phǐi taaj-hǒoŋ* (ghost of someone who has died a sudden death), *phǐi taaj phaaj* (ghost or spirit of a dead banana tree, or of someone who has died unexpectedly, especially during childbirth), and *phǐi taaj thɔ́ɔŋ klom* (ghost of a dead expectant mother). To die suddenly, violently, accidentally, prematurely, or in childbirth (i.e. *taaj-hǒoŋ)* is to die an inappropriate, inauspicious, or unprepared death (cf. Delaney 1977:263-95). This is a "bad death" because one cannot focus their accumulated merit or concentrate on appropriate thoughts as they leave this world, nor can they reap the complete benefits of merit transferred from attending loved ones. Also, by the unanticipated nature of the death, a monk will not be present to act as a death-guide and help the dying person recite the "threefold refuge" (seeking solace in Buddha, the teachings, and the monastic order).

To refer to victims of those have died giving birth, *phǐi taaj phraaj* can be used interchangeably with *phǐi taaj thɔ́ɔŋ klom. Phǐi taaj phraaj* may also be used to refer to a dead banana tree, especially one dying in the process of bearing fruit. Apparently a banana tree is the only plant that may take the *phǐi taaj phraaj* term. *Phǐi taaj thɔ́ɔŋ klom* can never be used to refer to any plant.

F. K. Lehman (personal communication) suggests that *phǐi taaj thɔ́ɔŋ klom* may be a euphemism for *phǐi taaj phraaj.* However, among our informants this is not clear; some informants believe that *phǐi taaj thɔ́ɔŋ klom* is more fearful than *phǐi taaj phraaj.*

Figure 1 indicates that the organizational scheme used by our informants to order Thai spirits is not a formal taxonomy. One reason is that the inclusion relations of many of the terms create a structure that is only partially hierarchical. For example, as mentioned before, *phǐi pàa* and *câaw pàa* may be used interchangeably by some informants and are not necessarily related by class inclusion. Also, we are left with many terms that cannot be accounted for within the taxonomic framework (listed below the double line in Figure 1). In addition, informants seem to use a wide variety of criteria in grouping spirits together (cf. Casagrande and Hale 1967). For example, *phǐi hàa* and *phǐi sòg* are grouped together because they are diseases, *phǐi krasyy, phǐi pɔɔb,* and *phǐi ka?* because they eat the internal organs of the body, and *phǐi prèed* and *phǐi piisàad* because they are both spirits of the underworld. Finally, problems of cross-referencing like those mentioned above cannot be accounted for in a formal taxonomic framework. Though this kind of diversity can be found in taxonomically ordered domains, the variation documented here is more extreme than previously noted in folk biological taxonomies (cf. Kay 1969; Burling 1964; Berlin, Breedlove, and Raven 1966, 1973).

A useful way to view the relations among *phǐi* is in comparison with Thai spatial structure of the world. The main heart of the community is the *mùu-bâan* (village), which is surrounded by the *thûŋ-naa,* consisting of rice paddies (*naa*) and areas of uncleared forest or jungle (*thûŋ*) which will become cultivated as needed. Outside the *thûŋ-naa* is the *pàa* (forest or woods), a wild, unfriendly, dangerous area, especially at night.

pàa	wild	dangerous
thûŋ-naa	semi-domesticated	less dangerous
mùu-bâan	domesticated	friendly

Phǐi thûŋ (spirits of the *thûŋ* field) and *phǐi naa* (spirits of the rice paddy) are usually thought of as a group by informants, in contrast to *phǐi pàa* and *phǐi bâan.* Three particularly gruesome *phǐi* prowl in the *thûŋ-naa: phǐi ka?, phǐi pɔɔb* and *phǐi krasyy.* All these *phǐi* are said to eat the internal organs of the human body.[9] The sea and fresh water are another significant element of the world's structure, and correspondingly another group of *phǐi*—*phǐi thale* (spirit of the sea) and *phǐi náam* (spirit of the water)—have jurisdiction over oceans, lakes, rivers, and streams. Besides these "earth-*phǐi*" there is another dimension of contrast evidenced by the clearly labeled sky spirits (*phǐi fáa*) and spirits of the underworld (*phǐi naróg*). This model of the world is given in Figure 2.

Conclusions

Knowledge is organized on the basis of principles relevant to, and emergent from, experience. Such orderings may be as trivial as a shopping list or as complex as a pantheistic cosmology. What they all do, however, is fulfill the need to organize data so that it may be recalled, or communicated to others, in an understandable way.

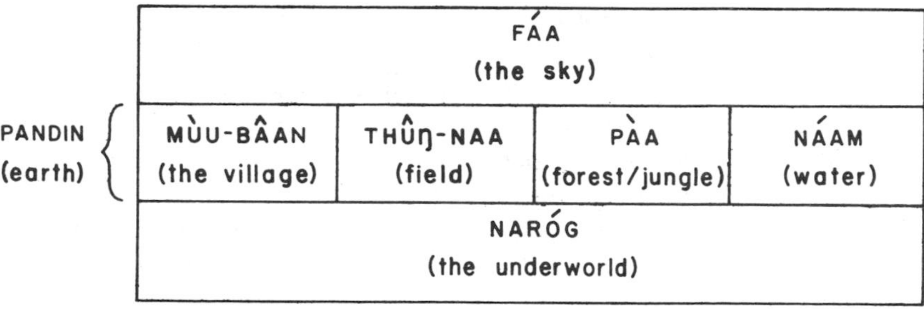

Figure 2. Thai Model of the World

Tyler (1978:257-58) claims that in an analogy an already developed mode of organization is applied to some other, totally different domain. One common analogical technique correlates world concepts with their usual spatial location, a device often used for both memorization and learning. For example, someone may write a grocery list by imagining themselves walking through their local supermarket looking for things they need. The resulting organization of words on the list is an analogue of the organization of things in the store. Applying this notion to ethnographic data, it is possible that concepts may be related on an analogy with body parts, physical-spatial relationships, or geographic location. This is evident in our analysis of the Thai spirit world.

Basso (1967:348-49) has noted that a nonbiological folk classification in Apache—a taxonomy of automobile parts—shows a structure analogous to Apache human body-part classification. For example, "headlights" corresponds to "eyes," "electrical wiring" to "veins," etc. Indeed, this similarity in structure between human and automobile morphology has been the basis of new vocabulary items in Apache via semantic extension of body-part terminology. Data such as Basso's, as well as our own work on Thai spirits, lead us to speculate that the elements of nonbiological folk knowledge are often ordered through analogy with some other physical or natural or metaphysical system. Thus car parts in Apache are ordered using the human body, and various Thai spirits using a cosmological view of the natural world.[10]

While it is likely that body parts, location, or even animal characteristics provide a wide range of possible analogies for those organizing nonbiological knowledge, this does not imply that all members of a culture must always see the same analogy and thus make the same structural organization. On the other hand, the rationale of a structural typology might be like a double arrow reflecting back on its analogous components, and in turn reinforcing them. Thus the organization of *phǐi* reflects, but also substantiates and supports, the Thai cosmological view of the sky, earth, and underworld.

Finally, it is now easier to see why not every term elicited fits into our typology. The remaining *phǐi* form a sample of a pool of terms that may be used in other organizational structures, based on other analogies, at other times, for other occasions. The ritual specialist or exorcist undoubtedly has a different conception of *phǐi* (perhaps based on their malignity, habits, or what objects are needed to drive them away) than a farmer. As many *phǐi* are associated with plants, it would not be too surprising if some other *phǐi* typologies would follow, in part, from the way Thais order the botanical world. The consensus on our typology, however, leads us to suspect that the village analogy with the Thai view of the world is a common, salient way many Thais may view spirits in many situations.

NOTES

We wish to thank Cecil H. Brown, Joseph B. Casagrande, Janet W. D. Dougherty, and F. K. Lehman for their thoughtful reading, helpful comments, and detailed criticisms of earlier drafts of this paper, even though their positions did not always agree with ours. The remaining limitations, of course, are our own. We also wish to thank Penny Van Esterik, who generously shared with us an unpublished manuscript of her work on Thai guardian spirits.

The data on Thai spirits were gathered from five Thai informants, two men and three women, temporarily residing in the United States. Two informants were from the Lampang area and three were from Bangkok. Interviews were conducted by Yoddumnern, a native Thai, who is currently working on her Ph.D. in anthropology at the University of Illinois.

The transcription system used in the text is that found in the standard reference by Haas (1964). To facilitate comparison with the other sources cited (who all used different transliterations), we should mention that our *c* is similar to the English /*č*/, *j* represents the semivowel /*y*/, and *y* is an unrounded high central vowel (sometimes transcribed as *u* or *ü* in other places). Vowel length is represented by repetition of the symbol, and tone is indicated by the usual diacritics.

1. Those who are experts on Buddhism may note some inconsistencies and lack of details in various parts of our discussion. This is partly because we have made some generalizations for the sake of brevity. It must be remembered, too, that none of our informants is a religious specialist. As Keyes (1977:170) mentions, "Full descriptions of Buddhist cosmology are contained in texts that could probably be found in most village-monastery

libraries. It is unlikely, however, that many villagers would be able to give anymore elaborate description of the cosmological classification than I have given here" (a brief description of about a half-dozen pages). See Leach (1968) and Terwiel (1976) for other discussions of "practical" religion and behavior.

Also, as can be seen from several of the articles in this volume, folk knowledge is not always consistently ordered, but often "emerges" from a situation. Though a theological canon may provide guidelines for a culture, each individual's beliefs within this framework may be quite disparate.

2. Our informants differed with Textor (1960:180), who claims "all but the filth ghost are derived from, or are associated with, death." They believe, for example, that all plants and animals have spiritual essences and therefore, presumably, *phǐi* as well. F. K. Lehman (personal communication) mentions that, rather than being associated with death, *phǐi* are separated from the *khandha* (Pāli term for the bundles of five properties of sentient beings; cf. Sanskrit *skandha*) of sentient beings of the normal birth-state.

3. Avoiding becoming a *phǐi* (or at least certain kinds of *phǐi*) is desirable because the living might fear you or a sorcerer may try to harness your supernatural powers. Also, because merit can only be made by humans, being a *phǐi* is a detour in advancing toward higher rebirths.

4. The individual's relationship to the deceased seems to determine how that person's spirit will be viewed. For example, a granddaughter would most likely view the spirit of a fond grandfather as benevolent regardless of the merit he allegedly earned. Others in the village, however (enemies, business competitors, etc.) might be quite convinced of his malevolent status.

5. Textor (1960:227-28) admits that he is not sure whether it is a *phǐi* or a *winjaan,* or some other type of spiritual essence, that his informants are perceiving during possession. The types of spirit possession found in rural Thailand, and the current medical and psychological problems associated with these beliefs, are discussed in Suwanlert (1976).

6. Even though the whispering ghost does not usually take the *phǐi* title, *phraaj krasib* is a true *phǐi* (because *phraaj* already means ghost or spirit, "*phǐi phraaj krasib*" apparently is redundant).

7. *Câaw thîi* is a *phǐi,* albeit one with rather high status (cf. Anuman Rajadhon 1954, 1976). Certain supernatural beings are given the prefix *câaw* (*câaw* = lord, prince, elevated *phǐi*). Because of their special power or benevolence, these *phǐi* are given more respect than other spirits. Our informants usually thought of these *phǐi* as being guardian spirits of an area (e.g. *câaw khǎw,* the mountain god or goddess; *câaw phɔ̂ɔ-làg myaŋ,* the guardian spirit of Bangkok or other large cities). Anuman Rajadhon (1954) believes there is a special class of supernatural beings—*câaw phǐi*—who are half ghosts or spirits (*phǐi*) and half deities (*theewadaa*).

8. It should be noted that in spite of some limitations Brown's work has raised extremely interesting questions and stimulated much debate. For a defense of his taxonomy, see Brown (1979, 1980).

9. These spirits were not placed under "semi-domesticated area *phǐi*" in the main schema even though they occupy the *thûŋ-naa.* To place them

directly under the covert category "semi-domesticated area *phǐi*" would have given each of these three *phǐi* equivalence with *phǐi thûŋ* (spirits of the *thûŋ* field) and *phǐi naa* (spirits of the rice paddy); informants were reluctant to do this. However, to place the covert category "internal-organ-eating *phǐi*" under "semi-domesticated area *phǐi*" would have implied a tripartite division of the *thûŋ-naa* spirits: *phǐi* of the *thûŋ* field, *phǐi* of the rice paddy, and *phǐi* that eat internal organs. This was unsatisfactory for informants. The fact that *phǐi krasyy, phǐi pɔɔb,* and *phǐi ka*ˀ all prowl in the *thûŋ-naa* was incidental to most informants, and not sufficient criterion for establishing a category to contrast with *phǐi thûŋ* and *phǐi naa.*

Lately, especially in highly developed areas like Bangkok, much of the *thûŋ* has been cleared for planting. It is likely, then, that city dwellers and young people might not always make such clear distinctions between *phǐi thûŋ* and *phǐi naa,* as more and more of the *thûŋ* disappears. This may alter the relevance of this spatial analysis for ordering Thai spirits.

10. Tambiah has also noted analogies with respect to spirits and classifications in Thai. For example, the human host and its possessor, *phǐi paub,* appears to be analogous to the female and the placenta (1970:319).

REFERENCES

Anuman Rajadhon, Phya
1954 The Phi. *Journal of the Siam Society* 41:153-78.
1969 *Rŷaŋ Phǐisǎa Theewadaa.* Bangkok: Prakano.
1973 The Story of Thai Marriage Customs. *Asian Culture Quarterly* 1:55-62.
1976 Chao Thi: Village God of Thailand. *Asian Culture Quarterly* 4:64-71.

Basso, Keith
1967 Semantic Aspects of Linguistic Acculturation. *American Anthropologist* 69:471-77.

Berlin, Brent
1972 Speculations on the Growth of Ethnobotanical Nomenclature. *Language in Soceity* 1:51-86.
1974 Further Note on Covert Categories and Folk Taxonomies: A Reply to Brown. *American Anthropologist* 76:327-31.
1976 The Concept of Rank in Ethnobiological Classification: Some Evidence from Aguaruna Folk Botany. *American Ethnologist* 3:381-99.

Berlin, Brent, Dennis Breedlove, and Peter Raven
1966 Folk Taxonomies and Folk Classification. *Science* 154:273-75.
1968 Covert Categories and Folk Taxonomies. *American Anthropologist* 70:290-99.
1973 General Principles of Classification and Nomenclature in Folk Biology. *American Anthropologist* 75:214-42.
1974 *Principles of Tzeltal Plant Classification: An Introduction to the Botanical Ethnography of a Mayan-Speaking Community in Highland Chiapas.* New York: Academic Press.

Boehm, Christopher
1980 Exposing the Moral Self in Montenegro: The Use of Natural Definitions to Keep Ethnography Descriptive. *American Ethnologist* 7:1-26.

Brandon, G. S. F.
1970 *A Dictionary of Buddhism.* Compiled from his *A Dictionary of Comparative Religion* by T. O. Ling. New York: Charles Scribner's Sons.

Brown, Cecil H.
1979 Variability, Cognitive Reality, and the Principles of Classification and Nomenclature. (Reply to Van Esterik.) *American Ethnologist* 6:407-8.
1980 Nonbiological Classification Reconsidered: A Response to Durrenberger and Morrison. *American Ethnologist* 7:184-87.

Brown, Cecil H., et al.
1976 Some General Principles of Biological and Non-Biological Folk Classification. *American Ethnologist* 3:73-85.

Burling, Robbins
1964 Cognition and Componential Analysis: God's Truth or Hocus-Pocus? In Stephen Tyler, ed., *Cognitive Anthropology,* pp. 419-28. New York: Holt, Rinehart and Winston.

Casagrande, Joseph B., and Kenneth Hale
1967 Semantic Relationships in Papago Folk-Definitions. In Dell Hymes and William Bittle, eds., *Studies in Southwestern Ethnolinguistics,* pp. 165-93. The Hague: Mouton.

Conklin, Harold C.
1962 The Lexicographic Treatment of Folk Taxonomies. In Stephen Tyler, ed., *Cognitive Anthropology,* pp. 41-59. New York: Holt, Rinehart and Winston.

Delaney, William Phillip
1977 Socio-cultural Aspects of Aging in Northern Thailand. Ph.D. dissertation, University of Illinois, Urbana.

Dougherty, Janet W. D.
1978 Salience and Relativity in Classification. *American Ethnologist* 5:66-80.

Durrenberger, E. Paul, and John Morrison
1977 A Theory of Analogy. *Journal of Anthropological Research* 33:372-87.
1979 Reply to Brown. *American Enthnologist* 6:408-9.

Haas, Mary R.
1964 *Thai-English Student's Dictionary.* Stanford, Calif.: Stanford University Press.

Hage, Per
1972 Müncher Beer Categories. In J. Spradley, ed., *Culture and Cognition: Rules, Maps, and Plans,* pp. 263-78. San Francisco: Chandler.

Harris, Marvin
1975 Why a Perfect Knowledge of All the Rules That One Must Know

in Order to Act Like a Native Cannot Lead to a Knowledge of How Natives Act. *Journal of Anthropological Research* 30:242-51.

1979 *Cultural Materialism: The Struggle for a Science of Culture.* New York: Vintage.

Hunn, Eugene

1975 *Cognitive Processes in Folk Ornithology: The Identification of Gulls.* Working Paper no. 42. Berkeley: Language-Behavior Research Laboratory, University of California.

1976 Toward a Perceptual Model of Folk Biological Classification. *American Ethnologist* 3:489-507.

Kay, Paul

1969 Comments on Colby. In Stephen Tyler, ed., *Cognitive Anthropology,* pp. 78-90. New York: Holt, Rinehart and Winston.

Keesing, Roger M.

1972 Paradigms Lost: The New Ethnography and the New Linguistics. *Southwestern Journal of Anthropology* 28:299-332.

1974 Theories of Culture. *Annual Review of Anthropology* 3:73-97.

1979 Linguistic Knowledge and Cultural Knowledge: Some Doubts and Speculations. *American Anthropologist* 81:14-36.

Keyes, Charles F.

1977 *The Golden Peninsula: Culture and Adaptation in Mainland Southeast Asia.* New York: Macmillan.

Kirsch, A. Thomas

1977 Complexity in the Thai Religious System: An Interpretation. *Journal of Asian Studies* 34:241-66.

Leach, E. R., ed.

1968 *Dialectic in Practical Religion.* Cambridge: Cambridge University Press.

Lehman, F. K.

1974 Foreword. In Paul Ballonoff, ed., *Mathematical Models of Social and Cognitive Structures,* pp. vii-xvii. Urbana: University of Illinois Press.

Lindstrom, Monty

1975 California Wine Categories. *Anthropological Linguistics* 17:273-85.

Noah, Randall

1979 Ethnoscience and the Grape: Further Inquiry into Nonbiological Folk Classification. *Journal of Anthropology* 1:65-79.

Potter, Sulamith Heins

1977 *Family Life in a Northern Thai Village: A Study in the Structural Significance of Women.* Berkeley: University of California Press.

Quinn, Naomi

1974 Getting Inside Our Informants' Heads. *Reviews in Anthropology* 1:244-52.

Spradley, James

1970 *You Owe Yourself a Drunk: An Ethnography of Urban Nomads.* Boston: Little, Brown.

Spradley, James, and Brenda Mann
1975 *The Cocktail Waitress: Woman's Work in a Man's World.* New York: John Wiley.

Spradley, James, and Davis McCurdy
1975 *Anthropology: The Cultural Experience.* New York: John Wiley.

Suwanlert, Sangun
1976 *Phii pob:* Spirit Possession in Rural Thailand. In William P. Lebra, ed., *Culture-bound Syndromes, Ethnopsychiatry, and Alternative Therapies,* pp. 68-87. Honolulu: University Press of Hawaii.

Tambiah, S. J.
1968 The Ideology of Merit and the Social Correlates of Buddhism in a Thai Village. In E. Leach, ed., *Dialectic in Practical Religion,* pp. 41-121. Cambridge: Cambridge University Press.
1970 *Buddhism and the Spirit Cults in Northeast Thailand.* Cambridge: Cambridge University Press.

Terwiel, B. J.
1976 A Model for the Study of Thai Buddhism. *Journal of Asian Studies* 35:391-403.

Textor, Robert B.
1960 An Inventory of Non-Buddhist Supernatural Objects in a Central Thai Village. Ph.D. dissertation, Cornell University.

Tyler, Stephen A.
1978 *The Said and the Unsaid: Mind, Meaning, and Culture.* New York: Academic Press.

Van Esterik, Penny
1978 Reply to Brown. *American Ethnologist* 5:404-5.
1979 Reply to Brown's Response. *American Ethnologist* 6:408.
1982 Interpreting a Cosmology: Guardian Spirits in Thai Buddhism. *Anthropos* 77:1-15.

7

Taskonomy: A Practical Approach to Knowledge Structures

Janet W. D. Dougherty and Charles M. Keller

Ethnoscientific research has contributed significantly to the comparative study of man's classification of natural (and occasionally social) phenomena (Berlin, Breedlove, and Raven 1973, Berlin and Kay 1969, Rosaldo 1972, M. Brown 1978, Bulmer 1968, Frake 1961, Hunn 1976). However, extensions of this classificatory framework to artifactual material have been particularly problematic (Brown et al. 1976, Rosch et al. 1976).[1] Currently, a diversification of research strategies is developing in the field of cognitive anthropology that builds upon the earlier work and establishes a new focus on conceptualization rather than on language. Our concern here is to account for the productivity evident in human behavior. As such, our emphasis is cognitive, not linguistic.[2]

Our discussion is intended to demonstrate three main points, two of them substantive, one methodological. Beginning with the premise that information is organized for much of everyday activity on the basis of goal-oriented tasks and strategies (Schutz 1964, 1971; Miller, Galanter, and Pribram 1960; Schank and Abelson 1977), it is shown that (1) everyday activity requires recognition and manipulation of distinctions not codified in naming; (2) a task at hand determines features of relevance for conceptualization; and (3) as strategies for action, organizations of knowledge are particularistically oriented, and the processes of organization are productive. As individuals behave they create and recreate organizations of aspects of their knowledge relevant to a task at hand. The investigation of cognition described here is based upon the technological activity of blacksmithing. It draws upon the blacksmithing expertise of Keller, which includes an ap-

An earlier version of this chapter appeared in *American Ethnologist* 9:763-74, 1982. It is reprinted by permission of the American Ethnological Society and the authors.

prenticeship in 1976 and four subsequent years of practice, and upon observations and interviews with blacksmiths of the American Southwest over a five-year period.[3] The mode of analysis we develop is not unique to blacksmithing. Any mundane project and attendant strategies will play a similar role in establishing relevance for conceptual organization.

Task-Oriented Constellations of Knowledge

In investigating the knowledge of blacksmithing, it soon becomes evident that there are numerous ways in which relevant knowledge is organized and reorganized within a system of open possibilities (Schutz 1971:81). Open possibilities suggest shifting, flexible, creative organizations of knowledge. This "open" quality frustrated our initial ethnosemantic inquiries. Once extensive inventories of named categories of tools, products, and materials had been collected, we proceeded to investigate the ways in which these named units are conceptually interrelated. Interviews proceeded as follows: "Given all these tools, can you sort them on the basis of some natural groupings?" or "Of these three tools, which two go together?" The consistently elicited response was, "For what?" Without a particular task as the basis for cognitive organization, the blacksmith relies upon principles generally relevant to blacksmithing: for example, "things that can be used as they are" versus "things that can be used without much additional work" versus "things that were once something but are now scrap."

More specific probing for a basic organizational system based on language, such as that suggested in the work of Brown et al. (1976) or Rosch et al. (1976), seemed to push the informant to make irrelevant decisions. Questions like "Is a cross-peen a kind of hammer?" or "Is a sledge hammer a kind of hammer?" or "Is this [holding a claw hammer] a kind a hammer?" were considered odd by practicing blacksmiths. "Nobody talks about it that way" was a common response. These early interviews, coupled with observation of natural conversations in the blacksmith shop, failed to point to basic linguistic units and the relations of contrast and inclusion among them as primary conceptual dimensions.

Concerned by the lack of reliance on ready-made named categories, we sorted tools using a linguistic template for the organization of categories. In the context of a working shop, with the tools present, they were sorted into clusters based on their common labels. *Hammers,* including ball-peen, claw, sledges, mallets, and a variety of others, were separated from *saws,* including hacksaws, coping saws, a Japanese carpenter's saw, and cross-cut and rip saws. Similar units of *tongs, clamps,* and *chisels* were segregated as well.

One blacksmith queried about the logic of this organization tried to make the point that this was only one of a large number of possible ways to think about the tools. "We could sort them into tools with wooden handles, single pieces of metal, pivoted metal tools, and multicomponent tools, too. . . ." Without some sort of goal direction or task, these sortings seem irrelevant to task-oriented blacksmiths.

The linguistic sorting is the result of applying a general classification scheme that solves the task and is consistently based on patterns of naming. Such general classification schemes may be employed by an analyst to create a context for sorting that an informant can work within if required to, even though it is not necessarily useful during specialized activity. The assumption, common in ethnographic semantics, that conceptualization frequently parallels such linguistically based clustering (Frake 1969:28, Berlin et al. 1973:214-16, Kay 1970:19) is one we cannot make. To better understand the relationship between speech and other cognitive activity, we turn to an investigation of a system of specialized knowledge.

We discard the notion of the basic morphological/linguistic hierarchy as central to the cognitive organization of blacksmithing and, in what follows, examine the kinds of organization that do make sense to blacksmiths at work. Here we return to the notion of open possibilities—to the productive organization of information on the basis of a particular context. The first relevant (and broadest) organizational system to emerge during our investigation is based on the proper location for each tool in the shop. Every tool has a place based upon associations for common jobs, component materials, shape, availability with respect to fixed elements such as the forge and the anvil or post drill, and physical features of the shop. The location-based system is task-oriented. It is used when specific tools are selected and also when tools are replaced during the task of cleaning up.

Tools are organized on the basis of proper location in a way that cross-cuts the structures based on naming patterns. Some hammers go in one place, some in another; some files go with the rivet header on the anvil stump, others go elsewhere; bending forks, crescent wrench, pliers, and hacksaws, linguistically unrelated, are grouped together as tools belonging on the vise post. Common labels do not constrain proper placement.

The locational system of conceptual organization does involve shallow hierarchy. Within the context of putting things away or retrieving them, labeled units such as *stump tools, drill press rack tools,* and *fire tools* emerge. These are usually idiosyncratic labels for clusters of tools based on location. The names are not necessarily shared even by smiths in the same shop, but develop individually for personal, cognitive organization in the working situation, or for ease of reference during an interview with the anthropologist. Variable as the linguistic labels are, however, these names do refer to useful clusters of tools. As analysts, we might represent such organizations as taxonomic trees. Such hierarchies should be treated only as analytical conveniences. They suggest a permanence or context-free validity that is inappropriate for genuine taskonomy. The organizations of knowledge, in short, need a task-oriented contextual frame. An alternative representation would situate the clustering of tools appropriately in the context of location within a shop. Such a context-specific, locational image, and the tool assignments within it, while messier than taxonomic trees, more closely reflects the smith's conceptual organization and the project-oriented (locational) relevance of this body of knowledge.

The locational clustering of tools is unique among organizations of tools for the smith in two ways. First, it is the only organization that includes all the tools in the shop at a given point in time. Second, it provides a consistent framework out of which the smith selects items for other task-specific constellations. This locational scheme is not constant, but may be revised as the tool inventory or other relevant variables change.

What about other conceptual schemes? We suspected that another broad organizational system might be based on the primary function of tools. Outside the context of any particular job, tools might be classified by their primary function. *Hardy, chisel, hacksaw, cut-off saw,* and *cutting torch* are among the tools primarily used for cutting; *tongs, clamps,* and *vise* are primarily used for holding; *hammers* and *wooden clubs* are primarily used for pounding. An abstract system of classification based upon such functional distinctions can be produced by a knowledgeable smith. Similar classification schemes are commonly reproduced in the organization of merchandise in hardware stores.

Like the linguistic hierarchy, however, this system is too general for the everyday activities of a blacksmith (although it may be relevant to the owner or employee of a hardware store). This classification system broadly based on function is inappropriate for the blacksmith in two ways. (1) It is artificially comprehensive in its attempt to incorporate a total universe of blacksmithing tools. (2) It is at the same time artificially narrow in its failure to incorporate the materials, processes, and products associated with the primary functions of smithing. In other words, it is inadequate to explain the productivity and variation typical of tool use because it focuses only on the categories of tools themselves (see Agar 1974).

Our continued investigations led us to characterize knowledge structures as constellations of conceptual units arising in response to a task at hand. The basic principles of such organizations are functional relations. Like Agar (1974), we see the task or process orientation as of primary importance in the organization of complex systems of knowledge; unlike Agar (1974), we draw attention to the significance of unnamed conceptual distinctions as an important part of such systems or constellations. These constellations are held together only while immediately relevant (Fillmore 1978 hints at the importance of such contextual associations in his discussion of frame semantics).[4] A Santa Fe blacksmith aptly refers to this productive organization and reorganization as follows: Having decided what shape you want the iron to take, "as you are standing taking a nice good heat, . . . plan the next step. What tools do you need? Are they in reach?" Each step requires a constellation of tools in association with materials, processes, and a notion of the desired end point. The first-order concern is to decide what shape the metal is to take and what materials are appropriate; following from that is a consideration of means and implements.

One example of a constellation derives from a common goal for the blacksmith of increasing the length and/or width of a section of iron by decreasing its thickness, referred to as *drawing out.* One set of means to this end is *fullering,* a process which involves making regular depressions in a hot iron rod and subsequently hammering down the intermediate ridges to produce a narrower rod of greater length than the original. With this goal in mind, and with fullering as the selected process, a relevant constellation includes: raw material selected on the basis of the job, a particular hammer or hammers, either an anvil horn or fuller depending on the blacksmith's preference, the dimension of the material, possibly a pair of tongs matched to the dimensions of the iron rod, and a wire brush to remove the scale from the metal.

A more complex example is evident in making a fleur-de-lis. In this task a rod is pointed and spread to a picket point. The tip of the picket point is cut with a hot chisel and the sections below drawn out and bent to form the arms. This involves first using the hammer and anvil and selecting a hot chisel (either straight or curved) and a pair of pliers. The piece would be hot rasped after the picket point was made and wire brushed after each heat. Each microepisode requires a unique association of notions of process, materials, implements, and desired end point, embedded within the larger conceptual constellation of making a fleur-de-lis. The constellation derives from the sequence of operations the smith goes through and the tools and materials incorporated into those operations.

A distinct constellation emerged for one smith in the task of twisting a pair of brackets to hold a hand rail. Here we quote an apprentice:

> I used half-inch rod and heated and hammered the center so it was semi-square. I heated it again and quenched the end and clamped it in the vise. I grabbed the opposite end with a small pipe wrench and walked around to give the twist. It was a nice soft twist because of rounded shoulders from semi-squaring the rod. I reheated the rod and straightened it with a big wooden club on a stump. That way by using soft stuff the twist wasn't distorted. Quenching was to keep the vise from mashing the round part when it was clamped. Then I heated it again and bent it with a fork to a 90° angle [to finish the bracket].

Enumerating such constellations of knowledge could go on. The process of formation is productive, and novel circumstances lead to novel constellations. The blacksmith's knowledge must include detailed representations of the features of processes, products, materials, and tools that mutually influence one another in the creation of unique constellations oriented to particular tasks.

Such constellations of knowledge are fundamental. The knowledge organized into constellations is not retrievable from a morphological/linguistic hierarchy, or from a general classificatory system based on primary function. Constellations of knowledge, such as that for drawing out an iron rod or making a fleur-de-lis, account for productive behavior by providing an overriding notion of ends and means, which in combination with appropriate materials provide a basis for the selection and interrelating of a set of tools. Each element of a constellation is related to and influences each other element in nonhierarchical fashion. Constellations are ephemeral, being pulled together and held in mind only as long as appropriate for a given task. There will be individual variation in the formation of constellations oriented to a given end and situational variation in the specific materials and tools incorporated into a sequence of operations. Any individual tool or material may occur in multiple constellations.

Some constellations recur as the situations for their use recur, and these may become established "recipes" (see Goodenough 1963). The blacksmith's knowledge includes recipes for typical procedures such as fullering; typical sequences of operations oriented to a specific end product, such as making a fleur-de-lis; and typical arrangements, such as proper location. While such recipes may come to be relied upon habitually, like more productive constellations they may be modified and oriented to particular characteristics of a task at hand. In the example of twisting brackets described above, general recipes for the process of twisting and for the requirements of brackets form the basis of a unique task-specific constellation.

Noncorrelation of Named Classes to Conceptual Units

No one set of features consistently informs decisions involved in the production of constellations. Features are selectively focused upon as a task demands. As Randall (1976:552) points out, a particular situation directs the selection of "a contrast set of characteristics which is both sufficiently general to achieve a practical and safe result and sufficiently specific to accomplish one's purposes efficiently." Relations of contrast are crucial in the formation of constellations of knowledge, but the specific dimensions of contrast constantly shift as the overriding notions change.

This productivity is not reflected in naming. For example, a particular hammer may be selected for some task on the basis of the shape and size of its face. A small round face makes sharp depressions in hot iron and spreads the metal equally in all directions; a long narrow face makes sharp straight depressions and spreads the metal perpendicular to the axis of the peen; a hammer with a round face of a particular radius might be chosen to match the curve of a place on the horn of the anvil to produce matching depressions on opposite faces of the hot iron; a flat hammer face produces a flat surface. Weight of the hammer also enters into the decision making, becoming a crucial feature for selection if a piece of iron is to be driven into a cavity or if a very large dimensioned material is being shaped. Such differences, crucial to the everyday processes of blacksmithing, are not consistently correlated with labeled classes of hammers.

Similarly, the smith is not constrained by a given inventory of tools, but is largely free to create new tools as the need arises. For example, tongs are manufactured to hold standard stock endwise and sideways. If a special shape stock is used, or a standard size significantly modified, the blacksmith can reforge the jaws to create a new set of tongs. The discontinuities evident in a tool inventory at any given point in time are perceived not as fixed boundaries within which one must work but as the arbitrary result of tools assembled for past tasks.

In other cases tools need not be manufactured for novel situations, but objects intended (and named) for some other purpose may serve a blacksmith's needs.[5] In making a gun spring, for example, one smith used a small sardine can for a tempering container, and the can well served the needs of the task. Another illustration of this kind of improvisation appears in Pirsig's (1975:50-51) *Zen and the Art of Mo-*

torcycle Maintenance. The author offers to tighten his friend's motorcycle handle bars using a piece of an aluminum beer can as shim stock. Although the friend indignantly refuses the offer, the aluminum can is perfect as stock for shims.

Named classes then are inadequate as the sole guide to the conceptual units relevant to everyday behavior. The members of a named class can be described by numerous features, relatively few of which are crucial to class definition. In the course of performance attention will be focused differentially on specific features appropriate to the strategies for action, regardless of the importance of these features for category definition. By the very standardization crucial to naming, the named classes fail to reflect the productivity evident in behavior.

Other Task-Oriented Conceptual Organizations

As we have argued, specific task orientations provide the meaningful features in line with which constellations as conceptual organizations are developed. The nature of the task then determines the nature of the relevant features. Tasks of identification usually require recognition of morphological/perceptual features, while other tasks, such as those we have been discussing, tend to rely on features functionally related to specific activity. The latter have been illustrated in the discussion of constellations.

Knowledge relevant to blacksmithing also includes perceptually based systems of classification. These systems hold across a wide range of contexts for blacksmithing. They are less subject to particularistic orientation than the constellations discussed above. The more standardized of these classification systems provide guidelines for decisions that recur across task-oriented contexts. Two such classification schemes are focused on color, reflecting distinctions of temperature, malleability, and hardness.

The color spectrum relevant for normal forging of iron ranges from *grey* through *low red* to *orange, light yellow,* and *white.* As the iron is heated, it gradually reaches an incandescent red described as low red. From this point the metal is glowing and its color moves through the indicated named spectrum as its temperature increases. The color tells the smith how malleable the iron is. If it is overheated, a molecular change takes place; the iron burns and is no longer workable. If it is worked at too low a temperature, the metal will become brittle and crack. This classification of the color spectrum as a reflection of temperature and malleability allows the blacksmith to monitor his working conditions. The knowledge is relevant to forging in general. One smith, advising his apprentice, commented, "A blacksmith who works between a bright orange and a low red usually can work faster because he doesn't have to leave the iron in the fire so long." Such knowledge, applicable across a wide range of contexts, is amenable to standard linguistic expression.

Like the normal forging spectrum, tempering colors apply consistently across contexts. As a result, it is also advantageous for the linguistic coding of this spectrum to be consistent for one smith from one task to another and across smiths. These systems of classification are associated with control over the malleability of iron. This is a task orientation common to all situations of forging. The conceptual structure embodying this knowledge can therefore remain constant. Because of the consistent nature of relevant distinctions, standardized names—in this case color designations—are useful.

A similar reliance on consistent morphological features occurs again (as might be expected) in a domain where recognition is the primary task orientation: that of coal and its by-products as it burns. Coal is the fuel used in forging. Before it is burned, the coal is referred to as *green coal.* The burning process produces *coke, clinker,* and *ash*, each of which must be identified and distinguished from the green coal in the forge pan so that each can be treated appropriately. Green coal appears black, angular, dense, and shiny. It is hard to ignite, does not produce as much heat as coke when it burns, and is very smoky.

Coke is the coal from which certain gases have been driven by the heat of the fire, concomitantly producing other changes. Coke appears dark, grey, rounded, porous, and dull. It ignites with reasonable ease and burns hot, with little smoke. In the forge the fire consumes coke (produced from burning the green coal) and produces clinker and ash. The green coal around the fire is continually being converted to coke, which is periodically fed into the fire to replace that which has been burned.

Clinker is lighter grey than coke, frequently accumulates at the bottom of the fire in a spongy, sticky mass, and has glassy inclusions. When a large mass of clinker has formed, its presence is revealed by an ineffective fire and by a mass at the base of the fire that glows yellow in contrast to the bright orange of the coke. Clinker often cements together pieces of ash and impurities into a mass that blocks the flow of air into the fire. In some forges it is possible to rotate a shaker and allow the clinker and ash to fall into an ash dump; in others it is necessary to clean the fire by removing ash and clinker with a spoon, leaving just enough glowing material to avoid extinguishing the fire.

Ash is a light grey, gritty material that has not been consolidated by clinker. It is blown up out of the fire by the blast of air from the blower and falls back into the coke and coal mixture around the fire. If it is not removed periodically, it accumulates to the point that the fire's effectiveness is reduced as a result of the low density of fuel in the forge.

Here, features of color, shape, size, texture, density, and shine are consistently employed in distinguishing coal and its by-products. Identification of these elements is crucial to the maintenance of an effective fire. As a result, the organization of relevant knowledge is constant across contexts. Because the task of identification remains constant, the relevant features for making distinctions can remain consistent across contexts. As with the functionally oriented constellations of knowledge discussed earlier, the nature of the task determines the features of relevance. The broad contextual applicability of the perceptual distinctions makes useful, standardized labels for the conceptual units: green coal, coke, clinker, and ash.

Conclusion

The set of named classes, and the interrelations among these names, cannot be taken to indicate a basic conceptual organization or a fixed set of units within which the blacksmith is constrained to operate. Labeled concepts do not provide a privileged, acontextual background system that is differentially tapped during the process of smithing. (If there is such a neutral framework for the blacksmith, it is the locational classification.) Named classes reflect only one possible way of interrelating a variety of basic elements relevant to blacksmithing.

Reliance on distinctions encoded by common labels occurs for the knowledgeable smith in two cases: (1) when a task occurs across a broad range of contexts, and (2) when the smith is attempting to communicate to a less informed other. In the first case a set of distinctions will be consistently relevant; and, as in the case of the color spectrum or coal distinctions, these concepts are likely to be consistently named. In the second case the smith must use labels shared in common with the nonsmith, but the inference that such named distinctions reflect consistently salient conceptual distinctions for the practicing smith is not justifiable.

Named distinctions reflect classes with broad contextual relevance. As such they must be sidestepped or further specified in any specific activity for which the named units fail to encode dimensions of context crucial for the task-oriented project of the moment. What leads to highly effective means of blacksmithing is flexibility in classification. There is no one basic structure to which we can turn as the key to the practice of blacksmithing. Blacksmithing, like other behavior, is characterized by productivity.

We offer an anti-Whorfian argument that is very different from the universalist conclusions previously derived from ethnoscientific work (Berlin and Kay 1969, Berlin et al. 1973). Our investigation leads us to argue that everyday technological activity requires attention to individual processes, entities, features, and their potential relationships in the constant production of new constellations of knowledge. There is a set of named distinctions reflecting elements of the universe that are generally taken for granted: *ball-peen, hammer, half-round file, small sardine can.* Tasks require attention to particular attributes of the members of these classes in the production of new categories that cross-cut these named classes (for related results see Burnham and Clark 1955, Lantz and Stefflre 1964).

It is the particular characteristics of a task, of a set of procedures, and of individual implements and materials that are the focus of awareness. The named class to which an object belongs for purposes of standard reference in general classification schemes has little influence over its occurrences in other constellations of applied knowledge. It matters little whether a wooden club (common in blacksmiths' shops but usually unnamed) is linguistically grouped with hammers because it pounds, or is separated from them because it does not have a transversely attached head. What does matter, when an iron rod needs to be pounded, are features of relevance oriented to the particular tasks: the relative softness or lightness of the wooden club or the radius and curvature of a hammer face.

Recipes may result from habitual constellations: these may be individual or culturally specific, but they are not dependent upon primary linguistic designations. Japanese and American smiths, if asked to produce a fleur-de-lis, would probably approach the task differently. They would do so not because they label their tools differently but because their customary approaches to forging differ.

Finally, we must constantly beware of imputing to the minds of others the categorical or cognitive relationships that we construct from data elicited from such others. In *Argonauts of the Western Pacific,* Malinowski (1961:229-30) warns the ethnographer against systematizing conceptual organizations, for "this represents neither the native's mind nor any other form of reality." It is well known, and generally accepted, that organizations of knowledge postulated on the basis of elicited responses to directed interviewing must be carefully interpreted in the study of cognition. Freedman (1970:169), in discussing Siassi kinship, argues that "the contemporary [Siassi] patriline is merely an ethnographical artifice." In her autobiography Mead (1972:199) reports taking individuals through complete census materials: "They could respond to a genealogical tree with a systematic kinship statement. But it turned out that this was not the way in which they used kinship at all." And Randall (1976:545) reports the surprise he encountered from informants when they were faced with the logical implications of the knowledge he elicited from them concerning marine food chains. As Schutz (1964:72-73) points out, everyday behavior is characterized by apparent inconsistency and contradiction (see also Leiter 1980:6-7). Human behavior is not simple; the cognitive systems underlying behavior are complexly rational. We have tried to take one step toward understanding the task-oriented, practical creativity that this complexity generates.

NOTES

1. Cecil Brown (1979:407) argues that the principles of taxonomic organization he focuses upon do not have clear implications for "cognitive reality."

2. This is not to deny the importance of linguistic research in anthropology, but to point up its relevance to our own interest in cognition and productive behavior.

3. Keller worked with three key informants, all of whom are self-employed professional blacksmiths, and participated in observation and discussion with at least seven other blacksmiths at blacksmithing conventions or workshops. Interviewing in these contexts was informal discussion directed with Keller's research goals in mind. Dougherty interviewed Keller as a blacksmith using a more formal format and at some length.

4. The data that suggest our constellations are derived from interviews with smiths. The descriptions are necessarily incomplete and, as a result of the requisite verbalization, tend to overemphasize labeled units. This is unavoidable because of the research procedures and because our task is written communication. Nonetheless, the flexibility and particularistic emphasis of elements within the task-oriented constellations should be clear.

5. In this context, note 8 in Brown et al. (1976:84) is enlightening. Kolar found that informants were capable of generating unusually large numbers of labels for tools after observing that "almost anything could be a tool."

REFERENCES

Agar, Michael
1974 Talking about Doing: Lexicon and Event. *Language in Society* 3:83-89.

Berlin, Brent, Dennis E. Breedlove, and Peter Raven
1973 General Principles of Classification and Nomenclature in Folk Biology. *American Anthropologist* 75:214-42.

Berlin, Brent, and Paul Kay
1969 *Basic Color Terms: Their Universality and Evolution.* Berkeley: University of California Press.
Brown, Cecil
1979 Variability, Cognitive Reality and Principles of Classification and Nomenclature. *American Ethnologist* 6:407-8.
Brown, Cecil, et al.
1976 Some General Principles of Biological and Non-Biological Folk Classification. *American Ethnologist* 3:73-85.
Brown, Michael
1978 From the Hero's Bones: Three Aguaruna Hallucinogens and Their Uses. In Richard Ford, ed., *The Nature and Status of Ethnobotany,* pp. 119-36. Ann Arbor: University of Michigan Press.
Bulmer, Ralph
1968 Karum Classification of Frogs. *Journal of the Polynesian Society* 77:333-85.
Burnham, R. W., and J. R. Clark
1955 A Test of Hue Memory. *Journal of Applied Psychology* 39:164-72.
Fillmore, C.
1978 The Organization of Semantic Information in the Lexicon. In D. Farkas, W. M. Jacobsen, and K. W. Todrys, ed., *Parassession on the Lexicon,* pp. 148-73. Papers from the Chicago Linguistic Society.
Frake, Charles
1961 The Diagnosis of Disease among the Subanun of Mindanao. *American Anthropologist* 63:113-32.
1969 The Ethnographic Study of Cognitive Systems. In Stephen Tyler, ed., *Cognitive Anthropology,* pp. 28-41. New York: Holt, Rinehart and Winston.
Freedman, Michael P.
1970 Social Organization of a Siassi Community. In T. C. Harding and B. J. Wallace, eds., *Cultures of the Pacific,* pp. 159-79. New York: Free Press Division of Macmillan Publishing Co.
Goodenough, Ward H.
1963 *Cooperation in Change.* New York: Russell Sage Foundation.
Hunn, Eugene
1976 Toward a Perceptual Model of Folk Biological Classification. *American Ethnologist* 3:508-24.
Kay, Paul
1970 Some Theoretical Implications of Ethnographic Semantics. *Current Directions in Anthropology* 3, pt. 2:19-31.
Lantz, D., and V. Stefflre
1964 Language and Cognition Revisited. *Journal of Abnormal and Social Psychology* 69:472-81.
Leiter, K.
1980 *A Primer on Ethnomethodology.* London: Oxford University Press.
Malinowski, B.
1961 *Argonauts of the Western Pacific.* New York: E. P. Dutton.

Mead, Margaret
1972 *Blackberry Winter.* New York: William Morrow.

Miller, G. A., E. Galanter, and K. H. Pribram
1960 *Plans and the Structure of Behavior.* New York: Holt, Rinehart and Winston.

Pirsig, Robert M.
1975 *Zen and the Art of Motorcycle Maintenance.* New York: Bantam Books.

Randall, Robert A.
1976 How Tall Is a Taxonomic Tree? Some Evidence for Dwarfism. *American Ethnologist* 3:543-53.

Rosaldo, Michelle Z.
1972 Metaphors and Folk Classification. *Southwestern Journal of Anthropology* 28:83-99.

Rosch, Eleanor, et al.
1976 Basic Objects in Natural Categories. *Cognitive Psychology* 8:382-439.

Schank, R., and R. Abelson
1977 *Scripts, Plans, Goals and Understanding.* Hillsdale, N.J.: Lawrence Erlbaum Associates.

Schutz, A.
1964 *Collected Papers II: Studies in Social Theory.* The Hague: Martinus Nijhoff.
1971 Choosing among Projects of Actions. *Collected Papers,* vol. 1. The Hague: Martinus Nijhoff.

B. LEARNING: A Consequence of Social Interaction

The chapters herein point out the implications of different learning situations for the ways in which concepts may be organized.

8

"Requiem for the Omniscient Informant": There's Life in the Old Girl Yet

James Shilts Boster

This paper addresses the problem of describing a cultural system in the face of informant disagreement. Though ethnographers have been aware of variation for a long time (e.g. Dorsey 1884, cited in Sapir 1938), they often solved the problem by ignoring it, describing cultures as though they were uniformly shared (for examples see Pelto and Pelto 1975:2). In the last 20 years increased attention has been paid to intracultural variation, especially in the ways people classify phenomena in their natural and social environments. This emphasis on classification is appropriate because a shared understanding of the referential meaning of words seems to be essential to most other forms of human communication. There have been reports of informant variation in such diverse areas as Buang clan membership assessments (Sankoff 1971), in Dene bird classification (Gardner 1976), in Ndumba plant knowledge (Hays 1976), in Tzintzuntzan hot-cold classification (Foster 1979), and in Tlaxcalan ceramic classification (Kempton 1981), to list a few. This paper will respond to the pessimistic conclusions of one of these studies of variation: Gardner's (1976) article "Birds, Words, and a Requiem for the Omniscient Informant." Gardner emphasizes the differences between individual cognitive life histories and the absence of a cultural standard or norm: "We have evidence that sharing is patterned in a way that makes it unproductive and perhaps unreasonable *in this particular instance* to define culture in terms of an average (cf. Sankoff 1971), the shared (Werner and Fenton 1970), the sum (Wallace 1961, 1970; Werner and Fenton 1970), or a mean around which there is variation (D'Andrade n.d. [1970])" (Gardner 1976:459; emphasis in the original). This finding leads him to reject

Werner's construct of the omniscient informant and with it the idea that an ethnography should be an encyclopedic description of all that is known by a people (Gardner 1976:459; cf. Werner 1969, Werner and Fenton 1970).

Contrary to Gardner, I believe it is premature to bury the omniscient informant. While an assumption of cultural homogeneity may be naive, the emphasis on variation should not be carried to the point of denying the possibility of a coherent cultural description. Using evidence from Aguaruna manioc classification, I will argue for the existence of a cultural system in spite of great cognitive diversity among informants. My starting point is Wallace's observation that a certain amount of cognitive diversity is necessary to the functioning of society (Wallace 1961:35). The problem is to reconcile Wallace's idea that individuals build their own mental maps of the world with the notion that this learning is culturally conditioned. I will show that cognitive diversity is organized in a way that reflects the dynamics of the cultural system, that deviations from a consensus are patterned according to the sexual division of labor, individual expertise, and membership in kin and residential groups.[1]

Background

The Aguaruna Jívaro are a forest-dwelling tribe of the northern Peruvian *montaña.* They subsist by gardening, fishing, hunting, and collecting forest products. Manioc (*Manihot esculenta*) is far and away the most important crop, contributing about 60 percent of the calories in the diet (Berlin and Berlin 1978:26). The starchy root is prepared boiled, roasted, and as manioc beer. This crop also makes up roughly 80 percent of the individual cultivated plants in the gardens.

Aguaruna gardens are principally a female domain. Male participation in gardening is limited to the clearing of new gardens and the care of a few cash crops. The day-to-day garden activities of planting, weeding, harvesting, as well as the selection of new manioc varieties, are done by women. Aguaruna subsistence and division of labor are typical of that described for most South American lowland tribes (Steward 1948). Traditionally, the Aguaruna settlement pattern was highly dispersed, with little social organization above the household. This situation is described by Harner for the related Ecuadorian Jívaro (Harner 1972). Now the majority of Aguaruna live in communities that have been established around schools.

Problems of Method in Studying Variation

This section addresses three methodological issues in the study of variation. The first is the relevance or importance of the domain studied. More than a year of fieldwork devoted to the study of manioc may appear a little extreme to those who know it only as the source of tapioca pudding. However, this crop is of paramount importance to the Aguaruna, as important as maize is to the Maya or rice to the Chinese. In studying variation, it is essential to investigate what is important to the informants, not just what is important to the ethnographer.

The problem is exemplified by Gardner's comment that the Dene are highly variable in their naming of the tassel or bell on the throat of a moose (Gardner 1976:447). The question is, do the Dene feel responsible for maintaining an extensive anatomical vocabulary for moose or were the elicited terms made up on the spot? Without an explanation of why moose tassels should be important to the Dene, the reader has no reason to believe that the absence of a stable term means anything at all. Given the importance of manioc to the Aguaruna, the degree of variation in manioc identification is surprising.

A second issue is the adequacy or realism of the stimuli used in variation studies. The question is whether the variability observed is a fact about the informants or a consequence of the characteristics of the stimuli. For example, Kay has pointed out that much of the ambiguity of Brazilian racial classification claimed by Harris (1970) may stem from the anomaly of the stimuli, line drawings that mix and match various racial characteristics (Kay 1978:85). Gardner has a similar but less flagrant problem in using book illustrations as stimuli for Dene bird identifications rather than stuffed or living specimens. In contrast, the stimuli used in this study were highly representative since they were mature plants growing in an experimental garden. Although it is the manioc root that is eaten, the above-ground portion of the plant provides the basis for distinguishing the varieties. The salient characteristics that help in the identification tasks and in day-to-day gardening include leaf shape, petiole (leaf stalk) color, stem color, and plant branching pattern. There is no significant difference between the experimental stimuli and those growing in any Aguaruna garden.

A third issue is the choice of the kind of variability to be studied. Gardner counts as variation in Dene bird classification words that appear to be alternate pronunciations of one another. For example, Gardner (1976:448) states that his first five informants identified the ruffled grouse as: /etsetsuę/, /etsets*uę/, /ets*ets*eśa/, /Θ*ets*uę/, and /ets*uęts*uę/. Without glosses, it is difficult to tell whether the variation is in categorization or in category labeling. Variation in category labeling may be interesting in its own right, but it is not relevant to the issue of cognitive diversity. There is similar variability in the pronunciation of Aguaruna manioc names: one type was called variously *ujákag*, *uják*, and *ujám*. Informants readily agreed that all expressions referred to the same kind of manioc. Since I was interested in the variability of people's categorization rather than of category labels, all of these variants were treated as the same. Similarly, some of the common varieties had named subtypes. These subdivisions were ignored in this study so that all identifications could be compared at the same folk taxonomic rank (cf. Berlin 1976). This was accomplished by developing a dictionary that recoded more than 700 distinct expressions into 127 category codes.

Data Collection

In order to investigate Aguaruna manioc identification, two experimental manioc gardens were planted. The first garden had 61 supposedly different[2] varieties of manioc given to me by Aguaruna women. For the second garden, six women provided examples of the 15 most common varieties. Data were collected by guiding informants one by one through the gardens, stopping at each plant and asking, *wajḭ́ máma aíta*, "What kind of manioc is this?" The two experimental gardens differed greatly in the difficulty they presented to informants. The first garden of 61 different varieties called for very fine discriminations, while the second garden, with its 15 most common varieties represented six times apiece, presented far fewer difficulties. This is reflected in the fact that informants disagreed about the identity of the plants in the first garden far more than they did in the second. Because of this difference, the manioc identification tasks in the first and second gardens will be referred to in the balance of this chapter as the "hard" and "easy" tasks respectively. A total of 58 women participated in the hard manioc identification task and a total of 43 women and 21 men participated in the easy task.

Data Analysis

The goal of this paper is to show that there is a single shared Aguaruna system of manioc identification through an analysis of the pattern of variation in naming of manioc varieties. This approach is similar to one used by Cancian when he argued for the psychological reality of a prestige scale he had constructed (Cancian 1963). Cancian observed that when his Mayan informants erred in their statements about the religious roles or "cargos" another had undertaken, they confused adjacent ranks of his prestige scale. However, there are two important differences between Cancian's problem and my own. First,

Cancian was attempting to determine something about the world as seen by his informants, while I am more interested in learning about the informants themselves. Second, it was usually possible for Cancian to determine what cargos an individual had actually undertaken. Hence he could justifiably describe informants' statements that differed from his determination as informant *error*. There is no way for me to know for certain the "correct" names of the specimens in the gardens, or even if there are correct names. This paper must show that the Aguaruna believe and act as though there are correct names[3] for the manioc plants without assuming that correct names exist.

For the purposes of this analysis, it does not matter which names informants use to identify a plant, just whether they happen to agree with the others. Ultimately, the only data considered are whether pairs of informants agree on the identity of particular plants. Two measures have been computed that summarize these primary data. The first measure, *proportion of agreement,* indicates the amount of agreement between pairs of informants. The number of times a pair of informants agree on the identity of a plant is summed for all stimuli in an identification task and divided by the total number of stimuli. The second measure, *overall agreement,* is an informant's average proportion of agreement with the rest of the population. This measure will be shown to reflect an informant's overall manioc knowledge or expertise.

I will begin the analysis by showing the overall patterns of agreement between informants in the manioc identification tasks. The overall patterns are represented here with cluster diagrams, shown in Figures 1 and 2. Each terminal node of the diagram represents a different informant.[4] The informants have been clustered by their proportional agreement; informants who agree a great deal with each other are joined before those who do not. For example, in Figure 1 informant numbers 52 and 48 agree with each other 62 percent of the time and are the first to be joined. In contrast, informants 26 and 49 agree only 21 percent of the time with each other and even less with everyone else, so they are the last to join. The position of each informant in these cluster diagrams can be specified by two parameters: position along the spine of the diagram and distance down from the spine. Position along the spine reflects overall agreement; informants at the left agree more often with other informants than those at the right. Overall agreement can be thought of as a measure of the approach or departure of an individual from the group consensus. Distance from the spine reflects the extent to which a small group of informants agrees with each other more than with the general population.

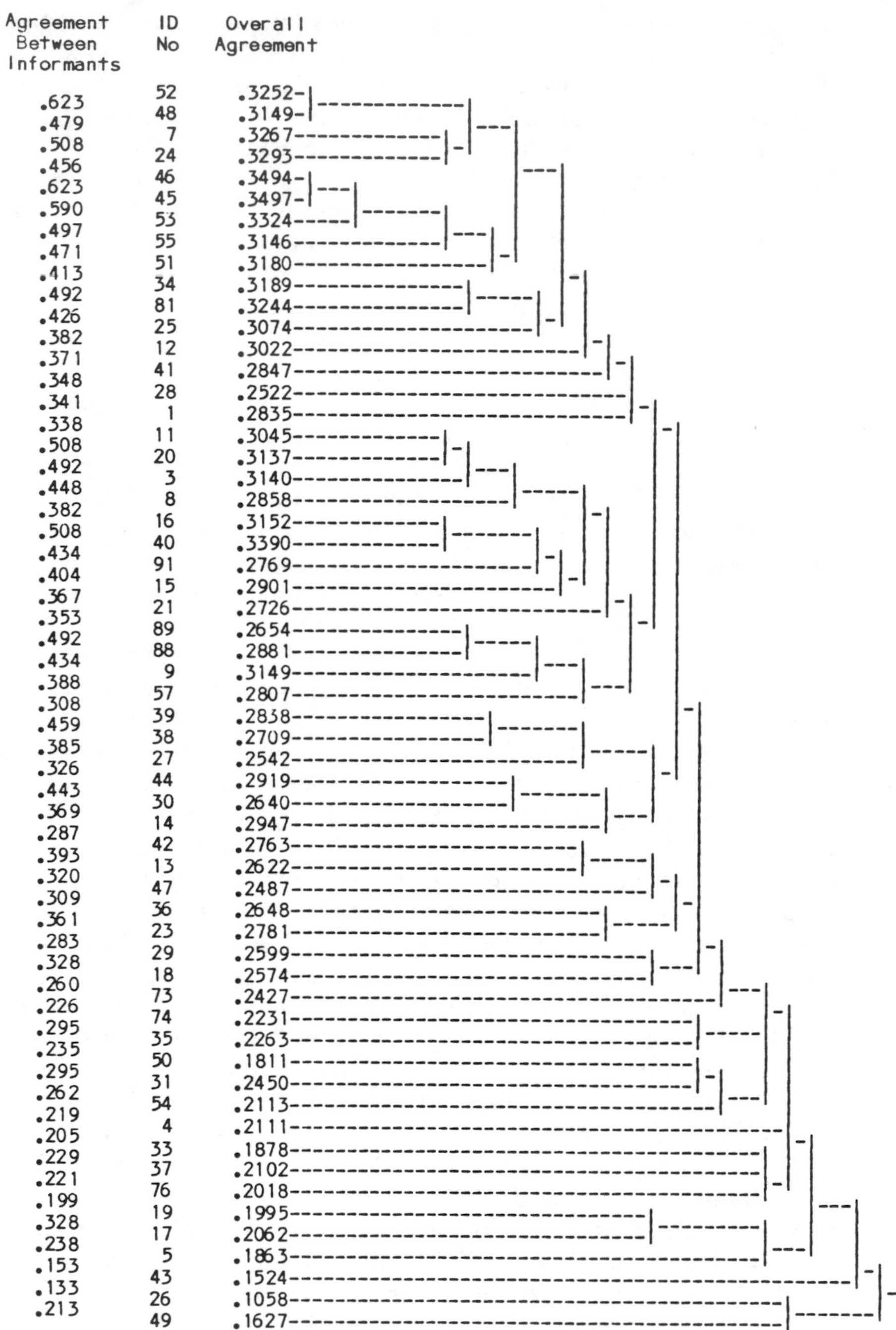

Figure 1. Clustering of Informants in the Hard Manioc Identification Task

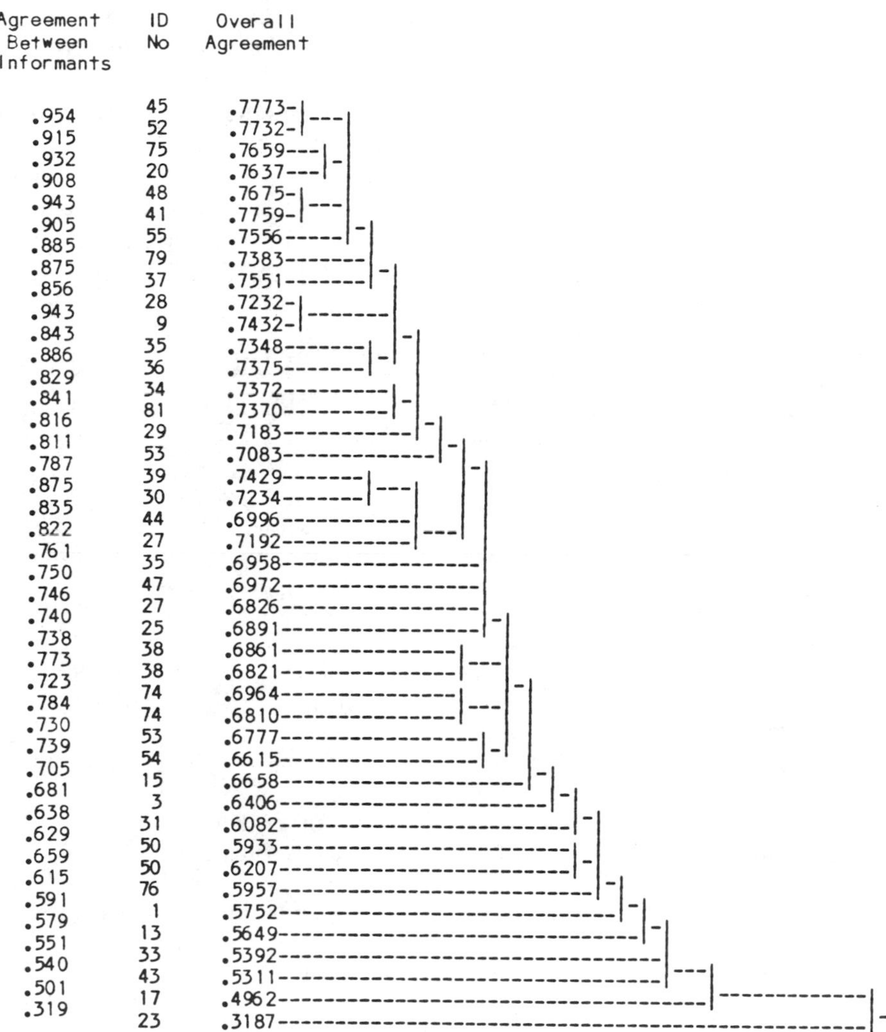

Figure 2. Clustering of Informants in the Easy Manioc Identification Task

The two cluster diagrams are not alike in the relative importance of these parameters. Figure 1 shows a number of clusters of women who share high agreement independent of the general consensus. These clusters are usually made up of closely related women, as seen in Table 1. Figure 2 is dominated by the general trend of approach or departure from the consensus along the spine. Departures of small groups from the consensus are far less conspicuous. The few that exist are shown in Table 1.

In order to interpret the patterns of agreement displayed in Figures 1 and 2, it is useful to consider what they would look like if there were (a) universal agreement, (b) random naming, (c) agreement patterned by social affiliations, or (d) agreement patterned by individual expertise. In the case of universal agreement, it would be clear that there was a single culturally shared model, since all informants would

Table 1. Kin Relations between Members of Clusters

Cluster	Pair	Relation
	Hard Manioc Identification Task	
52-48	52-48	mother-daughter
7-24	7-24	mother-daughter
46-45-53-55	45-53	co-wives
46-45-53-55	46-55	sisters
46-45-53-55	53-46	mother-daughter
46-45-53-55	53-55	mother-daughter
81-34	81-34	mother-daughter
11-20- 3- 8	3-11	sisters
11-20- 3- 8	3-20	sisters
11-20- 3- 8	11-20	sisters
11-20- 3- 8	8- 3	mother-daughter
11-20- 3- 8	8-11	mother-daughter
11-20- 3- 8	8-20	mother-daughter
39-38-27	39-38	mother-daughter
39-38-27	27-29	mother-in-law–daughter-in-law
39-38-27	27-38	grandmother-granddaughter
44-30	44-30	mother-daughter
29-18	29-18	sisters
	Easy Manioc Identification Task	
45-52	45-52	sisters-in-law
81-34	81-34	mother-daughter
39-30-44-27	44-30	mother-daughter
39-30-44-27	27-39	mother-in-law–daughter-in-law
39-30-44-27	27-44	sisters

give the culturally appropriate name of each plant. Little would be learned by looking at the cluster diagram, since all informants would join in one large cluster immediately. Conversely, if informants applied names at random, it would be equally clear that there was no shared model because informant agreement would be virtually nil. Again the cluster diagram would be uninteresting, all informants remaining isolates from one another. If there were strong social differentiation, informants would agree with all members of their social group and would disagree with everyone from other groups. One would conclude that there were as many cultural models as there were social groups. The diagram would be composed of a number of distinct clusters.

The observed patterns of informant agreement are closest to what would be expected if there were a single set of categories learned to varying degrees, the last alternative. In other words, it appears as if a cultural model of manioc identification exists, and some people know it better than others. This result is not conclusive, since some aspects of the patterns of agreement resemble what would be expected if each kin group had their own private set of names. In the balance of this paper I will demonstrate that agreement reflects knowledge of a cultural model by showing that agreement is patterned in the way that one would expect such knowledge to be patterned. The procedure used is to segment the pattern of agreement into interpretable components. I will show that most of the variation between informants can be explained by factors that reflect differential knowledge: age, sex roles, and opportunities to learn. Factors that reflect idiosyncratic differences of opinion between people are less important. While some of the variation can be attributed to differences between kin groups, very little can be attributed to consistent personal idiosyncrasy. Even kin group differences may be a result of differences in exposure to and knowledge of the rare varieties.

Differences in Identification by Sex Role

The greatest contrast between groups of informants in manioc naming is that between men and women. Women know manioc and men do not. This is not a subtle social fact that required elaborate testing to discover. Men volunteered that they could not distinguish manioc varieties and seemed to feel no compulsion to learn. Some men refused to participate in the manioc identification task because it would be senseless to go through the exercise of trying to identify plants they knew nothing about.

I emphasize this fact because it is clear in this case that departure from the consensus means relative ignorance. Of the 43 women and

21 men who participated in the easy manioc identification task, there were only four exceptions (two men, two women) to the rule that all of the women had higher overall agreement than all of the men. The probability that the disparity between the rankings of men and women could have occurred by chance alone is effectively zero (Mann Whitney U = 49).

This difference in manioc knowledge is part of the general intellectual and physical division of labor between the sexes. In a preliminary study, in which men and women were asked to name a wide variety of plants along a trail, men agreed on the names of the forest plants to a far greater degree than did women (Boster 1977). This will be referred to as the general plant identification task. Similarly, in bird identification tasks men agreed more often than women on the names of the forest birds (Berlin, Boster, and O'Neill 1981). These differences in agreement can be readily interpreted as differences in knowledge, attributable to the contrast of the Aguaruna man's role as hunter and gatherer of forest products with the woman's role as gardener. Social role affects not only a person's experience with and motivation to learn a particular group of organisms, but also participation in situations in which the culturally appropriate name could be shared and learned. Aguaruna women are frequently involved in discussions of the qualities and characteristics of manioc varieties while gardening. This activity enables them to approach a consensus on what each variety should be called. The men, even if they can distinguish the varieties, are unable to name them consistently because they have neither the need nor the opportunity to learn the names.

This social interpretation is strengthened by the fact that the difference between the sexes in the bird and plant tasks was not uniform over all of the organisms identified. There was very little difference between the sexes in naming the most culturally important plants and birds, since everyone agreed on their names. All informants, regardless of sex, also disagreed more often on the names of the less important organisms. However, the difference between the degrees of agreement of men and women was greatest when the organisms to be identified were important to only one of the sexes. The disparity between the sexes in the manioc identification tasks was much greater than on the bird and plant identification tasks and much more consistent across the specimens. Women knew all of the manioc varieties better than the men.

Differences in Identification by Individual Expertise

The relationship between the intellectual and physical division of labor is not only an interesting social fact but helps confirm the inference of a cultural model from consensus. Consensus is patterned in the way expertise should be. Up to this point only the expertise of the sexes has been compared. A stronger test of the relationship between knowledge and consensus is whether the ranking of individuals is consistent between tasks. If overall agreement does reflect differential knowledge, one would expect that the ranking of informants within each sex would be constant across tasks, indicating their relative skill as folk biologists.

This expectation seems to be borne out. Overall agreement scores in the general plant identification task were highly correlated with agreement scores in the manioc identification tasks. The Pearson correlation of women's overall agreement in the general plant identification with the hard manioc identification task was .573 ($N = 25$, $p < .001$), and the correlation with agreement in the easy manioc identification task was .556 ($N = 20$, $p = .005$). There seems to be a significant relation between women's performance in the three tasks. For men, the correlation between agreement on the general plant task with the easy manioc task was just as high ($r = .673$), but the number of informants was too low to permit a definite conclusion ($N = 6$, $p = .071$).

This is a very important result. It suggests that there is a component of skill in plant identification that carries over from task to task, a skill probably involving not only experience and motivation but also native intelligence and natural pattern-matching ability. This skill is also reflected in a strong correlation between scores of women in the two manioc identification tasks. Table 2 presents a correlation matrix showing the relationship between overall agreement in these naming tasks and some variables chosen to reflect general experience. It will be noted that the correlations given above are not the same as the

Table 2. Correlation Matrix of Agreement Scores and Other Characteristics of Female Participants in Three Identification Tasks

	General Plant Task	Manioc Hard Task	Manioc Easy Task	Schooling	Age Class
Manioc hard task	.354				
Manioc easy task	.594	.602			
Schooling	−.357	−.817	−.415		
Age class	.519	.391	.394	−.433	
Number of varieties recalled in interview	.390	.291	.359	−.310	.352

corresponding entries in Table 2. This is because the correlation matrix in Table 2 has been computed on a constant subset of 18 informants, omitting those informants who did not participate in all three identification tasks.

As shown in Table 2, the agreement scores of women are correlated with the age of the informant and the number of varieties they recalled in interviews. It is interesting that one of the best predictors of disagreement is schooling. Women who had gone to school agreed very little with others in manioc identification. A possible explanation is that an Aguaruna girl placed in school is deprived of her education as a horticulturalist with her mother in the garden. It is also the youngest women who have been to school, so that the effect of schooling may be partially confounded with the effects of youth and inexperience.

Further evidence that agreement reflects knowledge of a cultural model can be found by examining the extremes of a ranking of informants by overall agreement. Agreeing the most in most manioc identification tasks are mature women who are married to the most prestigious men in the community. These women were noted for their maintenance of a large diversity of manioc varieties, since they acted as distributors of certain rare varieties to other women in the community. Agreeing the least are a number of very young, recently married women. One of these had the reputation of being too lazy to maintain her own garden. She had lost her mother at an early age and may never have learned proper gardening skills.

Differences in Identification by Kin Group

This section will explore why some groups of informants agree more with each other than with the rest of the population. As was shown in Table 1, most of the small clusters of informants are composed of closely related women. The pattern is strongest among women who have the highest overall agreement, which suggests that closely related women agree on the rare plants only if they agree about the common ones.

Close kin agree with each other on the names of manioc varieties because they exchange both knowledge of the varieties and the varieties themselves. Agreement in naming reflects the pattern of the transmission of cultural knowledge. The most important kin relation in this transmission of knowledge is that between a mother and daughter. From an early age, girls help their mothers in the gardens and learn their principal occupation: manioc cultivation. At marriage, when the daughter begins to work her own garden, most of the varieties are taken from her mother's garden. Even after marriage the work group of mother and daughter is not entirely broken up, since mother and daughter often work together in each other's gardens. The tendency to matrilocal residence after marriage helps ensure that this work group is not split apart. A man's skills and tools as hunter are far more portable than a woman's as gardener because in Aguaruna society hunting is usually not a group activity. Sisters also share a great deal of knowledge about manioc, both by virtue of having learned from the same source and by working with each other. The relationship between sisters-in-law is moderately important, since in addition to exchanging brothers in marriage, female cross-cousins often exchange manioc varieties. If a married couple returns to the husband's original place of residence, the relationships between female in-laws become more important. In this case most of the varieties of the incoming bride are given to her by her husband's female kin. Finally, women share a certain amount of knowledge about manioc just by virtue of living in the same community.

In order to test the expected importance of kin relations on degree of agreement, stepwise multiple regressions were performed, treating the agreement between two individuals as the dependent variable and the type of kin relation linking them as a series of independent presence-absence variables. The regessions were carried out on three sets of data: the hard task using all informants, the hard task eliminating the informants with the lowest overall agreement, and the easy task. Table 3 shows the results of each of these regressions. Only those variables entering at the .05 significance level are shown.

The results of the multiple regression confirm the subjective interpretation of the cluster diagrams (Figures 1 and 2). Kin relations are a better predictor of agreement on the hard task than on the easy task and a better predictor among the best informants than among the informants overall. The ordering of importance of these kin relations, as suggested by their order of entry into the multiple regression equation and the values of *beta,* also accord with what might have been expected. Their ordering in the hard task limited to the best informants is shown in the middle of Table 3. That order is: (1) mother-daughter, (2) full sisters, (3) sisters-in-law, (4) co-wives, (5) village co-residents.

The difficulty of the task and the skill of the informants seemed to amplify the importance of the closest social links. In the easy task, or with less skilled informants, broader social relations were more important. In particular, village co-residents is fifth in importance in the hard task limited to the best informants, second in importance in the hard task with all of the informants, and most important on the

Table 3. Multiple Regression of Agreement on Kin Relations

Variable	Hard Manioc Task with All Informants, *N* = 1,654 Pairs					
	F to Enter	Prob	Multiple *R*	*R* Square	Simple *R*	Beta
Mother-daughter	31.0	.000	.136	.018	.136	.127
Village	17.4	.000	.169	.029	.120	.074
Sisters-in-law	11.9	.001	.189	.036	.097	.088
Full sisters	12.2	.001	.206	.043	.089	.085
Co-wives	10.2	.001	.220	.049	.080	.077

Variable	Hard Manioc Task with Best Informants, *N* = 821 Pairs					
	F to Enter	Prob	Multiple *R*	*R* Square	Simple *R*	Beta
Mother-daughter	49.6	.000	.239	.057	.239	.231
Full sisters	25.6	.000	.292	.086	.167	.164
Sisters-in-law	12.3	.000	.315	.099	.107	.102
Co-wives	10.3	.001	.332	.110	.102	.099
Village	6.3	.012	.342	.117	.161	.085

Variable	Easy Manioc Task with All Informants, *N* = 904 Pairs					
	F to Enter	Prob	Multiple *R*	*R* Square	Simple *R*	Beta
Village	5.8	.016	.080	.006	.080	.053
Sisters-in-law	4.1	.044	.104	.011	.076	.074

easy task. In other words, as the difficulty or role specialization of an identification task increases, total agreement declines, the difference between the sexes increases, and the importance of close kin relations also increases.

Though this may appear a complicated conjecture, I believe the underlying model is fairly simple. An individual can be considered to have a number of identities: a member of a society, an actor in a sex role in that society, a member of a household, and an individual. Different amounts of knowledge are shared at each of these layers. A certain amount can be presumed of any adult member of the society. That and more can be assumed as an actor in a sex role. Still more is shared between closely related people. Finally, certain knowledge is unique to the individual. As the difficulty or specialization of an identification task increases, agreement at all of the layers decreases but not at equal rates. Sharing at the most general layers falls off most quickly. Thus there is an apparent succession in the importance of these layers of identity depending on the difficulty of the task. On the easiest task, the naming of common cultivated and protected crops at the folk generic rank, all adult members of the society are in near complete agreement. The outermost layer, societal identity, is most important. On the slightly harder tasks, whether naming forest trees or common manioc varieties, sex-role identity is most important. On even harder tasks, such as naming rare manioc varieties, membership in small kin groups grows in importance. Finally, on an extremely difficult task the only agreement would be internal to the informant, although even this would be quite low.

These layers of identity correspond to the various social contexts in which knowledge is transmitted or shared. Each of the previously mentioned groups (considering the individual for the moment as a social entity of one) has associated with it particular modes and intensities of sharing of information.

One way that the social contexts of communication could have consequences for patterns of sharing of linguistic codes is evident in the pattern of shifts in referential level to manioc. The two levels considered here are the folk-generic and specific ranks (Berlin 1976): manioc in general (*máma*) and kind of manioc respectively. Appropriate level of reference shifts according to the speaker's sexual-social role and the context in which reference to manioc is being made.

Part of the context that influences how a plant specimen will be identified is the diversity of other plants from which the specimen must be distinguished. One can change this context experimentally by choice of stimuli. In the easy manioc identification task, all informants, male and female, responded with names of kinds of manioc; they did not feel it appropriate to name each of the 90 manioc plants with the single general term *máma*. This level of reference was forced by the design of the test.

The general plant identification task provided a context in which level of reference was not so severely constrained because the example of manioc was only one of 102 different cultivated and wild plants to be identified. In this task all but two of the 30 male informants identified the manioc with a general term. When women were guided in the task by male assistants, 17 of the 25 also identified the manioc with a general term, though eight identified it as a kind of manioc. However, when women were guided by a female assistant, all but one of the seven identified the specimen as a kind of manioc. The probability of this skewing occurring by chance alone was less than .0001 (Chi square = 19.36, d.f. = 2). In spite of the fact that the general term *máma* was sufficient to distinguish the example of manioc from all other plant specimens in the task, it was clearly more appropriate for a woman to refer to manioc with something more specific than the generic name for manioc when speaking to another woman.

It seems that women use their expectation of the background knowledge of their hearer in choosing the form of reference to manioc. Thus women are usually more specific in manioc reference when talking to other women than when talking to men. This shift in referential level according to the speaker's judgment of the background knowledge of her hearer both reflects and perpetuates a situation in which women know more about manioc than men.

Differences in Identification by Personal Idiosyncrasy

There remains the question of whether variation is within people or between them, whether the differences observed between individuals stem from differences in their cognition or merely reflect the inherent variability of each individual responding to different contexts (cf. Sankoff 1971:404-7). This difference is crucial to the question of the degree to which culture is shared. If within-informant variation is high in comparison to between-informant variation, apparent differences between people can be interpreted as an artifact of this inherent variability. One could say that in spite of the apparent variation, there is a sharing of a general cultural model. On the other hand, if informants are internally consistent but systematically differ from one another, it is apparent that they do not share a single model.

The answer to this question depends on the context of the test made to decide it. The choice of cultural domain and stimulus material, the difficulty of the task, and the skill of the informants are all factors that will influence what kind of pattern of variation is observed. One could construct tasks that would appear to demonstrate any of a large range of theoretical positions ranging from pure idiosyncrasy to total cultural homogeneity. Although the question of the extent to which culture is shared in general is undecidable, it is possible to determine the degree of sharing of specific cultural subsystems. In the case of variation in the identification of Aguaruna manioc varieties, I reiterate that there appears to be a single cultural model shared by most adult Aguaruna women because a substantial proportion of the variation between informants, unexplained by differences in knowledge, is attributable to within-informant variation. This point can be supported by examining the pattern of within-informant variation.

Only six informants in the easy identification task were retested, but the patterns that emerge from their responses are striking. There are three major findings. First, the agreement of informants with other informants increases in the retest (matched sample $T = 2.03$,

$p < .05$). This indicates that either the plants were easier to identify in the two-month interval between test and retest or that the informants learned in the interim. In either case change is in the direction of the general consensus. Second, informants agree with themselves more often than they do with others, but not much more. Depending on the choice of the statistical test used to measure this effect, the difference may or may not be considered significant (single sample $Z = 1.143$, $p = .126$, matched sample $T = 7.87$, $p << .001$).[5] This indicates that the level of within-informant variation is of roughly the same order of magnitude as between-informant variation. Third, within-informant agreement is strongly correlated with between-informant agreement ($r = .922$, $p = .004$). In other words, informants who agree with others were more likely to agree with themselves.

This third finding is the strongest evidence that agreement means knowledge. Informants who are internally consistent are also those who agree most often with others. I believe that the most reasonable interpretation of this relationship is that inconsistency in naming reflects the informant's uncertainty. The fact that the level of within-informant agreement is only slightly higher than between-informant agreement allows the interpretation that residual between-informant variation, unexplained by other factors, may be in large part a product of within-informant variation. The fact that the two are correlated helps confirm that interpretation.

Summary

I have shown that there is a single Aguaruna model of manioc identification and that deviations from the model are patterned according the sexual division of labor, membership in kin and residential groups, and individual expertise. In the course of this demonstration the patterns of agreement observed in identification tasks have been related to the social contexts of learning and speaking about manioc. It was suggested that different degrees of agreement corresponded to different layers of social identity and also to different modes and intensities of communication about manioc. These layers were: adult member of the society, mature woman, close kinswoman, and the individual. The variation between individuals can be explained at all of these layers. However, an examination of the pattern of within-informant agreement revealed that little of the variation between informants could be explained as a result of personal idiosyncrasy. This helped confirm the inference of cultural knowledge from consensus.

One implication of this work is that the now-maligned practice of using key informants may not be so bad after all. In the case of Aguaruna manioc identification, one could pick informants who have more knowledge of the cultural model than others. These older women approach Werner's ideal of the omniscient informant in that their knowledge of manioc represents a "union of individual competences" (Werner 1969:333). Deviations from their identifications can be considered mostly the results of either performance errors or ignorance. A careful ethnographer might have chosen these women to interview on the basis of a knowledge of the rest of the society. The problem is that only by studying variation could the ethnographer be assured of having made the right choice.

This work has outlined a method for confirming the ethnographer's choice of informant. The method determines whether a cultural standard exists by examining the way in which cognitive diversity is organized. It is related to a number of techniques that exploit error (Cancian 1963), conflict (Turner 1957), and misunderstanding (Garfinkel 1967) to gain a better understanding of the cultural system. I suspect that many cases of informant disagreement have a pattern similar to that documented here. Though speculative, this suspicion is testable.

NOTES

This paper is a modified version of chapter 4 of my dissertation (Boster 1980). The field research was conducted in north-central Peru between July 1977 and Sept. 1978 as part of the Segunda Expedición Etnobiológica al Río Alto Marañón. The research was funded by the National Science Foundation (grant no. BNS 7916746), with Brent Berlin as principal investigator. Travel was supported by grants from the Tinker Foundation administered through the Center for Latin American Studies at Berkeley. I am grateful to Mike Agar, Brent Berlin, Harold Conklin, Janet Dougherty, Eugene Hammel, Paul Kay, Willett Kempton, Susan Niles, Katherine Woolard, and Oswald Werner for comments and criticism. I am also indebted to Susan Niles for the title. Any errors of fact or interpretation in the text are my own.

1. I am not the first to discover that there are social correlates of informant variation. All of the empirical studies cited above mention social factors that help explain the patterns of informant variation. Gardner is one of the most thorough in his list of possible factors, including age, sex, kinship, degree of acculturation, and many others (Gardner 1976:458-59). Given that Gardner and I recognize the same kinds of explanatory factors and are dealing with similar amounts of informant variation (if anything, there is more variation in Aguaruna manioc identification than in Dene bird classification), I believe that we are describing comparable situations and that the analysis developed here would apply to the Dene with only minor changes. Though

I respect Gardner's care in restricting his statements to the Dene, I doubt that the Dene are a special case of extreme cognitive individualism.

2. A stem was accepted for planting only if the woman presenting it identified it differently from those already planted. I say "supposedly different" because this procedure allowed the possibility that other women would regard the new stem as identical to one already planted.

3. It appears that many Aguaruna women believe there are correct names for manioc varieties. When I told women that others named a particular plant differently than they did, they usually responded that the others were wrong. However, the following example illustrates why it is not clear that agreement necessarily should be equated with correctness. I planted in the first test garden a stem I was told was *masěgmish,* a variety that comes from a neighboring drainage. Most of the informants in the identification task called the plant *mamáyakem,* a local variety which it resembled. Only the woman who had given the stem to me in the first place called it by her original name. It did not appear that she was using the two names synonymously, since she called the example of *mamáyakem* in the test garden by its local name. It is not clear to me whether the "correct" name in a case like this is the most common name or the name offered by the owner. This example suggests that the enterprise of attempting to discover with absolute confidence the correct name of every plant is futile. Fortunately, problem cases like this were rare; much more frequently the majority opinion seemed to represent the expert opinion. While it might not be possible to equate consensus with correctness in every case, in the aggregate it seems the most reasonable assumption.

4. The algorithm used to generate the cluster diagrams was average link clustering as implemented by Donald Olivier's Fortran program AGCLUS. This algorithm has the advantage of reducing the tendency toward chaining observed in single link clustering (Everitt 1974:15, Sneath and Sokal 1973:228-40). Informants who were retested appear twice in Figure 2. In half of the cases (38, 79, 50) they are grouped with their retest selves. The other retested informants were numbers 27, 35, and 53.

5. The single sample Z test treats all informant agreements as a population and asks whether the observed sample of within-informant agreements could have been drawn from it. To reduce the problem of dependence of between- and within-informant agreement, the second trials of each informant have been eliminated. The number of between-informant agreement scores is high enough ($N = 666$) to allow one to treat its standard deviation (.143) as the population standard deviation. Again, if the comparison is made in this way, the difference between within- and between-informant agreement (.073) is within the normal spread of between-informant agreement ($Z = 1.14$, $p = .126$).

If the problem is treated as a matched sample comparison, a different conclusion is drawn. This design treats the mean agreement of each informant with all others as one observation and agreement of each informant with herself as the other. The result of this test suggests that there is a significant difference between within-informant agreement and mean between-informant agreement (mean difference = .076, standard deviation of difference = .022, matched sample $T = 7.87$, $p << .001$). But the sampling distribution of these two variables are quite different, since the variance of the mean agreement is low in comparison to the variance of the population of agreement scores on which it is based. For this reason, I prefer the first of these tests, the single sample Z test. Regardless of the statistical test used, it is fair to say that informants do not agree with themselves much more often than they do with other informants.

REFERENCES

Berlin, Brent
1976 The Concept of Rank in Ethnobiological Classification: Some Evidence from Aguaruna Folk Botany. *American Ethnologist* 3:381-99.

Berlin, Brent, and Elois Ann Berlin
1978 Etnobiología, subsistencia, y nutrición en una sociedad de la selva: Los Aguaruna (Jíbaro). In Alberto Chirif, ed., *Salud y nutrición en sociedades nativas,* pp. 13-47. Lima, Peru: Centro de Investigación y Promoción Amazónica.

Berlin, Brent, James S. Boster, and John P. O'Neill
1981 The Perceptual Bases of Ethnobiological Classification: Evidence from Aguaruna Jivaro Ornithology. *Journal of Ethnobiology* 1:95-108.

Boster, James
1977 Inter-informant Variation in Aguaruna Plant Classification. Paper presented to the 23rd Annual Meeting of the Kroeber Anthropological Society, Berkeley, Calif.
1980 How the Exceptions Prove the Rule: An Analysis of Informant Disagreement in Aguaruna Manioc Identification. Ph.D. dissertation, University of California, Berkeley.

Cancian, Frank
1963 Informant Error and Native Prestige Ranking in Zinacantan. *American Anthropologist* 65:1068-75.

D'Andrade, Roy
1970 Culture Shared and Unique. Paper presented at the 69th Annual Meeting of the American Anthropological Association.

Dorsey, J. O.
1884 Omaha Sociology. Bureau of American Ethnology, Bulletin no. 3, pp. 211-370.

Everitt, Brian
1974 *Cluster Analysis.* London: Heinemann Educational Books.

Foster, George
1979 Methodological Problems in the Study of Intracultural Variation: The Hot/Cold Dichotomy in Tzintzuntzan. *Human Organization* 38:179-83.

Gardner, Peter M.
1976 Birds, Words and a Requiem for the Omniscient Informant. *American Ethnologist* 3:446-68.
Garfinkel, Harold
1967 *Studies in Ethnomethodology.* Englewood Cliffs, N.J.: Prentice-Hall.
Harner, Michael J.
1972 The Jivaro: People of the Sacred Waterfalls. Garden City, N.Y.: Doubleday/Natural History Press.
Harris, Marvin
1970 Referential Ambiguity in the Calculus of Brazilian Racial Identity. *Southwestern Journal of Anthropology* 36:1-14.
Hays, Terence E.
1976 An Empirical Method for the Identification of Covert Categories in Ethnobiology. *American Ethnologist* 3:489-507.
Kay, Paul
1978 Tahitian Words for Race and Class. In *Rank and Status in Polynesia and Melanesia: Essays in Honor of Professor Douglas Oliver.* Publications de la Société Océanistes, no. 39. Paris: Musée de l'Homme.
Kempton, Willett
1981 *The Folk Classification of Ceramics: A Study of Cognitive Prototypes.* New York: Academic Press.
Pelto, Pertti J., and Gretel H. Pelto
1975 Intra-cultural Diversity: Some Theoretical Issues. *American Ethnologist* 2:1-18.
Sankoff, Gillian
1971 Quantitative Analysis of Sharing and Variability in a Cognitive Model. *Ethnology* 10:389-408.
Sapir, Edward
1938 Why Anthropology Needs the Psychiatrist. *Psychiatry* 1:7-12.
Sneath, Peter H., and Robert R. Sokal
1973 *Numerical Taxonomy: The Principles and Practice of Numerical Classification.* San Francisco: W. H. Freeman.
Steward, Julian, ed.
1948 *Handbook of South American Indians,* vol. 3: *The Tropical Forest Tribes.* Smithsonian Institution, Bureau of American Ethnology, Bulletin no. 143. Washington, D.C.: U.S. Government Printing Office.
Turner, Victor W.
1957 *Schism and Continuity in an African Society.* Manchester: Manchester University Press.
Wallace, Anthony F. C.
1961 *Culture and Personality.* New York: Random House, 2d ed., 1970.
Werner, Oswald
1969 The Basic Assumptions of Ethnoscience. *Semiotica* 1:329-38.
Werner, Oswald, and Joann Fenton
1970 Method and Theory in Ethnoscience or Ethnoepistemology. In Raoul Naroll and Ronald Cohen, eds., *A Handbook of Method in Cultural Anthropology,* pp. 537-78. Garden City, N.Y.: Natural History Press.

9

Actions Speak Louder than Words

John B. Gatewood

> Unless you can use your Image to do something, you are like a man who collects maps but never takes a trip.
>
> Miller, Galanter, and Pribram (1960:2)

Anthropological interest in cognitive systems has ramified to such an extent that some may be unclear about what cognitive anthropology is. Keesing (1974) circumscribes the subfield by contrasting it with structural and symbolic anthropology, all three being based on an ideational conception of culture. The Laboratory of Comparative Human Cognition (1978) takes a different tack and enumerates three areas of active research: testing for psychological salience, studying folk classifications, and modeling decision processes. Others, for example, Bock (1980) and Casson (1981), provide more complete surveys including both historical derivations and current areas of interest.

The most conspicuous absence in such listings of research interests is a genuine concern with *action*. Cognitive anthropology remains closely affiliated with linguistics, both in terms of the importation of formal models and in that lexicon and verbal reports constitute the principal data. With few exceptions, anthropologists have been slow to confront the problems posed in describing systems of action and in relating cognition to action. Most have been content to pursue their inquiries into the structure of static, atemporal, semantic relations.

The disregard of action in cognitive anthropology is symptomatic of the more fundamental lack of concern with the temporal dimension of knowledge. Because we tend to focus on human beings as *understanding*-systems to the exclusion of human beings as *acting*-systems, we lose sight of the fact that cognizing, thinking, and knowing take time just as much as do easily observable actions such as running, winking, and fidgeting. Response time (latency) is a critical variable in physiologically oriented research (e.g. Goodglass 1980). Similarly, response time has been used, along with other measures, as an indicator of relative salience (e.g. Rosch et al. 1976, Lucy and Shweder 1979). But in these studies the focus is on the speed of passive assimilation and response to stimuli rather than on the sequencing, timing, and coordination of the ongoing flow of thought and action. Researchers in the area of nonverbal behavior (e.g. Condon and Ogston 1967; Condon 1979; Birdwhistell 1970; Kendon 1970, 1973; Chapple 1970) have developed techniques for studying the coordination of behavior in social interactions, but they do not attempt to chart the equally complex flow of thoughts and feelings that, presumably, transpire in concert with the overt behaviors. Who asks how long it takes to have an idea, think a thought, feel a feeling? Indeed, there are few counterexamples to Arbib's critique: "For many linguists and anthropologists, concepts are static entities to be isolated. Many anthropologists are not interested in cognitive processes, in other words in the dynamics, but in learning as much as possible of the cognitive categories enforced in a culture at any one time. A cognitive system is then not dynamic, but rather some sort of static world view, or picture, or map" (Arbib 1970:332).

The issue is how human knowledge is linked to, meshed with, part of human action. Because actions transpire—they are extended in time with characteristic sequencing and durations—a necessary first step toward resolving this issue is to be concerned with the temporal properties of knowledge structures as well as of actions. Failure in this regard engenders a rigid separation between competence-cognition-knowledge on the one hand and performance-action-behavior on the other (e.g. Chomsky 1957, 1965). This, in turn, gives rise to an image of human beings as passive interpreters of their lives, as severe split personalities whose knowledge only monitors their behavior, who spin endlessly in the vicious cycle of behave-interpret-behave-interpret. In this view the human being is reduced to an overintellectualized creature whose behavior arises of its own accord only to become grist for a disembodied and alienated mind. Knowledge is divorced from action. Cognitive psychology, too, has yet to deal with this matter: "A classic problem for most cognitive approaches has been that their constructs typically do not explain how thought is turned into action" (Fischer 1980:523).

In what follows I take an initial step toward relating knowledge and action in anthropological accounts: I describe in much-abbreviated fashion one person's cognitive organization of an action system. The description is not intended as a simulation model of cognitive/action processes, and knowledge structures are not specified in the forms typical of artificial intelligence work (e.g. Axten and Fararo 1977, Rumelhart and Ortony 1977, Schank and Abelson 1977, Palmer 1978, Kieras 1981). Rather, I am concerned with how one person represented his job routine to himself—how he organized his work in order to know what to do next in a highly sequenced group activity—and how this organization developed concomitantly with his skill level. Clearly, this will not solve the problem of how knowledge underlies action, but it is a starting point insofar as the description preserves at least the sequential aspects of both cognitions and actions as well as sketching their ontogenetic development.

The case comes from my three seasons of experience as a paid crew member on Alaskan salmon boats. The work of putting the seine (type of net) in the water, holding it open to entrap fish, and retrieving the gear is called "making a set." It requires the coordinated work of from five to eight crew members, and it takes about one hour. The operation is repeated from five to twelve times per working day, the exact number depending on various factors.

Because the phenomenon involves breaking down a process into events or episodes, the case resembles Agar's (1974, 1975) study of addicts' verbal segmentation of "getting a fix." In seining, however, very few temporal phases of the work are encoded in the collective jargon. As a result, my description is concerned largely with unlabeled cognitive categories and how they are related to the way people talk about seining. Each crew member constructs his own cognitive representation of his work (including its segmentation into episodes), and these personal constructs only partially correspond with those encoded in the collective representations of the work.

Ethnographic Background to Salmon Purse Seining

Purse seining is a variety of net fishing. The top of the net has floats attached to keep it at the water's surface, and the bottom of the net is weighted. The seine can be closed at the bottom by pulling a free-running line that is threaded through rings attached to the weight line. Closing the seine is rather like closing an old-fashioned lady's purse by pulling its strings. In this way fish are trapped, not gilled.

In southeast Alaskan salmon seining the purse seines are 250 fathoms long (ca. 457.2 m) and about 90 feet deep (ca. 27.4 m). Because the seine is so heavy and difficult to manage in the strong tides, all major manipulations of it are done with mechanical aides. Chief among these are the two boats, which drag and hold open the seine. The main boat is about 55 feet long (ca. 16.8 m), and the power skiff is about 16 feet (ca. 4.9 m). In addition to the boats themselves, seiners use a power winch to pull in the purse lines and a Puretic power block to hoist the seine onto the deck.

Crews range in size from five to eight, skipper included. Most boats have crews of six: one skipper, one cook, one skiff driver, and three deck hands. These are the relevant roles when making a set. At most other times the significant distinction is simply skipper versus crew member.

The salmon seine season lasts from roughly mid-July through September, and seining is tightly regulated by the Alaska Department of Fish and Game. Legal seining is specified in terms of both when and where. Each week during a season the ADF&G announces "openings," and the seine boats leave port for the open areas. An opening usually lasts from 36 hours to several days, and the boats stay out in the fishing areas this whole time, unloading their catches each evening to tender boats. During openings the work day may be as long as 20 hours (in accord with the long daylight hours of the latitude in summer). On the other hand, after the seine is mended on returning to port, seiners do no work whatsoever for a few days, until the next opening.

I refer the reader to Browning (1974), Langdon (1977), and Gatewood (1978, 1983a, 1984) for more general ethnographic information, including photographs and drawings of seining hardware. Here our concern is with the central operation of seining—making a set—and not with other aspects of the work. Below is a description providing the crudest outlines of what happens when seiners perform their main task. This is the sort of story I would tell an interested tourist or a mildly curious friend; that is, it is my *narrator's account:*

> Well, to begin with, there are six people who do all the work. The skipper stays on the main boat and runs the show, the skiff man maneuvers the power skiff around, and the other guys are deck hands. When the skipper gives the order to cut loose, the skiff man and one of the deck hands take off in the skiff with one end of the seine. They go out and hold the net open so that the fish swim into it. It is a long net, about a quarter-mile or so. When the skipper thinks it is time, he tells the skiff to bring its end of the seine back to the main boat. Now, the seine is in a big circle with both ends tied to the main boat. Two guys start pursing up the bottom of the seine by wrapping a line which is run through rings attached to the bottom of the seine around the drums of a power winch on the boat. This closes the bottom of the seine so that the fish cannot swim out. While they are "pursing," as it is called, two others guys

> are running around doing assorted things to keep the seine from getting tangled. The one fellow who went for a ride in the skiff is back on deck by now. When the pursing is finished, we hoist up the bottom of the seine and drop it on the deck. Now, the fish cannot get out. All that is left to do is haul in the seine until there is just a little (or big!) bag of fish in the water, then hoist the fish up and drop them on deck. Then, we pitch the fish into the hold, clean up, and get ready for the next set.

The description above is infused with my current functional comprehension of the collective work. The focus of such a narrator's account is what happens to the seine as the crew collectively manipulates it in the water. This is *not* the way a seiner organizes his job routine while doing the work. The narrator's account stems from a reflective, functional manner of thinking and is from the posture of an informed observer. When doing one's job routine, it is quite unnecessary to know why one pulls up a line and ties it around a cleat, for example, only that it must be done at a particular time. Presumably, someone at some time understood the why of each job. My point is that any given seiner need not understand his work in terms of functional rationales. One does one's jobs because the skipper or an experienced deck hand has told him to do so. Even with my academically fostered propensity to ask functional questions, I did not understand why I did several jobs until my second and even third season. The problem when working is not communicating the collective effort via word-pictures complete with rationales but, rather, knowing what to do next. The narrator's perspective, once developed, may assist in the formation of a worker's cognitive organization of his job routine, but it is not identical with the personal construction. It is with and through such personal constructions that seining is accomplished.

The Cognitive Organization of Purse Seining

When first exposed to purse seining, one finds it difficult to see the big picture, the larger pattern that all the various little things people are doing carry along. This is true from the vantage point of a spectator, and it is painfully true for a "rookie" (novice seiner) who is trying to participate in the bewildering array of tasks. The initial conception of the work is quite different from what eventually develops as the work becomes more familiar.

Prior to commencing work, the prospective rookie has heard most of the seining jargon referring to phases of making a set, he has probably heard several narrator's accounts of what to expect, and he is familiar with the visual appearance of the boats and their hardware.

However, he is only slightly more knowledgeable than the reader is now.

The evening before my first opening our skipper finally gathered us together on deck and formally announced the job assignments for the season. In close paraphrase his speech was something like: "Well, let's see. Darrell, you and Richard will do the pursing up this year. You two [Sk'eg and John] do the other things. Sk'eg, you're the skiff man with Frank. Richard, you'll do the web again; John, you do corks; Sk'eg the leads; and Darrell, you do what you did last year." This terse, jargony speech was the first and last time that jobs were assigned by authoritative decree. If you cannot figure out what seining is like from the skipper's assignments, then you know how I felt that night, because it did not mean much to me either. I had expected some sort of lecture on the operation of making a set. Instead, I got a semicoded message and the obvious prophecy, "You'll see tomorrow."

The next morning we were the second boat in our vicinity to make a set. We waited in line while the boat ahead of us held open its set, and I eagerly watched what its crew members were doing. When their skiff headed back to its boat, we began maneuvering. Richard released the skiff on the skipper's command, and Frank whirled the skiff around and headed for the shoreline with his end of our seine.

While we held our seine open, I received more detailed descriptions of what would happen in the first few minutes after our skiff returned. I was supposed to help Richard start one of the purse lines going around the stern-side winch drum. I was to stand holding the boat tow line and wait for Richard to lower it after Frank had steered the skiff out of the set. I should then unfasten the double block from the boat tow line and pull it down to the deck and fasten it to the cleat so it would not swing freely in the air. Then, Richard would untie the boat tow line from the winch niggerheads, and I must very quickly push the line over to the stern-side davit pulley, put it in, and shut the pulley's clasp. Once the boat tow line was through the davit pulley, Richard could begin pursing it up.

Of course, their instructions that morning were very different from this written account of them. They did not bother naming parts of the hardware, nor did they explain the purpose of each task I was assigned. Rather, they just told me to do several things in a linguistic form similar to: "Put that [point] through there [point]." All I got from their instructions was a vague advance warning that things were going to get very hectic and very busy. I concentrated on my responsibilities: getting the yellow line above my head (the boat tow line) freed from the double block and through the davit pulley (that one right →). If I did that, other folks would take care of everything else.

The skiff returned, and everything progressed according to the plan. I put the yellow line through the davit pulley and shut the clasp. Then, as the adrenalin was pumping through my body, things got very strange very quickly. What were those others things I was supposed to be doing?

About this time I abandoned my arrogant hopes of being a participant-observer. I had all I could handle trying to participate. Skipper began yelling succinct, entirely ambiguous orders like, "Pull up that line!!" Sk'eg (also a rookie) and I both jumped toward the general direction of Skipper's pointing and commenced fondling lines until one of us hit upon the correct one. Then we tugged away at it. Just when we were feeling we must be doing a good thing, Skipper yelled another equally clear instruction, and we let go our line to jump for the second one. This brought a rapid verbal evaluation of our overall mental capacities. Eventually Sk'eg and I divided and conquered—each to his own line—and Skipper's agitation began to dissipate.

The set continued even though Sk'eg and I were part of the action. He and I were very eager but very ignorant. Our work required constant monitoring by Skipper (which is why he was upset with us), but we finished that first set and made about five more that day. The following day we made six sets, and the first opening was over.

During the two days of my first opening I developed a distinctive mode of organizing my work. After the first set everything from shutting the davit pulley's clasp to the beginning of "hauling gear" (bringing the seine over the Puretic power block and making cork, web, and lead piles) was just a blur. I was unable to remember clearly what I had done or when. However, by the end of the first day, i.e. six sets, I began to see my work (a) as a routine, and (b) as a single-leveled array of separate "little tasks," each of which had to be mastered in and of itself.

This initial organization seems to be typical of rookies. In this stage of development rookies are often oblivious to what other crew members are doing, and they are completely absorbed in their own thoughts, work, and anxieties. Provided the rookie has the beginnings of a good seining ethos, his inner turmoil can be seen on his confused but eager face. My own worries were whether I could remember everything I had somehow gotten done the previous set, whether I could remember when to do what, and whether the jobs I had done the previous set were expectable parts of my evolving routine or peculiar to the contingencies of that set. I also knew that my position on the boat was in the balance: if I did not gain control of my work within the next couple of openings, I would be fired.

Before too long (roughly on the order of eight to sixteen sets), the rookie who is going to make it as a seiner manages to get his responsibilities under control. He can tie lines around cleats and rigging pins quickly. He knows where the busy and congested spaces are. He knows not to stop the operation just because some jellyfish is burning on his face. And he knows what he is responsible for doing and when he should do it. Typically, this understanding involves a simple memorization after the fashion, "First 1 do job_1, then I do job_2, then I do job_3, . . . , then I am finished." In other words, this first level of understanding is in the form of a *string of beads.*

The string-of-beads organization, though quite simple, is itself rather miraculous because job responsibilities and the division of labor are evolving during the same time. For example, if I had been provided with a detailed list of "my jobs," I am confident I could have memorized it thoroughly before making my first set. But no such list is provided. Furthermore, there are no dress rehearsals or practice runs in advance of the real event.

Despite the mass of confusion (from the rookie's vantage point), a normal human being seems capable of coping with the flux and transforming it into routines, and this is in addition to mastering each task. However, if a rookie with only a few sets' experience were asked merely to recite his job routine, he would not be able to answer with any degree of certainty. Mental rehearsals can hasten this form of mastery, and, indeed, Sk'eg and I verbally practiced our respective routines all the way back to port after our first opening. The language of such rehearsing, whether spoken out loud or inwardly, tends to follow Vygotsky's (1962) general observations: there is a very high ratio of verbs, in the present tense. Yet not all of one's actions are represented verbally, outwardly or inwardly. Rather, one experiences visual imagery and muscular tensions appropriate to certain actions, but can only grope for words to express these inner thought-feeling flows. Such was the case as Sk'eg and I tried to articulate our job routines to each other, and I have the same problem every time I try to write about seining, though the more often I write, the easier it becomes, because I have built up a stable repertoire of labels, names, and expressions.

In addition to mentally rehearsing my routine, I stumbled upon a simple trick which made remembering what to do next much easier, though still in the string-of-beads organization. I spatialized the temporal relations of my job routine. Instead of trying to remember which job followed which job, I transformed the problem and memorized which spaces I occupied in what order. This was particularly appropriate because my routine required that I make a simple circuit around the boat's perimeter. I got this flash of insight during my second opening, and it dramatically improved my temporal awareness and mastery. This spatial mnemonic for temporal relations was most significant during the first half of my rookie season. After that I began to think of my work in yet different ways, and though I persisted in recognizing my dance around the boat, its mnemonic function declined.

I do not know if other seiners develop spatial mnemonics similar to the one I devised. Be that as it may, they commonly develop some sort of string-of-beads organization, and they continue thinking this way until they become confident of their accuracy. After 20 to 30 sets a rookie can recite his routine easily and fluidly (if in awkward language forms) as well as perform it gracefully. But by this time two things have also happened: (a) he has developed additional ways of representing his work to himself, and (b) he is not likely to think of himself as a rookie any longer.

During my own period of rapid learning I had the feeling that two levels of understanding were slowly coming together. On the one hand, the jargon a rookie has heard since his arrival (e.g. making a set, pursing, hauling gear) is beginning to be more than mere words. The jargon has served to loosely organize seining even before he started working, but now the expressions have deeper meanings. On the other hand, little things, unnamed chunks of activity, have riveted the rookie's attention away from the big picture crudely provided in the jargon, and these little things have surprised, confused, and frustrated him until he finally masters each one. The large-scale overview of seining given expression in the collective representations does not mean very much to the beginner, and the small-scale fragments of the process dominate one's thinking but provide no comprehension despite their vividness. Both visions concern the same process, both have merit, but initially they remain two distinct and seemingly unrelated perspectives.

With experience, the two organizations mesh and interpenetrate. When this is achieved—however it happens—the rookie is not only able to *do* his work and *recite* his routine but also imagines that he has begun to *comprehend* seining. The tunnel vision characteristic of the beginner, lost in the details of his own responsibilities, gives way to a broadened view of the operation as a whole. Now, in addition to telling tourists what seining is all about (a narrator's account), the partially experienced seiner can relate his job routine with all its little tasks to that same story. This new form of organization is reflected in the subjective experience, in an increased ability to decipher another person's work on a different boat, and in increased awareness of what fellow crew members do at different times during a set.

The nature of this relation between job routine and the operation as a whole is not, as many readers may suspect, a matter of understanding the purpose of one's work. Functional comprehension develops piecemeal and usually long after the seiner has constructed the sort of cognitive organization sketched above. As mentioned previously, I did not discover the purpose of some jobs until my third season, yet I was regarded by my skipper and fellows as a skilled coworker. The beginning of seining comprehension is a matter not of functional understanding but, rather, of establishing temporal correspondences between the elements of one's routine and the major functional phases of making a set. Such temporal linkages do not in themselves reveal the purpose of any given little task, however, because the functional phases indicated in a narrator's account are accomplished by ensembles of little tasks performed by perhaps several crew members. In other words, narrators' accounts describe seining at a much higher scale than what constitutes the immediate reality for someone working on deck.

Relating the little tasks of one's job routine to the functional phases of a narrator's account is not unidirectional in effect. If the association provides comprehension of the little tasks, it also enriches the meaning of the jargon and narrator's account. I once listened patiently to a person who had never been seining tell a tourist what happens when making a set. His account differed in no significant way from the story I would have told, yet I submit that he did not know what he was talking about. To him, it was "loose talk" (Gatewood 1983b), just words strung together in a colorful manner. He had never experienced a sampling of the little tasks that are so vivid and dominating to even partially experienced seiners. After a couple of openings a rookie not only can talk a good set but he knows what it means to make a set. As he relates the specifics of his job routine to the operation as a whole, the jargon takes on deeper meaning. With experience, hauling gear, for example, becomes more than just a colorful addition to one's vocabulary and acquires all sorts of connotations. These connotations resonate through muscles that flex and contract in new ways. Thinking about hauling gear conjures moods of complex inner tensions. And these matters are distinct from simple linguistic mastery of the expression. When these kinds of feelings, these inner flowings, become patterned and regular through repeated activation, the seiner thinks of hauling gear in a more than linguistic framework. Now it is a temporal segment, an expression pregnant with meaning, a natural phase of seining. Its meaning is lodged in muscles as well as words.

Every seiner I questioned, with one exception, had developed a segmentation of the process of making a set. The single exception proves the rule in that he was also regarded as the most inept seiner imaginable. The generality of segmentation is interesting in itself and begs explanation. Why should seiners develop intermediate levels of organization between the little tasks and the process as a whole? Why should their initial, string-of-beads organization be superseded and reorganized in accord with some higher-order temporal segmentation.

One answer to these questions can be formulated by viewing the segmentations as the solution to a cognitive problem. In this view the problem for a seiner doing his job routine can be framed as knowing what to do next. Indeed, this is a felt problem during the first part of the rookie season. Segmentations solve this problem because it is easier to remember an ordering if the elements being ordered are hierarchically organized rather than single-leveled. This can be deduced with the algebra of permutations (see, for example, the case of the two watchmakers in Simon 1973). And, in point of fact, seiners find it easier to remember their job sequence once making a set has become internally represented as consisting of distinct temporal segments rather than a simple linear order of little tasks. However, once such segments have been constructed, the original problem is no longer felt as the same problem. It is not that remembering is easier but that, within the bounds of a segment, one does not have to remember consciously at all. Nonetheless, segments solve the original cognitive problem, whether in the same terms or by transforming the problem itself. Hence, the difficulty of knowing what to do next can be regarded as a functional motivation for the construction of segmentations. Of course, this motivation does not determine *which* segmentation; rather, it lies behind any and all segmentations.

Segmentations are not simply replications of the collective representations. A given segment is not merely a linguistic expression with expanded meaning, common to all seiners. Rather, each seiner constructs his own version of the natural phases of a set. Figure 1 illustrates the segmentations of three crew members who worked together. The labels of the segments are their own phrasings. Capitalized labels indicate expressions that are also common jargon. An expression in quotation marks signifies that the seiner's label for the segment derives from the jargon although he did not do the work so specified. For example, John used "pursing" as a segment label even though he did not purse, and Darrell used "hauling gear" but did not do this work himself.

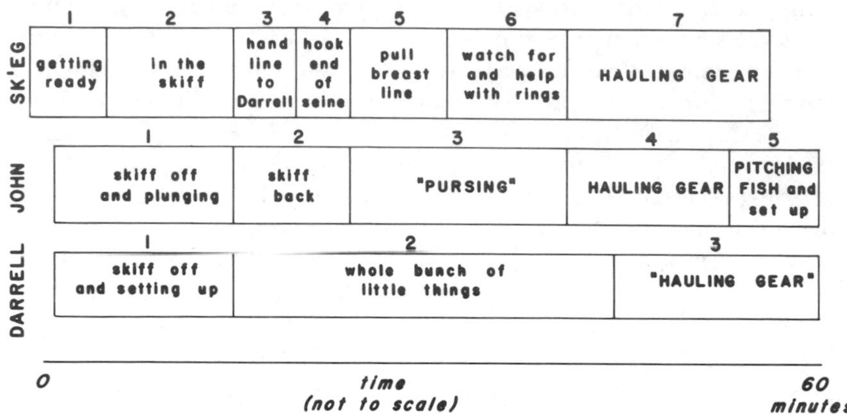

Figure 1. Varying Segmentations of "Making a Set" by Three Members of the Same Crew

The diversity depicted in Figure 1 runs counter to two rather widely held views in anthropology: (a) that cognitive sharing is a prerequisite for successful social interaction and even more so for cooperative activities, and (b) that cognitive organization is simply internalized collective representations. Why would seiners working on the same boat, having to coordinate their individual work efforts with one another, develop different representations of the natural phases of seining? We have already seen a functional motivation for constructing *some* segmentation, but why would segments differ even in their temporal boundaries from one crew member to another?

Especially during one's first season there is a strong element of faith on the part of the rookie that the system is good and not itself the source of fouling. When fouling does occur, the good rookie blames himself and not the tradition. This strong sentiment is most often expressed as the belief that so long as each person does his work, everything will go right. Of course, this presumes that the division of labor has covered all necessary work and that the boat's equipment holds together. The point is that a crew member's faith in the seining tradition frees him to wear blinders, to fixate on just his own responsibilities. This attitude partially accounts for the variation in segmentations because it has the effect of isolating one's own work from that of the crew as a whole. Thus, although one's work must articulate at many points with others', the cognitive organization of one's work is a private concern. So long as a seiner gets his work done properly and in time, how he organizes his routine does not concern anyone else.

Two factors—faith in the seining tradition and the functional advantage of multileveled cognitive organization—make it appropriate and wise, respectively, for a crew member to segment *his job routine* into phases. What remains to be explained is why seiners construct the segments they do and why each feels his is the natural way of breaking the whole process into episodes.

Normally, if a classification is natural, one would expect others to share it. Yet, as already noted, there is variation in what is perceived as natural, even among people working closely together in a collective activity. To understand how the various segmentations can all appear to be the natural way of carving seining, i.e. at its joints, one must realize also that: (a) no one talks about these things in naturally occurring situations; rather, they are brought into the public sphere only by questioning; (b) no one would argue the correctness of his own version over other versions; and (c) each segmentation is natural in terms of the organization of a single crew member's routine, and it only partially pertains to and derives from that routine's relations to the collective work. As job routines vary, so do the segmentations. Figure 1 illustrates this point: Darrell, Sk'eg, and John did different things while making a set, and their segmentations, their personal representations, reflect these differences (see Gatewood 1978:134-50 for detailed descriptions of the various job routines). The same point is supported another way by comparing one person's segmentations from different seasons when he had different routines.

As illustrated in Figure 2, my segmentation of making a set the

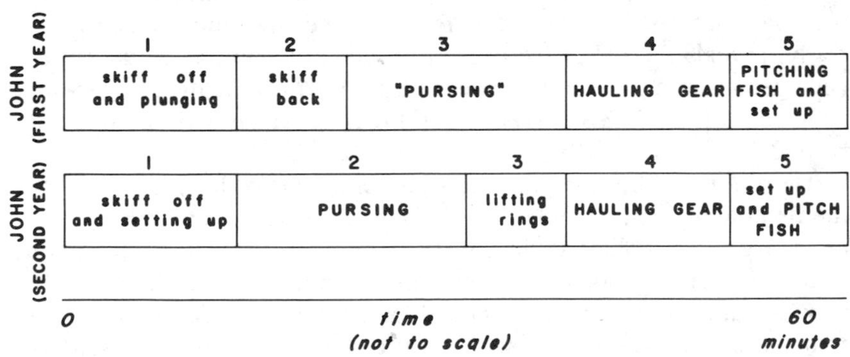

Figure 2. Varying Segmentations of "Making a Set" by the Same Crew Member from Two Consecutive Seining Seasons on the Same Boat

second year was rather different from that of the first year. Because I was deck boss the second season, my first segment was dominated by the responsibility to make sure everything was prepared for the skiff's return rather than by the task of plunging. Also, since I was pursing on the inside drum of the power winch, I felt that pursing began almost immediately on the skiff's arrival and that pursing was the dominant job of that time period. By contrast, in my first season I had many little jobs associated with the skiff's return (getting the boat tow line through the davit pulley, etc.), and pursing was merely a heuristic for the third time segment, after the skiff had gotten clear of the set. The other differences shown in Figure 2 are similarly related to differences in my job responsibilities one year compared to the next.

The diversity in segmentations is thus understandable as deriving from differences in job routines. Each crew member has his own job routine, and this is reflected in his segmentation of it. The question arises whether two people having the same routine would thereby also have the same segmentation. In other words, is there a one-to-one correspondence between job routine and segmentation? My data are insufficient to answer this, but my feeling is that the relation is many-many. As Spiro (1951:37-41) argues at a general level each person enters a situation with a perhaps unique history, and that history is vital to understanding the person's response. Therefore, merely having the same job routine—in itself an unlikely happenstance—would not necessarily predict having the same segmentation.

Segmentations function to organize all the little tasks each seiner does and thereby facilitate knowing what do to next. They are not directly reflected in a seiner's narrative account of what happens while making a set. Such an account (for example, the one offered previously) reveals the collective representations of seining—how seiners represent seining to one another—but not necessarily the personal representations. Personal representations organize actions, not narratives.

Despite the difference between personal and collective, some segments take at least their labels, if not their precise temporal boundaries, from the collective jargon. Furthermore, the process of constructing segmentations involves an interaction between the collective representations and the specifics of one's routine. Hence, I suggest that seiners construct their segmentations as some kind of resolution between two quite distinct modes of cognitive organization. These two modes are:

1. *Socially standardized but vague jargon.* The collective representations of the work (encoded in the jargon and processually revealed

in narrators' accounts) are learned first. They are ontogenetically prior to familiarity with the actual work of seining. They serve to organize the process as a whole into functional phases according to how the crew, as a collectivity, manipulates the seine. These collective representations are public and verbal. They are the terms in which seiners represent seining to each other. But such representations lack concreteness. They impose analytical distinctions and create temporal phases that are clearly understandable but not experientially vivid action segments.

2. *Specifics of a given job routine.* These are variable, both from crew member to crew member and from year to year for the same person. The components of job routines are initially felt as little tasks, discrete and coherent action units, which are organized in simple linear sequence. These little tasks may or may not be labeled (in either external or internal speech), but it is in terms of these that seining is actually done. Despite their vividness and subjective definiteness as chunks of action, they do not provide any sense of the process as a whole.

Resolving these two modes is not simply a matter of mapping the set of little tasks into the functional phases of a narrator's account. If it were, then each crew member's segmentation would have the same number of segments and the boundaries of segments would be mutually aligned because seiners give remarkably comparable renditions in their narrative accounts of what happens when seining. However the resolution occurs, it happens during the rookie season. In subsequent seasons there is a tendency to modify prior segmentations directly rather than to repeat the constructive process anew. For example, when I started my second season, I did not begin at the beginning: I was not a rookie again. Instead, I assimilated my new job routine with existing segments and accommodated discrepancies as necessary. Figure 2 illustrates this in an oblique way: the temporal boundaries between Segments 1 and 2, 3 and 4, and 4 and 5 remained constant from the first year to the second despite substantive changes in the segments themselves.

To this point, I have spoken of segments only as categories of time and action. But they have properties above and beyond those deriving from the whole-part relation vis-à-vis the little tasks they organize. Focusing on temporal boundaries is the easiest way to demonstrate diversity and highlight their categorical qualities. However, segments are differentiated from one another substantively as well. They cohere as *psychological* units in the following ways:

1. *A segment has temporal continuity.* A segment does not occur, subside, and recur in the same set. Although there may be affinities

between portions of different segments, a segment is a temporally continuous episode within the process of making a set.

2. *A segment has a characteristic emotional tone or ethos.* The characteristic emotional tone is a regular part of a segment's performance. It is also active, though less intensely, when reliving the segment in memory. Part of the awareness of a segment comes from its specific, fairly regular mixture of emotions. (In saying a segment has a characteristic ethos, I refer to its psychological manifestation within the individual and not to the tone of crew interactions during that period of time.)

3. *A segment has a characteristic unified action mode.* A unified action mode, once fully developed, constitutes a fluid fabric in time. The person is aware of "getting ready" to enter into such a mode and is aware of "emerging" from it. But when engaged in its characteristic activities, he will be unconscious of it. The little tasks within a segment flow smoothly into one another and only rarely require conscious effort to remember what follows. By contrast, at the boundaries of segments, one typically has to think about where he is in the set and reorient psychologically to the upcoming, next segment. The little tasks within a segment are felt to be in some significant sense the same kind of work.

There are intermediate and different kinds of cognitive structures ranging in scope between the segment and the little tasks. Some of these are described elsewhere (Gatewood 1978:470-75). Here I have concentrated on distinguishing segments as a level of cognitive structuring and on tracing their developmental sequence and consequences. A segment is a coherent, not necessarily shared, psychologically felt unit of behavior that functions to organize small-scale actions. The organizing function is accomplished in at least several ways. First, segments categorize little tasks in time. This relation of part to whole and the concomitant hierarchical organization make knowing what to do next while seining much easier. Second, segments relate little tasks to large-scale and often causal understandings of the seining operation. So long as the little tasks remain in their initial string-of-beads organization, they have little, if any, subjective significance as purposive events. With the development of a segmentation, however, the causal significance of each little task is easier to discern, both in terms of its special and isolated function and in its effect in combination with other jobs. Third, segments facilitate comprehension of the temporal interrelations among different job routines on the same boat and thereby improve crew coordination.

Conclusions

From the foregoing, several points emerge that extend beyond the confines of Alaskan salmon seining. Seining is a convenient example in which I can document interindividual variation in cognitive organization despite a common core of collective representations. In similar fashion, though from less grandiose circumstances, most of my actions are cognitively organized by unlabeled and largely unreflected upon categories of behavior that are not necessarily shared with other participants in my culture. When I ride a bicycle, brush my teeth, smoke a pipe, or play pool, I do not think these actions in words; rather, I do them in terms of unconscious action sequences. By reflecting upon these actions, I am able to recognize the existence of psychological events and episodes that would otherwise go unnoticed. Further, I am capable of formulating linguistic expressions to designate these hitherto unconscious flows of thought and action. But both the recognition and the labeling are capabilities independent of the actions themselves.

A focus on standardized linguistic behavior does not necessarily capture the pertinent cognitive phenomena underlying actions unless one assumes: (a) that language encodes all that is important in action, and/or (b) that collective representations are the basis of each person's cognitive organization—that there is cognitive sharing owing to a common ontogenetic development from language to action segmentation. My experience with and account of seining belies both of the suppositions. Not all cognitive categories are linguistically encoded.

In seining, I was provided with a crude cognitive map of making a set before the work commenced. Then I became familiar with the work itself and found it consisted of an incomprehensible array of little tasks. I had words for meaningless actions, and I had meaningful actions with no words. This was the initial state of affairs. As I reflected upon my work, struggling to improve my mastery, I constructed a personal representation of my routine. This personal mode of portraying seining to myself became linguistically formulated (primarily in inner speech) and even incorporated some of the collective representations. But it remained a *personal* construct, not equivalent to the collective mode of representing the work when conversing with others. Because the cognitive organization of work may differ from its collective representations, interindividual differences are free to arise.

Differences in cognitive organization do not impede collective action. As Wallace (1961) argues generally and I have described for one case, social life is a matter of orchestrating diversity, not replicating uniformity. Making a set together, coordinating work sequences, does not depend upon shared understandings of what is happening. The development of a seiner's cognitive organization is directed not by some transcendental need to share meanings but by the practical constraints of coordinating his actions with those of his fellows. His actions, and theirs, speak louder than words.

Accounting for action is the problem for cognitive sciences. Thinking, speaking, moving are all forms of action: they are dynamic processes whose specific forms are susceptible to culturing. Here I have concentrated on but a small part of this bigger problem; I have focused on how a person represents his actions to himself. Actions are underlain by personal rather than collective representations. The constituent cognitive structures may or may not be labeled, and, if labeled, these may or may not derive from collective speech forms. Further, cognitive structures, like more observable behaviors, transpire. Hence, in any depiction or diagram of cognitive phenomena there should always be a time line (Witz 1976, Witz and Easley 1975), and we must collect data using methods that record the temporal aspects of thoughts and actions. Congruent with this view, I suggest we change our analytical language habits. Rather than speaking of ideas, concepts, categories, and links, we should speak of flows, contours, intensities, and resonances. By including the temporal dimension in descriptions of cognitive phenomena, our models will explicitly preserve the fundamental temporal properties of the referent psychological behavior and, thereby, be working toward a reconciliation of knowledge and action.

NOTE

I would like to thank Catherine Cameron, Mary Douglas, Robert Rosenwein, and David Schenck for their critical comments on earlier versions of this paper. Janet Dougherty, the editor of this volume, was especially helpful in offering suggestions and encouragements. The general way of thinking about cognition manifest in this paper derives from ideas of Klaus Witz and F. K. Lehman, though, of course, they are not responsible for how I have interpreted them.

REFERENCES

Agar, Michael

1974 Talking about Doing: Lexicon and Event. *Language in Society* 3:83-89.

1975 Cognition and Events. In M. Sanches and B. Blount, eds., *Socio-*

cultural Dimensions of Language Use, pp. 41-56. New York: Academic Press.

Arbib, Michael A.

1970 Cognition—A Cybernetic Approach. In P. Garvin, ed., *Cognition: A Multiple View,* pp. 331-48. New York: Spartan Books.

Axten, Nick, and Thomas J. Fararo

1977 The Information Processing Representation of Institutionalized Social Action. In P. Krishnan, ed., *Mathematical Models of Sociology,* pp. 35-77. Sociological Review Monograph no. 24. Hanley, Great Britain: J. H. Brookes.

Birdwhistell, Ray L.

1970 *Kinesics and Context: Essays on Body Motion Communication.* Philadelphia: University of Pennsylvania Press.

Bock, Philip K.

1980 *Continuities in Psychological Anthropology: A Historical Introduction.* San Francisco: W. H. Freeman.

Browning, Robert J.

1974 *Fisheries of the North Pacific: History, Species, Gear and Processes.* Anchorage: Alaska Northwest Publishing.

Casson, Ronald W.

1981 General Introduction. In R. Casson, ed., *Language, Culture, and Cognition: Anthropological Perspectives,* pp. 1-10. New York: Macmillan.

Chapple, Eliot D.

1970 *Culture and Biological Man: Explorations in Behavioral Anthropology.* New York: Holt, Rinehart and Winston.

Chomsky, Noam

1957 *Syntactic Structures.* The Hague: Mouton.

1965 *Aspects of the Theory of Syntax.* Cambridge: M.I.T. Press.

Condon, W. S.

1979 Neonatal Entrainment and Enculturation. In M. Bullowa, ed., *Before Speech: The Beginnings of Interpersonal Communication,* pp. 131-48. New York: Cambridge University Press.

Condon, W. S., and W. D. Ogston

1967 A Segmentation of Behavior. *Journal of Psychiatric Research* 5:221-35.

Fischer, Kurt W.

1980 A Theory of Cognitive Development: The Control and Construction of Hierarchies of Skills. *Psychological Review* 87:447-531.

Gatewood, John B.

1978 Fishing, Memory, and the Stability of Culture Complexes. Ph.D. dissertation, University of Illinois, Urbana-Champaign.

1983a Deciding Where to Fish: The Skipper's Dilemma in Southeast Alaskan Salmon Seining. In M. L. Miller, special ed., *Culture and Marine Affairs.* Theme issue of *Coastal Zone Management Journal* 10:347-67.

1983b Loose Talk: Linguistic Competence and Recognition Ability. *American Anthropologist* 85:378-87.
1984 Cooperation, Competition, and Synergy: Information-Sharing Groups among Southeast Alaskan Salmon Seiners. *American Ethnologist* 11:350-70.

Goodglass, Harold
1980 Disorders of Naming Following Brain Injury. *American Scientist* 68:647-55.

Keesing, Roger M.
1974 Theories of Culture. *Annual Review of Anthropology* 3:73-97.

Kendon, Adam
1970 Movement Coordination in Social Interaction: Some Examples Described. *Acta Psychologica* 32:101-25.
1973 The Role of Visible Behavior in the Organization of Social Interaction. In M. von Cranach and I. Vine, eds., *Social Communication and Movement: Studies of Interaction and Expression in Man and Chimpanzees,* pp. 29-74. New York: Academic Press.

Kieras, David E.
1981 Knowledge Representation in Cognitive Psychology. In L. Cobb and R. M. Thrall, eds., *Mathematical Frontiers of the Social and Policy Sciences,* pp. 5-36. Boulder, Colo.: Westview Press.

Laboratory of Comparative Human Cognition
1978 Cognition as a Residual Category in Anthropology. *Annual Review of Anthropology* 7:51-69.

Langdon, Stephen J.
1977 Technology, Ecology, and Economy: Fishing Systems in Southeast Alaska. Ph.D. dissertation, Stanford University.

Lucy, John A., and Richard A. Shweder
1979 Whorf and His Critics: Linguistic and Nonlinguistic Influences on Color Memory. *American Anthropologist* 81:581-615.

Miller, George A., Eugene Galanter, and Karl H. Pribram
1960 *Plans and the Structure of Behavior.* New York: Holt, Rinehart and Winston.

Palmer, Stephen E.
1978 Fundamental Aspects of Cognitive Representation. In E. Rosch and B. Lloyd, eds., *Cognition and Categorization,* pp. 259-303. Hillsdale, N.J.: Lawrence Erlbaum Associates.

Rosch, Eleanor, et al.
1976 Basic Objects in Natural Categories. *Cognitive Psychology* 8:382-439.

Rumelhart, David E., and Andrew Ortony
1977 The Repesentation of Knowledge in Memory. In R. Anderson, R. Spiro, and W. Montague, eds., *Schooling and the Acquisition of Knowledge,* pp. 99-135. Hillsdale, N.J.: Lawrence Erlbaum Associates.

Schank, Roger C., and Robert P. Abelson
1977 *Scripts, Plans, Goals and Understanding.* Hillsdale, N.J.: Lawrence Erlbaum Associates.

Simon, Herbert A.
1973 The Organization of Complex Systems. In H. Pattee, ed., *Hierarchy Theory: The Challenge of Complex Systems,* pp. 3-27. New York: George Braziller.

Spiro, Melford E.
1951 Culture and Personality: The Natural History of a False Dichotomy. *Psychiatry* 14:19-46.

Vygotsky, L. S.
1962 *Thought and Language.* Trans. and ed. E. Hanfmann and G. Vakar. Cambridge: M.I.T. Press.

Wallace, Anthony F. C.
1961 *Culture and Personality.* New York: Random House.

Witz, Klaus G.
1976 Conceptualizing Behavioral Development. In *The Developing Individual in a Changing Word,* vol. 1: *Historical and Cultural Issues,* ed. K. Riegl and J. Meacham, pp. 79-88. Chicago: Aldine.

Witz, Klaus G., and J. A. Easley, Jr.
1975 A New Approach to Cognition. Manuscript. Champaign: Committee on Culture and Cognition, University of Illinois.

10

Imitating Ban Chiang Pottery: Toward a Cognitive Theory of Replication

Penny Van Esterik

1

"Hey, lady, want to buy a three-thousand-year-old Ban Chiang painted pot?"

"No? Well, how about a Ban Chiang pot with a pretty new design?"

"No? How about a new pot with an even better Ban Chiang design?"

"No? Then, how about a Ban Chiang T-shirt?"

(Bangkok, October 1973)

This young salesman in a popular tourist shopping center in Bangkok is attempting to sell more than illicit antiquities from northeast Thailand. He is trying to sell a system of design that has been identified as Ban Chiang, named after the village of Ban Chiang in Udorn Province, northeast Thailand, where painted pottery of great age bearing these designs was first discovered, in the 1960s. The site has recently been excavated by the Thai Fine Arts Department and the University of Pennsylvania Museum, taking over from pot hunters and amateur excavators who threatened to destroy the site entirely. Summarizing from the brief reports published (cf. Gorman and Charoenwongsa 1976): Ban Chiang was occupied from about 3500 B.C. to 250 B.C. by rice farmers skilled in bronze metallurgy and ceramic production. Excavation of the low cemetery mound revealed a ritual pattern of extended burials with extensive grave goods, including bronze axes and moulds, crucibles, bracelets and wire necklaces, iron implements, pottery vessels, animal and human figurines, and substantial quantities of animal bone (Higham 1975:257). The decorative techniques used on the pottery change through time. Black incised and burnished pottery is earliest, followed by cord marked, incised and painted ware, red on buff painted pottery, and finally a cruder red slipped and burnished ware (Gorman and Charoenwongsa 1976:26). This pottery was directly associated with human burials and may be considered funerary ware. As the supply of authentic painted pottery from this region dwindled and as laws restricting the sale and transport of antiquities became more strictly enforced, production of forgeries increased both in the vicinity of Ban Chiang and in Bangkok.

The words of the street vendor appear to be of little concern to an anthropologist studying design, since they indicate little or nothing about the vendor's knowledge of Ban Chiang designs. On the other hand, the quotation reveals two assumptions that he or his superior holds about the nature of design. First, the statement indicates that he or his superior can recognize Ban Chiang designs when they see them on painted pottery vessels. Second, it indicates that someone has gone beyond mere recognition to create a new and "better" Ban Chiang design. Both recognition and imitation imply that design is an organized system of knowledge.

Elsewhere (Van Esterik 1976) I have tried to define this system of knowledge in some detail based on examinations of Thai collections of Ban Chiang painted pottery, arguing for the need to abstract a cognitive system, a system of knowledge and belief that underlies behavior (Chomsky 1968:4). A cognitive theory of design production looks at the possible theories that artists might construct for creating and interpreting their artistic behavior. Although these theories remain unavailable to the analyst, and in large part to the artists themselves, they should be acknowledged in the analyst's explanation of design. By hypothesizing that an artist constructs a theory utilizing design rules of the kind suggested here, an analyst can talk about things that are important in a study of artistic behavior, namely the range of acceptability of designs, possible ambiguous representations, the source of variation in designs, innovation, and imitation. Here I want to examine the process of imitation using modern Ban Chiang vessels painted in the 1970s. While the subject of the forging of antiquities is interesting in its own right, my primary objective in this paper is to suggest ways that imitation can further our understanding of human cognitive processes.

2

> "The essential feature of art forgery is not imitation but the intention to deceive."
>
> (Tietze 1948)

Anthropologists have paid scant attention to understanding the cultural process of imitation. Imitation can best be explored as one expression of the process of cultural transmission and replication of codes or patterns from one individual to another through time and space. A thorough study of the process of imitation should include examination of socialization, acculturation, mimicry, parody, and archaism, all processes related to cultural transmission. However, in this preliminary effort attention will be focused on authenticity and the intent to deceive.

The research problem requires a discussion of recognizing, evaluating, and classifying imitations. Following a description of the production of imitations, we can suggest ways to link this process to broader issues in cognitive studies.[1]

Recognizing Imitations

During the course of research on collections of painted pottery from Ban Chiang, I had occasion to make judgments that certain designs were imitations of real Ban Chiang designs. Both modern artists and unscrupulous salesmen were inspired to recreate these designs for a variety of reasons. Yet recognition of fake designs on my part was an educated guess. Once I had grasped the overall design principles, it became impossible to recall and retrieve the parts and arrangements of the design that triggered the recognition. As I learned what to look for, I became more able to discriminate between designs but less able to identify my reasons. Recognition may have been triggered through identification of a set of defining attributes, or it may have been an all-or-nothing, seat-of-the-pants intuitive evaluation. Hardin's work (1977:112) in another context confirmed a similar problem. Individuals asked to identify the work of other artists in a Tarascan village were able to identify the artist's work but could not say how they were able to identify the painter of any particular vessel. Any time that I failed to recognize a forged design, I would unavoidably be broadening the definition of the "authentic" design class. The imitations, then, influenced the analysis and interpretation of the authentic designs. Each time a forgery is mistaken for an authentic design, it becomes easier for another similar forgery to be included as a member of a particular design class. In the following analysis I will be discussing both modern copies of old pots and pots decorated in the style of Ban Chiang.

The Real Thing

Most vessels photographed in 1973-74 were from collections made in the region of Ban Chiang in the late sixties and early seventies. Very few of these collections contained repainted vessels, although I believe that most vessels for sale in Southeast Asia and elsewhere now have been repainted. This essay is not based on the authentic Ban Chiang vessels, which are illustrated and described elsewhere (Van Esterik 1976, 1979; You Di 1972; Gorman and Charoenwongsa 1976). Nevertheless, the following points should assist the reader in following the argument.

Ban Chiang painted pottery is commonly beige slipped with a dark red painted design on body, neck, or pedestal segments. The pedestal and neck segments are decorated separately with simple band designs. The body designs are described by reference to a limited number of operations that produce design fields. Most significant for purposes of classification are symmetry operations, which are clearly described in Shepard (1971) and Washburn (1977). Briefly, designs are classified according to whether they are based on the motion of reflection (making a mirror image), or rotation of a design element around a pot, or by the combination of reflection and rotation to produce radial figures.[2] Most Ban Chiang designs are composed of asymmetric spirals, concentric designs exhibiting bilateral symmetry, and sigmoid or curvilinear lozenge designs that utilize the most complex symmetry operations possible (class 7). Structurally, the designs are elaborated bands with upper and lower boundaries elaborated.

Evaluating Imitations

How do imitation Ban Chiang painted pots differ from real Ban Chiang painted pots? While there are technical tests for distinguishing age from appearance of age, the problem of time is more complex, for new designs are painted on old pots, old designs appear on new pots, new designs appear on new pots, and old designs on old pots. How can genuine and originals be evaluated? To simplify our problem, we can identify two periods of artistic activity: T_1 is the second millennium B.C.; T_2 is the 1970s. But we have no adequate stylistic test to decide when a design was created.

Many imitations can be identified by the materials from which they are constructed. Cheap souvenirs are usually newly constructed from local clays and modern paints. Designs may also be reproduced on paper, plastic, or cloth. But new designs may also be applied to old vessels or modifications of authentic vessels. Another criterion is cost, with authentic vessels costing up to $5,000 and imitations usually available much more cheaply. Yet this criterion is also unreliable, since some vessels with modern designs command equally high prices, are treated as authentic, and are displayed in museums.

The intention of the artist is another dimension of contrast. But intentions are not readily observable in the objects themselves and have to be inferred from social interaction. The original Ban Chiang artists produced painted designs on vessels that had meaning as parts of burial rituals. In Mary Douglas's terms, these painted objects were ritual adjuncts (1979:65). Objects with "Ban Chiang" designs are currently produced for sale. These modern artists do not intend to produce ritual objects. Modern artists creating Ban Chiang designs have two distinct tasks at hand. The first task is to create a product that will deceive buyers into thinking they have purchased authentic Ban Chiang vessels, an illegal activity. The second task is to create a product that will remind buyers of Ban Chiang painted pottery. Such imitations are genuine souvenirs. While artists may not intend to deceive their audience, middlemen might make false claims for the products they sell. Thus products that are produced with no intention to deceive may become "forgeries without forgers" in the hands of salespersons.

The last dimension of contrast concerns the design structure itself. This has proved the most difficult dimension to use in differentiating authentic and imitation designs for both theoretical and practical reasons. I analyzed the design structure of Ban Chiang painted pottery in my thesis (1976), producing a set of rules of design production that could be used to generate three classes of Ban Chiang designs (spiral, concentric, sigmoid). Although the imitation designs were important for the production of design rules, I did not explore their design structure in detail there. Below, I outline briefly the first two steps in the analysis of Ban Chiang design, which provided the background necessary for the third step, leading up to the present essay.

Step one:

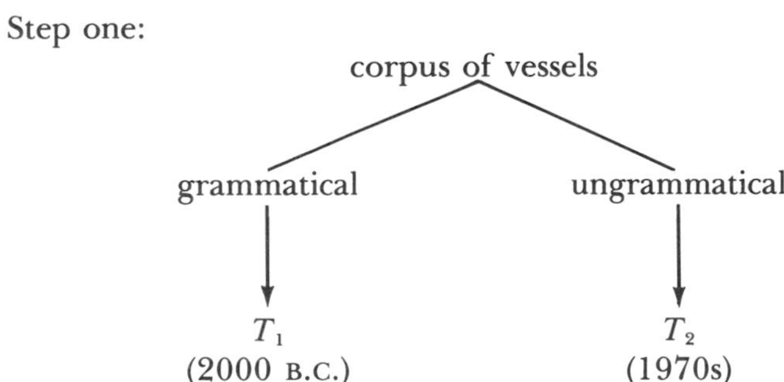

Based on a linguistic analogy, designs that could be interpreted by reference to a proposed theory of design production were called grammatical; those that could not were considered ungrammatical. I attempted to separate vessels with painted designs into authentic and forged on the basis of grammaticality.[3] This proved impossible, since the proposed rules of well-formedness failed to distinguish authentic from forged vessels. Both grammatical and ungrammatical occurred in both time periods.

Step two:

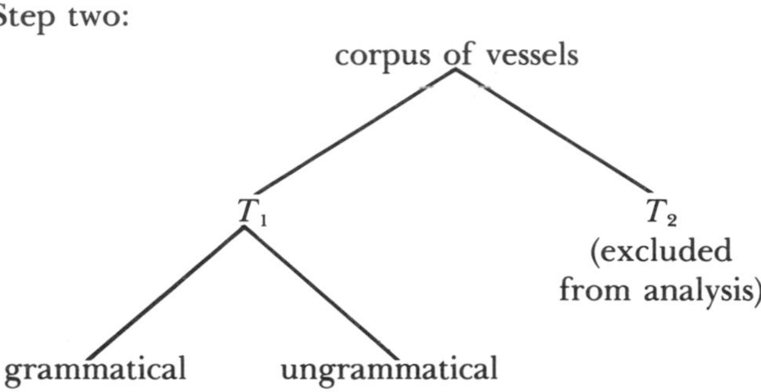

In this second step I used modern designs simply to suggest and evaluate possible design strategies that a Ban Chiang artist might have used to construct the authentic Ban Chiang designs. In this way the existence of imitations provided a natural experiment for testing design strategies, since some imitation designs broke specifiable rules of design production. Modern imitations were excluded from the design analysis and briefly described prior to step three (Van Esterik 1981).

Step three:

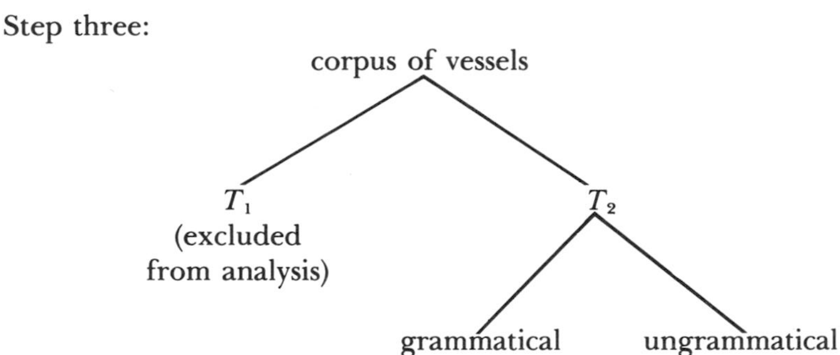

In this essay attention has shifted back to these modern vessels and designs, excluding the original designs from analysis except as they illustrate an argument about a modern design. But T_1 remains the reference point for evaluating the grammaticality of the modern designs. Ungrammatical designs made in the seventies may utilize design fields, design elements, or symmetry operations that differ from the original Ban Chiang designs. These changes may result from deliberate rule deletion, addition, or transformation, or from an incomplete understanding of the original design. In addition, some artists may intend to innovate and create a totally new design theory, producing a souvenir that is labeled Ban Chiang but is otherwise unrelated to Ban Chiang designs.

In evaluating these designs, I realize that I still fall short of constructing a testable theory to differentiate real from all imitation designs.[4] In fact, it is possible that I have misattributed designs. This present attempt is an intermediate step to explain imitation designs. Using external criteria (interviews with artists, wet paint, statements of salesmen, manufacturing techniques, etc.), I am taking as a starting point a number of vessels that display the artistic efforts of modern artists in order to examine the process of imitation.

Classifying Imitations

Archaeologists are concerned with categorizing objects to answer certain questions about cultural processes. With no living informants, they cannot emphasize the relations among named categories, but they can and do create taxonomies based on other criteria. When biological principles have been extended to nonbiological classification of objects such as cars and tools (Brown 1976), the resulting taxonomies have been criticized for being counterintuitive, arbitrary, unrelated to behavior, and unproductive (Van Esterik 1978:404-5, Durrenberger and Morrison 1979:408-9). Analogous arguments by archaeologists about the construction of artifact typologies contrast the empiricist view that artifacts have inherent meaning discoverable by an archaeologist with the positivist view that classificatory systems are imposed by the investigator (Hill and Evans 1972:233, 252). In order to address the problem of imitations, I will classify modern Ban Chiang designs to produce working definitions. Categories cannot explain processes, but they can be used to clarify discussions of complex questions.

	no intention to deceive	intention to deceive
grammatical designs	replica	fake (forgery)
ungrammatical designs	reproduction	copy

Replicas are constructed in a new medium and are not intended by the artist to represent authentic Ban Chiang vessels. The designs are not intentionally innovative and attempt to reproduce Ban Chiang designs as faithfully as possible.

Reproductions are constructed in a new medium and are legal souvenirs or reminders of Ban Chiang painted pottery. The designs are intentionally innovative but reminiscent of Ban Chiang designs.

Fakes (or forgeries) utilize old unpainted vessels from Ban Chiang or elsewhere. They are painted to reproduce the design on one particular pot. Both artist and salespersons intend to represent the objects as authentic Ban Chiang painted pottery.

Copies utilize old unpainted vessels from Ban Chiang and elsewhere. They may also be constructed from new materials. They are identified as authentic Ban Chiang painted pottery and are innovative in design structure.

Imitations may occasionally be used as a general term to refer to fakes, copies, replicas, and reproductions. The boundaries of these categories are permeable, since there are degrees of grammaticality and degrees of intentionality.

3

> "If fools did not go to market, cracked pots and false wares would not be sold."
>
> (Jean Le Malchanceux)[5]

Reproductions

We know most about the process of manufacturing legal souvenirs of Ban Chiang painted pottery. The most successful enterprise in the mid-seventies was Ban Chiang Products, founded by the trained artist Krachang Chansang. He recognized the artistic and commercial potential of these designs and provided inexpensive, colorful, and legal souvenirs by painting what he called Ban Chiang designs on new vases, ash trays, water jars, posters, and clothes. Vessels were made to his specifications in a village northeast of Bangkok, near Khorat. The vessel shapes and designs were chosen by Krachang from articles illustrating and describing the vessels (e.g. You Di 1972). Although he began by matching an appropriate design to vessel shape, he is largely guided by what sells best. He draws the primary design unit of the body first in pencil, paints it, and then fills in the secondary designs or fillers later, or gives it to his apprentice to complete. Spirals and sigmoid units he finds most difficult, and it took him over a year to be able to draw spirals freehand. One complex design based on sigmoid units took him so long to construct that he decided to drop the design from his repertoire and develop a vastly simplified version which his female assistant can mass produce. He does not have a catalog of primary design units and fillers, but his work is analytical to the extent that he recognizes the need to "break down" and "figure out" the designs before they can be easily or accurately copied.

It would be unfair to Krachang's enterprising spirit not to mention the Ban Chiang clothing he designed. He paints the designs with washable red and black paint on buff cotton cloth and constructs dresses, jackets, and bikinis for sale in tourist shops. The designs are often applied to inappropriately shaped design fields, but small fillers often resemble design elements popular in the painted pottery tradition.

In the mid-seventies his products were prominently displayed in department stores, tourist shops, and government craft stores. Produced in a new medium and quite innovative, these products are intended to remind people of Ban Chiang, not deceive them. It is unlikely anyone could mistake the wheel-turned pottery with its bold red and beige designs for authentic Ban Chiang painted pottery. Nevertheless, there are points of resemblance in these reproductions.

In the vessels illustrated in Figure 1, Krachang has used spirals on necks, pedestals, and bodies, making no attempt to replicate the design layout of Ban Chiang vessels. On Vessel 178, for example, he uses double spirals on the neck band, but the linking lines are much longer than a Ban Chiang artist's. But on the body of the vessel the spirals are not linked at all. A double line runs around and between the spirals but stops (with an unacceptable line abutment) without ever enclosing acceptable spiral units. He has, however, drawn enclosure lines separating the three decorative zones of the vessel, a common operation in the construction of Ban Chiang designs when the design is against a buff background. Krachang has reversed the strategy by defining unpainted enclosures against a red background, instead of the more common painted line against a buff background.

On Vessel 199 there are no lines linking the spirals, but a field is created between adjacent spirals. This Krachang fills with an appropriate filler, although the surface representation is much more static and balanced than spiral designs with lines between them. The neck design is his own simplification of a Ban Chiang meander. The pedestal provides a large decorative zone filled with an inappropriate concentric design. A common vessel shape alteration in original Ban Chiang vessels is the enlargement of the neck segment. Krachang reverses this and often enlarges the pedestal segment. This vessel is about 40 cm high, while the remaining vessels are only about half that size.

It is not hard to imagine the skill that Krachang had to acquire to

Figure 1. Ban Chiang Spiral Designs. Top row, original vessels; middle and bottom rows: Ban Chiang reproductions.

render the fine-line double spirals of Vessel 173. Again, the spirals are not linked, although the fillers are an acceptable alternative for spiral designs. They are common in concentric designs and Krachang borrows from that model of design production just as the original Ban Chiang artists interpreted some spiral designs by reference to a concentric model of design production.[6]

Vessel 171 utilizes the multiple-line spiral with the lines converging on a single point. Note, too, the "shadowing" or perspective-line shading that is common in multiple-line designs. The band above the double spiral band on the neck is a recognizable Ban Chiang filler, as is the hooked "heart" motif on the pedestal. Krachang has a good stock of these low-level design details, and they give an aura of authenticity to his designs in spite of his great innovations in design layout.

Replicas

Other companies produced Ban Chiang souvenirs for a wealthier market. In 1974 at least one factory was producing a glazed celadon product advertised as Ban Chiang celadon. This attractive green glazed ware does not replicate the vessel shapes of Ban Chiang painted pottery. However, the designs themselves are accurate simplifications of Ban Chiang designs. It is possible that the designs which conform most closely to those on authentic vessels are produced of materials which most clearly differentiate the modern souvenir from the authentic vessel. One wonders what else this artist does with his talents when not sketching designs on celadon ware.[7]

The utilitarian pottery in use in the villages in the vicinity of Ban Chiang has been affected by the popularity of the prehistoric pottery in the region. Local potters added the shapes of the prehistoric pottery to their domestic inventory. Some vessels resembled the black incised vessels that predated the painted pottery in the region. One potter reported that his customers often provided pictures of the incised design and vessel shape they preferred, and would order 20 to 50 vessels at a time. While the artist may be producing replicas for souvenirs, these customers may be trying to market the vessels as authentic. Generally, the incised designs were greatly simplified from the original geometric shapes.

Neither reproductions nor replicas are particularly profitable. Both are very reasonable in price, and the demand for these products is decreasing. In 1981 they were not displayed in department stores and rarely encountered in tourist shops. As one salesperson complained, "No one knows about Ban Chiang any more." The market for these products is closely linked to a continuing interest in and knowledge about Ban Chiang. After a flurry of articles in newspapers in the mid-seventies, the site has received less publicity. The availability of the occasional fake or copy as the number of authentic vessels on the art market decreases may serve to rekindle interest in the pottery and increase the demand for souvenirs to remind the public of Ban Chiang.

Copies

Artists with the requisite skills for reproducing Ban Chiang designs accurately are much more likely to apply their skills in the production of more profitable if illegal copies intended to deceive the buyer. While it was not difficult to discuss the design process with the artists and salespeople producing souvenirs, artists who claimed that their modern imitations were authentic old vessels were difficult or impossible to interview. For example, several knowledgeable Thais referred to the fact that students from a Bangkok art college produced excellent copies of Ban Chiang painted pottery and also repainted old vessels with Ban Chiang designs. Some antique shops in Bangkok employed artists to repaint designs on old and new pottery, and to reconstruct Ban Chiang vessels from assorted sherds, pedestals, and rims.

More artistic opportunities are available to artists who make no attempt to reproduce a particular design but, rather, produce a design "in the style of" the Ban Chiang artists. These artists inevitably put their own artistic personalities into their work, thus revealing their design preferences. They seldom follow the layout or the symmetry operations employed by the original Ban Chiang artists. Rather, modern artists have constructed their own theories of design production utilizing the primary design units (spirals, concentric units, etc.) favored by the original Ban Chiang artists. Having less experience with the symmetry operations favored by these artists, the copyists tend to simply translate design elements or use another lower-level symmetry motion, avoiding the more complex longitudinal and transverse reflection, and alternate rotation and transverse reflection, used in the original designs.

Artists with less familiarity with the original Ban Chiang layouts often produce designs that then become prototypes. They may imitate these secondary derivations in their own work and inspire other artists to follow a prototype twice removed from the original designs. These artists then are no longer interpreting Ban Chiang motifs, rather the motifs of yet another artist who is familiar with the construction of individual motifs, although not with the total design layout. This process would be of great interest to study, but artists of this caliber are reluctant to discuss their craft.

When the copyists attempt to reproduce a common motif, such as the Ban Chiang meander, their lack of familiarity with the motor habits involved in performing certain symmetry operations becomes apparent by their awkward and simplified designs. The upper body field of one group of imitations illustrates an attempt to produce a line based on bifold rotation and transverse reflection, the most complex symmetry rules, but an alternate derivation is possible for this design, based on bifold rotation. The artist who produced these imitations has used this latter, simpler derivation, building the design up from bifold rotation by the addition of suitable line segments. One advantage of higher-level symmetry rules is that the designs can also be built up from lower-level symmetry rules with no loss in design complexity to produce the same design fields. Thus a band derived from bifold rotation can also be rendered by a single, continuous, wavy line. This simplified band design is particularly appealing to copyists.

Another artist's work is characterized by careful attention to such details as line composition, background, and enclosures. He has recognized that sigmoid designs should be enclosed by a band of dentate triangles above and below the primary design unit of the body. However, he places the lower band of dentate triangles on the pedestal of his pots, not the body. The design elements are not enclosed in any higher symmetry figure. These elements are accurate fillers for sigmoid designs, but the artist has not enclosed the figures in any way, as the original Ban Chiang artists would have.

The copyists in Bangkok and the vicinity of Ban Chiang are skilled artists inspired by the uniqueness of the Ban Chiang designs and the unprecedented opportunity to dupe the purchaser, both foreign and Thai, whose curiosity has been aroused by this site.

Fakes

Fakes or forgeries are probably created both in Bangkok and the vicinity of Ban Chiang. But the artists in the village of Ban Chiang have the best opportunity for extensive contact with the authentic painted designs. They learn details of design construction from reconstructing and repairing original vessels. They paint new vessels after they are fired, or repaint old vessels that have faint or no painting visible, using the iron oxide paint nodules found in the ground along with the burials. Less skilled craftsmen modify or reconstruct vessels in order to increase their selling price. The commonest modifications include cutting the top half of restricted vessels off to form perfect unrestricted vessels, joining two pedestals together to form a complete bowl, and filing rims off smooth to sell as a perfect vessel. It is quite common to find vessels restored inaccurately, or vessels almost "created" from a mosaic of spare sherds. These latter vessels were given away free as "bonuses" to regular customers.

Artists have developed exceptional skill at rendering perfect fakes. One artist's mother reported that her son found the unpainted vessel in Ban Chiang but "knew" what design should be on it. This knowledge he gained from repairing vessels, and he was referred to as one who "understood" the designs best. Were it not for the fact that the paint was still wet, the vessel would have been photographed and described as an authentic Ban Chiang painted pot. Although technical analysis could reveal that the painting was recent, the design differs from an original Ban Chiang design in only the minutest details such as a ruler-straight line or an awkward line abutment. Even the line quality resembled that on authentic vessels, demonstrating the expertise these artists had developed by the mid-seventies.

Two additional vessels repainted by the same artist both employ a crossed link, which is an elaboration not found in the context of bulging pedestals of original Ban Chiang designs. Similarly, the vessel is composite contour, with a separate decorative zone on the neck. This alteration in the shape of the decorative zone of the body may have tempted the artist to elaborate the space with wavy line fillers, an elaboration that is also incompatible with bulging pedestals. These last two vessels may have been repaired using the wrong pedestal, or the artist may have been following a model not present in this sample. Whatever the case may be, this artist shows exceptional skill, and his work no doubt graces many museum displays. Other examples of near perfect fakes of Ban Chiang designs were found on new pots and unpainted pots from later historical periods.

4

> "When it comes his time to act he is not copyist but a fluent practitioner. Perhaps, like the learning singer of epics or chanter of sermons, he passes through an apprenticeship of imitation. But at maturity, like the best of epic singers, he is reliant not on one original, but on a competence constructed out of numerous of originals."
>
> (Glassie 1975:67)

What can the existence of imitation Ban Chiang designs tell us about cognitive processes? Goodman recognizes that fakes present practical problems for curators and collectors but concludes that the theoretical problems they raise are even more acute (1968:99). These theoretical problems can be related to concerns of cultural anthropologists, particularly those who include cognitive processes in their explanations of human behavior. For example, the existence of fake and real objects raises the issue of intracultural diversity (Pelto and Pelto 1975). To what extent are members of the same object class imitations of one another? The authors in *The Individual in Prehistory* (Hill and Gunn 1977) also emphasized individual variation in the production of objects. Similarly, Mary Douglas (1979) looks at *The World of Goods* not to categorize the objects but to understand their use as communicators and definers of social relationships.

In the study of complex design the insights of two authors provide a starting point for examining cognitive processes. In her study of Tarascan pottery Hardin (1977:111) found that individual differences in style were due to differences in the organization, content, and order of painting. Each painter possessed a slightly different theory of design, with the result that only the most skilled painters with exceptional control could deliberately copy another painter's style (1977:135). Washburn identified another problem as a result of deliberate copying of designs that was not understood. She found instances of false counterchanged designs caused by artists who did not understand that perfect counterchange requires alteration in color of the same shaped elements as well as alteration in color of any series of elements (Washburn 1977:84).

If perception is a constructive process, we expect that "the more skilled the perceiver, the more he can perceive" (Neisser 1976:93). Others (Rosch 1976, Dougherty 1978) have argued that the state of knowledge of the people who are categorizing influences the categorizing. Taking this assumption, consider first how the state of knowledge of the original artists creating the Ban Chiang designs would differ from that of the modern artists recreating related designs, and second, how these two bodies of knowledge are organized. I have argued elsewhere (Van Esterik 1976) that the original Ban Chiang artists constructed their theories of design production from observing a range of completed contemporary vessels, watching artists construct and decorate a vessel, practicing the motor habits used to paint the designs, and from hearing stated instructions, advice, or criticisms from a more accomplished artist. Their task at hand, closely linked to the cultural context in which they worked, was to produce an appropriate Ban Chiang painted vessel. Appropriateness, in this case, would be partially defined by meaning attributed to the vessel in the context of burial ritual by both artist and audience.

Each artist would have possessed technological, social, and symbolic knowledge in addition to a set of rules of design production and a set of motor habits or patterns used to make and decorate pottery. These broad patterns of knowledge could be stored as procedural knowledge. Ban Chiang artists may be expected to have shared certain cultural premises about designs and to experiment with a similar range of symmetry operations, since they would learn design production by undergoing broadly similar patterns of artistic socialization. This training might encourage them to attend to the global properties of designs (their overall appearance) as opposed to the local properties or details in isolation (Hofstadter 1979:372).

Variation among designs produced by different artists and by the same artists at different times would be expected. Like Hardin's Tarascan artists, we would expect differences in personal style and the creative manipulation of design rules. Design information, then, would be stored as plans or schemata that would enable the artist to perceive present events and store information about past ones (cf. Neisser 1976:62). These artists possessed images of finished designs and strategies for action rather than cognitive maps of designs, layouts or lists of alternative design elements. By proposing the more active construction of design theories, we can account for rule play and ambiguity in these designs (Van Esterik 1979), for both artist and audience must be able to interpret alternate representations of designs.

The modern forgers (and anthropologists or analysts) must construct their theories of design production very differently. They have the opportunity to observe either a random collection of Ban Chiang painted pottery or descriptions and illustrations of what analysts have defined as typical Ban Chiang vessels. Forgers do not have nor would they recognize a representative set of all the designs they imitate. They can acquire the motor habits necessary to produce these designs by practicing drawing design elements. Many of them gain recognition skills from reconstructing broken vessels. But they lack the opportunity to watch a living artist construct and decorate a pot or advise others on the process. Since they are removed from the cultural context that attributes religious meaning to the painted pottery, these modern artists paint for an audience that cannot provide feedback on the appropriateness of a particular burial urn. Their theories of design production are evaluated by a single standard—what sells, either as a souvenir or as an imitation of Ban Chiang painted pottery.

The artists working in the seventies to construct Ban Chiang designs have learned about these designs in a different cultural context. Their acquisition of design knowledge is undoubtedly different from the original Ban Chiang artists. One consequence of this difference is that the modern artists, regardless of their motivations, attend to different features of the designs. These modern artists lack experience with the symmetry operations preferred by the Ban Chiang artists (cf. Washburn 1977). They ignore symmetry as an organizing principle or rely on bifold rotation, the symmetry operation most easily recognized by humans (Corballis and Beale 1976:11). These modern artists may attend to different parts of the design because of differences in their experience and training.

The best of these artists possess what Berger and Luckman (1966:40) call "recipe knowledge" of designs—knowledge limited to pragmatic competence in routine performance. Artificial intelligence research might refer to this as declarative knowledge, knowledge stored explicitly as in an almanac or dictionary, acquired as a result of attention to local properties or details as opposed to global properties or overall sweeping vision (Hofstadter 1979:363, 376).

The grammatical designs produced in the seventies cannot be said to be generated from the same set of rules as the grammatical designs produced in the second millennium B.C. Instead, designs such as those on Vessel 969 and other perfect fakes are generated by efforts to replicate the original finished product. These forgeries are of particular interest to art historians. From the perspective of aesthetic theory, the designs do not "go" anywhere. The artists run no risk of artistic failure for they have no freedom of choice (cf. Meyer 1967). Perfect fakes, for example, simply follow their model slavishly, for there is only one way that the design can be duplicated exactly. And, as the discovered forger knows, there are limitless numbers of ways that the design can be altered. While the copyist has a mental image of the product he or she wants to create, or perhaps a rule-governed theory of design production distinct from that used by Ban Chiang artists, the forger works not from a mental vision or a theory but from a concrete finished object which, with great effort, can be reproduced. There is no room for variation in forgeries, but it is possible that a skillful artist could "mass produce" a number of identical perfect fakes.

The replicas and reproductions produced as souvenirs or reminders of Ban Chiang are related to the original designs in two different ways. First, they may be generated by a new set of production rules. Their connections with Ban Chiang designs are tenuous at best, often limited to the label identifying the design as Ban Chiang, the color combination of dark red on buff, or the use of the same primary design unit (e.g. spirals). Alternatively, any imitation can be made to resemble Ban Chiang designs by the addition of small design elements commonly used in the pottery. These traits which may serve to identify the design as Ban Chiang can be seen on fakes, copies, reproductions, and replicas. They represent design traits that are discrete, distinctive, and relatively simple to reproduce. That is, it is possible to achieve skill in rendering them quite quickly. They might be stored as a list of alternate design elements much as a lexicon lists words. In Neisser's (1976) terminology, they may represent landmarks in artists' cognitive maps of Ban Chiang design. It is these landmarks that serve to remind the audience of Ban Chiang or the designs on Ban Chiang painted pottery.

Modern artists are successful at producing both forgeries and souvenirs because knowledge of Ban Chiang designs is not widespread. The audience for their products has few means of evaluating the designs they see. In the face of a diminishing supply of authentic Ban Chiang painted pottery and a dearth of analysis and publicity on the painted pottery,[8] we might predict an increase in the number of fakes and copies and a decrease in the number of replicas and reproductions in the years ahead.

Faking It

One difficulty with sharing work in progress is that the author may be unable to see the forest for the trees, while the readers may be left with only a hazy outline of both. To minimize this, I will summarize the implications of this work on Ban Chiang imitations.

First, the trees . . .

1. Imitations help us view the real differently.

2. Imitations are not a single class, but must be differentiated into several categories (e.g. replicas, fakes, reproductions, copies).

3. Forgers and the original Ban Chiang artists learn about, attend to, and store knowledge of design differently.

4. A perfect fake is made from a real object model and displays a genuine Ban Chiang design.

5. Copies are made from an image of the final product plus a theory of design production that differs from the theory of the original Ban Chiang artists.

6. Replicas and reproductions are genuine souvenirs produced from knowledge of design elements without understanding the rules for combining the elements.

7. Recognition of imitation is a cognitive skill based partially on intuition concerning the total overall appearance, and partially on the identification of defining attributes.

And the forest . . .

1. Humans desire links with the past in everyday life. They are willing to accept reasonable facsimiles when the more desirable or more authentic is unobtainable. These pots are symbols of Thailand's prehistoric past. Yet they are both reconstructed and reinterpreted to communicate to an audience 3,000 years later.

2. The process whereby symbols are interpreted and reinterpreted

is observable both in the past and the present—both in material culture and in social interaction.

3. Humans regularly make judgments about whether people's behavior is genuine or forced, appropriate to a particular time and place or inappropriate.

4. Imitation, as part of the process of cultural transmission, accounts in part for stability in cultural systems.

5. But imitation should not be viewed as the opposite of creativity. For cultural innovations to be transmitted, they must be imitated. There must, then, be a close relation between imitation and creativity.

NOTES

1. I have begun an expanded treatment of this subject, placing the process of imitation more directly in the context of past anthropological theory.

2. I follow the terminology of Shepard (1971), who identifies the seven classes of regular band patterns as (1) translation, (2) longitudinal or horizontal reflection, (3) transverse or vertical reflection, (4) bifold rotation, (5) longitudinal and transverse reflection, (6) slide reflection and alternate rotation, and (7) alternate rotation and transverse reflection. Classes 5 and 7 are more complex operations and are particularly popular among the Ban Chiang artists (see Van Esterik 1979).

3. I am grateful to Charles Keller and Warren Peterson, who refused to let me sweep the imitations under the rug.

4. When site reports are available from Ban Chiang and more imitations have been identified, it may be possible to construct a more powerful theory that will differentiate real from imitation designs.

5. This quotation opens Clifford Irving's book, *Fake* (1969). It is very possible that the quote itself is a fake, since he provides no citation and I have uncovered no Jean Le Malchanceux in a superficial search.

6. See Van Esterik (1976:156). Put simply, spirals are constructed to look like concentric designs. The end of the spiral is masked and at first glance the design appears to be a concentric design.

7. I suspect that many Bangkok artists produced both legal and illegal imitations, but I have no evidence of this.

8. To date, there are no site reports from Ban Chiang. The tragic death of the principal investigator, Chester Gorman (7 June 1981), may further complicate the immense task of analysis and publication.

REFERENCES

Berger, P. L., and T. Luckmann
  1966 *The Social Construction of Reality.* Garden City, N.Y.: Doubleday.

Brown, Cecil H., et al.
  1976 Some General Principles of Biological and Non-Biological Folk Classification. *American Ethnologist* 3:73-85.

Chomsky, N.
1968 *Language and Mind.* New York: Harcourt, Brace and World.
Corballis, M. C., and I. L. Beale
1976 *The Psychology of Left and Right.* New York: John Wiley and Sons.
Dougherty, Janet W. D.
1978 Salience and Relativity in Classification. *American Ethnologist* 5:66-80.
Douglas, Mary, and B. Isherwood
1979 *The World of Goods.* New York: Basic Books.
Durrenburger, E. Paul, and John W. Morrison
1979 Letter to the editor. *American Ethnologist* 6:408-9.
Fu, Marilyn, and Shen Fu
1973 *Studies in Connoisseurship.* Art Museum, Princeton University.
Glassie, H.
1975 *Folk Housing in Middle Virginia.* Knoxville: University of Tennessee Press.
Goodman, Nelson
1968 *Languages of Art.* Indianapolis: Bobbs-Merrill.
Gorman, Chester, and Pisit Charoenwongsa
1976 Ban Chiang: A Mosaic of Impressions from the First Two Years. *Expedition* 18:14-26.
Hardin, Margaret
1977 Individual Style in San Jose Pottery Painting: The Role of Deliberate Choice. In James N. Hill and Joel Gunn, eds., *The Individual in Prehistory.* New York: Academic Press.
Higham, C. F. W.
1975 Aspects of Economy and Ritual in Prehistoric Northeast Thailand. *Journal of Archaeological Sciences* 2:245-88.
Hill, James N., and Joel Gunn, eds.
1977 *The Individual in Prehistory.* New York: Academic Press.
Hill, J. N., and R. K. Evans
1972 A Model for Classification and Typology. In D. L. Carke, ed., *Models in Archaeology.* London: Methuen.
Hofstadter, Douglas
1979 *Gödel, Escher, Bach: An Eternal Golden Braid.* New York: Vintage Books.
Irving, Clifford
1969 *Fake! The Story of Elmyr de Hory.* New York: McGraw-Hill.
Meyer, L. B.
1967 *Music, the Arts, and Ideas.* Chicago: University of Chicago Press.
Neisser, Ulric
1976 *Cognition and Reality.* San Francisco: W. H. Freeman.
Pelto, P., and G. Pelto
1975 Intra-cultural Diversity: Some Theoretical Issues. *American Ethnologist* 2:1-19.

Rosch, Eleanor, et al.
1976 Basic Objects in Natural Categories. *Cognitive Psychology* 8:382-439.
Shepard, Anna O.
1971 *Ceramics for the Archaeologist.* Publication 609. Washington, D.C.: Carnegie Institution.
Tietze, Hans
1948 *Genuine and False: Copies, Imitations, Forgeries.* New York: Chanticleer Press.
Van Esterik, Penny
1976 Cognition and Design Production in Ban Chiang Painted Pottery. Ph.D. dissertation, University of Illinois, Urbana.
1978 Letter to the editor. *American Ethnologist* 5:404-5.
1979 Symmetry and Symbolism in Ban Chiang Painted Pottery. *Journal of Anthropological Research* 35:495-508.
1981 Cognition and Design Production in Ban Chiang Painted Pottery. Center for International Studies, Southeast Asian Series, Monograph no. 58. Athens: Ohio University Press.
Washburn, D.
1977 *A Symmetry Analysis of Upper Gila Area Ceramic Design.* Papers of the Peabody Museum of Archaeology and Ethnology, vol. 68.
You Di, Chin
1972 The Prehistoric Culture of Ban Chiang. Bangkok: Fine Arts Department (in Thai).

SECTION III

Systems of Cultural Knowledge

All of the authors of the chapters in this final section illuminate the role of language and word meaning in the organization of systems of cultural knowledge, and emphasize the emergent quality of understanding. The former theme is central to the papers of IIIA. The latter theme is most clearly developed in the papers of IIIB.

Giving language a central place in their analyses, the authors develop distinct approaches toward the modeling of aspects of cognition. In IIIA, Quinn argues that the complex semantics of "key words" simultaneously frames and generates culturally appropriate goals crucial to the processes of understanding, expectation, and planning. White and D'Andrade look to word meanings, particularly to redundant and overlapping themes, as an indication of tacit premises for culturally appropriate action. They argue that the semantics of a set of interrelated terms cohere in a cultural folk theory that provides commonsense "outlines of reality" to guide the interpretation of experience. In more traditional fashion, Randall and Colby each build models for the conceptual representation of integrated systems of cultural knowledge as semantic networks. Common to all these papers is a concern with the role language plays in crystalizing *a priori* conceptual schemata by which experience is largely ordered (Scheler 1980). In IIIB, Agar and Hobbs let the structure of discourse suggest a project-oriented model for the purposeful organization and expression of life history data. Brown emphasizes the pragmatic and contextualized bases of language use for analyses of cultural knowledge. Finally, Holland explores discourse as reflections upon one's self and others. Common to these latter chapters is a concern with a mutually constitutive relationship of language and culture.

Systematically organized concepts or conceptual schemata are continually involved in individuals' efforts at interpretation, at making sense of experience as it happens. Useful knowledge about the world in process is systematically stored and subsequently reapplied as it is appropriate to emerging experience. All the papers in this section describe organizations of knowledge consistently applicable to the interpretation of social action. Schank and Abelson (1977) call this "background knowledge," which is organized in "higher-level" knowledge structures. With a different metaphor, Holland in her paper refers to "deeper" levels of cultural knowledge.

At the same time that these chapters deal with the structure of schematic cultural knowledge, the authors of IIIB emphasize the process of understanding and interpretation in everyday tasks such as identifying a magical stone (Brown), or telling one's life story to a listener (Agar and Hobbs), or evaluating others and their behavior in the course of daily interactions (Holland). Agar and Hobbs and Brown illustrate a dialectical relation between knowledge schemata and interpretation, suggesting that organizations of knowledge applied in interpreting events are selected as they are relevant to explicit emerging content. Such organized cultural knowledge provides a framework that enables one to make sense of a developing scenario by making available the implicit knowledge which structures the ongoing event. As we saw in Section II, hypothesis testing is evident at the focus of awareness. A match of knowledge structure with experience is confirmed or rejected by a constant mental checking of schema-based predictions against the ongoing activity. In the process, specifics of an example may become incorporated into a conceptual representation, elaborating the underlying framework. In this way the schemata themselves can be reorganized or elaborated by the particular instances in which they guide interpretation.

A view of conceptual change begins to emerge in the consideration of a dialectical relation between schemata and experience (Agar and Hobbs, Colby). Any instance of identification may modify the relevant mental representations (see also Dougherty and Keller, Van Esterik, and Lehman in other sections of the volume). In each instance of identification the relevant conceptual hypotheses are subject to verification, revision, or rejection. A conceptual representation may be simultaneously verified in the process of categorization and modified or elaborated in light of newly emergent attributes. Much of this change goes on unattended, but, as Holland points out, a situation in which one is forced to recognize a need for redefinition or reorganization, one that she designates as a "symbolic encounter," may have a particularly powerful effect on the individual involved. This perspective provides an account of change as an inherent property of cultural knowledge in use. This is much like the phenomenon of cultural drift cited in the introduction to this volume. Within the limits set by our innate capacities, cultural knowledge is continually in flux, being reconstituted by the very experience it categorizes.

Cognitive phenomena are flexible and productive constructions that emerge in the continual interactions of their users.

The problem of change is not unrelated to the issues of individual variation and cultural consensus. It is within the individual that the mutual modification of cognitive structure and perceived experience takes place. And it is from the pool of individual variability that larger directions of change emerge. However, for the most part individual variation is inherent in the operation of a cultural system, and is not necessarily indicative of directed or lasting social change. Quinn, White, and D'Andrade (and Gatewood, whose paper appears in Section II) address this issue. They argue that "collective representations" or "shared knowledge" operate as organizational frameworks that allow individuals to interpret experience and to communicate their understandings to one another (cf. Geertz 1973). Quinn (and Gatewood) goes on to argue that the collective representation is given content by the specifics of individual behavior, which vary with time, interest, and experience. It is the function of the collective representations to encompass this variation and to facilitate cooperative interaction.

NOTE

The orientation of this introduction reflects the careful suggestions of Naomi Quinn and Dorothy Holland, who are, of course, not responsible for its final form.

REFERENCES

Geertz, Clifford
1973 *The Interpretation of Cultures.* New York: Basic Books.

Schank, Roger, and Robert Abelson
1977 *Scripts, Plans, Goals and Understanding.* Hillsdale, N.J.: Lawrence Erlbaum Associates.

Scheler, Max
1980 *Problems of a Sociology of Knowledge.* London: Routledge and Kegan Paul.

A. SCHEMATA AND SEMANTICS: Language-Based Systems of Cultural Knowledge

These chapters emphasize the role of language and word meaning in the organizational systems of cultural knowledge.

11

Steps toward an Ethnosemantics of Verbs: Complex Fishing Technique Scripts and the "Unsaid" in Listener Identification

Robert A. Randall

How do people understand discussion of complex work tasks? Presumably, they identify the task being talked about, and then use their knowledge of the task to "fill in" what has been left unsaid (cf. Tyler 1978). But how do people identify the task being talked about? Presumably, either tasks are identified directly because they are named by conventionally labeled verbs and verb-object combinations, or they are identified indirectly because an inference can be drawn from discussion about the task.

We know very little, however, about the ethnosemantics of such verbs. Despite their pivotal role in the organization of sentences and in the categorization of socially standardized behavior, we still know little either about specific verb domains in specific languages or about the semantics of verbs cross-culturally. We are, therefore, a very long way from understanding how people interpret what people say about what they do.

In order to improve this situation slightly, I propose to examine here some of the task identification processes Northern Sinama[1] speakers use to understand discourse about a domain of economically important southern Philippine fishing techniques. After outlining some of the issues raised by a "fishing story," I consider how Schank and Abelson's artificial intelligence theory of "script headers" (1977) might be used to explain the fishing technique identification processes prerequisite to inferential understanding.

Schank and Abelson do not discuss culturally standard names for activities, but nevertheless their view of script headers accounts surprisingly well for the Sinama names used to identify fishing techniques. The exceptions to this general applicability, however, are numerous enough to warrant some modifications in their theory. In particular, a large number of highly similar fishing activities are routinely identified by mention of some unique or unusual attribute. By contrast, if such unusual attributes are not mentioned, the technique is identified by assuming that it lacks such unique attributes. Although it has been frequently remarked since the early days of communication theory that the unusual is more informative than the usual, too little has been made of this in ethnosemantics. Here, though, I intend to show that the distinction between the usual and the unusual is crucial to understanding what fishermen say about their work.

To properly appreciate some of the difficulties in developing an ethnosemantic description of fishing technique verbs, it may be useful to begin by trying to understand an old fisherman's 'story' about 'moneymaking' a few days earlier. In what follows I have provided a literal line-for-line gloss of the Sinama. Although one can easily improve the English and make the material much more intelligible with parenthetical cultural information, doing so would make much less obvious the inference processes Sinama speakers must normally engage in.

Making Money

My speech at my wife, "Oh my wife, overthere get ready and heat early this sunclimb. Hooking we-not-you with our-all's children. Weak are we-all. There aren't any of our-all's essentials. Oh Abirin, Oh Imbang, help me. Launch the canoe, we-all hook the sunclimb. There aren't really our-all's essentials." Father to one, "Accompanying me, Imbang and Rang. A threesome we-not-you hooking."

Then, when hooking we-not-you, to the sea: paddling we-not-you. Then, when paddling we-not-you, said Imbang, "Make vigorous you-all paddling so that not late at the current." When reach we-not-you at sea, a depth about 20 double-armspans, making cease we-not-you at sea. Steer-on-the-current I at the rear. Says Imbang, "Drop we-all, Dad, hooks here." . . . Oh, striking already my-hook. When gathering in already . . . what? . . . an emperor—like this. Said I, "Makes good."

So, drop his also by him. Therefore, drop mine already also by me. Accompanying each other we-not-you striking. By "the netlike" at his, at me a triggerfish. Said, "Badluck for my hooks." The one that strikes at me a triggerfish, at him a "netlike." So then, hooking again-and-again we-not-you. Oh! Gathering in that-child-of-mine from the bow, counting already. Like what? When gathering in a lot already . . . uh . . . when yanking by me, a "spiny tetradontoid" at mine already. If like this, only be "roast-hashed-fried."

Now then, that child of mine, a lot could catch that one. About one hour we-not-you hooking. Says they, "Oh Dad, better we-all be quick homing. A lot already we-all able to get." Says I, "Why we-all homing?" "There's not, Dad, our Clinton. Deadline-beating we-all the Clinton; cause-to-accompany we-all to Lamitan. 'There's,' it's said, 'departing Uncle Daru?' He's departing to Lamitan. Make exchange, Dad, for lansones. Make exchange we-all for manioc . . . rice if there's the buying already reaching like that, Dad." . . .

So then, far already we-not-you. Drifted by the current already. "Dad, can-be-late we-all." Says I, "Child, make vigorous yourself paddling." When making vigorous already paddling, broke that paddle. "Oh God," I said, "Why already?" "Father, because your instruction to me 'Make vigorous that paddling.' " "Oh God, not already sell our-all's fish unless already I strongly paddle. Oh my breath." Expelling my breath. Accordingly, coughing still I already. "If like that," said the children, "suffering we-all."

Now, all-of-a-sudden, somewhat-made-to-accompany we-not-you at the ebb: The ebb—quick, really, we-all. The children: "Bundle already you-all." So, accordingly, overthere to bundle the fish. Three bundles only, but many bundling. The price already, one bundle: three pesos. . . .

When arriving we-not-you already to the edge, boatwashing already I the canoe. When boatwashing we-not-you the canoe, in not very long, lift-launching already Daru? So says I, "Cause-to-accompany already our fish." . . .

The 'story' is superficially, at least, an attempt to relate an unusual incident that happened a few days earlier. It also, I think, had a more profound meaning, but for the moment let us ignore this aspect of the communication and focus on the difficulty we outsiders have understanding relatively simple parts of the story.

Even if I were to rearrange the story's syntax, supply tense affixations where there are none in Sinama, and explain, for example, why a fisherman might 'still be coughing' (tuberculosis) or why not having a "Clinton" might require haste (a Clinton is a type of double-outrigger dugout canoe having plywood sides and a Clinton-type inboard engine, and is used for transporting fish between islands), it would still be difficult to understand many of the inferences expected from the listener by the speaker.

Consider, for instance, that just when they were trying to paddle vigorously and had broken one of their paddles, they managed to catch an ebb current and make it to the beach in time to send their fish with a departing fish carrier. How would one know from what is actually conveyed in the last paragraph of the story that an 'ebb' was the current necessary to get them home quickly? Presumably because one knows that ebbs go eastward, are strong, predictable currents, and that *the type of fishing being done is done west of the beach.*

And how does one know what type of fishing was being done? Some Samal might be familiar with our storyteller's usual fishing activities, but even so, knowledge of possible Sinama fishing techniques makes it easy to identify from cues in the narrative the fishing technique being used. The man and his children were doing what Samal call *agpissi allaw* (literally, 'to hook daytime'). Furthermore, of the two day-hooking techniques done at sunclimb, we can be sure the technique known as *aglaway allaw* 'to spiderweb daytime' was not being used for at least three reasons: because three people never go *aglaway* in one dugout (they would tangle lines); because emperors, "netters," and the like are not usually caught in the *aglaway* technique; and because the fisherman would probably not have used the ambiguous term 'hooking' to tell his children what they were going to do if he intended to do the type of hooking known as *aglaway.*

By "elimination," therefore, listeners would be expected early in the story to infer that the one- or two-hook technique was being used. Since this is almost always done west of the beach at a shoal known as 'Current-lee', most listeners would visualize the canoe and its surroundings early in the story, and then instantly draw the correct inference about the result of an ebb when the last paragraph was uttered.

What seems clear from the above, and from any number of other such texts, is that one cannot understand what is being said about Sinama fishing techniques without considerable information not ordinarily available to the outsider. Unlike color, plants, and any number of other domains that have been studied, however, fishing techniques need not be categorized by attributes of universal relevance. The obvious ethnosemantic question is, then, how might knowledge of such complex, culturally localized tasks be described with sufficient precision to explain the function of particular verbs in particular texts?

Identifying Fishing Scripts

If one agrees with the computer interpretation-of-text theories being developed by Schank and Abelson and others (1977), one might argue that the fisherman and listener share a 'day-hooking' script (or what I have elsewhere called a routine action plan [1977] and Goodenough [1981] calls a routine).[2] According to them: "A script is a structure that describes appropriate sequences of events in a particular context. A script is made up of slots and requirements about what can fill those slots. The structure is an interconnected whole, and what is in one slot affects what can be in another. Scripts handle stylized everyday situations. . . . Thus, a script is a predetermined, stereotyped sequence of actions that defines a well-known situation" (1977:41). Certainly, 'day hooking' is a "culturally consensual" (p. 55) "standard sequence" that the fisherman has "been through many times" (pp. 37-38), and obviously, something like a script is used to infer the location of the canoe prior to catching the ebb current and thereby understand the story. But how does one know what script to invoke?

Schank and Abelson argue, "The rules for activating a script are dependent on certain key concepts or conceptualizations when found in certain contexts" (p. 48). The conceptualizations or *script headers* they found studying their own restaurant eating are of four types (p. 49). For example, *being hungry* and *wanting food* are "precondition headers" for restaurant scripts because they are routine goals restaurant scripts are used to obtain. Similarly, in the fisherman's story 'get essentials' is a precondition header that tells the listener that the narrative is probably about a 'cash acquisition' script such as 'hooking.' 'Hooking emperorfish,' on the other hand, is a precondition header that tells the listener that a bottom-fishing script is being used.

By contrast, 'using hooks' is an "instrumental header" that suggests a 'getting fish' script, and 'drifted by the current' is an instrumental header suggesting 'drift fishing techniques.' The time ('sunclimb') and the place where the hooking was done ('20 fathoms') are what Schank and Abelson called "locale headers" because they tell us that certain 'day-hooking' scripts are being discussed. Finally, Schank and Abelson mention a fourth type of script header called "the internal conceptualization header." In the story 'being struck by a fish' might be such a header because it commonly occurs in fishing scripts, but Schank and Abelson's description of this header is not precise enough to be certain.

But how well do these script headers help identify the script the fisherman is using? In this case, knowing that the activity occurs at sunclimb, at sea 20 fathoms deep, and aims at acquiring bottom fish such as emperors, is sufficient to identify the script being used. No single one of these script headers, however, is sufficient by itself. More important, as I have already observed, it is the absence of a standard *aglaway* technique name that, more than anything else, tells us, as the children addressed in the story, what script is being referenced.

What is clearly necessary, then, is a general explanation of how Sinama listeners use script headers to determine which of several fairly similar techniques are being discussed. Schank and Abelson argue that different "restaurant tracks" are made less ambiguous by unique script headers such as *Big Mac, Italian food, McDonald's,* and so forth. There may be some truth to this position, but if so, why, for example, would not *some chicken* or *McBride's* be good script headers as well? Schank and Abelson do not directly discuss this issue, but the answer seems fairly obvious. *Big Mac, Italian food,* and *McDonald's* are good script headers not only because they indicate instruments, preconditions, and locales for culturally consensual scripts, but also because such script headers are parts of culturally consensual *names* for scripts. The place, then, to search for Sinama fishing technique script headers is in the standard nomenclature of fishing techniques.

Sinama Fishing Technique Terms and Their Nomenclature

Many well-studied semantic domains consist of categories having names with no folk etymology. We do not ask Americans, for example, why names such as *father, red, she, oak,* and so forth are appropriate to the categories they name. Many verbs, by contrast, have names that speakers of the language can easily justify: *to plow,* for example, is *to use a plow,* and *to fence,* in one usage at least, derives from *the goal* the activity attempts to achieve. Many verb names, including those standing for Sinama fishing techniques, have transparent etymologies, so one can, with a little caution, use such folk etymologies in developing a theory of script headers. In what follows I will use literal glosses in single quotes wherever the etymology is obvious.

If one asks a Samal, "What are the important ways to make a living?" one way they are sure to mention is 'acquire cash.' One main way to get cash is 'to get sea food,' and there are more than 52 substantially different techniques for doing this.[3] Elsewhere, I have shown that in one village the *active* repertoire of complex and time-consuming seafood acquisition techniques can be characterized by a rather large hierarchical taxonomy (Randall 1977:355-63). In all, 69 terms are used to designate, with varying degrees of generality, the full repertoire of techniques.

By my count, 40 techniques are usually referred to by monomial names. These are in several respects similar to what Berlin (1976; cf. Berlin, Breedlove, and Raven 1973) has called "generics" and Rosch and Mervis have called "basic categories" (1975). Eleven of these seafood acquisition techniques are further subdivided into 24 binomially labeled, more specific techniques and two of these are even further subdivided into distinctive techniques labeled by complex phrases.

Generics and subgenerics are grouped into more general categories as well. There are eight general categories of seafood acquisition. One general category, *agdadaing* (literally, 'to fish repeatedly'), is immediately subdivided both into generic categories and into several suprageneric categories as well. The suprageneric 'to poison fish' seems to be intermediate in generality between the more general fish acquisition category and the generic types of fish poisoning, but the other suprageneric fishing terms appear to have a different origin. Several important generic category names may be used in a more general sense to refer to all techniques employing similar material means. 'To net,' for example, usually refers to a technique for netting garfish, but it can also be used more generally to refer to any net-fishing technique. Similarly, 'to hook' usually refers to ordinary single-hook daytime handline fishing, but is frequently used as well to refer to any hooked handline technique.

Within the general 'hooking' category, moreover, still other suprageneric distinctions can be made. *Agpasakkad* is a residual category that ordinarily refers to night bottom fishing not in any particular location. It is generalized sometimes to designate any night bottom fishing. As well, the economically important night, anchored, scad fishing technique known as *aglaway* may be used to designate other hooking techniques that employ a multiple-hook handline, even though they are not anchored, do not seek scad, and are done in the daytime.

Even a cursory study of the names used to designate Sinama seafood acquisition verbs makes it obvious that fishing technique names emphasize many different characteristics of fishing techniques. Of the generic verbs, some are named for a precondition header specifying the goal being sought. There are, accordingly, verbs to acquire tidal life, tuna, and striped barracuda. Many other technique names, moreover, emphasize instrumental headers: namely, the distinctive material means used in capture. There is, for example, 'to weir,' 'to multi-hook,' 'to net,' 'to fish pot,' and so forth.

A few other techniques, however, emphasize not the headers Schank and Abelson have identified but activities performed during the technique. Thus, in 'to jiggle [a shrimp lure for squid],' the name calls attention to the way the line is moved. In others the position of the line is singled out, as in 'to throw,' 'to quasi tow,' 'to [vertical] handline.' In still another the position of the hook on the bottom receives attention. While these are locatives, they do not refer to the locale of the activity and therefore are not exactly what Schank and Abelson call "locale headers."

Even further from Schank and Abelson's classification of headers are 'decoying' and 'joining together.' 'Decoying' is sometimes called 'fooling the *Loligo* squid' because, *without hooks,* this squid will attach itself to virtually anything bright enough. 'Joining together' is so named because it requires large numbers of people to surround a school of fish and then drive them into a net, weir, or other capture device.

One finds a similar situation upon examining the binomially named fishing techniques. Some 15 terms, for example, are of the form "Means + X," where X is either the goal being pursued (such as 'poisoning fish' or 'cotton-netting mackerel'), or the time of the activity ('speargunning daytime,' 'hooking daytime'), or the location of the activity ('hooking at the dropping place'). These names, then, in close conformity with Schank and Abelson's observations about script headers, combine instrumental headers with locale or preconditional headers.

There are, again, a few techniques named differently: 'multihook drifting,' 'anchoring daytime,' and '[vertical] handling barracuda' might appear to conform to the Schank-Abelson hypothesis on script headers. 'Drifting,' however, is a direction-controlling technique; 'anchoring' is an instrumental header because it is a means to prevent movement, not—except indirectly—because it is a means to catch fish; and, although 'vertical handlining' may seem to emphasize the instrumentality for catching fish, informants insist the name derives from the importance of keeping the handline vertical in the sea.

Despite such exceptions, however, the vast majority of fishing technique names are what one would expect if Samal were following a simple nomenclatural rule: where possible, name the technique for the "rig" (i.e. *pangolloʔan* or means of acquisition) used. Only if the techniques cannot be easily named for the rig should the name emphasize some other distinction. Thus, for example, in 'fishing,' 'decoying,' and 'joining together' there are so many alternative means commonly employed that no one fishing rig could be used in the name. By contrast, in 'tidal gathering' only hands are used to pick up mollusks and other tidal life, so there is no distinctive means of capture at all.

Schank and Abelson say nothing whatever about nomenclature. Nevertheless, with respect to what I have discussed so far about fishing technique nomenclature, Schank and Abelson's observations about script headers seem overwhemingly supported. There are, however, a large number of techniques that cannot be monomially named for the rig because another technique uses the same instrument of capture and *is* named for it. In such cases a listener who depends solely on an instrumental header for script identification could easily mistake the technique being discussed.

Such mistaken identification would be particularly likely with 'hooking' and 'multihooking' because there are so many techniques using hooks and multihook rigs. But misidentifications would also occur, for example, if one thought the shrimp lure 'jiggling' technique mentioned earlier were being discussed when 'to shrimp' was referred to. Even though 'jiggling' uses a shrimp lure, it cannot be called 'to shrimp' because another *Ilex* squid acquisition technique also uses a shrimp lure and is called 'to shrimp.'

If one studies the use of fishing technique terms, it becomes obvious there are at least three ways to nonemclaturally distinguish two or more techniques employing the same rig. The easiest way to name two techniques after a rig is to subclassify the techniques by combining the rig with distinct locale or precondition headers. 'Jiggling,' for example, was referred to by some as '[use] shrimp daytime' and was contrasted with '[use] shrimp nighttime.' Similarly, 'dipnetting' is subdivided into 'dipnet Indian anchovy,' 'dipnet full-bodied anchovy,' and 'dipnet mullet'; 'cotton netting' is divided into 'mackerel' and 'herring' subcategories; and 'speargunning' is subdivided into day and night varieties.

Alternatively, one can simply subclassify the type of rig and then name the techniques after the specific rig subtype. Several of the suprageneric categories discussed earlier—such as 'hooking,' 'netting,' and 'fish poisoning'—are subdivided into techniques named respectively for specific types of hook rigs, nets, and fish poisons.

Both of the above ways to name fishing techniques conform to Schank and Abelson's observations about script headers fairly well. The names are concatenations of instruments, goal preconditions, or locales, and each uniquely identifies the script being discussed. There is, however, an important set of techniques not so named and identified. Rather, such techniques are identified not so much by what they name as by what they *fail* to name.

Techniques using the same rig are often binomialized (or "marked") when they are less common, while the monomial (or "unmarked") form refers to the common technique. There are several examples of such marking in the repertoire of fishing technique names, but the best example is the set of economically important techniques named for the *laway* multihook rig (and perhaps for its 'spiderweb' appearance).

In Figure 1 I use the diagramming method developed by Geoghegan (1973:439) and Quinn (1981:419) to show how modification of the head verb (such as 'hooking' and 'multihooking') changes technique identification. Note in particular the distinction between the overtly named contrasts in the literal glosses of fishing technique

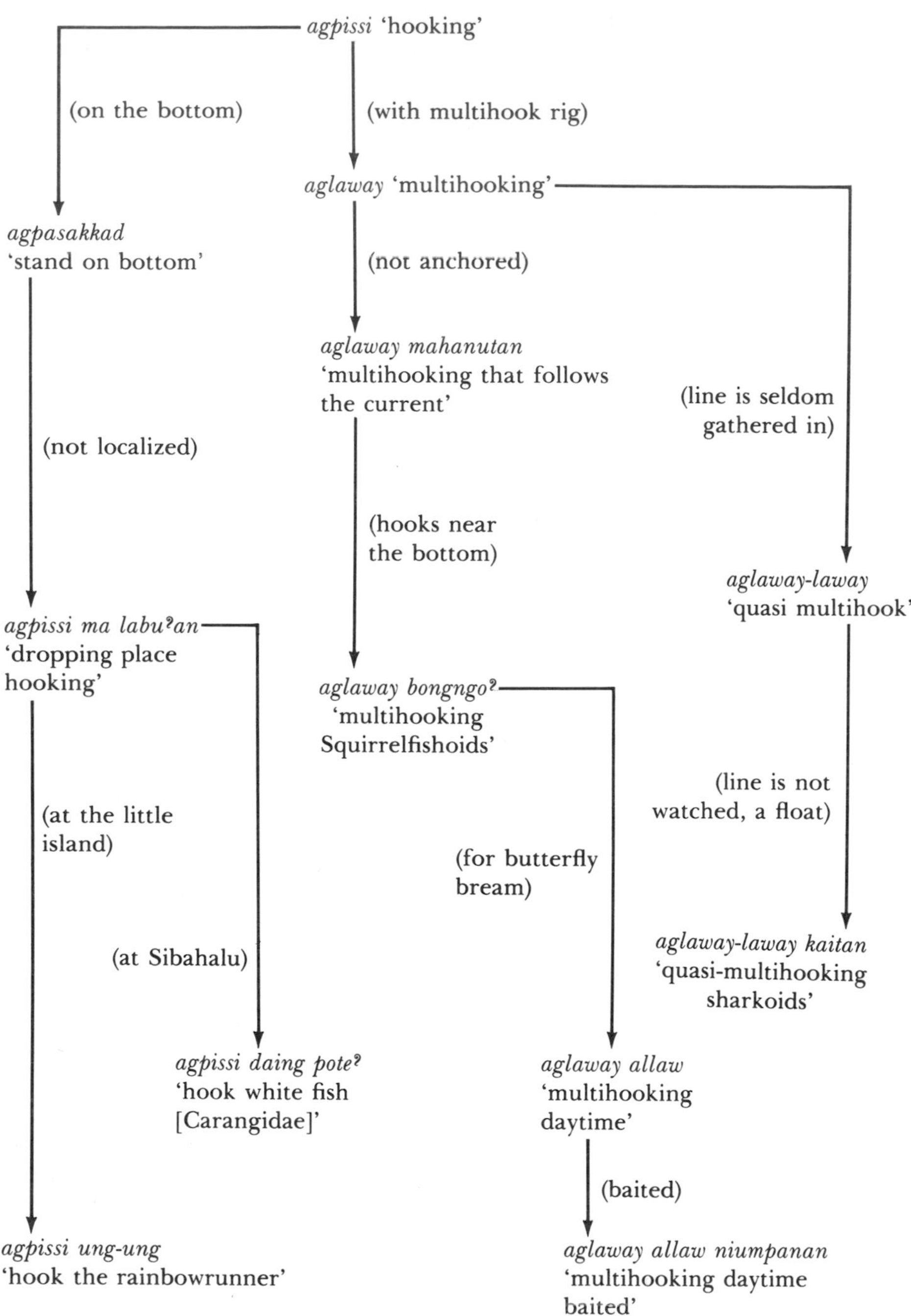

Figure 1. Covert and Overt Marking Relations in Hooking Nomenclature

names and the entailed covert distinctions fishermen regard as extremely important (in parentheses next to arrows). Thus, although *aglaway allaw* in the bottom right of the figure might be categorized as a type of *aglaway* (because it uses the *laway* rig) and might be further categorized as a type of 'hooking' because the *laway* rig has hooks, it would not be referred to simply as *aglaway* or as 'hooking' because these names suggest very different techniques.

If one only considered the overtly marked contrasts, *aglaway allaw* would appear to differ from *aglaway* proper only because the former occurs in the day and the latter at night, but, as the diagram makes clear, there are important, often unspoken differences. The two techniques differ not only because *aglaway allaw* is a daytime technique and therefore does not use a pressure lantern to attract fish, or any of the lengthy procedures and costly means this entails, but also because it follows the current with hooks near the bottom, in search of butterfly bream. *Aglaway*, by contrast, is a mid-water, anchored technique that catches a type of scad. One can tell therefore that a 'day *aglaway*' script is being discussed not only if the speaker uses the standard name but also if *aglaway* and 'day' (or subdivisions such as 'sunclimb') or *aglaway* and 'bream' (or a fly used to catch bream) are mentioned.

More important, if, as in the fisherman's story, a standard name such as *aglaway* is not mentioned, listeners assume some simpler type of hooking is being discussed. If none of the covert or overt markers used to modify *aglaway* are mentioned, Samal assume that the technique being discussed is the standard, night, anchored, mid-water, sinker-at-end, flies-for-bait, bag-eyed scad catching technique from which most people make most of their money.

Schank and Abelson recognize a similar problem of script identification when they point out that stories typically relate events that are unusual with respect to standard scripts (1977:45, 57-67, 166), but they do not generalize this perspective in developing a theory of script headers for restaurant scripts that are highly similar. What seems obvious, then, is that their concept of script headers fairly well describes an important part of conventional fishing technique reference, but it incorrectly assumes that scripts are identified solely from information conveyed explicitly by script headers. With Sinama fishing, at least, some scripts are identified not just from an instrumental script header but also from *assumptions* about what the speaker would have added if they had any other script in mind.

But how does one describe what a speaker might have added if he had another script in mind? Fishing techniques involve scripts of such enormous size that they are probably stored in memory generatively (Randall 1977:321-45). They typically differ from each other in numerous ways, so there are potentially many ways to designate a script as an unusual one. What is needed, then, is a description of the important similarities and differences among fishing techniques.

The Attributes of Fishing Technique Terms

As is well known, psychologists, linguists, and anthropologists have for decades been developing various versions of attribute theory in order to specify how somewhat similar categories are differentiated (cf. Bruner, Goodnow, and Austin 1956, Fodor 1977:144, Kay 1969). In general, the idea has been to take some set of conceptually similar nouns (objects) or adjectives (qualities) and determine what attributes (characteristics, components, dimensions, considerations) are used to distinguish among them. Attempts have been made to determine the relative importance of these attributes both in judging the similarity of the categories (e.g. by multidimensional scaling; Rose and Romney 1981) and in selecting a category to use (e.g. by information processing flow charts; Geoghegan 1971, 1973). More recently, it has also become clear that attributes such as the *hue* of a *color* or the *shape* of a *mug* are not partitioned into a set of mutually exclusive features but, instead, represent an ordinal scale of features ranging from "best example" to "not an example" (cf. Berlin and Kay 1969, Kay and McDaniel 1978, Kempton 1981, Rosch 1973).

With the exception of a small domain of English *lying* verbs analyzed in Kay and Coleman (1981), and a few other efforts (cf. Frake 1969, Agar 1974), there is, however, virtually no research on the attributes of verbs, and none at all on domains of the size, complexity, and unfamiliarity of Sinama fishing techniques. It is by no means obvious, therefore, that attribute theory is even applicable to such domains.

What happens if we try to discover the attributes of Sinama fishing technique terms? Considerable interviewing of fishermen regarding differences and similarities between techniques[4] makes it clear that such terms can be differentiated by a large number of distinctive attributes. It would be too cumbersome to describe the whole domain in such detail, so in what follows I will focus on the handlining techniques most relevant to the story we considered earlier.

Handlining techniques differ in the time they are performed (day, night), the location where the fishing is done (from shore, at some shoal, near shore at some location, or on a known drift tract). The bait can be placed on the surface of the sea, or below, either on the bottom or in-between. Fishing at night usually implies some sort of illumination either to attract fish (lantern) or to permit bait perception (moon); fishing from shore implies casting to get the bait in the sea; fishing on the surface implies some sort of boat movement to keep the bait on the surface and therefore make it appear pelagic; fishing below surface requires some sort of sinker to get it down.

Bait can be 'live' (i.e. recently so); it can be a feather or hair fly (of many types), or an aluminum lure, or a shrimp made out of wood, or a pandanus fish-shaped lure. To make flies and lures effective, they must be moved through the water either vertically or horizontally. Thus fishermen who are not paddling (or using an inboard) must jiggle, raise and lower, or slowly gather in the line, unless it is so light it will move in minor currents. Live bait, on the other hand, must be caught, prepared, and lowered on a hook. When one feels a fish pull the line, one 'yanks' to impale the hook in the fish's mouth, then gathers in the line, removes the fish, and then replaces the bait.

Hooks and nylon line are purchased ready-made in a variety of sizes depending on the size of the fish being sought. Low-numbered hooks and large-numbered lines are for large fish and the reverse is true for small fish. Lines designed for small fish can have numerous hooks, but lines designed for large fish should, for obvious reasons, have a few at most. Frequently, if the fish being sought can bite through nylon, the hook is attached to the mainline with iron wire leader; for the smaller, less toothy fishes, nylon is used. If there is more than one hook, nylon leaders must be used to attach each hook to a leaderline, and since lines with such leaders become easily twisted and tangled, a swivel is used to attach the mainline to the line holding the leaders.

Those techniques requiring sinkers use lead or iron mostly, but two techniques use basalt and coral. In the first case basalt rather than metal is used because the sinker must be discarded once the rig reaches the bottom. This is done by tying the basalt to a coconut leaflet, then snagging the leaflet on the fish hook at the end of the handline. Once the hook reaches bottom, the line is yanked, freeing the hook from the leaflet, and thereby leaving a sinkerless hook and fly wafting in the bottom currents. The coralline rock, on the other hand, is used because it is available in much heavier pieces than the basalt and could not be duplicated with metal except at great expense. The purpose of such a large sinker is to keep the line completely immobilized in a bottom hole.

Usually sinkers are located at the end of the line. The only exceptions are the coconut leaflet used to attach the basalt sinker, the net used to attach the coralline sinker, and a single technique where the sinker is placed at the midpoint of the handline in order to permit a more horizontal placement of the multihooked line in mid-water depths.

Virtually all techniques require constant monitoring of the line for fish activity. Fishermen keep their hands on the line so they can feel 'a bite' or notice any changes in 'weight.' For live-bait techniques fishermen also bring the line to the surface frequently to check the bait's appearance. In the 'quasi-multihook' techniques, however, the line is seldom checked. With the 'sharkoid' variant of this technique, in particular, the line is tied to a float and may even be left overnight.

Finally, fishing techniques usually differ in the type of fish being sought. The goal of the technique obviously affects the choice of means, location, and so forth, but it also implies considerable additional variation that fishermen do not mention when asked about important differences among techniques. For example, some fish are dangerous enough that they must be landed with a gaff, and others must be grasped very carefully because they have very sharp dorsals. Techniques differ also in the clock times, the nights of the lunar month, the current strengths, and the monsoon times that they can be productively pursued. Fish also differ in sale price, the way they can be cooked, the rate at which they deteriorate, and the way deterioration is prevented. All of these factors affect the method employed. There are, therefore, many ways other than technique naming for a speaker to convey to a listener what fish were being sought.

In Table 1 I have abbreviated the main handlining term attributes in a standard form. If one examines the relation of names to attributes, it becomes clear that the information conveyed by the handlining subset of fishing technique terms does not support the claim about the communication process underlying either the Schank-Abelson notion of script headers or most versions of exemplar theory. The names are what they are, not because the categories they name differ from each other on numerous attributes the way *foxes,* for example, differ from *raccoons* or *couches* differ from *chairs* (cf. Rosch and Mervis 1975), or because the names derive from highly informative instruments, goal preconditions, or locales. Rather, what stands out in the table is the large percentage of cases where a unique or unusual attribute of the technique contributes the name.

In Table 1 I have placed an asterisk beside all attributes that either contribute to the name or are not associated with more than one other technique. For the eight multihooking techniques, I have also placed asterisks beside attributes that are unique among multihooking techniques.

Table 1. Attribute Definitions of Sinama Handlining Terms

GLOSS	TIME	FISHING PLACE	# OF HOOKS	TYPE OF HOOK	LINE LENGTH	LINE SIZE	BAIT TYPE	BAIT LOCATN	VERTICL BAIT MOTION	HORIZN BAIT MOTION	LEADER	SINKER	LOCATN OF SINKER	LINE IS WATCHED ?	FISH CATCHING GOAL
1. (USE)SHRIMP (**)	NITE	NR SH A	4-6	ON LURE			*SHRIMP	SURFC	D.N.A.	SLOW	NONE	LEAD	LURE	WATCH	ILEX SQUID
2. JIGGLE (*)	DAY	SHOAL B	4-6	ON LURE			SHRIMP	MID-W	*JIGGLE	DRIFT	NONE	LEAD	LURE	WATCH	ILEX SQUID
3.DECOY/SL GATHER (*)	NITE	SHOAL C	* 0	NONE	*5 FATH		*FEATH	MID-W	*SL GAT	DRIFT	D.N.A	LEAD	LURE	WATCH	*LOLIGO SQUID
4. THROW (*)	DAY	* SHORE	1-2	SMALL		THIN	LIVE	TIDAL				LEAD	END	WATCH	TIDAL FISH
5. (USE) PANDANUS(*)	DAY	SHOAL D	1	#13		80/100	*PANDAN	SURFC	D.N.A.	FAST	IRON	NONE	D.N.A.	WATCH	SPAN.MACKEREL
6. QUASI-TOWING (EX)	NITE	SHOAL E	1			80/100	LIVE	*SURFC	D.N.A.	SLOW	IRON	LEAD	LEADER	WATCH	SPAN.MACKEREL
7. AGSALID (?)	DAY	SHOAL F	1	11/13	40 FTH	80/100	LIVE	SURFC	D.N.A.	SLOW	IRON	LEAD	LEADER	WATCH	SPAN.MACKEREL
7. AGSALID GARFISH(*)	DAY	SHOAL G	1	11/13	40 FTH	80/100	LIVE	SURFC	D.N.A.	SLOW	IRON	LEAD	LEADER	WATCH	*GARFISH
8."TUNAING" BONITO(*)	DAY	SHOAL H	1	SMALL	20 FTH	THIN	FLY	SURFC	D.N.A.	FAST	NONE	NONE	D.N.A.	WATCH	*BONITO,ETC.
8.TUN.BNTO.INBOARD(*)	DAY	SHOAL H	1	ON LUR	20 FTH	THIN	ALU FLY	SURFC	D.N.A.	*V.FAST	NONE	NONE	D.N.A.	WATCH	*BONITO,ETC.
8. "TUNAING" TUNA (*)	DAY	SHOAL H	1	LARGE	20 FTH	THICK	FLY	SURFC	D.N.A	FAST	NONE	NONE	D.N.A.	WATCH	*THUNIDAE FAM
8.TUN.TUNA INBOARD(*)	DAY	SHOAL H	1	ON LUR	20 FTH	THICK	ALU FLY	SURFC	D.N.A.	*V.FAST	NONE	NONE	D.N.A.	WATCH	*THUNIDAE FAM
9."TUNA." SQURLFSH(*)	DAY	SHOAL I	1				FLY	SURFC	D.N.A.	FAST	NONE	NONE	D.N.A.	WATCH	*SQUIRRELFISH
10.FALLNG COC LEAF(*)	DAY	SHOAL J	1				FLY	BOTTOM	*WF CUR	DRIFT	NONE	*BASLT	*LEAF	WATCH	BOTTOM FISH
11.DAY ANCHORING (**)	DAY	SHOAL K	2-3	11/13		#100	LIVE	BOTTOM	NONE	*ANCHOR	IRON	*CORAL	* NET	WATCH	*MAL TREVALLY
11.NITE ANCHORING(**)	NITE	SHOAL L	2-3	11/13		#100	LIVE	BOTTOM	NONE	*ANCHOR	IRON	*CORAL	* NET	WATCH	BOTTOM FISH
12.STAND ON BOTTM(EX)	NITE	DRFT TR	1				LIVE	*BOTTM	NONE	DRIFT	NONE	LEAD	AT END	WATCH	BOTTOM FISH
13.DROP PLACE HK(*)	NITE	*NR SHR	1		10 FTH		LIVE	BOTTOM	NONE	DRIFT	NONE	LEAD	AT END	WATCH	BOTTOM FISH
13.WHITE FISH HK(*)	NITE	NR SH M	1		10 FTH		LIVE	BOTTOM	NONE	DRIFT	NONE	LEAD	AT END	WATCH	*CARANGIDAE
13.NOSEY HOOKING(*)	NITE	NR SH N	1		10 FTH		LIVE	BOTTOM	NONE	DRIFT	NONE	LEAD	AT END	WATCH	*RNBOW RUNNER
14.(VERT)HANDLINE(*)	NITE	DRFT TR	1	14/15	15 FTH	*50/60	LIVE	*SEE $	NONE	DRIFT	IRON	LEAD	LEADER	WATCH	SPAN.MACKEREL
14.HANDL BARRACUDA(*)	NITE	DRFT TR	1	SMALL	15 FTH	THIN	LIVE	*SEE $	NONE	DRIFT	NONE	LEAD	AT END	WATCH	*BARRACUDA
15.DAY HOOKING (EX)	*DAY	DRFT TR	1	19-25	20 FTH	8/10	FLY	BOTTOM	NONE	DRIFT	IRON	LEAD	AT END	WATCH	*BOTTOM FISH
16.GANG RIGING (?)	NITE	DRFT TR	1	23-25	15 FTH	8/10	FLY	MID-WA	UP&DOWN	DRIFT	IRON	LEAD	AT END	WATCH	BAGEYED SCAD
* * * * * *	* *	* *	* *	* *	* *	* *	* *	* *	* *	* *	* *	* *	* *	* *	* * * *
17.MULTI-HOOKING(*)	NITE	SHOAL P	*30-UP	23-25	15 FTH	8/10	FLY	MID-WA	UP&DOWN	ANCHOR	NYLON	LEAD	AT END	WATCH	BAGEYED SCAD
17A.TOWED MULTIHOOK(*)	NITE	SHOAL P	*30-UP	23-25	15 FTH	8/10	FLY	MID-WA	UP&DOWN	ANCHOR	NYLON	LEAD	*MID	WATCH	BAGEYED SCAD
17B.DRIFT MULTIHOOK(*)	NITE	*DRF TR	10	23-25	10 FTH	8/10	FLY	MID-WA	UP&DOWN	*DRIFT	NYLON	LEAD	AT END	WATCH	BAGEYED SCAD
17C.SQURLFSH MULTIHK(*)	NITE	NR SH Q	10	SMALL	10 FTH	THIN	FLY	BOTTOM	UP&DOWN	DRIFT	NYLON	LEAD	AT END	WATCH	*SQUIRRELFISH
17D.DAY MULTIHOOKNG(*)	*DAY	SHOAL R	10	SMALL	10 FTH	THIN	FLY	BOTTOM	UP&DOWN	DRIFT	NYLON	LEAD	AT END	WATCH	BUTRFLY BREAM
17D.BAIT DAY MULTIHK(*)	*DAY	SHOAL S	5	SMALL	10 FTH	THIN	*LIVE	BOTTOM	NONE	DRIFT	NYLON	LEAD	AT END	WATCH	BUTRFLY BREAM
17E.QUASI-MULTIHK(*)	DY&NT	SHOAL T	10	SMALL		THIN	LIVE	MID-WA	NONE	ANCHOR	NYLON	LEAD	AT END	*NT WAT	MISC.FISH
17F.QSI MLHK SHARK(*)	DY&NT	SHOAL U	5	LARGE		THICK	LIVE	MID-WA	NONE	* FLOAT	NYLON	LEAD	AT END	*NT WAT	*SHARKOIDS

ABBREVIATIONS:

* DESIGNATES AN ATTRIBUTE USED IN THE NAME
(*) FISHING TERMS WHOSE NAMES DERIVE FROM ATTRIBUTES UNIQUE TO THE TECHNIQUE OR GENERAL TYPE OF TECHNIQUE
(**) TERMS NAMED FOR ATTRIBUTES FOUND IN ONE OTHER TECHNIQUE
(?) TERMS WHOSE ETYMOLOGY IS UNCLEAR
(EX) TERMS WHOSE NAMES DERIVE FROM COMMONLY OCCURRING ATTRIBUTES; EXCEPTIONS

$ = BAIT IS LOCATED VERTICALLY BELOW BOAT AT MID-WATER.
OTHER ABBREVIATIONS IN THE TABLE: ALU FLY= ALUMINUM FISH-SHAPED LURE;BASLT=A BASALT ROCK; DRFT TR= A DRIFT TRACK OVER A KNOWN SEA BOTTOM; MID-WA=MID-WATER; NR SH A = A FISHING LOCATION NEAR SHORE AT POINT A; SL GAT=TO SLOWLY GATHER IN THE LINE; VERTCL= VERTICAL; WF CR= WAFTING IN THE CURRENT WITHOUT SINKER;NT WAT=NOT WATCHED; MAL=MALABAR

There are 32 handlining terms in the table, but some are minor variants of others. In order, therefore, to get some quantitative estimate of the degree to which unusual attributes create names, it seems reasonable to count handlining techniques that are quite different from each other. In the table, therefore, I have designated minor variants of a technique by the same reference number (extreme left of the table). In addition, two techniques (ref. nos. 7 and 16) have names whose etymology is unknown, so there is no way to determine whether their etymologies derive from unusual characteristics of the technique.

Of the techniques in the table, 15 types are substantially different from each other and have a known etymology. Of these 15, ten are named for attributes found in no other technique type and two are named for attributes found in only one other technique type. In the table I have designated them by an asterisk (*) if the attribute is unique and by a double asterisk (**) if the attribute is found in only one other technique type. Only three techniques, by contrast, are exceptions (EX in the table) because they take their name from attributes found in three or more technique types. By inspecting the table, it is clear that these techniques could not be named for their unique attributes because none of their attributes are unique or even uncommon.

It might be supposed that the descriptive statistics cited above would be different if some of the technique subtypes had not been excluded from the analysis. Number 17c, 'squirrelfishoid multihooking,' for example, has a unique attribute among the multihooking terms because it catches squirrelfish and similar fish. But it is not unique as a handlining term because no. 9, 'tuna-ing squirrelfishoids,' also catches the same fishes. Since the eight multihooking terms are nomenclaturally distinguished from the other handlining terms by their common unique attribute—the presence of numerous hooks—there is no reason to further distinguish the multihooking techniques from other hooking techniques. Rather, a speaker's problem is to nomenclaturally distinguish the multihooking techniques from each other. Within the multihooking category then, each subtype nomenclaturally singles out an attribute unique to multihooking.

It would be interesting to determine whether other large domains of complex behaviors are usually talked about by their odd traits, and it would be interesting to learn which properties an unusual attribute must have to be nomenclature material. My suspicions are that unusual attributes of complex tasks derive from innovative solutions to problems, but this is just speculation until we know more about verbs.

Concluding Thoughts and Some Second Thoughts

At the outset I asked how people understand discussion of complex work tasks, and I used a fisherman's story about 'Making Money' to illustrate some of the problems of script identification one must solve before one can understand understanding. I summarized data on more than 50 Samal fishing techniques, and showed that fishing technique names have many of the characteristics recent artificial intelligence work attributes to "script headers." At the same time, though, there are frequent occasions where the *absence* of a specialized term or other distinguishing characteristic is used in script identification. Analysis of such distinguishing characteristics shows that among techniques employing highly similar means of capture, technique names do not especially emphasize exemplary combinations of attributes, nor does the Schank-Abelson classification of "script headers" seem to explain things. Rather, among very similar techniques it is *unique* or *unusual attributes* that are frequently used as names and, presumably, as script headers.

Before closing, it may be advisable to inject a note of caution concerning the very rudimentary view of fishing verb understanding I have provided above. Being able to identify the 'day hooking' script the fisherman was talking about is an essential step in understanding his story, but it is by no means *sufficient* for such understanding. There is, I think, persuasive evidence that the story is only superficially about some unimportant 'day hooking' problems of a few days earlier. Rather, the story is about the problem of 'making a living' by hook fishing.

Early in my fieldwork, when I first transcribed and glossed the fisherman's story, I thought the format to be a fairly obvious account of a slightly atypical work day. It was only several months later, after I had asked every fisherman in the village, "What would you do if you had 5,000 pesos (about $700)?" that I fully realized what people thought of fishing. An answer to my question could have been 'Bank the money' or 'Build a good house' or 'Go to Mecca,' but every fisherman said he would use the money to leave fishing (Randall 1977:218). Samal fishermen uniformly say fishing 'is not exactly a good way to make money.' And they—including our storyteller—especially dislike 'day hooking' because it makes so little income for the work. Accordingly, only the old, young, or sick try to make money at it.

By doing day hooking, choosing to talk about it, and then emphasizing the lack of essentials, the unlucky catch, the hard paddling necessitated by not having an inboard canoe, the broken paddle, the exacerbated cough, and the barely adequate sale price (as well as numerous other hardships mentioned in other stories), the fisherman managed to tell what he thought of 'day hooking.' Only by identifying the day hooking script as a least preference, and by knowing that 'day hookers' *routinely* lack the essentials, get near-useless fish, must paddle 'vigorously' because they cannot afford an inboard motor canoe, and barely 'reach' minimal necessities, can one appreciate why the fisherman wanted to tell about a broken paddle and the resultant exacerbated cough. Rather than merely tell 'a good story about fishing,' the fisherman almost certainly was trying to 'teach an American' that an announced admiration for Samal fishing was 'naive' (*inosente*). In any event, if this were the message, it would be no different in substance from what Samal fathers frequently tell sons who want to get in a canoe.

All of this is to say that script header theory must be modified if it is to play a central role in the understanding of understanding. On a number of levels, Samal fishermen who are communicating rely not so much on what they say as on what they *would have said* if the unusual were the case. 'Multihooking' is not just an instrumental header but also a *usually performed* activity; the fisherman's story is not just about 'day hooking' but also about the inappropriateness of life as it is *usually performed.* In some cases, therefore, a listener may be able to *identify* a script by what is said without necessarily getting the point; in other cases a listener may not even be able to identify the script solely with the information contained in the script header. As Tyler has argued so persuasively (1978), one must know what is unsaid if one expects to understand what is said.

NOTES

1. In this paper all references to "Sinama" are meant to refer to the language of the Basilan Strait, Southwestern Mindanao Samal I have been studying since Aug. 1971. Much of the fishing terminology discussed in this paper is variable from island to island, so the data should be considered directly applicable to one island. There is no reason to believe, however, that the explanation advanced in this paper would be any different if it were based on data gathered elsewhere in the region. The research reported here has been supported at various times by the National Science Foundation, the UC Berkeley Institute of International Studies, and a University of Houston Research Initiation Grant.

2. More recently, Abelson (1981:719) has distinguished between the script and the "action rule." The action rule appears to be a policy whereby a particular script is appropriately selected. Given this revised terminology, what have been called routines or routine action plans by anthropologists would appear to be an amalgam of scripts and action rules.

3. A fishing technique count of 52 is only approximate. Some techniques differ from each other in just a few relatively superficial ways while others are highly distinctive. If one included known obsolete techniques, techniques known but inapplicable where the fishermen lived, or techniques known but not done owing to lack of expensive equipment, the list of techniques could be expanded considerably, especially if the knowledge of all fishermen were pooled. On the other hand, by considering techniques that are variants of each other to be the same, one could contract the list of techniques considerably. The technique count of 52 therefore represents what I take to be the common active repertoire of techniques different enough to require significant independent practical learning.

4. The differences and similarities among fishing technique categories were determined by several methods. One informant was given a nearly complete series of triad questions of the sort "Of the following three 'occupations' X, Y, Z, are there two different from that one?" After an answer was obtained, the informant was queried as to why two were more similar. I also at another time asked, "What is it that is called X?" and obtained definitions of the terms. I also have several hundred pages of interviews concerning various fishing techniques. With all of these types of information, I have detailed interviews with one informant, corroborating interviews with three to five others, and spot sampling checks on some data with others. I have no reason to think the data I report are either unrepresentative or subject to significant local variation.

REFERENCES

Abelson, Robert P.
1981 Psychological Status of the Script Concept. *American Psychologist* 36:715-29.

Berlin, Brent, and Paul Kay
1969 *Basic Color Terms: Their Universality and Evolution.* Berkeley: University of California Press.

Bruner, Jerome S., J. J. Goodnow, and G. A. Austin
1956 *A Study of Thinking.* New York: John Wiley.

Fodor, Janet Dean
1977 *Semantics.* Cambridge, Mass.: Harvard University Press.

Frake, Charles
1969 Struck by Speech: The Yakan Concept of Litigation. In Laura Nader, ed., *Law in Culture and Society.* Chicago: Aldine.

Geoghegan, William
1971 Information Processing Systems in Culture. In Paul Kay, ed., *Explorations in Mathematical Anthropology.* Cambridge: M.I.T. Press.
1973 *Natural Information Processing Rules.* Monographs of the Language Behavior Research Lab. Berkeley: University of California.

Goodenough, Ward
1981 *Culture, Language and Society.* 2d ed. Menlo Park, Calif.: Benjamin Cummings Publishing Co.

Kay, Paul
1969 Comments on Colby. In Stephen Tyler, ed., *Cognitive Anthropology.* New York: Holt, Rinehart and Winston.

Kay, Paul, and Linda Coleman
1981 Prototype Semantics: The English Word *Lie. Language* 57:26-44.

Kay, Paul, and Chad K. McDaniel
1978 The Linguistic Significance of the Meanings of Basic Color Terms. *Language* 54:610-46.

Kempton, Willett
1981 Category Grading and Taxonomic Relations: A Mug Is a Sort of Cup. In R. Casson, ed., *Language, Culture, and Cognition.* New York: Macmillan.

Quinn, Naomi
1981 A Natural System Used in Mfantse Litigation Settlement. In R. Casson, ed., *Language, Culture, and Cognition.* New York: Macmillan.

Randall, Robert A.
1977 Change and Variation in Samal Fishing: Making Plans to 'Make a Living' in the Southern Philippines. University Microfilms 77-31511.

Rosch, Eleanor
1973 On the Internal Structure of Perceptual and Semantic Categories. In T. M. Moore, ed., *Cognitive Development and the Acquisition of Language,* pp. 111-44. New York: Academic Press.

Rosch, Eleanor, and Carolyn B. Mervis
1975 Family Resemblances: Studies in the Internal Structure of Categories. *Cognitive Psychology* 7:573-605.

Rose, Michael, and A. Kimball Romney
1981 Cognitive Pluralism and Individual Differences: A Comparison of Alternative Models of American English Kin Terms. In R. Casson, ed., *Language, Culture, and Cognition.* New York: Macmillan.

Schank, Roger, and Robert Abelson
1977 *Scripts, Plans, Goals and Understanding.* Hillsdale, N.J.: Lawrence Erlbaum Associates.

Tyler, Stephen
1978 *The Said and the Unsaid.* New York: Academic Press.

12

Toward an Encyclopedic Ethnography for Use in "Intelligent" Computer Programs

Benjamin N. Colby

We are rapidly coming to the point where "intelligent" computer programs will be of practical use in handling information accessed through computers. A major impediment in the development of such programs is the lack of an ethnographic component. In a system designed to simulate text comprehension, it is not enough to include syntactic parsers and semantic rules. There have to be presuppositional statements as well. These statements are essentially ethnographic. Text comprehension programs require many such statements, which together constitute ethnographic chunks or, as others have referred to them, "long-term memory components." So far these ethnographic chunks have been created by computer programmers in an *ad hoc* manner without any guiding ethnographic principles or theories.

In anthropology, ethnographers are concerned about the requirements for increasingly greater precision and higher levels of sophistication in their ethnographic statements. There are many tools available for accomplishing this task that have been constructed by programmers in artificial intelligence. If anthropologists can develop a theory of ethnographic description that would satisfy the requirements of language comprehension programs, they would open up a new field that aims for a higher level of ethnographic standards than past traditions have aspired to.

I suggest here some activities that cognitive anthropologists might engage in toward the development of such a new subfield within our discipline. While my primary emphasis will be on the analysis of texts collected by the ethnographer, I also want to emphasize the importance that the ethnographer's own contextual experience in the society being studied will have. Thus, while much of what an ethnographer might do would involve feeding various kinds of texts into a computer, it is also necessary to recognize that the anthropologist's own contextual understanding can be drawn upon in computer representations that will assist the analysis of the texts. In other words, various tools of artificial intelligence can be used both for organizing the data of a text and for organizing ethnographic statements made by the anthropologist.

I shall speak of this new approach as text ethnography, the description and modeling of culture through the study of recorded human speech (which is transcribed as a text by the ethnographer). The subject matter includes all that has been of traditional ethnographic interest: beliefs and values, social organization, role behavior, child rearing, religious practices, economics, and the rest.

A Discourse Research System

The analysis of text can be aided by a computer system developed as a prototype at the University of California at Irvine, called the Discourse Research System (DRS). This system uses three elements: features, rules, and frames (James and Colby 1979). Features are simply the components of meaning a word can contain. For instance, the word "chair" can include in its feature definition the qualities of being inanimate, as being a manufactured article or artifact, and as being a piece of furniture (a full-feature definition is not necessary for most of the purposes we have in mind). Accordingly, we can list these features for chair in brackets, the plus sign indicating a feature's presence: [+inanimate +artifact +furniture]. DRS also includes features of syntactic class (+noun, +verb), cohesion features (+deictic, +nonspecific), and associational features (from word association norms). The features for chair would thus be expanded to contain: [+noun +specific +table]. Of course, the word "chair" has many secondary meanings as well. For example, "the chair" can refer to a person presiding at a meeting. Secondary features which define these additional meanings can be included with the more frequent primary ones. The presence of these features is necessary for the application of rules and for assigning words to particular locations in knowledge structures or frames. The computer system reads a text, looks up every word in a feature dictionary, and inserts a feature list after each word. All further analysis is based on this expanded text.

Even with an expanded feature system such as ours, however, the types of relations covered are small in number compared to what might possibly exist. In our Discourse Research System the feature,

+furniture, is linked to the entry word, *table*, in a "kind of" relation. A table is a kind of furniture. This could be represented as a relation with two terms: (kind-of, table, furniture). But our feature dictionary simply lists the second term of the relation, with the relation itself presupposed. For association norms, where chair has the relation of "commonly associated" with "table," the dictionary listing simply includes the feature without specifying the type of relation.

The second component of DRS is a rule-building facility. A rule in DRS consists of a pattern and an action instruction that is contingent upon the appearance of that pattern in a text. The pattern can be a literal string of words or a group of features or a mixture of the two. For example, if one wishes to define a rule, DRS presents the analyst with three categories of information: variables, pattern, and action. Take the following rule:

variables: X, Y
pattern: 'The' X&+noun +be Y&+adj.
action: 'The' Y X

Words enclosed in quotes are to be taken as literal strings. The & sign is used to bind a variable to whatever word has the features that are indicated in the pattern.

DRS, if given the sentence "The tree is green," will apply the above rule and write "The green tree." Rather than carrying out such transformations, the most frequent action used is to assign words, features, or other elements to knowledge structures that are organized in networks of frames, as illustrated later.

The third component consists of frames. Frames are basically data structures. They can be of several types. The most important ones are sentence, situation, text, and text-world frames. Sentence frames map out conceptual relations, demarcate clause boundaries, identify themes, indicate case relations and other things that make up the meaning of a particular sentence. Situation frames represent the current state of the world at any particular point in a text. Text frames model the rhetorical structures of the text and such higher-level phenomena as plot or eidochronic structure (Colby 1973). Text-world frames model the ethnographic knowledge gained from a text. Beaugrande and Dressler (1980) define the text world as the cognitive content activitated by a text.

We can think of frames as a set of categories with empty slots to be filled with specific instances or values of each category. Frames can be embedded within other frames or can relate to frames in some other manner. Frames contain pointers to other frames so that networks can be created. Each frame can have one or more titles that indicate both the type of frame and the type of information kept in it.

Through the use of features, rules, and frames, the original discourse is translated into a general conceptual representation in a cluster of structures. Some of these are temporary structures (situational frames) that are eliminated or condensed along the way of the story line, similar to the actual fading in memory of the details of a story as the story comprehension progresses from start to finish. In other structures the processing goes beyond the text to represent long-standing beliefs and procedures (text-world frames). Such long-standing structures (as opposed to the occasional frames representing particular situations in space and time) are both created and referred to while the comprehension of a text progresses. Since our primary interest is the building of an ethnography rather than text comprehension itself (usually the major goal in artificial intelligence), it is the long-standing knowledge structure, the text-world frame, that commands ethnographic attention. Both text comprehension and a text ethnography require each other in a kind of bootstrap process as one wends his way through discourse. Text ethnography must therefore attend to both processes, the former as a means of accessing the latter.

How DRS Can Be Used

While these long-standing structures are of special interest to us as ethnographers, I will use a simpler analytical purpose to explain in more detail how our Discourse Research System operates. In the Anthropology Lab at UC Irvine we are interested in developing new forms of content analysis in order to do cross-cultural studies of the effects of hostility levels among different peoples.

To give an example of what might be done with the system, we will take an excerpt from a Maya dream collected by Robert Laughlin in Zinacantan (Laughlin 1976:21, Dream 5) and see how one might go about measuring hostility in terms of the Gottschalk and Glesar (1969) scales. In the process of measuring hostility, different types of conceptual relationships can be worked out to yield a qualitative as well as quantitative picture. This picture (i.e. data arranged in frames) can be used as a point of departure for further analyses *sans* computer. Thus the computer assists the anthropologist in some particular task by organizing and counting data that would otherwise not be available except on a very small scale.

Here is a sample text to be analyzed: "Then a cow arrived there. The children threw lots of stones at it. The owner of the cow came. The children got a good bawling out. The children got mad and threw stones at the owner of the cow, too. The owner of the cow was scared. He fled. And even I was terribly scared because they almost hit me with the stones, too."

The first step is to assign the words features from the feature dictionary. The words of the first sentence can be given something like the following features:

Sentence Word	*Features*
Then	(function word, relational, time adverbial, temporal)
a	(function word, article, deictic, nonspecific, singular)
cow	(entity, noun, singular, animate, animal, domesticated, milk, meat, pasture)
arrived	(event, verb, past, movement, directional)
there	(function word, relational, reference, demonstrative, selective, circumstance, location)

After assigning features, one applies rules that will analyze the text in terms of various communicative or textual characteristics before getting to the actual content. For instance, one can develop rules for identifying the major clauses of the sentences, rules to determine the mood (i.e. interrogative, imperative, or declarative) of each clause, clause-theme identification rules (Halliday and Hasan 1976), head-noun identification rules, subject identification rules, and cohesion rules including those of pronominal reference.

For example, after pronominal reference rules have been run, the text sample will look something like the following: "Then a cow arrived there. The children threw lots of stones at it (cow). The owner of the cow came. The children got a good bawling out. The children got mad and threw stones at the owner of the cow, too. The owner of the cow was scared. He (owner) fled. And even I (narrator) was terribly scared because they (children) almost hit me (narrator) with the stones, too."

Now the text is ready for thematic analysis (note: unless specifically identified as "clause theme," "theme" designates a unit of meaning that has some extended duration, frequent appearance, or focus either in a text or in the search image of an analyst).

Since we are using the system for measuring hostility, we may take the second sentence and imagine a number of alternative sentences of the same general pattern:

1. The children threw lots of stones at it (cow).
2. The children threw lots of stones in the lake.

3. The children threw stones in his face.
4. The children threw the knife away.
5. The children threw the man's cane away.

The first, third, and fifth sentences indicate some form of hostility (in most cases where we would imagine these sentences to apply; of course, a contextual analysis might suggest cases in which these assumptions might not hold, but we are developing frequency indices, not a logical structure that admits of no exceptions). The second sentence is neutral with respect to hostility; for the sake of argument, the fourth sentence may be considered a weak "protective."

In all these cases the semantic component, *direction,* which becomes activated by the verb "throw," is realized by a single function word (preposition) or a function word followed by other function words or by modifiers or, finally, by a noun. In the particular case of "throw," the major weight of thematic determination rests on these tail-end words and phrases. A series of rules is set up to handle them:

Motion.location Rule 1 (called by the appearance of the verb "throw"):
If
. . . "in" . . . [+body.part+animate] then 1 Aggression
. . . "in" . . . [+inanimate] then 0 Aggression
. . . "at" . . . [+animate] then 1 Aggression
. . . "at" . . . [+inanimate] then 0 Aggression
. . . "away" . . . then apply Aggression.case Rule 1
etc.

Aggression.case Rule 1
If
object.modifier = +possession then 1 Aggression
else object = +danger then 1 Protection

The scores are kept in one of several types of *frame* (see Minsky 1975 for discussions of different versions of frame representation). Frames can be located within frames. Within the smallest frames are *fields* that can contain whatever value a rule may place in them. What is selected to fill these frames and fields depends on the focus of the investigation and the rules that the investigator makes up. Frames can be used as a storehouse of knowledge, or to cluster different categories of rules, or to represent a particular situation located in time and space. How frames are used is entirely up to the investigator and the special research task.

Frames are a starting place for new kinds of studies involving unusual insights about ethnographic texts and native statements that can be subsequently formalized by the analyst and tested on other textual materials. In the example just given, a set of rules works directly on the text to provide numerical scores. Another approach would be a two-step system where rules fill out conceptual frames and another set of rules analyzes the content of the frames to determine special scores.

While the system can be used to transform texts in various ways, its main purpose in anthropological work is to construct representations of selected aspects of meaning according to any number of possible designs or architectures. The possibility of constructing a variety of architectures is one of its major advantages. For an example of one kind of architecture, see Table 1. The situation frame in the diagram is amplified in Table 2. A situation frame may remain active over a number of clauses and sentences until a major shift in setting, subject, or subject-theme relationships occurs. The subframes and fields of such a frame are filled only when the text in question provides the information or only for certain types of information the investigator is concerned about.

Unlike the General Inquirer system of content analysis (Stone et al. 1966), in which many word categories or "tags" are determined in a single pass, the system described here uses a very large dictionary from which small special-purpose dictionaries for single variables or clusters of variables can be built. Every time a cross-cultural study is run on a set of texts, a special code book containing DRS rules can be developed for that particular set of variables. In this process a folktale can be thought of as a sequence of events and situations. When a particular situation involves the concept being studied in some way, it will be mapped out by hand by filling out the relevant parts of a situation frame. A checklist for developing such a frame is shown in Table 2. What an actual frame for some particular concept might look like is shown in Table 3. The concept illustrated, *envy*, figures prominently in the body of texts from which the cow and stones sample text was drawn.

Frames such as the one in Table 3 are used for deeper-level interpretations if one is concerned about mapping out hostility relationships in more detail. Associated with this frame are rules that are activated when a word concerning dislike or envy occurs in the text. These rules attempt to fill out the frame and insert the filled-in frame somewhere within the situational frame.

Once a series of these frames have been filled out, they will be examined to see what particular types of words are used as clues for the essential concepts. Further steps will involve a set of rules similar to, but somewhat more formal than, those of McClelland (1961) and McClelland et al. (1972).

The feature approach to word definition is ideal for building knowl-

Table 1. Example of the Kind of Overall Architecture that Might Be Constructed with the System

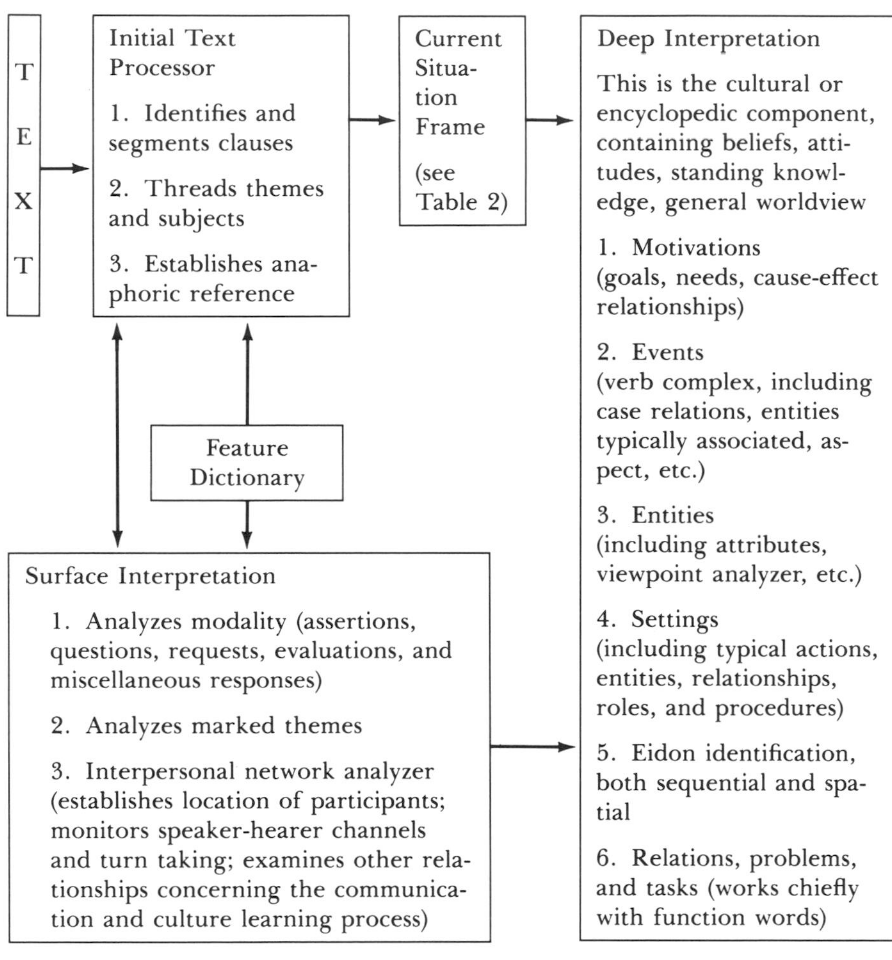
T E X T
Initial Text Processor
1. Identifies and segments clauses
2. Threads themes and subjects
3. Establishes anaphoric reference
Current Situation Frame
(see Table 2)
Deep Interpretation
This is the cultural or encyclopedic component, containing beliefs, attitudes, standing knowledge, general worldview
1. Motivations (goals, needs, cause-effect relationships)
2. Events (verb complex, including case relations, entities typically associated, aspect, etc.)
3. Entities (including attributes, viewpoint analyzer, etc.)
4. Settings (including typical actions, entities, relationships, roles, and procedures)
5. Eidon identification, both sequential and spatial
6. Relations, problems, and tasks (works chiefly with function words)
Feature Dictionary
Surface Interpretation
1. Analyzes modality (assertions, questions, requests, evaluations, and miscellaneous responses)
2. Analyzes marked themes
3. Interpersonal network analyzer (establishes location of participants; monitors speaker-hearer channels and turn taking; examines other relationships concerning the communication and culture learning process)

Table 2. Frame Checklist

1. Setting
   - Space
   - Time
   - General ambience
   - Behavior setting (Roger Barker)
2. Participants
   - Animate
     - Motivations, attitudes, attributes (including potentialities)
     - Current state
   - Inanimate
     - Attributes, location
3. Processes (events, actions)
   - Case relations
   - Event hierarchy and sequence relations
   - Multiple (reciprocal, nonreciprocal, simultaneous, nonsimultaneous, embedded, etc.)
   - Goal linkages
4. Motivations and problems
   - Unfulfilled goals
   - Lacking attributes
   - Mismatch of existing situation with desired situation
5. Aspect
6. Perspectives and viewpoints
7. Focus and salience list
   - Identification
   - Position
   - Choice
   - Reason
   - Process
   - Contingency
   - Attribution

edge structures with pattern-invoked rules such as those of DRS. But such knowledge structures are likely to be rather meager without a more complete kind of ethnographic dictionary to draw upon. Such a dictionary can be built with DRS in a kind of bootstrap operation.

Ethnographic Dictionary Building

Because the world is coded differently in the languages of different cultural systems, anthropologists have usually paid close attention to

Table 3. Sample Frame for *Dislike* or *Envy*

Subject	*Target* ________
location ________	
strength ________	
Reasons (of subject)	
Target has	
attribute ________	location ________
possession ________	strength ________
relationship ________	
	Problems (attributed to, or caused by, subject)
Desires	
Subject wants target to	
Lose attribute ________	________
possession ________	________
relationship ________	*Actions* (target considers or takes corrective action)
Stop acting ________	
Change from positive	________
state to: ________	________
Subject wants to do X to target ________	

dictionaries and native semantic organization. This concern was formalized in the ethnoscience movement where the focus was on the interrelations of semantic features in such vocabulary domains as astronomy (Goodenough 1953), color (Lennenberg and Roberts 1956, Conklin 1955, Berlin and Kay 1969), and kinship terms (Goodenough 1956; Lounsbury 1956; Wallace and Atkins 1960; Romney and D'Andrade 1964; Kronenfeld 1973, 1980) and a variety of other folk taxonomies (Conklin 1962, Nida 1975). This work has continued among anthropologists in the use of multidimensional scaling techniques (Romney, Shepard, and Nerlove 1972, Burton and Kirk 1977), regression analysis (Lave 1972), and computer simulations (Colby and Knaus 1974, Werner 1978). It has also been taken up by psychologists (Miller and Johnson-Laird 1976).

What is needed is a special kind of ethnographic dictionary, one that goes beyond a list of features and also one that goes beyond common dictionary definitions. For example, take a standard dictionary definition for table:

> ta'ble: n. 1, an article of furniture having a flat top supported by legs. 2, a plane surface; a level tract of ground; a plateau. 3, food served; fare. 4, persons gathered at a table. 5, an arrangement of written or printed information for classification in small space. 6, a list. (Morehead and Morehead 1961)

The value of an ethnographic dictionary over the standard type just quoted would be in its having detailed information that is presupposed by natives but not always by the anthropologist. This more complete kind of information is also the kind that artificial intelligence programs are likely to require. While this is a major reason for interdisciplinary work between anthropology and artificial intelligence, so far the only noteworthy works in this area by anthropologists using an AI approach are Eike Hinz (1978) and Oswald Werner (1978).

The making of an ethnographic dictionary would be an enormous task, but much of it could follow an automated procedure that abstracts some aspect of a word's meaning from the context of other words in the text. This would require activating a procedure that creates a partial definition for a word whenever the word appears in that text. For example, there might be a large set of "of" relation rules that looks for different strings of words containing "of." Each case would be classified according to a specified pattern of features. With each successful find or match of the pattern, a partial dictionary definition can be entered for one of the words in the "of" phrase. For example, one "of" rule might take the phrase "the edge of the table" and set up a dictionary entry for *table* as follows: *table*—has an edge.

In DRS a rule that can do this looks like the following:

variables:	X Y
pattern:	. . . +det . . . X&[+noun +location] "of" +det . . . Y&+noun
action:	Y "has a(n)" X ⇒ Dictionary

The two key terms (the first with the features, +noun and +location, the second with +noun) are identified as variables X and Y to be used in the action that takes the words matched, carries out a transformation, and sends it to the dictionary. The rule, of course, will not work on just any pattern of words containing an "of" somewhere in it. The pattern matcher will only match an "of" phrase that is preceded by a noun which contains a feature of location. Clearly there will have to be many different "of" rules including different types of features for some of the words in the "of" phrase. Thus, if one seeks to find a counterexample, it is necessary to pay particular attention to the features involved.

By taking high-frequency function words and retrieving a wide range of sentences that contain them, rules can be set up which place information in the dictionary that is rarely found in ordinary definitions. That a table has an edge is so obvious in our cultural system that there is no need for it in a standard dictionary definition. It is presupposed. Yet presupposed information is often not obvious to an ethnographer in some exotic society, and of course it is not obvious to a computer.

The rules that would build such a dictionary will often require the use of quite specific semantic features. Further editing will usually be necessary: the ethnographer or native sits at a terminal and reviews the automated definitions while a text is read and the definitions are formed. An optional characteristic of the system is to add the full sentence exemplifying the word to the definition entry. A "finished" ethnographic dictionary would thus have a set of defining characteristics for each word along with the examples of the words as they are used in sentences. In addition to a dictionary, one also ends up with an unusual kind of semantic grammar consisting of the rules that were used in the automated dictionary build procedure.

Individual variation can lead to multiple representation, which might be useful in studies of informant variation. But since these concepts are dealt with in particular contexts, the reliability of informant variation should not be a serious question: the matter is a question of semantics that presumably is widely shared. In other words, unless the analysis is particularly motivated toward the question of informant variation for some theoretical reason, a study of informant variation in this context is probably a case of misplaced precision.

Situational Representation

The process of text comprehension and the following of topic flow depend on a means of extracting information from a text and building up a dynamic mental "picture" of the situation. This picture I see as existing primarily in the short-term memory (STM) as a "window" that moves through the story line. Creating such a picture involves a complex interaction between the patterns in the text, various processing systems of the brain, and long-term memory (LTM) (Becker 1973).

For anthropologists LTM constitutes nothing less than the entire mental component of the cultural system that an individual operates in. Since anthropologists have been centrally concerned with representing the LTM (essentially in the form of an ethnography) in new, more formalized ways, there is much that the relevant AI approaches can offer them. Conversely, anthropologists would be valuable assets for AI research groups because a main problem in AI work is the lack of adequate LTM components. In fact, the various knowledge structures used by Schank and Abelson (1977) might be called mini-ethnographies. However, their characterization of roles and themes is *ad hoc* and uninformed by anthropological work. The LTM can be approached only through an adequate representation of what happens in STM, particularly in modeling the current context of situation for a text. In reading through a narrative text, any point in that text can be represented in a situational frame (see Table 2).

An Ethnographic Encyclopedia

Neither a dictionary nor a situational representation constitutes an ethnography. While there may be some argument about what exactly does constitute an ethnography, most anthropologists would agree that it would have to go beyond a list of lexical definitions, no matter how extensive and rich such definitions might be. Going beyond would presumably mean a treatment of broader topics (Pelto and Pelto 1973, 1978), the traditional "economics," "religion," "rituals," "material culture," "child-rearing practices," and the like. In short, an ethnography would be like an encyclopedia, but focused on a single society.

I suggest that, through the computer-aided study of texts, an ethnography be organized around roles and settings and that roles and settings, in turn, be organized around processes and situations, the situations including causes, goals, and results of the processes. This notion has been developed in Colby and Colby (1981). At a still higher level such information could be organized into themes, perhaps as Schank and Abelson have suggested (1977). Roles have a focal importance in anthropology because they lie at the intersection of two frames of reference, that of the individual and that of society. The plans or procedures that characterize a particular role are among the many behaviors of an individual's repertoire. The patterns resulting from these plans or procedures as carried out by a group of individuals are generalized in accounts of social structure and institutions.

Roles usually are not considered apart from the settings or situations in which they normally are activated. When role attributes and role procedures are observed, they are always observed in situations that have at least some elements in common. There must be, then, a human pattern-abstracting system that identifies these common elements and gives them contextual significance with respect to the relevant role attributes and procedures. By abstracting the attributes and procedures associated with various roles and by observing the actions of other people in a particular setting, one can infer what their motivations or goals are, while by knowing their goals, and the setting, one can guess what they may plan to do.

Once several text ethnographies have been constructed and a series of role sets has been identified, the reference point for these roles can be shifted from the individual to the setting or situation that evokes them. For example, after preparing several text ethnographies (e.g. after extracting information from the text-world frames for a collection of folktales of some society), we may have a list of roles utilized in the stories by the different characters. Associated with each character may be anywhere from one to ten or more roles he has used in the course of a story. Now, instead of sorting the roles by character, we can shift to situation type and sort the roles according to the situation in which they are used. This reference shift carries us from a focus on the individual mind to a focus on types of contexts, milieus, and social groupings.

One of the problems in working with role systems is that there can be embedding and multiple membership of components of the roles. Certain role elements might fit in a number of different types of roles, so that until further information becomes available, they remain ambiguous. But with the use of a frame network, this complexity can be handled.

An organization of roles and settings is illustrated in the following hypothetical representation (Table 4) of the role of maize farmer among the Ixil Mayans of Guatemala. The three frames are at the top level. Each item has a series of pointers, one of which links the process to subprocesses, others (not shown) to the appropriate setting. Other types of frames in the network will depend upon a particular analytical purpose. (This particular example was not derived from an actual computer analysis of a text.)

These frames can be taken as a starting point for a computer program that models the procedures of a role process. If the procedures are undeviating, that is, if they consist of a single string of events, they can be compared to scripts (Schank and Abelson 1977). If they involve multiple paths, then each path can be seen as a plan (Schank and Abelson 1977) or the end production of a cultural grammar (Colby 1975). This network of scripts, plans, and grammars, whether organized by roles or settings (or possibly some other category depending upon one's analytical purpose), can be thought of as part of an ethnographic encyclopedia.

If frames like those of Table 4 can be derived from native texts, we may possibly be closer to "cultural reality" than if we try to work out a role system based on our own observations. Thus, through text

Table 4. Roles and Settings for Maize Farmer

Role Frame: Maize Farmer

Settings: Fields
Route among house, granary, and fields
General neighborhood
Granary and patio
House

Processes: Clear land
Recruit help
Perform ritual
Plant →
Weed
Harvest
Store

Process Frame: Plant Maize

Subprocesses: Plan planting day
Recruit planters
Enlist kitchen help
Prepare food for planters
Pour seed corn for planters
Walk to field with seeds and planting stick
Leave extra seed and gear at corner of field
Proceed in line with other planters parallel to line of fall
Eat →
Return to planting procedure
Leave field, return to house
Provide evening meal to helpers

Process Frame: Eat

Subprocesses: Receive bowl for washing hands
Wash
Pass bowl on
Receive bowl for rinsing out mouth
Rinse
Pass bowl on
Receive and eat food
Receive and drink atole and coffee
Give thanks/acknowledge thanks

ethnography, we may be closer to an emic (culturally real categories) than an etic (predetermined or *ad hoc* categories) description.

Some Issues

The Use of Primitives

The requirements of an artificial intelligence system and those of cognitive anthropology differ significantly. A common approach in artificial intelligence (e.g. Schank and Abelson 1977, Wilks 1979) is to reduce words of fairly high information content to primitives. The particular primitives used in this scheme, however, are *ad hoc. Ad hoc* primitives are perfectly acceptable from the engineering approach of artificial intelligence. But they are not acceptable in cognitive anthropology, where native categorizations, features (components), and relations are crucial. A different approach is needed that is more consonant with cognitive anthropology, one that preserves information and avoids arbitrary pruning of information. Such a different approach is the use of the words of the texts in organized frames such as those already mentioned, rather than the recoding of words into semantic primitives. In the frame approach emphasis shifts to the nature of the frame itself. Yet, even so, each text word has added to it a feature "definition" that has much of the utility of semantic primitives, with the added advantage that the features are not entirely *ad hoc.* Many of these features are derived from linguistic analysis, some from psychological studies. Another difficulty with the reduction of words (particularly high-frequency words) is that it is harder to assign marking relations and determine rhetorical structures. Marking relations are a key to determining basic topics and comments of sentences, paragraphs, and entire texts. With loss of control over the marking relations there is loss of control over some of the textual component of a text.

As Minsky suggests, a study of sentence comprehension is an ethnographic effort. He points out, for instance, that very little of the meaning of "trade" is captured in the following:

First Frame:		Second Frame:	
A has X	B has Y	B has X	A has Y

According to Minsky, "trading normally occurs in a social context of law, trust, and convention. Unless we also represent these other facts, most trade transactions will be almost meaningless" (1975:240). I think that there is no really good reason for throwing away information by reducing sentences to a series of semantic primitives. The use of features *along with* the original words is preferable. Sentence comprehension would then begin with an *adding to*, rather than a subtracting from, the original text. In addition to the word features, what we add to the text is the pragmatic component, all the cultural knowledge that we keep in our heads to understand our world.

Transformations

Another major issue is the utility of transformational generative grammar for text ethnography. If one looks at texts in terms of thematic structures, a simple transformational approach that assumes a string to be the surface manifestation of some inner kernel does not deal with anaphoric reference and general textual or rhetorical structures. The approach by Chomsky goes beyond the single sentence only with difficulty because it visualizes transformations as being produced from simple kernels. Recently there has been a discussion of this issue as it relates to artificial intelligence. In a radically new approach Knaus (1978b) rejects transformational generative grammar and other grammars based on constituent ordering. Such grammars fail to deal adequately with spoken sentences, which are usually regarded as ungrammatical, that is, as broken off, having new sentence insertions and sentences with repeated or deleted constituents, etc. Knaus's solution is to take chunks as basic elements. A chunk is a list of attribute-value pairs. During language understanding chunks are moved around in STM. New chunks can be added to existing ones. One chunk can be used as the value of some attribute in another chunk. In anaphoric reference this process extends into a longer-term memory. Knaus discusses the design consequences of time and memory constraints and suggests how a chunking parser can map sentences into case grammar deep structures while living within the constraints.

Some Crucial Desiderata

The studies by Grimes (1975) and Longacre (1968) have shown how important the question of overall textual structure is for text ethnography. Much of the work by Halliday and Hasan (1976) constitutes a major contribution to it. The importance of the textual (or rhetorical) structure lies not only in the need for a systematic handling of the text content and purpose as a prerequisite for content analysis but also in establishing a link between the narrative or expositional logic and a more global logic of human behavior and purpose. Further, the textual structures provide us with clues about the internal organization or chunking into what has been vaguely described as schemata.

A very promising way to learn about rhetorical predicates and similar higher textual-level chunks is in the study of narrative recall, where different types of narrative structure, from plot content to dramatic emphasis, can be revealed through the mistakes of the subjects. An entirely new field dealing with these matters with interesting and diverse approaches is beginning to open up (Mandler and Johnson 1977, Norman et al. 1976, Rumelhart 1975). The most significant work by an anthropologist so far is that of Rice (1978). In Rice's study subjects were given stories with different sections missing to see how different elements of a story's structure affected comprehension and recall.

Conclusion

With text ethnography I believe we can get much better ethnographic reliability. Describing the underlying philosophy and values of a society without distortions and bias is impossible. But we can try to approximate a hypothetical "true" or culturally real description. Such a task presents problems of greater or lesser severity depending on one's approach. Text ethnography should allow more precise description than has been the case. Further, anthropologists are more likely to agree on the results. Thus both validity and reliability are improved. In so doing it should help to place discipline on a firmer scientific footing and provide a useful structure for psychology, linguistics, and other disciplines that utilize texts.

Text ethnography need not work only with "edited" text. Nor is there any reason why the analysis should be limited to the text being studied. The anthropological observer and the computer can interact to provide background material that is necessary for the interpretation of the text being studied. Depending on the purpose of the study, this interpretative element of the observer can be distinguished from the material derived directly from a text. Edited text rather than casual conversational text is easier to use for obvious reasons. A conversational text between two native speakers will have many elliptical elements that would have to be explained by the observer or by the native in some exegesis. Rather than the observer's commentary or the native exegesis, one can use a native text that has been filled out in the edited form. But even here background information will be needed, and we are talking about a question of degree. There will be background information that cannot be supplied in the interpretation of any particular text segment. However, in dealing with hundreds or thousands of texts, an information system can be built up that can then supply interpretive data for otherwise elliptical texts.

We are dealing with a complex interactive process. DRS can be a learning system that produces world knowledge from a text, or it can be a comprehending system that produces an ethnographic interpretation of a text. Finally, DRS can be used more fundamentally as a system to develop rules applicable in the above two systems.

The kind of ethnographic analysis described here will clearly have to be developed to a very substantial extent in the next 25 to 50 years as we move into a new age of communication and information processing. Such work requires a team approach. One might characterize it as "high-information anthropology." But whether cognitive anthropologists choose to move in this direction or whether psychologists, linguists, and artificial intelligence people will have to become ethnographers in their place remains to be seen.

REFERENCES

Beaugrande, Robert-Alain de, and Wolfgang Dressler
1980 *Introduction to Text Linguistics:* London: Longman.

Becker, J. D.
1973 A Model for the Encoding of Experiential Information. In R. C. Schank and K. M. Colby, eds., *Computer Models of Thought and Language.* San Francisco: Freeman.

Berlin, Brent
1971 *Speculations on the Growth of Ethnobotanical Nomenclature.* Language-Behavior Research Laboratory Working Paper no. 39. University of California, Berkeley.

Burton, Michael L., and Lorraine Kirk
1977 Meaning and Context: A Study of Contextual Shifts in Meaning of Maasai Personality Descriptors. *American Ethnologist* 4:734-61.

Colby, B. N.
1973a A Partial Grammar of Eskimo Folktales. *American Anthropologist* 75:645-62.
1975 Culture Grammars. *Science* 187:913-19.

Colby, B. N., and Lore Colby
1981 *The Daykeeper.* Cambridge, Mass.: Harvard University Press.

Colby, B. N., and Rodger Knaus
1974 Men, Grammars and Machines: A New Direction for the Study of Man. In M. Black and W. A. Smalley, eds., *On Language, Culture, and Religion: In Honor of Eugene A. Nida.* The Hague: Mouton.

Conklin, Harold C.
1955 Hanunóo Color Categories. *Southwestern Journal of Anthropology* 11:339-44.
1962 Lexicographical Treatment of Folk Taxonomies. *International Journal of American Linguistics* 28:119-41.

Goodenough, W. H.
1953 *Native Astronomy in the Central Carolines.* University Museum Monographs. Philadelphia.

1956 Componential Analysis and the Study of Meaning. *Language* 32:195-216.

Gottschalk, L. A., and G. C. Gleser

1969 *The Measurement of Psychological States through the Content Analysis of Verbal Behavior.* Berkeley: University of California Press.

Grimes, Joseph E.

1975 *The Thread of Discourse.* The Hague: Mouton.

Halliday, M. A. K., and Ruqaiya Hasan

1976 *Cohesion in English.* London: Longman.

Hinz, Eikc

1978 *Analyse aztekischer Gedankensysteme: Wahragelaube und Eerziehungsnormenals Alltagstheorie sozialen Handelns.* Wiesbaden: Franz Steiner Verlag GMBH.

James, M. L., and B. N. Colby

1979 *The DRS-77 Instructional Manual.* School of Social Sciences, Orangeback Series, Scientiarum Ancillae 1, University of California, Irvine.

Knaus, Rodger

1978 Parsing with Short Term Memory Constraints. Paper presented at COLING-78, International Conference on Computational Linguistics, Bergen, Norway, 14-18 Aug.

Kronenfeld, David B.

1973 Fanti Kinship: The Structure of Terminology and Behavior. *American Anthropologist* 75:1577-95.

1980 Particularistic or Universalistic Analyses of Fanti Kin-Terminology: The Alternative Goals of Terminological Analysis. *Man* 15(n.s.):151-69.

Laughlin, R. M.

1976 *Of Wonders Wild and New: Dreams from Zinacantan.* Smithsonian Contributions to Anthropology no. 22. Washington, D.C.: Smithsonian Institution Press.

Lave, Jean C.

1972 *A Decision-Model of Choice of Referential Relationship Terminology.* Social Sciences Working Paper no. 11. University of California, Irvine.

Lenneberg, E. H., and John M. Roberts

1956 *The Language of Experience: A Study in Methodology.* International Journal of American Linguistics Memoir no. 13.

Longacre, Robert E.

1968 *Discourse and Paragraph Structure.* Santa Ana, Calif.: Summer Institute of Linguistics.

Lounsbury, F. G.

1956 A Semanatic Analysis of the Pawnee Kinships Usage. *Language* 32:158-94.

Mandler, Jean M., and Nancy S. Johnson

1977 Remembrance of Things Parsed: Story Structure and Recall. *Cognitive Psychology* 9:111-51.

McClelland, David C.
1961 *The Achieving Society.* Princeton, N.J.: Van Nostrand.
McClelland, David C., et al.
1972 *The Drinking Man.* New York: Free Press.
Miller, G. A., and P. N. Johnson-Laird
1976 *Language and Perception.* Cambridge, Mass.: Harvard University Press.
Minsky, M.
1975 A Framework for Representing Knowledge. In P. Winston, ed., *The Psychology of Computer Vision.* New York: McGraw-Hill.
Morehead, Albert, and Loy Morehead
1961 *The New American Webster Handy College Dictionary.* New York: New American Library.
Nida, E. A.
1975 *Componential Analysis of Meaning.* The Hague: Mouton.
Norman, D. A., et al.
1976 *Explorations in Cognition.* San Francisco: Freeman.
Pelto, Pertti J., and Gretel H. Pelto
1973 Ethnography: The Fieldwork Enterprise. In John J. Honigmann, ed., *Handbook of Social and Cultural Anthropology.* Chicago: Rand McNally.
1978 *Anthropological Research: The Structure of Inquiry.* 2d ed. Cambridge: Cambridge University Press.
Rice, Grace Elizabeth
1978 The Role of Cultural Schemata in Narrative Comprehension. Ph.D. dissertation, University of California, Irvine.
Romney, A. Kimball, and R. G. D'Andrade
1964 Cognitive Aspects of English Terms. In A. Kimball Romney and R. G. D'Andrade, eds., *Transcultural Studies in Cognition,* pp. 146-70. Special issue of *American Anthropologist,* vol. 66.
1972 *Multidimensional Scaling: Theory and Applications in the Behavioral Sciences.* Vol. 1: *Theory;* vol. 2: *Applications.* New York: Seminar Press.
Rumelhart, David E.
1975 Notes on a Schema for Stories. In D. Bobrow and A. Collins, eds., *Representation and Understanding Studies in Cognitive Science,* pp. 211-36. New York: Academic Press.
Schank, Roger C., and Robert P. Abelson
1977 *Scripts, Plans, Goals, and Understanding.* Hillsdale, N.J.: Lawrence Erlbaum Associates.
Stone, Philip J., et al., eds.
1966 *The General Inquirer: A Computer Approach to Content Analysis.* Cambridge: M.I.T. Press.
Wallace, Anthony, and J. Atkins
1960 The Meaning of Kinship Terms. *American Anthropologist* 62:58-80.
Werner, Oswald
1978 The Synthetic Informant Model: On the Simulation of Large Lex-

ical/Semantic Field. In Marvin D. Loflin and James Silverberg, eds., *Discourse and Inference in Cognitive Anthropology: An Approach to Psychic Unity and Enculturation.* The Hague: Mouton.

Wilks, Yorick
1979 Making Preferences More Active. *Artificial Intelligence* 11:197-224.

13

"Commitment" in American Marriage: A Cultural Analysis

Naomi Quinn

An enduring question in anthropology has concerned the nature of culture. Cognitive anthropology inherited from its parent school, ethnoscience, its own distinctive answer to this question: culture is shared knowledge. One chronicler of the modest intellectual history of cognitive anthropology, Roger Keesing, set this history in perspective when he suggested (1974:77) that far outlasting ethnoscientific absorption with systems of folk classification has been "a new and important view of culture as cognition" in which "cultures are seen as systems of knowledge." This view is most explicit in the various writings of Goodenough, and especially in this now familiar passage cited by Keesing: "A society's culture consists of whatever it is one has to know or believe in order to operate in a manner acceptable to its members. Culture is not a material phenomenon; it does not consist of things, people, behavior or emotions. It is rather an organization of these things. It is the form of things that people have in mind, their models of perceiving, relating, and otherwise interpreting them" (1957:167).

Whatever it is that one does have to know or believe to pass oneself off as a member of one's culture, however things, people, behavior, and emotions may be organized in the mind, whatever people's models of perceiving, relating, and interpreting these things may be—all remained unspecified in Goodenough's definition. Rather, the definition unfolded an ambitious theoretical program.

Cognitive anthropologists began to turn from their original questions about the taxonomic and paradigmatic structure of categorization systems, to broader concerns with the organization of knowl-

An earlier version of this chapter appeared in *American Ethnologist* 9:775-98, 1982. It is reprinted by permission of the American Ethnological Society and the author.

edge. They began to contemplate the various kinds of structures which must be posited to account for all that people know: for example, in Goodenough's own (1971) discussion of the interaction among propositions, beliefs, values, rules, recipes, routines, and customs; in D'Andrade's treatment of the organization of belief systems (D'Andrade 1972); and in a variety of proposals for recognition of the primary or vital role of particular conceptual structures such as propositions (Kay 1973), events (Frake 1977), and structured sequences of behavior settings (Frake 1975). Most recently, some of these anthropologists and their students have directed detailed research efforts to questions about the organization of knowledge, and have pressed toward a unified theoretical statement. In these pursuits cognitive anthropology converges with other fields in a newly fashioned multidisciplinary effort called cognitive science, which takes the issue of the representation of knowledge as a central concern. In delineating the role of culture in the organization of knowledge, this branch of anthropology now finds itself in a position to make a unique contribution to cognitive science.

This paper deals with one structure, here called a "scenario word," which plays a part in organizing knowledge. And it assumes that one important way in which cultural understanding comes to be shared, and the way in which the knowledge embedded in scenario words is shared, is through learning to speak a common language. This is, of course, an unabashedly Whorfian claim. But the following analysis benefits from lexical semantic theory that postdates Whorf considerably and permits a more precise description of how words can organize understanding.

The present paper emerges from research on people's understandings of an important everyday concern: their own marriages. In this research a small number of individuals (husband and wife in eleven marriages) have been interviewed separately and extensively about their marriages (a rough average of 15-16 hour-long interviews per person).[1] The analysis here rests on that portion of the interview material which has been transcribed to date—the first eight hours with each interviewee. Occasional segments from later interviews were also transcribed and analyzed when they were identified as containing relevant material.

The interviews themselves were patterned as closely as possible after ordinary conversations, the interviewer following the conversational lead of the interviewee and providing each interviewee the maximum opportunity to say all he or she had to say on the topic. Thus the interviews contain substories (about the interviewee's marital experiences) in what Linde (n.d.) has called the individual's "life story."

That is, they focus on the place of marriage in the interviewee's life. While the interview context is somewhat unusual, the stories which the interviewee tells in this context are similar, but not identical, to what transpires in naturally occurring conversations with one's friends, family, spouse, and oneself. What is told to the interviewer, then, in Linde's (ibid.:7) words, is one "cross-section of a speaker's life story." While this cross-section certainly does not reveal all that a given individual thinks about his or her marriage, it is representative of how that individual thinks.

What people know about an interpersonal relationship such as marriage is hardly systematic. A range of knowledge is brought to bear on a diverse set of cognitive tasks such as interpreting another's behavior, selecting and monitoring goals, decision making and planning, which arise in various contexts. Yet some of this knowledge has to do with broad understandings of the nature and point of the relationship itself, and it is this knowledge upon which the current research focuses.

Certain abstract words such as "commitment," "relationship," "fulfillment," and "love," which recur across the transcripts of different individuals, play an important role in understanding the point and nature of marriage. This paper offers an analysis of interviewees' use of the word "commitment" (and its verbal form, "commit"), a word that is employed by a majority of the spouses interviewed and occurs a total of 283 times in 90 interviews. "Commitment" became the object of analytic attention because of the frequency of its use in this material, and because of a seeming paradox in the manner of its use. Interviewees took for granted the interviewers' grasp of the meaning of this word and resisted requests to define it more closely. Yet inspection of the following interview excerpts should convince the reader that "commitment" can mean different things to different interviewees.[2]

1W-3 It really made me think. I had to sit there and think, "Gah." You know, "Am I really doing the right thing? Do I really love him enough to *commit* myself?" With this other guy over here that I thought I loved at one time telling me not to do this [GET MARRIED].

2W-5 I think it's harder for the *commitment* to break down than it is for the relationship and that's what causes a lot of bitterness and heartache when you break up with someone.

6H-11 But it just kind of occurred to me that I was going to propose to her when I saw her next. This—that I was going to make a *commitment,* you know.

5H-3 I think she is very *committed* to making our relationship and marriage work well. I think she works harder at that than I do.

5W-1 When I was dating anybody, they had to be completely *committed* to me, or finished. I didn't care, I wasn't waiting around for them to say, "Some day," or anything, they had to—right on the line.

6W-1 And as soon as I could convince them that the *commitment* was there, although the marriage was not, then they were very happy. And they—the more they saw us together then they realized that we really were quite committed to each other and that we would make the same type of effort to make it work whether we were married.

These statements suggest, but do not begin to exhaust, the variety of usage in our interview material.

It will be argued in detail that three alternative syntactic patterns of striking regularity in these data, and certain metaphorical and other linguistic features highly consistent with this syntax, mark three distinct senses of the word "commitment" as it is used in the context of American marriage. These three polysemous senses are themselves subordinate to a fourth, more general sense reflected in other usages. The superordinate sense encompasses all of the subordinate senses rather than differentiating among them. These three subordinate senses are: that of PROMISE (or PLEDGE); that of DEDICATION (or DEVOTION); and that of ATTACHMENT (or BOND, or TIE). Here small capitals have been used to indicate that these are not words but concepts—basic or underlying meanings—most closely captured in the American English word or words. Whether these concepts are themselves decomposable into other concepts, or whether they constitute primitive notions in an American folk psychology, is not addressed here. Because the words "promise," "dedication," and "attachment" come closest to saying what these concepts mean, there has come to be a partial mapping of syntax and metaphor belonging to these words onto the word "commitment." When used in each different sense, "commitment" takes the usage of another English word closest to that sense.

But there is more to the argument, which goes on to say that these three subordinate senses of "commitment," and no others, occur in the context of American marriage because of the way in which they are related to one another. This claim leans on an approach to word meaning suggested by Fillmore (1977a and b) and Langacker (1979). Fillmore asserts that "meanings are relativized to scenes" (1977a:59, 1977b:84), so that "when you pick up a word, you drag along with it a whole scene" (1977b:114). Illustrating this notion with verbs from the domain of commerce, he argues "that a word like buy or pay activates the scene of the commercial event; that everybody who understands the word knows what are the various components and aspects of such an event; and that a speaker's linguistic knowledge of the verb includes that knowledge of the grammatical ways in which the various parts of the event can be realized in the form of the utterance" (1977a:73). He goes on to sketch a cognitive basis for this view of word meaning: "Now when I say that meanings are relativized to scenes, what I mean is that we choose and understand expressions by having or activating in our minds schemes or images or memories of experiences within which the word or expression has a naming or describing or classifying function" (1977a:74). These scenes include, as well as individual memories, "schemata of concepts, stereotypes of familiar objects and acts, and standard scenarios for familiar actions and events that can be spoken of independently of given individuals' memories of experiences" (1977b:126).

Langacker carries this approach to a consideration of nouns, speaking of an "established functional assembly" (1979:10-11) akin to Fillmore's standard scenario, and illustrating this notion with the word "orphan":

> It tells a whole story in a single word, a story based on a functional assembly of kin relations and the life cycle. . . . This is an established functional assembly because people know that death occurs and often reaches both parents while their offspring is still relatively young. The word orphan designates an entity that plays a particular role in this conceptual complex. . . . Not only is its designation restricted to the person in the offspring role, but it is further restricted to that person in a particular time frame, subsequent to the death of the parents but prior (say) to maturity. (Ibid.)

A parallel analysis of the word "commitment" is argued here. The three subordinate senses of "commitment," PROMISE, DEDICATION, and ATTACHMENT, are related as different aspects of one interpersonal relationship. "Commitment" differs from "orphan" in being a story, not about a social status and the circumstances of a life cycle that surround it, but about a social institution, the speech act (PROMISE) that initiates it, and the entailments of this act: a state of intentionality (DEDICATION) and a relationship to another person (ATTACHMENT). Unlike the commercial event analyzed by Fillmore but like "orphan" in Langacker's example, the story of "commitment" is told in a single word. By contrast to "orphan," the word "commitment" has a more complex structure that is reflected in its variant usages. Finally, like both "orphan" and the terms for commercial transactions, "commitment" can be considered part of what Langacker calls an "established functional assembly" because American English speakers share the usages of this word, usages which carry shared understanding of a "scenario" that includes the speech act and its standard entailments for American marriage. In other words, those an anthropologist might choose, "commitment" embodies cultural knowledge. While the linguists cited above are primarily concerned with how this knowledge is employed in word understanding, the present application of their approach points mainly in the other direction, to the role of words that contain such knowledge, in the understanding of experience. Parenthetically, however, the present analysis has an important implication for linguists' understanding of polysemy: that polysemous senses of the same word, seemingly arbitrary when taken out of all the different contexts of its use and lumped together, demonstrate their relatedness within the specific contexts in which usage has evolved.

Eleven unhelpful cases of the quotative use of "commitment" (as in "I guess that's what I mean by 'commitment'") and another 31 cases in which the word's referent is only tangential or wholly unrelated to marriage (e.g. commitment to career, children, leisure activities, causes, or issues) were set aside. Of the remaining 241 cases amenable to analysis, 32 take a global or superordinate sense of the word "commitment" in reference to marriage, while 195 can be argued to take one of the three more particular or subordinate senses of the word. Twelve additional cases seem to combine two subordinate senses. Two last cases will be explained as variants borrowed from usage more typical of contexts outside of marriage. The analysis rests on four kinds of evidence: (1) syntactic regularity, (2) metaphorical usage, (3) formulaic language, and (4) sense of utterance. As will be seen, these criteria for assignment overlap in many of the actual usages to be examined. The persuasiveness of this analysis must be judged on the weight of all these pieces of evidence taken together.

Usage of "commitment" in its superordinate sense affirms the appropriateness of this notion in the context of marriage, without further specifying its entailments. As the following example suggests, such usages often make clear that commitment is central to what marriage is all about:

2H-1 We felt strongly enough about each other and we were both oriented towards marriage as, you know, a way of life. The thing to do, whatever. And, so that was for us the expression of *commitment.* You know, were we willing to get married and accept whatever, you know, the legal and social aspects that go along with getting married?

Each of the three subordinate senses of the word is more specific. These different subordinate senses correlate with three alternative patterns of syntax that help to distinguish them. An idea of the regularity and distribution of this syntactic patterning can be gained from the fact that, in these data, 101 cases can be unambiguously assigned to one or another of the three syntactic patterns—38 PROMISE, 17 DEDICATION, and 46 ATTACHMENT.

Using the convention that *X* and *Y* are persons, the agent and beneficiary respectively, and *a* is a thing that takes the patient role, these three patterns may be represented as follows:

1. *X* makes a commitment/It is a commitment to *Y* to do *a*/that *X* will do *a*.
2. *X* is committed/It is a commitment to *a*/to doing *a*.
3. *X* has a commitment/is committed/commits self to *Y*.

Below, each of these three patterns is illustrated in turn: Examples of syntactic pattern 1:

2W-7 Basically, that kind of a leap was saying that we were making a *commitment* together, that we were going to stay together, that we were going to try and make a go of our relationship permanently. For all intents and purposes. You know, I've explained, I think, already our idea of permanence is not permanent, permanent, permanent.

7H-1 I guess we looked at ourselves, each other, a little more seriously. I felt that we had made the—a real *commitment*. I mean even more so than we had before because we had exchanged—we had—we'd said to each other in front of all our closest friends and family at that ceremony, we had written the ceremony ourselves.

6H-2 I think the marriage commitment is slightly different and that it is a *commitment* to grow old together, have children, and, you know, intermix, and so forth.

4W-1 And I think the other thing that's changed has been our—just our *commitment* to communicate; our *commitment* to work things out and to share. And I think that makes a big difference.

5H-7 Perhaps part of our *commitment* to continually evaluate where we are is some sort of awareness of that phenomenon. That the greatest liability to our relationship is to not work on trying to get a good sense of where we are. If I let her alone and don't try and she leaves me alone, we might satellite far enough away so we're not sure what's in between us.

4H-1 I'd say that we got serious sometime after we made the *commitment* to get married. Once we got married that was a *commitment* to at least figure out how to get serious.

Examples of syntactic pattern 2:

2W-1 The word "commitment" strikes a chord in me. You know, like it just—it goes fairly deep. It feels like, if I'm *committed* to something, I'm going to—I feel strongly about it. I feel strongly enough that I'm not going to let it go easily, be it a relationship, a cause, a friendship—something that I believe in. I take my beliefs seriously and I act on them. I don't like to say one thing and do another.

3W-12 To cherish me and the children and the relationship. I think he feels totally *committed* to doing that. At least as much as I feel *committed* to doing that. I've never felt like he would be more willing than I was to say, "Oh, let's just break it up." Or anything like that. I've never felt that.

6H-2 By that time the communication really had broken down and both people were *committed* to entirely different and conflicting things. A total flip flop of where they had been. Which in our case didn't happen, fortunately.

4W-1 I would say it's a *commitment* to our marriage, a *commitment* to wanting to make our marriage work, wanting to put the effort into making it work. I think it's very easy to—I think it's very easy for people to let a marriage slide. Just slide right down the tubes. There's so many odds against it anyway.

Examples of syntactic pattern 3:

1W-1 And what's to say you're too young to be married, just because you're *committed* to someone, I mean, you know, and you—if you love them enough what difference does it make if you're married or not married?

2W-2 I sat down and I tried to—I said, "Look, I really just—I need the emotional support of sleeping with him. We feel married already. We have the *commitment* to each other. Please, you know, let us do that."

7H-1 You know, you choose someone to live with who, in the same way as a marriage partner, is stimulating to you, who shares interests with you. It's not like you're married to them in the same sense. You're not—you don't have that kind of *commitment* because you just—they can move out anytime or you can move out.

3W-7 I think when we met, okay, I was a junior in college. He was the first boyfriend that I had that I really considered a boyfriend in a long-term kind of way. I had gone out with a lot of other guys and sometimes they had been my boyfriend for a while but none in terms of, "Hey, this is somebody I really want to settle down with who also think—feels that way about me." And to settle into that—also that kind of sexual relationship where you—you know, you're fairly *committed* to each other and this is the—you assume—. . . .
. . . Yeah. And, that like I say I think I fell in love with him in the ter—in the sense of being really not interested in anyone else once that came along.

Now, while some of the 101 usages exhibit the full syntactic pattern which they exemplify, others are abbreviated in the sense that one or another optional element of the syntactic construction is omitted from the particular utterance. Thus, for example, in constructions of the first type, *X, Y,* and *a* are optional, resulting in utterances such as the following:

7H-2 I wouldn't have made a *commitment* to a woman who didn't fit that kind of general image. (*a* omitted.)

6H-2 I guess it's [MARRIAGE] the *commitment* that now it's no longer just games and you can drop it, you know. You mean to be together—period. (*X* and *Y* omitted.)

2H-2 I definitely wanted to make such a commitment. . . . (*Y* and *a* omitted.)

Optional elements can be indicated notationally by means of parentheses. Thus the examples above can all be subsumed under the general pattern

1a. ((*X*) makes/It is) a commitment (to *Y*) (to do *a*/that *X* will do *a*).

The omissions are interesting in and of themselves because they reflect the speaker's choice of a perspective from which one or another element of a situation may be put in the foreground (Fillmore 1977a). In one context it may be the beneficiary of a commitment who is salient and therefore foregrounded by the speaker, as in the first example above. In another context the nature of the commitment may be at issue, or, in still another, the act of making it. Other elements of the situation are taken for granted and may be deleted from the utterance. Thus much variability in the use of the word can be accounted for by the concerns that lead speakers, both by selecting one or another subpattern (e.g. *X* makes a commitment . . . versus it is a commitment . . .) and by making or not making deletions optional in that subpattern, to foreground different aspects of their commitment. At the same time, this feature of language creates a problem in classifying certain usages of "commitment" which are so abbreviated by deletion that they cannot be unambiguously assigned to one syntactic pattern or another, because the undeleted syntactic elements are ones shared by two patterns.[3] There are nine such ambiguous cases.

Strikingly, however, the assembled usages rarely cross these syntactic patterns. Interviewees do not, for example, say such things as "We made a commitment to working at our marriage" (a combination of syntactic patterns 1, which uses the verb "make," and 2, which takes the gerundive), or the reverse, "We are committed to communicate with each other" (pattern 2, followed by pattern 1). Nor do they make such statements as the more normal-sounding "We had a commitment to marriage" (a combination of pattern 3 with pattern 2) or "We made a commitment to our marriage" (patterns 1 and 2 combined). While readers may feel that some or all of the above are perfectly good English, in fact they simply are not said in these interviews. By comparison with the 101 usages that conform unambiguously to one of the three syntactic patterns, and the nine additional ambiguous cases, only four usages mix syntactic patterns. Two of these rare mixed constructions are contained in the following segment, where the first usage combines patterns 2 and 3 and the second combines features of patterns 1 and 2:

4H-1 . . . both of us have deep *commitments* to the concept of marriage based on our backgrounds and upbringing. We couldn't have given that up once we made the *commitment* to it.

The fact that such mixed constructions occur at all, and the fact that they do not seem to violate our sense of grammaticality, are both compatible with the theory of polysemous meaning underlying this analysis. The three specific senses of the word "commitment" are, after all, closely related to one another, and to the superordinate sense of the word, as parts of a single scenario for marriage. So it should not be surprising that these senses can and do "run together," intermingling in particular utterances as they do, and more rarely, in a single usage of the word. Brugman (1981) has borrowed from prototype theory to suggest, in the analysis of a different kind of polysemous word—"over"—that within the supercategory of the word will be cases which exist on the edge of two subcategories—that is, between two subordinate senses. Since both senses are named by the same word, the issue of grammaticality does not arise.

The present analysis, unlike Brugman's, is based on frequencies of actual usage rather than intuitions about grammaticality. What requires explanation is the finding that speakers so infrequently use the word "commitment" to apply simultaneously to two of its specific senses, even though the syntactic constructions that resulted would be grammatical. That such mixing of its subordinate senses does not ordinarily occur in natural discourse about marital "commitment" may have the following explanation. These distinct subordinate senses of the word have arisen in the first place, we can suppose, to mark out the culturally recognized components of an experience (Brugman 1981). As long as speakers continue to agree that these are indeed the separate components into which the experience can be meaningfully segregated, they will tend to use that word in these separate focal senses in order to make, and not obscure, these culturally important distinctions. At the same time, as Brugman stresses, these different aspects of experience go by the same name, rather than different names, because they are related.

Thus, to restate the claim being made, when interviewees offer such statements as "We made the commitment to get married" and "We were making a commitment together, that we were going to stay together," they are using "commitment" in the sense of PROMISE. When they say, "We are deeply committed to marriage and family" or "It's a commitment to wanting to make our marriage work," they are using the word in the sense of DEDICATION. And when they say such things as "We were really committed to each other" and "Was I willing to commit myself to her?" they are using "commitment" in the sense of ATTACHMENT. While the three patterns of syntactic regularity distinguish many usages of "commitment," other usages can be assigned to one or another sense on the basis of additional, minor syntactic patterns to be considered next.

What are here called minor syntactic patterns contrast sharply with those already discussed in being highly infrequent; each may occur once or twice in the entire body of material under analysis here, and together they account for only seven cases. But these cases are all the more telling for their infrequency. It is as if interviewees, instead of drawing on the syntactic constructions they habitually use with the word "commitment," are more actively mapping the syntax of other words onto "commitment" to create new constructions. Thus, for example, one interviewee says,

2W-1 Commitment was made I suppose about the same time we decided to get married, but even when I said yes to his proposal, it was more of a yes to "I want to try and make our relationship work for as long as it can." I guess that's what I mean by "commitment," making—deciding—*committing* to each other that you're going to try your best to make the relationship work, that it's worth some struggle and pain, to keep it going.

This construction, of the form

4. *X* commits to *Y* that *X* will do *a*.

occurs only once, but employs a construction very natural with the word "promise." Likewise, one could substitute "promise" for "commitment" in the following two cases, which exhibit the pattern

5. The commitment of *a*/doing *a* . . .

2W-5 The specific *commitment* of living together [WOULD END]. . . . . . . Not the commitment to support each other because as long as he's a friend of mine, he's—I would still support him. I support my friends.

5H-4 I think the *commitment* of P.'s love to me, knowing P., in some sense I thought was written in stone somewhere. That "So she loves and she will love and Amen."

Still another construction occurs in four usages of "commitment" in what appears to be its ATTACHMENT sense; the preposition "with" is used in place of "to" to yield

6. *X* has a commitment with *Y*.

as in the statement

2W-1 And I really don't believe in the institution of marriage. I don't believe it's necessary. I believe if you have a *commitment* with the person that the piece of paper, the legal thing, is not necessary.

"With" is certainly a familiar syntactic alternative to "to" in constructions, not with the word "attachment" but with the synonyms "bond" or "tie," from which this syntax seems to be borrowed.

The evidence that interviewees treat "commitment" alternatively as PROMISE, DEDICATION, and ATTACHMENT is not only syntactic but also comes from an examination of metaphorical usage, and one usage of formulaic language, as well as from the senses of the utterances in which the word "commitment" is employed. This evidence often overlaps with syntactic criteria, but just as frequently permits assignment of a usage to one or another sense of "commitment" when syntactic evidence is ambiguous or absent. In the remainder of the analysis it has proven most manageable to treat each sense of "commitment" in turn.

Lakoff and Johnson (1980) have called attention to the pervasiveness of metaphorical thinking reflected in everyday language. They would probably agree, for example, that the use of "make" in such phrases as "make a promise" or "make a commitment" turns these acts of speech into objects. It is not intended here to force a distinction between syntax and semantics in classifying such usages by their syntactic pattern rather than their metaphorical sense. It is simply a diagnostic convenience to group the multiple instances of this syntactic pattern together and contrast them with other syntactic patterns. Other usages are more varied as to syntax, and can more conveniently be grouped by the pattern of borrowed metaphor which they display. Thus certain further metaphors specific to the act of promising treat a PROMISE as various particular kinds of object: a promise can be "given" and "kept," "lived by" or "forgotten" (some may want to argue that forgetting a promise involves a literal meaning of "promise" as a speech event that becomes a mental construct in memory). All of these usages typical with the word "promise" are appropriated by interviewees to describe marital commitment:

7H-1 I think you can make a commitment from day one. . . . . . . It just takes—use the word—it takes work to keep the *commitment.* Because of other factors that enter into a relationship or your life.

7H-2 To maintain it or to make it real you have to give some kind of *commitment* to that person, that you will be with them. You will stay with them, you know, through the good times and the bad times. Just like it says in those traditional vows.

4H-2 She was feeling a deep commitment, which I admire her commitment, to her mother, and she was on the verge of forgetting the other *commitment.*

The sense of "commitment" as PROMISE is marked not only by borrowed metaphor but by the borrowing of what Fillmore (n.d.) calls "formulaic language." Two speakers seem to be mapping the expression " . . . NOT make any promises" onto "commitment" when they say

1W-1 And he was kind of in limbo, as he told me later, you know, he was going to school, finishing up his meat-cutting school, whatever you want to call it. And he was waiting to pass his exams before he—because he would be getting a big raise. And he didn't want to—didn't make any *commitments* until he had this raise, or was sure he was going to be a meat cutter.

2W-1 For about four months at least we didn't make that commitment verbal at all. We didn't say anything to the effect, we both were essentially free to see anyone else and I think we had stated that, too. That if either one of us felt like seeing someone else that was all right at that point because we hadn't made any *commitments,* monogamous commitments or anything else, it was just—but we wanted to spend—I mean, we were both interested enough in the relationship that we wanted to spend all our time together.

These usages of "commitment" share with utterances such as "I can't make any promises, but I'll try," the conjoining of a negative verb form, the word "any," and the plural form of "commitment" distinctive of this particular formulaic expression. (Other pluralizations of "commitment" are rare in these data, and almost always used in the sense of multiple ATTACHMENTS to different people.)

Interesting indirect evidence for "commitment" as PROMISE is provided by examples in which "commitment" is explicitly treated as an act of speech:

2W-1 For about four months at least we didn't make that *commitment* verbal at all. . . .

5H-4 I think the *commitment* of P.'s love to me, knowing P., in some sense I thought was written in stone somewhere. . . .

6W-1 And it's a very lovely, very simple ceremony. You just sit quietly and then we stand and say our vows and you can say anything. We chose the standard one which is just a very simple sentence-long *commitment.*

While such statements do not all differentiate between PROMISE and other speech acts that might conceivably be the basis for this usage of "commitment," they do clearly distinguish between "commitment" as a kind of speech act and the other senses of "commitment" to be discussed below.

When "commitment" is used in the sense of DEDICATION or ATTACHMENT, it seems to take on their attribute of being an internal state. Thus in these usages the word can take a common metaphor for internal psychological states in American English: it can be felt (13 cases). In its PROMISE sense a "commitment" cannot be felt; thus interviewees never say things like, "I feel a commitment to work at this marriage." They can and do say, however,

4H-5 At the very beginning of these tapes I remember saying how T. and I felt a deep *commitment* to marriage and family. . . .

Here "commitment" is being used in the sense of DEDICATION. Using "commitment" in the sense of ATTACHMENT, interviewees also make such statements as

2W-5 His is just a deeper level of the same process. He's someone that I've been able to get to a much deeper level with, the deepest of anyone that I know. But every relationship that I have is somewhere in that process. I feel very strongly—very *committed* to so many people.

Both the syntax (to *a* in the first usage, and to *X* in the second) and the modifiers taken by "commitment" ("deep" and "strongly" respectively, metaphorical usages to be discussed below) permit distinction between the DEDICATION sense of "commitment" in the first case above the ATTACHMENT sense in the second case. In four cases in which "feel" is employed, however, the remainder of the construction fails to distinguish unambiguously between these two senses. For example:

7H-2 Or the person, let's say, who solved the problem would—whose ego has been a little inflated would feel real good about themselves, you know, it would make them feel more *committed* because they did good and they feel good for what they did.

Other metaphors are more specific to one or the other sense of the word. In its DEDICATION sense "commitment" can be metaphorized as "deep," or "deeply felt," as in the phrase "I felt a deep commitment to marriage and family" above, and two additional cases. Another metaphor borrowed from DEDICATION is one that treats "commitment" as requiring continuous effort; this usage of "commitment" with the verb "maintain" occurs once in the material under analysis:

4W-7 Well, it's hard to pinpoint any time or any event. It [THE MARRIAGE] simply moved slowly. I think probably a part of it moving was developing a stronger commitment or a trust that somehow it could work out in the marriage, in the relationship. That it was worth trying to develop the independence and autonomy while at the same time maintaining the *commitment* to the relationship.

The sense of "commitment" as the directed, motivated intentional state conveyed by DEDICATION is overwhelming in the kinds of marital goals interviewees make commitments to and are committed to. Commitment is to marriage, family, the relationship—to serious goals such as raising a family and staying together:

3W-1 That [LIVING TOGETHER FIRST] was part of the process of deciding that that would happen. But I think in terms of a long-term *commitment,* it—if we had said to each other "Well we really are going to stay together for a long time, but we won't get married," that would have seemed silly to me. You know, I mean I was able to think in terms of our relationship, "Well, we'll settle down and we'll have children, we'll . . ." you know, there was some future kind of a thing, that "This is the way we're going to do it."

6H-12 Then there's two of us and then—and you have to like—and getting my degree, going through that whole thing and sticking with it, was partly a *commitment* to our relationship, you know, wan—thinking children in the future in a vague sort of way, you know, so by that point I was not—no longer feeling footloose and fancy-free either as I was when I was leaving India, you know, or wanting to be.

And commitment is to effortful goals, "to making our relationship and marriage work well," "to wanting to make our marriage work, wanting to put the effort into making it work," "to making our life very happy together," "to trying to stay together," "to continually evaluate where we are," "to at least figure out how to get serious," "to communicate . . . to work things out and to share," "that you're going to try your best to make the relationship work, that it's worth some struggle and pain, to keep it going," "that you will stay with them through the good times and the bad times," "that it's no longer just games and you can drop it."

The third sense of "commitment," ATTACHMENT,[4] invites a number of usages all drawn on the metaphor of an attachment or bond as a physical connection between people. Interviewees use this metaphor to locate their "commitment" to their spouses on several dimensions. For example, "commitment" can vary in strength (12 cases), as in the statement,

2W-5 As you grow together the commitment grows and the more time you spend you're developing on that. You know. Beginning a relationship the *commitment* is very weak at the very beginning when you first meet someone—*commitment* is extremely weak but there's a tiny bit of commitment there to either continue the relationship, you know, make an effort on it to make that person into a better friend. You know? Or drop them altogether.

Other adjectives vary "commitment," as "attachment" can be varied, in primacy (eight cases),

4W-3 And that we don't have the usual contract that folks have which is that this is a no-no, this will ruin everything, this means you've been unfaithful, untrue, unloyal, and all kinds of bad things. And that's obviously there because of the experiences we've had, because we've learned that you don't give up your basic *commitment*, that we haven't given up our basic *commitment* with each other and to each other in the process of having cared for, loved other people. That it's still there.

5H-5 There was a primary *commitment* to me and the relationship with F. was ancillary, may deal on areas that I didn't. But was largely additive and so that made it good and okay and reasonable and all that.

in duration (four cases),

6H-11 Well sort of ability to deal effectively with people on a certain level [IS QUITE COMMON IN AMERICA] but beyond that a real lack of commitment to other people. As persons, you know—individual kind of long-standing *commitments* to other people and, you know, I guess maybe that's why it's easier—easy to get married with somebody else, you know, and so forth and so on.

2H-2 Neither of us were afraid of permanent *commitment*. We weren't trying to play, you know, loose and keeping our options open or things like that. That w—neither of us were really interested in that.

and in type, which can be legal, as in the single case below,

1W-1 And, it's terrible, I'll say I trust him enough not to go out, yet I'm sure he trusts me but I was doing it. But we had no commitment, really. Not any kind of legal *commitment* or, it's different now, but then —

but is overwhelmingly emotional (nine cases), as in the following segment:

3W-12 That he has a right to have a wife who has the sort of emotional *commitment* to him that many couples seem to have, and one part of me says, "Well you probably do have at least as much emotional *commitment* to him as almost anybody would have but you don't have the mindless 'I'm in love' kind of losing yourself." Pu—surrendering your judgment and perspective and stuff like that. And some part of me must keep saying to me, "That's the way you're

> supposed to be in love, that's why you're supposed to be married that's the ideal, you know, that's what you *owe* to your husband."

A number of interviewees also speak of "commitment" as something which "is there" (11 cases). Unlike "commitment" in the sense of PROMISE, an act of speech which must be made, or "commitment" in the sense of DEDICATION, an internal motivational state one is in, "commitment" as ATTACHMENT is externalized as a physical bond existing "there" between two people:

1W-2 I knew I loved him when I was in college, but I still went out with other people, for a while. But I wouldn't have done it here in Burlington, where he would have found out and it would have hurt him unless I were going to tell him. Because we kind of—I mean it wasn't a complete *commitment,* there as far as, you know, we weren't seeing anybody else. You know we were kind of together all the time.

2W-4 It's further solidifying the commitment. . . .
. . . The *commitment*'s there, but the closer together we get, the stronger the commitment gets.

4H-2 I still, at the very beginning, I said, you know, right away we knew there was a *commitment.* And this was the same thing that was basically true about all these couples. I think they all got married thinking that this was the thing, the right thing to do and it made sense for them and it was real.

Other overlapping criteria, such as the sense of the first utterance above (which makes clear that exclusivity of attachment is at issue) and the metaphor of strength in the second utterance, are invariably consistent with this interpretation of "there" as referencing an attachment between spouses.

But this bond is not immutable. The same actions that can be performed on physical or metaphorical attachment can be performed on commitment. Not only can one actively "commit oneself" to another person in the same way one can attach oneself, but one can also threaten, give up, develop, intensify, continue, solidify, utilize, and build on a commitment (12 cases), in such observations as,

2W-4 The strongest commitment I have to anyone on this earth is the commitment that I have to C. . . .
. . . And, you know, if it came down to a friend that I had a commitment to versus the commitment to C., if I had to give up one of them, I would give up the *commitment* to the friend.

5H-4 I think it worked out that through miles of talking, with one another, on a lot of this, that it at least made sense to us and felt important to us to continue our *commitment* and our living together with one another.

Since attachment to another person is at the same time a human emotion engendered by the tie between people, it seems to take on physical properties in common with certain other feelings in American English. Not only can it be felt, but it also grows and otherwise changes in degree. "Commitment," in turn, takes on these metaphorical capacities (12 cases). Commitment can grow, strengthen, or, conversely, break down, in statements like,

2W-5 As you grow together the *commitment* grows. . . .

2W-5 I think it's harder for the *commitment* to break down than it is for the relationship. . . .

and the following interview segment, which illustrates explicitly the concrete sense of ATTACHMENT this husband has in mind:

7H-2 In a healthy marriage or in a healthy relationship, the *commitment* will follow an upward curve. I guess, bell curve [*sic*]. Steadily. And then it will probably level off at a certain peak and —. . . .
. . . and it'll reach a certain peak and it'll level off. Can't keep going on forever. It can go down, but in a healthy—you reach a healthy state of relating together. . . .
. . . I mean, yeah, between two people, you know, you only go so far. You know, without—you're not—you may be married, you know. You don't—you're not cemented together physically, you know. You can only get so close. And it's not good to get that cl—it's good to know your partner as well as you can know another human being possibly.

Finally, two further properties of attachment between persons which can be conveniently conveyed by the metaphor of physical connection are enduringness and exclusivity. When "commitment" is described in terms of either of these dimensions, this is taken as evidence for the sense of ATTACHMENT. The idea of enduringness is conveyed not only in modifiers such as "permanent," "long-standing," and "long-term" commitment discussed above but also in the sense of statements such as:

2W-1 . . . if I'm *committed* to something, I'm going to—I feel strongly about it. I feel strongly enough that I'm not going to let it go easily, be it a relationship, a cause, a friendship. . . .

7H-1 We may have been together for four or five years and it may seem like a long time to us, but look at people who've been married for fifty years and there you really see *commitment* or attempted *commitment*.

3W-12 It's not as much emotional *commitment* as I want to have because I would feel happy with—as I think K. deserves. I'm certainly committed emotionally but there *is* a part that I'm holding in reserve. There's that part that says, "Well there may come a time when I have to dissolve this relationship because I can't deal with it anymore." It's a realistic kind of thing.

7W-1 Well, I don't know, I was uncomfortable with how we—really sharing things without some kind of *commitment* back. And there were two issues that I felt. One was living together and—I had a certain amount of savings for my dissertation and I didn't want that used for anything but me and my dissertation. Especially for someone who might not be here the next week or the week after.

The feature of enduringness that interviewees impute to "commitment" allows these otherwise uninterpretable usages to be assigned the ATTACHMENT sense of the word. Not all of the interviewees who discuss "commitment" in terms of enduringness necessarily agree that it implies permanency. Some deliberately qualify their statements to allow for the possibility that the intention of staying together permanently may not always be realized.

For other interviewees commitment raises the issue of exclusivity:

1W-2 Because once I got married that was my complete, total *commitment*. I would never, I mean, that's what I was saying, if I were to get to where I wanted to go out with somebody else I'd leave him first.

5W-1 I mean he was crazy about me. I mean I just like it when somebody's crazy about me. They have to be crazy about me and like everything about me. And he was really pretty *committed*. He didn't date anyone else. I mean as far as I know he didn't date anyone else—and I didn't.

Six otherwise ambiguous cases can be assigned the sense of ATTACHMENT because the utterances in which "commitment" is used make clear this entailment of exclusivity. Some interviewees talk about the exclusivity of commitment in terms of monogamy or faithfulness, suggesting that sexual exclusivity may be at the core of the matter. All these variable views of enduringness and exclusivity are common ways of talking about attachments to people, imported into the meaning of "commitment."

At this point it is prudent to summarize the disposition of cases.

As already noted, 32 usages carry the most general, superordinate sense of "commitment." While syntax, metaphor, formulaic language, and sense of utterance may overlap, singly and together these criteria permit the assignment of 182 (of the remaining 209) usages to one or another of the three subordinate senses of "commitment." An additional nine syntactic constructions and four usages of "commitment" with the verb "feel" exhibit features consistent with their assignment to a subordinate sense of "commitment," but are ambiguous with respect to which sense they are to be assigned to. There are, in addition to the four cases of mixed syntax discussed earlier, another eight usages of "commitment" that mix a syntactic pattern appropriate to one sense of the word with a metaphor appropriate to another sense. An example of this latter kind of mixed usage is:

2W-5 The relationship has changed in a way that you no longer want to be solidly *committed* to living with that person.

which seems to combine DEDICATION syntax with a metaphor of ATTACHMENT. These eight cases can be compared with another 21 usages in which syntactic and metaphorical criteria overlap (e.g. "to the depth of commitment to doing it" or "I committed myself emotionally to him") and 14 usages in which two metaphorical criteria are concatenated (e.g. "a strong emotional commitment") to produce utterances consistent with a single subordinate sense of the word. Again, usages that combine two senses of "commitment" do occur but are in the minority. Speakers tend to, though they need not always, use the word in one or another of its distinct focal senses.

Two cases remain unaccounted for. These merit special attention because they do not fit the interpretation set out here at all, but invoke instead a sense of "commitment" common in everyday speech but virtually absent from talk about marriage: "commitment" as AGREEMENT or UNDERSTANDING. This sense is characterized by the snytax,

7. There is a commitment that *X* will do *a*.

and is represented in statements by two different interviewees:

4W-3 So that the assurance is there that J. is never going to one day just walk out the door, with anybody. And I'm never one day going to walk out the door, never say a word, never talk about anything. The *commitment* is there that we must talk about it no matter what it is. And really make some kind of effort to get an understanding of what's happening.

7W-1 But there would be some *commitment* that we were going to spend—that we intended to make it work, that we did intend to share the rest of our lives together. That was our intent. That we intended to be with each other forever.

Utterances of this form, like utterances employing "commitment" as a kind of OBLIGATION (for example, in the formulaic expressions "fulfill one's commitment" and "honor one's commitments"), and constructions of the form

8. *X* has a commitment to do *a*.

—senses which seem to occur very commonly in everyday usage—are conspicuous by their absence in these interviews. These senses of "commitment," and others, simply do not seem to be part of the marital picture. Possibly these senses foreground a contractual aspect of the word that is available for the characterization of some relationships but is either inappropriate or deliberately suppressed in conceptualizing the marital relationship.

Why are the three senses of "commitment" as PROMISE, DEDICATION, and ATTACHMENT packaged in a single word applicable to marriage? The relationship between PROMISE and DEDICATION is perhaps most transparent. In the context of marriage, a "commitment" is not just any promise but, as reflected in interviewees' statements of goals, a promise to do something effortful and ongoing—something very difficult over the long run. It is in this sense that interviewees speak of making "such a commitment" and "that kind of commitment." To carry out such a promise engenders a particular state of intentionality, a dedication to the trying. It is as if, for those who elect to use it, the notion of "commitment" frames the kinds of goals that are appropriate to American marriage—goals of staying together, having a family and raising children, working out a relationship with one another, and making one another happy. This interpretation, that PROMISE and DEDICATION are related by virtue of their combined relationship to goals—the promise to attain certain goals entailing the intention to pursue them—is borne out by the observation that these marital goals can be couched in either the syntax of PROMISE or the syntax of DEDICATION. Interviewees make statements of the form "We made a commitment to have a family" as readily as they make statements of the form "We are committed to having a family."

The nature of these goals involves the makers, not only in a long-term effort to keep a promise but in a joint effort to do so, and hence in a long-term relationship with one another. Making such a commitment to someone is at the same time attaching oneself to that person for the duration of time—whether this be conceived of as "forever" or only "as long as possible"—required for pursuit of the goals to which commitment has been made. The attachment is not intellectual, like commitment to an idea can be, or contractual, like commitment to an obligation. Its overriding sense is rather that of emotional attachment. In American folk psychology two people in joint pursuit of goals as important, effortful, and remote as making a family, making the marriage work, struggling to figure out what it is about or where each other is, or helping each other "through the good times and the bad times," do become attached, or grow more attached over time, emotionally. In sum, the word "commitment" tells a story about American marriage.

This complex relationship in which two senses of "commitment," PROMISE and DEDICATION, entail the third, ATTACHMENT, is reflected in a number of interviewee statements about the enduringness and exclusivity of their commitment that couple these features of ATTACHMENT to the senses of "commitment" as PROMISE or DEDICATION. Thus enduringness and exclusivity themselves figure among the goals to which a couple has made a commitment or which they are committed to pursuing. The goal of enduringness particularly is likely to be the logical consequence of other, long-term goals. Thus the commitment is made "that we were going to stay together, that we were going to try and make a go of our relationship permanently"; that "you will stay with them, you know, through the good times and the bad times"; "that now it's no longer just games and you can just drop it, you know. You mean to be together—period"; "to grow old together, have children, and, you know, intermix and so forth"; "that we intended to make it work, that we did intend to share the rest of our lives together." And interviewees say, "We couldn't have given this up once we made the commitment to it, without tremendous trauma"; "You know, this may last. This may be a permanent situation. Am I willing to make that commitment?"

An occasional interview segment captures even more completely this interrelationship among original promise, subsequent effort, and the expectation of resulting attachment between spouses. It is in the juxtaposition of several usages of "commitment" in such passages, rather than within a single usage, that speakers are most likely to shift from one polysemous sense of the word to another. The following interview excerpts are representative of such complex utterances. These three excerpts are reproduced in full because the discussions surrounding the word "commitment" and its several usages make one or both links between the three parts of the commitment scenario particularly explicit.

4W-3 I think we are *committed* to making our marriage work. Making the effort to do the best we can until some—unless at some point doing the best we can doesn't work—simply doesn't work, doesn't meet our needs, doesn't make anybody happy and that kind of thing. So that primary *commitment* to make the effort, to work, to work together, understand each other, I think is what I mean by our primary *commitment* to each other. There is no one else I feel that kind of *commitment* to. And I—there's no one else that J. feels that kind of *commitment* to. That's the most important *commitment* we have.

3H-5 I think that too often—that too many decisions are made without real thought; made on impulse, made on—made for reasons other than conscious decision that this is somebody you want to not just be with for the next week or the next night or the next ten minutes, but someone you want to be with for a long—extended period of time. And if you—if—it seems to me when you make a *commitment* to something like that, in human terms, when you make a *commitment* to another person, irregardless of who it is, whether it's going to be your wife, or your male lover or whoever in God's name it is, if you're going to make a human *commitment* to somebody then you ought to be prepared to live by the *commitment* and to do so because you want to, not because you feel obligated to.

8W-10 Yeah, when you said "commitment" that's, see, because it means something. Marriage is—these people who keep kidding themselves that living—what's the difference whether you're living together or you wrote something on a piece of paper? The difference is *commitment*. . . .
. . . It's an emotional *commitment*. I mean you have decided definitely that this is a person that you are going to exert yourself to spend your life with. You don't feel that little loophole. That, you know, if I get mad at him, well, you know—

Because knowledge of word use is shared, words carry culturally shared understanding, and abstract words such as "commitment," which organize complex relations among concepts, play a large role in such understanding. At the same time, word use accommodates considerable variation. The content of the PROMISE, the specific long-range goals a couple sets and tries to meet in their marriage, are widely variable. Likewise, the nature of the ATTACHMENT, for example, whether it is exclusive or only primary, whether it is forever or only "as long as it can work," or whether it grows over time or not, can vary. Moreover, knowledge of language may be shared, but its use is a matter of selectivity. Usage permits one or another of the three senses of "commitment" to be foregrounded or neglected in a particular marriage or a given context. Emphasis may be put on the goals of one marriage or the relationship between spouses in another. Finally, by electing not to use the word "commitment" an individual or a couple may reject the "commitment model" of marriage altogether.

A final important issue raised in this analysis has to do with the relationship, not between cognition and culture but between cognition and goals (and hence, indirectly, between cognition and behavior). In suggesting that "commitment" "frames" certain marital goals, this paper is introducing a rather important claim about how goals themselves are conceptualized. The claim is that knowledge structures which organize broad understandings about people's marriages and other interpersonal relationships, about themselves and other people, and about their lives are, at the same time, goal-defining knowledge structures. This is so because such broad understandings incorporate, among other things, understandings of what one wants out of, for example, a relationship, and how to get it. Thus in the present case the "commitment model" of marriage may engender expectations about what will happen to a couple in the natural course of their marriage—for instance, that their commitment to one another will grow stronger over time—and still other expectations about their own role in the outcome of their marriage—for instance, that in order to make the marriage work, they must be committed to trying to make it work.

In a book justly influential for the fresh and sweeping formulation of the organization of human knowledge that it undertakes, Schank and Abelson (1977) also relate goals to understanding. They distinguish three categories of broad understandings, which they call "themes"—interpersonal themes, role themes, and life themes—and they characterize these themes as bundles of related goals. The present analysis suggests that such a characterization is insufficient. In Schank and Abelson's formulation the "theme" is a single, overarching concept of an interpersonal relationship, such as the interpersonal theme MARRIED (p. 140); no notion is given as to how the goals bundled into this theme are organized by it. Here it is suggested that marital goals are organized, in part, by knowledge of the word "commitment." The particular part "commitment" seems to play is to constrain appropriate marital goals to the class of goals that are characteristically long-range and effortful.

"Commitment," however, does not fully specify the goals appropriate to American marriage. This ongoing research reveals that another type of knowledge structure—stable, underlying metaphorical models of marriage reflected in the language interviewees use—define individuals' marital goals still further (Quinn 1981). Thus, for example, a model of marriage as a DURABLE PRODUCT allows one husband to make the metaphors "we forged a lifetime proposition," "we have both looked into the other person and found their best parts and used those parts to make the relationship gel," "we made that the cornerstone," "they had a basic solid foundation in their marriages that could be shaped into something good," "our marriage was strengthened," "marriage is a do-it-yourself project," and others. Not surprisingly, this husband uses the word "commitment" to mark the priority of a goal engendered by this model: he says, "the commitment was to make that family work. You know, that this was going to be a solid thing." By contrast, a second husband, whose metaphorical expressions cluster around a model of marriage as a SPATIAL RELATIONSHIP, uses the word to emphasize the priority of another goal, one consonant with this latter model. He speaks of "our commitment to continually evaluate where we are" and "a commitment to making certain that we're pretty clear where each of us are in our growth, in our lives, in our living."

Thus marital goals gain specification by the conjunction of two different knowledge structures that contribute differently to the total understanding of the marital experience. Metaphorical models define these goals, and "commitment" prioritizes them. The word, in framing the kinds of goals and the degree of attachment appropriate to marriage, may influence the invention and acceptance of metaphors that adequately capture these features of the marital relationship. Interviewees, for example, are wholly disinclined to characterize marriage as A GAME, A SPORT, or any other activity that is relatively brief in duration and nonserious in intent. Reciprocally, individuals' selection of certain metaphors may dictate their use or disuse of the word "commitment," and the senses of "commitment" they choose to foreground. So metaphorical models of marriage as A DURABLE PRODUCT, A QUEST, AN INVESTMENT, GROWTH, A STRUGGLE, or A JOURNEY may encourage the foregrounding of the PROMISE and DEDICATION senses of "commitment," while metaphors of marriage as A PARTNERSHIP, TWO PATHS CROSSING, MUTUAL PARENTING, BEING A UNITED FRONT, BEING A PAIR, or BEING ONE may be more favorable to selection of the ATTACHMENT sense of the word. The story of these culturally shared metaphors for American marriage remains to be told.

NOTES

The research described was funded by a National Institute of Mental Health research grant (R01 MH330370-01). The results owe much to the skill and perseverance of Rebecca Taylor, research assistant to this project, who completed interviews with six of the eleven couples in the study, and a student, Laurie Moore, who completed interviews with a seventh couple. I cannot adequately thank the 22 anonymous husbands and wives who participated in the long interview process, and gave us an appreciation for their unique and beautiful ways of seeing their marriages. This paper has benefited immensely from exchanges with Claudia Brugman, Roy D'Andrade, Virginia Dominguez, Janet Dougherty, Dorothy Clement Holland, Paul Kay, George Lakoff, Catherine Lutz, Daniel Maltz, and Rebecca Taylor. Of course, none of the persons named above is necessarily committed to my ideas.

1. All interview segments in this paper have been regularized for stammers, stutters, elisions, slips of the tongue, and hesitations. Names of persons have been replaced by fictive initials, and place names have been changed. Each usage of the word "commitment" under discussion is italicized; all other occurrences of "commitment" in the same segment are neither italicized nor tabulated unless they too exhibit the pattern of usage under discussion. Occasionally, when a segment is difficult to interpret out of context, the sense of the relevant portion of the preceding interview is summarized and appears in small capitals, surrounded by square brackets. A line of dots between lines of interview indicates that the interviewer has interjected a comment. Dots before and/or after a segment indicate that this particular segment has been quoted more fully elsewhere in the paper. The code at the left of each segment contains, in order, an interviewee identification number, a W or an H to indicate wife or husband, and the number of that interview in the sequence of interviews with that individual. This information will allow the reader to compare women's usage with men's, as well as the utterances of a particular interviewee with one another. It would have been convenient to identify interview segments in a manner allowing readers to compare each interviewee's usages with those of his or her spouse. However, disclosure of such information posed a possible breach of confidentiality, since spouses themselves would then be able to identify their own spouses' interview segments.

2. All interviewees were residents of one town in the southeastern United States. All were native-born Americans, but couples were selected for diversity of geographic origin within the United States, ethnic and racial identity, occupation, education, neighborhood, and social network. Efforts to attain educational and occupational diversity were not wholly successful, with college graduates and to a lesser degree professionals predominating. Duration of marriage ranged from 1 to 27 years but concentrated somewhat more heavily at the lower end of the distribution. All of the marriages were first marriages. Diversity, rather than representativeness, was sought. The study aims to investigate how people organize knowledge rather than how any particular organizing principle varies across sociological categories such as gender or ethnicity.

3. For example, in the utterance,

5H-2 Oh, I think they were delighted. I think the extent of time that we were somewhat *committed,* the five year time of just kind of being in and out, bode well for them in the sense that I was not trying to sweep a young Miss off her feet, prematurely anyway. Or precipitously.

it is impossible to decide whether the couple is "somewhat committed" to each other (pattern 3) or to something, say, the relationship (pattern 2). And in

5H-4 I think it worked out that J. and I both perceived that we had very little idea of, in fact, what our *commitments* to one another involved. That we did not, in many ways, know ourselves particularly well relative to relationships.

there is ambiguity as to whether these commitments are ones that each spouse had to the other (as in syntactic pattern 3) or made to one another (as in pattern 1).

4. This sense of "commitment" would seem to correspond, roughly, to Schneider's (1968) characterization of American marriage as "for love, and forever," taken in conjunction with his famous definition of familial love, including marital love, as "diffuse, enduring solidarity." The similarity is certainly not coincidental, since Schneider, too, was working from what Americans said about marriage. But the present analysis is differently motivated. Schneider claims to have achieved "an account of the American kinship system as a *cultural system, as a system of symbols, and not as a 'description' at any other level,*" an account avowedly "*not* about what Americans *think,* as a rational, conscious, cognitive process, about kinship and family" (ibid.:18). I take this to mean, emphatically, that culture can be analyzed as a self-contained system independently of cognition (or conscious thought, anyway). I do not understand how culture can be treated independently of individuals' thinking about it, so I am motivated to describe the role of cultural knowledge in thought. I claim to have located certain shared knowledge (or cultural knowledge, which I am using synonymously) in the language Americans have available to think with. Thus the present analysis specifies that ATTACHMENT is shared by virtue of being part of the structure of the word "commitment." Of course, as this analysis will show, individuals apply such shared knowledge selectively to the interpretation of their own experience.

The description of culture in isolation from cognition and its treatment as a unitary, integrated, and self-contained system is a position weakened by Schneider's method, which is neither forthcoming with data nor explicit about procedures for getting from this interview data to the final account. He defends this method by saying, "The book is the data" (1980:124). But clearly, the extensive interviews on which the book rests are relevant too, and were these data subjected to systematic scrutiny, they would likely yield a much more complex and variable, less integrated and self-contained picture of American cultural knowledge about kinship than Schneider has drawn freehand. Inexplicably, he justifies the lack of data in his book by equating all data with apt illustration, saying: "I might be wrong in my analysis, but I was certainly not going to cheat, and using nice little quotes and convincing little illustrations was, I thought then and think equally strongly now, a form of cheating: it pretends to documentation when it is not that at all" (ibid.). I hope that the analysis presented here demonstrates the feasibility of doing something more systematic with these kinds of rich interview data than drawing on them selectively for apt illustrations.

REFERENCES

Brugman, Claudia

1981 Story of *Over*. Master's thesis, University of California, Berkeley.

D'Andrade, Roy

1972 Cultural Belief Systems. Report to the National Institute of Mental Health Committee on Social and Cultural Processes, November.

Fillmore, Charles J.

1977a The Case for Case Reopened. In *Syntax and Semantics*, vol. 8: *Grammatical Relations*, ed. P. Cole and J. Sadock, pp. 59-81. New York: Academic Press.

1977b Topics in Lexical Semantics. In R. W. Cole, ed., *Current Issues in Linguistic Theory*, pp. 76-138. Bloomington: Indiana University Press.

N.d. The Problem of Ungenerated Language. Unpublished MS.

Frake, Charles O.

1975 How to Enter a Yakan House. In M. Sanches and B. G. Blount, eds., *Sociocultural Dimensions of Language Use*, pp. 25-40. New York: Academic Press.

1977 Plying Frames Can Be Dangerous: Some Reflections on Methodology in Cognitive Anthropology. *Quarterly Newsletter of the Institute for Comparative Human Development* 1:1-7.

Goodenough, Ward H.

1957 Cultural Anthropology and Linguistics. In P. Garvin, ed., *Report of the Seventh Annual Round Table Meeting on Linguistics and Language Study*, pp. 167-73. Washington, D.C.: Georgetown University.

1971 *Culture, Language, and Society*. Addison-Wesley Module in Anthropology. Reading, Mass.: Addison-Wesley.

Kay, Paul

1973 Ethnography and Cultural Theory. In H. Siverts, ed., *Drinking Patterns in Highland Chiapas*, pp. 59-64. Bergen: Universitelsforlaget.

Keesing, Roger

1974 Theories of Culture. *Annual Review of Anthropology* 3:73-97.

Lakoff, George, and Mark N. Johnson

1980 *Metaphors We Live By*. Chicago: University of Chicago Press.

Langacker, Ronald W.

1979 Grammar as Image. Paper delivered to the Conference on Neurolinguistics and Cognition, Program in Cognitive Science, University of California, San Diego, March.

Linde, Charlotte
N.d. The Life Story: A Temporally Discontinuous Discourse Type. Unpublished MS.
Quinn, Naomi
1981 Marriage Is a Do-It-Yourself Project: The Organization of Marital Goals. *Proceedings,* Third Annual Conference of the Cognitive Science Society, pp. 31-40, Berkeley, August.
Schank, Roger, and Robert Abelson
1977 *Scripts, Plans, Goals and Understanding.* Hillsdale, N.J.: Lawrence Erlbaum Associates.
Schneider, David
1968 *American Kinship: A Cultural Account.* Chicago: University of Chicago Press. 2d ed., 1980.

14

Character Terms and Cultural Models

Roy G. D'Andrade

The terms by which we describe *character* in English contain a very general model of the human psyche. This model is composed of a relatively small number of features that define the internal mental states and external objects one needs to know in order to understand human behavior—at least in our culture. In this paper an outline of this model will be presented based on a correlational and semantic analysis of character term ratings.

A major assumption behind the analysis presented below is that one important way in which people learn complex cultural schemata is through language. More specifically, by learning the vocabulary of a language, one necessarily learns the distinctions that are embedded as semantic features in that vocabulary (Lenneberg and Roberts 1956). By analyzing the content and organization of the semantic features found in sets of interrelated terms, it is possible to discover cultural models learned by all competent speakers of the language. Such "lexically constituted" models may not include all the knowledge held by members of a culture about a particular domain. Such models do, however, have the virtue of being not just widely shared but *intersubjectively* shared, in that speakers of the language know that other speakers have the same—or similar—word meanings, and thereby also hold the same—or similar—understandings about the object of their descriptions.

My interest in character terms began some years ago, when I became convinced that the correlational analyses carried out by psychologists on character term ratings, which psychologists took to reflect facts about what goes with what in the world, actually reflected primarily the *semantic* relations between the words used in the ratings (D'Andrade 1965). Character terms are those terms that can be used to describe permanent aspects of a person's behavior. Examples range from morphologically simple terms such as "kind" and "smart" to complex terms like "unfriendly," "hard-working," and "happy-go-lucky." The number of character terms in English is very large: Allport and Odbert collected almost 18,000 such terms from the second edition of Webster's Unabridged Dictionary, while an even more exhaustive search by Warren Norman unearthed over 27,000 terms that could be used to describe a person's character. Using Norman's list and removing the obscure, unusual, and archaic terms, as well as those terms whose primary meaning lay outside the semantic field of human character, Lewis Goldberg found nearly 2,000 terms known by 90 percent of a sample of university undergraduates (Goldberg 1981).

It is important to note that there are many things we might want to say about someone's character for which there is no single word. For example, in English there is no common word that means "someone who always wants to be the center of attention," nor is there a common word that means "someone who has a good memory." Only part of what can be said about character has been "lexicalized" into single words in English. However, because the part of the cultural model that has been lexicalized is intersubjectively shared, it tends to have a basic "commonsensical" quality, as if it were an obvious outline of reality.

The 2,000 terms collected by Goldberg display considerable overlap in meaning, with many partial synonyms and antonyms. In order to construct a simple yet systematic description of "character" or "personality," the standard procedure in psychology has been to select a broad sample of terms and obtain ratings by respondents on scales made from these terms (respondents might be asked, for example, to rate themselves and people they know on each term according to a numerical scale running from "has this trait to unusual excess" to "does not display this trait at all"). Ratings obtained in this manner are then analyzed by factor analysis, cluster analysis, or other multidimensional scaling techniques to uncover underlying dimensions of character and personality.

The development of computers during World War II made feasible factor analyses of large sets of terms. By 1965, through the work of Warren Norman and others, it had become clear that the domain of character terms had five generally replicable factor dimensions. The terms used by Norman that define these five factors are presented in Figure 1.

In order to try to show that the Norman factors were the result of semantic and cognitive structures that were to be found in the minds of the raters rather than a reflection of underlying entities existing in the personality of the ratees, I undertook a research project

Figure 1. Norman Factor Dimensions for Character Terms

1. Surgency (Extroversion)
   talkative — silent
   sociable — reclusive
   adventurous — cautious
   frank — secretive

2. Agreeableness
   good natured — irritable
   cooperative — negativistic
   mild/gentle — headstrong
   jealous — not jealous

3. Conscientious
   responsible — undependable
   scrupulous — unscrupulous
   persevering — quitting
   fussy/tidy — careless

4. Emotional Stability
   calm — anxious
   composed — excitable
   not hypochondriacal — hypochondriacal
   poised — nervous

5. Culture
   intellectual — unintellectual
   artistic — nonartistic
   imaginative — simple/direct
   polished/refined — crude/boorish

in which respondents were asked to rate the semantic similarity of pairs of character terms, and these ratings were then factor-analyzed. The results of these factor analyses were almost identical to the results obtained by Norman, showing that the Norman factor dimensions could be obtained from semantic ratings, without using ratings on actual people (D'Andrade 1965). Hakel, in a similar study, used multidimensional scaling of semantic similarity ratings of character terms and obtained the same result (1974).

Thus, when people make ratings about how someone acts, the matrix of correlations between rating terms corresponds closely to the people's judgments about the degree of "similarity in meaning" between the various pairs of terms. Furthermore, the matrix of correlations between ratings, when these ratings are based on the rater's long-term memory, does not correspond at all well to the matrix of correlations obtained if specific behaviors are coded by observers from video-tape or direct observation, and the scores for frequency of behavior are intercorrelated across the persons observed. It appears that human memory is greatly affected by prior conceptions or schemata, and that people assume that "things which are alike" are usually "things which go together" (D'Andrade 1974, Shweder and D'Andrade 1980).

These findings indicate that the Norman classification corresponds to a semantically based folk classification of character terms, not to dimensions of human personality. However, the Norman classification, as it stands, is unsatisfactory as a taxonomic description, in that it does not make apparent any principle or system for partitioning terms. Why should "surgency," "agreeableness," "responsibility," "emotional stability," and "culture" be the major foci of character, rather than "individuality," "maturity," "dominance," "sexuality," and "achievement"—or many other characteristics? Usually, from the examination of a classification system it is possible to gain some insight into the features that produce the observed partitions. The Norman classification, as presented, is not illuminating.

Another potential objection to the Norman classification is that it is not clear whether the same groupings would emerge under different experimental conditions, or, more specifically, if the same groupings would emerge if the analysis was done on terms and phrases used frequently by ordinary people in describing character, rather than a set of terms selected by psychologists and rated by undergraduates. In order to investigate the classification of frequently used character terms and phrases by ordinary people, a study was undertaken of a sample of middle-class nonprofessional women in the San Diego area who were unsophisticated with respect to either clinical or academic psychology.

The ages of our respondents ranged from the early twenties to the late fifties. The sample was selected randomly from a household directory, and screened in a telephone interview for availability and cooperativeness. Income and occupational levels were not especially high, falling into the upper clerical brackets. Ethnic backgrounds were standard European in various fractionated blends and combinations. All our respondents had strong self-identifications as "Americans," all were Christian or Jewish, white, and married at least once. While this sample is a long way from a probability sample of U.S. adults, it does seem representative of one kind of American lifeway: that of the modest suburban white middle class.

The interviews consisted primarily of descriptions by the sample of respondents of people whom they knew. The interviewers elicited relatively long and detailed protocols for each person described, typically an hour or more of talk. The interviewers were nondirective, permitting the respondents to proceed as they choose. However, since respondents tended to describe people they liked, there was a requirement that at least a quarter of the people described should be people whom they did not like.

A total of 25 respondents were interviewed, each contributing 15 person descriptions, resulting in a total of 375 person descriptions.

All interviews were tape-recorded. Transcripts were made of the relevant interview segments. Names and other identifying information were deleted from the records to ensure anonymity.

The first step of analysis was to select frequently used descriptors. From each person description a list of descriptors was made, and a master list developed. We found that many of the descriptors were phrases that could not be broken into smaller units without changing or destroying their meaning; for example: "——is always doing things for other people" or "Anything you'd need,——would be right there to do it, even if it is an inconvenience." We also found that many descriptive phrases consisted of two or more close synonyms said together, as if they were a single term. For example: "——is a very thoughtful and considerate person" or "——is frank and honest." We decided to leave these synonym phrases intact, since the intention seemed to be to give a more precise description by using overlapping specifications.

A typical description contained from 30 to 80 descriptors. Many of these were similar in meaning, and appeared to be used to provide somewhat different perspectives on a smaller set of conceptual characteristics. Once this first phase of data collection was complete, descriptor phrases were grouped into narrowly defined sets of synonyms or near synonyms. The most representative and least ambiguous phrase was selected from each set by a panel of five judges. In a formal interview respondents were then asked to judge all the people they had previously described on each of the phrases. Respondents were asked to dichotomize their sample of people into those who had the trait more and those who had the trait less. These judgments were then treated as 0, 1 ratings.

To determine the way in which people classify or group together these character descriptors, descriptors were intercorrelated across all persons described, and the resulting correlation matrix was factor-analyzed using principal axes and varimax rotation. The first six factors accounted for 43 percent of the variance. The seventh factor would have accounted for less than 3 percent of the variance. The six factor results are presented in Figure 2.

In Figure 2 the character phrases are grouped according to the factor loadings. Labels, presented in small capitals, are given as approximate cover terms for each factor grouping.

Five of the factors found in the San Diego study show a strong correspondence to the Norman factors. The extra sixth factor, labeled "liberal/conservative," has been found in a number of other factor-analytic studies of person descriptions, but it is usually not included in analyses of character terms because a political orientation of this sort is thought to be more a matter of "attitude" than "disposition" (Cattell 1957).

In order to see how a different group of people might organize these phrases, a sample of 50 University of California undergraduates were asked to rate themselves and five people whom they knew on each of the phrases used in the previous study. Seven-point rather than dichotomous rating scales were used. These results are presented in Figure 3.

Figure 2. Factor Analysis of San Diego Women's Ratings of Others

CHARACTERIZING TERMS AND PHRASES	FACTOR LOADINGS F1	F2	F3	F4	F5	F6
EMOTIONAL INSTABILITY/STABILITY						
is emotional and easily upset	76	−12	0	−14	5	−9
feels sorry for himself/herself	72	4	−25	18	12	−5
is nervous and a worrier	72	6	2	4	−13	−1
is a bitter, complaining person	60	16	−37	12	6	−4
has some really basic problems	58	14	−25	18	15	−22
is very dependent on other people	52	−27	7	−2	−13	−22
is a very sensitive person	48	−24	19	23	−24	6
lives beyond his/her/their means	43	−3	−3	−5	38	−22
talks a lot about money	42	20	−7	−10	13	−36
has a lot of nervous energy	36	33	15	−3	19	−6
gets terribly angry	28	21	8	−3	22	3
is an active, outdoors type of person	−81	27	27	17	−15	31
is an easy-going type	−47	−15	32	20	15	−8
is a calm and collected type of person	−63	7	14	28	−5	−1
TASK PERFORMANCE						
is very ambitious	−6	68	3	−8	−4	−4
is domineering and authoritarian	32	62	−17	4	14	0
is very hard-working	−7	59	23	14	−28	−13
is an organizer	−7	58	−1	−23	5	31
is a good provider/housekeeper	−23	50	22	10	−20	4
is arrogant and tries to make other people feel inferior	31	46	−36	−8	35	−11
AGREEABLENESS						
is a warm and friendly person	−15	−4	62	−21	−1	2
I am comfortable with	8	−2	60	−2	−8	7
we have much in common	4	11	59	−1	7	25
is always doing things for other people	2	8	57	−6	−27	−1
is a good friend	2	−2	56	14	3	−1
has a good sense of humor	−25	4	51	−13	9	9
he/she enjoys life	−34	−1	49	−26	2	21

Figure 2. Continued

CHARACTERIZING TERMS AND PHRASES	FACTOR LOADINGS F1	F2	F3	F4	F5	F6
is frank and honest	−14	32	43	12	−3	−6
is very polite	−13	−7	43	6	−22	4
is practical with lots of common sense	−36	31	37	8	−25	10
lets their kids do anything they want	−11	0	−17	−15	2	−12
doesn't take care of how he/she looks	5	−17	−20	0	11	0
acts different—quaint, odd, strange	26	−4	−36	25	34	−4
INTROVERSION/EXTROVERSION						
is shy and hard to get to know	5	−9	0	59	1	3
a loner—doesn't get involved with people	17	12	−17	58	−4	−11
is involved in a lot of social groups	10	18	1	−40	7	15
talks quite a bit	19	2	10	−70	4	−14
LIBERAL/CONSERVATIVE						
is very liberal about drugs and politics	−7	−4	21	5	63	19
tries to go to bed with everybody	20	11	−6	2	54	−10
is selfish and takes advantage of people	34	20	−42	−5	45	−10
is quite naive and unsophisticated	29	−36	−8	21	−42	−18
is (likely to be) happily married	−16	3	30	−30	−43	4
life (likely to) revolves around children	21	14	3	−1	−50	3
is a person to whom religion is important	12	3	25	7	−53	9
is very conservative	−7	16	−7	36	−56	−20
CULTURE						
is well educated	−29	22	−5	−18	4	65
is quite intelligent	−39	28	11	−10	6	56
is from a good family	10	−13	28	7	−11	35
is a creative person	12	14	2	−4	7	30
is a social climber	25	24	−16	−32	11	−39
shows off that they have money	4	21	−9	−38	16	−42
is bigoted	18	30	−32	−21	−8	−48

Figure 3. Factor Analysis of College Students' Ratings of Others

CHARACTERIZING TERMS AND PHRASES	FACTOR LOADINGS F1	F2	F3	F4	F5	F6
AGREEABLENESS						
I am comfortable with	59	−46	−22	20	8	−14
is a good friend	59	−46	−9	26	−5	−28
is (likely to be) happily married	55	13	−15	33	19	−15
is a warm and friendly person	55	−38	−31	24	30	−17
we have a great deal in common	39	−26	−19	35	8	−32

Figure 3. Continued

CHARACTERIZING TERMS AND PHRASES	FACTOR LOADINGS F1	F2	F3	F4	F5	F6
is a person to whom religion is important	38	1	−1	26	−6	−32
has some really basic problems	−49	8	21	−24	−20	34
is a bitter, complaining person	−51	12	43	−34	−16	5
gets terribly angry	−51	−10	49	−17	12	−18
lives beyond his/her/their means	−58	−17	−4	1	−11	8
talks a lot about money	−58	5	9	−22	10	−8
is domineering and authoritarian	−59	4	16	−5	33	−49
shows off that they have money	−72	13	0	16	16	8
is selfish and takes advantage of people	−78	17	8	−24	6	−4
is arrogant and tries to make other people feel inferior	−78	20	13	−1	16	−4
CONSERVATIVE/LIBERAL						
is very conservative	−15	65	−9	2	−6	−7
is frank and honest	33	−47	−14	14	28	−28
is an easy-going type	13	−52	−36	27	−1	3
has a good sense of humor	32	−55	−21	44	14	−15
is very liberal about drugs and politics	−1	−61	−11	−12	1	16
EMOTIONAL INSTABILITY/STABILITY						
is emotional and gets easily upset	−14	1	79	23	−3	1
is nervous and a worrier	−4	7	73	2	−25	2
feels sorry for himself/herself	−24	11	60	−16	−24	24
has lots of nervous energy	−11	13	48	−16	46	−20
acts different—quaint, odd, strange	−45	20	47	−4	2	32
is quite naive and unsophisticated	14	42	47	−18	1	31
doesn't take care of how he/she looks	−15	−21	38	−18	6	7
is a calm and collected type of person	8	−15	−69	23	−25	0
CULTURE						
is well educated	5	−4	−32	80	−10	−24
is quite intelligent	11	−8	−25	79	−2	−21
is from a good family	24	16	−7	66	13	−7
is a creative person	−8	−37	0	61	−7	−14
is a very sensitive person	36	−39	26	58	−9	−17
is always doing things for other people	17	−28	4	50	13	−31
is very polite	35	13	−34	47	−19	−26
life (likely to) resolves around chidren	7	28	12	35	28	−25
is bigoted	−40	20	−6	−57	−7	12
EXTROVERSION/INTROVERSION						
talks quite a bit	−22	−7	20	−15	71	−11
is involved in a lot of social groups	0	24	−12	21	55	−25
is an active, outdoors type of person	−14	−14	4	14	53	5

Figure 3. Continued

CHARACTERIZING TERMS AND PHRASES	FACTOR LOADINGS F1	F2	F3	F4	F5	F6
enjoys life	19	−31	−44	25	49	−5
is a social climber	−36	36	−17	33	43	−2
a loner—doesn't get involved with people	−39	−6	25	2	−57	24
is shy and hard to get to know	−5	13	9	4	−64	−11
CONSCIENTIOUSNESS						
lets their kids do anything they want	−17	−15	−7	−5	−16	63
is very dependent on other people	29	20	14	4	14	52
tries to go to bed with everybody	−46	2	−9	−32	24	51
is very hard-working	15	−1	−30	46	11	−50
is a good provider/housekeeper	20	22	2	31	12	−55
is an organizer	−17	−1	−4	40	45	−55
is practical with lots of common sense	31	−18	−30	37	−21	−56
is very ambitious	2	1	−20	41	27	−60

Two things stand out in comparing the factor organization of the San Diego women sample to the U.C. undergraduate sample. First, the Norman factors plus the "liberal/conservative" factor are clearly identifiable in both groups. Second, the particular phrases that make up the factors differ in the two groups. For example, "liberalism" goes with "tries to go to bed with everybody" and "is selfish and takes advantage of people" in the San Diego women sample, but goes with "has a good sense of humor," "is an easy-going type of person," and "is frank and honest" in the U.C. undergraduate sample. These particular group differences in factor composition can be understood as reflections of subcultural differences.

The factor similarity of the work by Norman, Goldberg, and others using a variety of single-term scales, and the results reported here using complex phrases and two relatively different groups of respondents, indicate that the Norman factors are not an artifact of scale selection or a result limited to the college student population. While the Norman factors do not have the surface appearance of a good taxonomic system, they do have the important characteristics of robustness and generality. It seems unlikely that the Norman factors would show such factor invariance across different samples unless these factors had some strong correspondence to a widely held folk system of character classification.

To gain some understanding of what this folk system might be, an informal semantic analysis of a large set of character terms selected and analyzed by Lewis Goldberg was initiated. The set of terms used by Goldberg consists of 586 commonly used and understood character adjectives. These terms were written on cards and then grouped into categories on the basis of semantic similarity. Results from four subjects were obtained. Several things became apparent in carrying out this exercise.

First, the set of character terms contains a number of cross-cutting features. Features having to do with "good feelings," for example, are found in conjunction with features concerning interpersonal relationships ("warm," "affectionate"), with features that indicate "extroversion" ("merry," "cheerful"), and with features that indicate "emotional stability" ("confident," "optimistic"). Or, to take another example, terms that contain the feature of "talk" are found in conjunction with features that indicate "sociability" ("talkative," "gossipy"), "dishonesty" ("glib"), and "intelligence" ("articulate," "witty"). These crosscutting features make it possible to group terms in a number of alternative systems.

Second, some terms seem vague, referring primarily to some general aspect of "goodness" or "badness." Examples are terms like "mature," "involved," "shallow," and "childish." At first it seemed that such terms might function as something like taxonomic "upper-level" superordinates. This does not seem to be the case, however, since there are no subordinate or lower-level terms that describe different ways of being mature, involved, shallow, etc.

Another problem is that a number of groupings can be made on the basis of implications derived from the meanings of terms. For example, in the Norman factor classification "conceited," "snobbish," and "boastful" are placed on the negative side of the Agreeableness factor. However, the "disagreeableness" of "conceit," for example, is not a semantic feature of that term: one can be "conceited" and—in some cases—also quite "agreeable." It is just that in the usual course of things someone who is "conceited" is likely to talk about themselves as if they were very much better than other people, and this is likely to be considered "disagreeable." Since character terms are rich in implications, many cross-cutting implication-based groupings can be formed, and the problem becomes that of trying to determine which implications are salient to the group of people being studied.

One set of findings did emerge from the informal semantic analysis of the terms. In working with the terms, it became apparent that each of the five Norman factors corresponded to a very general category of human action. Listed below are the Norman factors, several exemplar terms, and the "category criteria" for each factor.

Norman Factor	Category Criteria
1. Surgency (talkative, sociable, adventurous)	The Expression of Internal States in Observable Behavior
2. Agreeableness (good-natured, cooperative, mild)	Behavior directed toward Other People
3. Conscientiousness (responsible, persevering, tidy)	Behavior related to doing Tasks
4. Emotional Stability (calm, relaxed, brave)	The Occurrence of Internal, especially Emotional, States
5. Culture (intelligent, creative, cultured)	Cognitive Abilities and Capacities

The term "Internal States" refers not just to "emotions" but also to "impluses," "needs," "desires"—to all those things about which one can be "expressive." The term "Task" refers to "work" or to "a job." Norman's Factor 5, Culture, is mislabeled. Most of the terms with high loadings on this factor have to do with "intelligence." Terms like "refined" and "sophisticated" also occur in this factor but have smaller loadings and are less frequent than terms like "intelligent," "smart," "wise," "creative," "insightful," and "contemplative."

In sum, the Norman factors tell us that people think, do tasks, feel, express their feelings, and orient much of their behavior toward other people. Such a system of categories does not create mutually exclusive groupings, so that some terms have high loadings on more than one factor. Being "assertive," for example, is a way of acting that is both expressive of one's internal state and oriented toward other people. Being "inventive" is both a way of doing a task and an indication of intelligence. Being "responsible" is both a way of doing tasks or duties and an action oriented toward other people. And being "possessive" simultaneously expresses an internal state, represents the occurrence of a feeling, and is oriented toward other people.

The categories that determine the Norman factors not only are not mutually exclusive but also are strongly interrelated. Thus the Surgency factor and the Emotional Stability factor both involve "internal states"—expressed behaviorally in one case, but not necessarily in the other. The Agreeableness factor is related to both the Surgency and Emotional Stability factors in that a number of internal states are, by their own definitions, aroused by or directed toward other people (e.g. "love," "jealousy," "hostility," etc.).

Another major property of the semantics of the Norman factors, and of character terms in general, is that there is an egregious component of "evaluation" in the terms and in the way factors are composed. As Rosenberg and others have pointed out, character terms may generally be considered to be varieties of ways of evaluating people (Kim and Rosenberg 1980). This emphasis on evaluation shows up clearly in the factor loadings, in that the highest loading terms tend to be highly evaluative. Thus "agreeableness" is a highly evaluative term by which one can describe how someone relates to other people, "intelligence" is a highly evaluative term by which one can describe how someone thinks, "emotional stability" is a highly evaluative term by which one can describe someone's emotional life, and "conscientiousness" is a highly evaluative term by which one can describe how someone does a job. The only one of the five Norman factors that is not saliently evaluative is Surgency, although, as we shall see, it has some highly evaluative subfactors.

This strongly evaluative component in character terms has discouraged those who have hoped to refine the ordinary language of character description and thereby create a rich scientific vocabulary for the study of human behavior. The evaluative component has proven so deep and ineradicable that no process of refinement has been able to develop an effective evaluation-free system built from natural language. However, it should be remembered that the natural language of character terms was created by and for ordinary people, and that one of the major needs of ordinary people is to determine how to react to what other people do—to approach or avoid, to reward or punish, to imitate or correct. The natural language system of character terms seems well suited to these purposes. What is interesting is that we have developed so many ways of being good and being bad.

In order to make as explicit as possible the taxonomic criteria that lie behind the Norman factors, a new set of factor labels is proposed: (1) Expressive Behavior, (2) Interpersonal Behavior, (3) Task Behavior, (4) Emotionality, and (5) Cognition. The informal semantic analysis described above also indicated that each of the five Norman factors was subdivided into a number of smaller clusters. In order to obtain a clearer picture of the composition of these subgroupings, factor analyses of the terms for each of the Norman factors were carried out.

Lewis Goldberg kindly made available a portion of his data, consisting of seven-point ratings of peers and self by 123 undergraduates on the 586 terms mentioned above. In order to assign terms to the five Norman factors, a factor-analytic study carried out by Goldberg of 475 of the terms combined into 131 synonym clusters was used. In this and similar studies Goldberg has found an unusual degree of stability in factor composition for the mean scores for synonym cluster across different samples of ratings (peer ratings versus self-ratings), methods of rotation (varimax rotation, oblimax rotation, Kaiser's Little Jiffy Method), and number of factors rotated (from four to thirteen) (Goldberg 1979).

Each of the 475 terms was assigned to one of the Norman factors on the basis of the highest loading of the synonym cluster. For example, the term "quarrelsome" was part of a synonym cluster composed of the terms "argumentative," "combative," "belligerent," "negativistic," "quarrelsome," "antagonistic," and "uncooperative." The mean scores for this cluster had its greatest mean factor loading on Norman's Factor 2, Interpersonal Behavior (−.74). Thus the term "quarrelsome" (and the other terms in this synonym cluster) were all assigned to Norman's Factor 2.

After the initial assignment of terms to the Norman factors, the entire corpus of 475 terms was examined, and all terms that had a clear semantic relationship to the defining characteristics given above for each of the Norman factors were assigned to that factor, even if the term belonged to a synonym cluster whose highest mean factor loading placed it in a different factor. For example, the term "sociable," which belongs to a cluster whose highest mean factor loading is with the Norman Factor 1, Expressive Behavior, also has a clear semantic reference to Norman Factor 2, Interpersonal Behavior, which is defined by behavior directed toward other people and was therefore also assigned to Factor 2.

Each set of terms was then subjected to a principal axis factor analysis (Veldman 1967). Twelve subfactors were extracted for Norman Factor 2. The other four factors each had ten subfactors extracted. Varimax rotations were carried out for 2, 3, . . . to the total number of subfactors extracted. Rather than trying to select the "best" or "most interpretable" rotation for each set of terms, the entire corpus of varimax rotation results was examined, and those variables that throughout all the analyses had very high loadings for the same groupings of terms were selected as "marker" variables for the various subfactors. Thus, for Norman Factor 1, Expressiveness, the variables found consistently to have the highest loadings to specific subfactors were the terms "daring," "talkative," "cheerful," "passionate," "straightforward," "irritable," "impulsive."

In order to show the general pattern of factor results, the original product-moment correlation coefficients were used to group terms under the marker variables. This was done by computing the correlations of all subfactor terms with the marker variables, and assigning each term to the marker variable with which it had the greatest absolute correlation. The overall results are remarkably similar to the results of the factor analyses with respect to the way the total corpus of terms is grouped and ranked, except that the correlation coefficients tend to be somewhat smaller than the corresponding factor loadings. In my view, this method of using marker variables and the original correlation coefficients is superior as a descriptive device to the standard matrix of factor loadings, since the correlation coefficients are more stable than factor loadings over changes in the composition of variables and sample differences.

These results are presented in Figure 4. To conserve space, only the three most strongly correlated terms, both positively and negatively, are presented for selected marker terms.

The results of the analyses of the subfactors confirms some of the conclusions of the earlier informal semantic analysis. The highly evaluative character of the overall system is replicated in the structure of the subfactors: all but two of the 33 subfactors are bipolar with clear "good" versus "bad" poles. Another conclusion from the semantic analysis that is also supported by the subfactor analyses is that a number of subfactors from different Norman factors show a high degree of content similarity; these subfactors move from one Norman factor to another depending on shifts in factor-related semantic emphasis. For example, emotional states related to "anger" are found in three of the Norman factors: in Factor 1, incorporated into the "expressive" behavior of being "irritable"; in Factor 2, incorporated into the "interpersonal" behavior of being "quarrelsome"; and in Factor 4, incorporated into the "emotional state" of being "perturbed."

As part of an analysis of character terms, Goldberg developed a semantically based general classification of 42 basic dimensions of character (Goldberg 1981). Goldberg's classification, using his marker terms for each dimension, is compared with the subfactor analyses in Figure 5. Other dimensions of the Goldberg system not found within any of the subfactors of the Norman factors are "liberal vs. conservative," "religious vs. irreverent," "sensual vs. prudish," and "masculine vs. feminine."

While there is some ambiguity about the composition of the subfactors, there is also enough convergence on a number of dimensions occurring both in the semantic analyses and in the factor-analytic studies to make possible discussion of the underlying model of the person that is lexicalized in these terms. From the results obtained

Norman Factor One
(Expressive Behavior)

daring		talkative	
.61 adventurous .60 bold .55 brave	-.41 unaggressive -.36 cowardly -.35 uncompetitive	.55 extroverted .55 sociable .50 social	-.64 quiet -.60 silent -.45 reserved
cheerful		**passionate**	
.65 merry .59 friendly .54 pleasant	-.44 unsociable -.37 joyless -.25 somber	.64 affectionate .62 warm .43 expressive	-.50 passionless -.46 unemotional -.33 unexcitable
straightforward		**irritable**	**impulsive**
.61 frank .57 direct .34 assertive	-.31 meek -.27 insecure -.25 prideless	.48 grumpy .47 moody .46 cranky	.37 impetuous .36 spontaneous .31 devil-may-care

Norman Factor Two
(Interpersonal Behavior)

warm		respectful	
.63 kind .62 affectionate .54 compassionate	-.52 cold -.46 insensitive -.44 unfriendly	.51 courteous .50 considerate .48 cooperative	-.46 impolite -.45 disrespectful -.41 rude
shy		**amiable**	
.70 bashful .53 withdrawn .45 reserved	-.47 extroverted -.44 assertive -.42 sociable	.43 cordial .36 genial .33 benevolent	-.41 ungracious -.40 harsh -.40 abusive
tolerant		**honest**	
.56 patient .28 uncritical .26 earthy	-.56 quarrelsome -.47 impatient -.44 explosive	.59 truthful .46 trustful .25 candid	-.54 dishonest -.39 deceitful -.34 distrustful

Norman Factor Three
(Task Behavior)

dependable		organized	
.74 reliable .63 responsible .43 practical	-.72 undependable -.65 unreliable -.47 negligent	.68 orderly .53 systematic .50 efficient	-.69 disorganized -.50 unsystematic -.44 careless
industrious		**precise**	
.43 purposeful .36 decisive .17 tenacious	-.39 unambitious -.38 aimless -.27 vague	.54 thorough .52 exacting .48 perfectionistic	-.42 sloppy -.32 haphazard

Norman Factor Four
(Emotionality)

confident		imperturbable	
.58 assured .41 optimistic .26 buoyant	-.42 timid -.41 shy -.39 withdrawn	.16 placid	-.31 irritable -.29 tempermental -.24 possessive
relaxed		**courageous**	
.44 easy-going .42 cheerful .32 natural	-.37 nervous -.28 high-strung -.28 bitter	.62 brave .48 strong .44 tough	-.40 cowardly -.26 fearful -.14 feminine

Norman Factor Five
(Cognition)

intelligent		logical		creative		contemplative	
.71 smart .67 knowledgeable .64 bright	-.62 unintelligent -.54 unintellectual -.37 ignorant	.49 rational .30 analytic .32 objective	-.47 illogical -.22 gullible -.18 foolhardy	.63 artistic .57 inventive .54 imaginative	-.67 uncreative -.64 unimaginative	.53 introspective .50 meditative .40 self-critical	-.45 unreflective -.32 imperceptive

Figure 5. Comparison of Subfactors with Goldberg's Classification System

Subfactors	Goldberg's Classification System
1. Expressive Behavior	
1.1 daring vs. unaggressive	daring vs. timid
1.2 talkative vs. quiet	talkative vs. silent
1.3 cheerful vs. joyless	zestful vs. somber
1.4 passionate vs. passionless	emotional vs. unemotional
1.5 straightforward vs. meek	tactful vs. tactless (?)
1.6 irritable	patient vs. irritable
1.7 impulsive	impulsive vs. restrained
	humorous vs. humorless
2. Interpersonal Behavior	
2.1 warm vs. cold	warm vs. cold
2.2 respectful vs. impolite	courteous vs. rude
2.3 extroverted vs. shy	sociable vs. withdrawn
2.4 amiable vs. ungracious	
2.5 tolerant vs. quarrelsome	lenient vs. fault-finding
	peaceful vs. belligerent
	accommodating vs. dominant
2.6 honest vs. dishonest	honest vs. dishonest
2.7 generous vs. charitable	generous vs. miserly
2.8 modest vs. conceited	
	trustful vs. distrustful
	unenvious vs. envious
3. Task Behavior	
3.1 dependable vs. undependable	reliable vs. unreliable
	responsible vs. careless
3.2 organized vs. disorganized	organized vs. disorganized
3.3 industrious vs. unambitious	ambitious vs. aimless
	energetic vs. sluggish
3.4 precise vs. sloppy	consistent vs. erratic (?)
4. Emotionality	
4.1 confident vs. timid	assured vs. self-effacing
4.2 imperturbable vs. irritable	patient vs. irritable
4.3 relaxed vs. nervous	
4.4 courageous vs. cowardly	
4.5 independent vs. prideless	
5. Cognition	
5.1 intelligent vs. unintelligent	intelligent vs. unintelligent
5.2 logical vs. illogical	rational vs. illogical
5.3 creative vs. uncreative	creative vs. uncreative
5.4 contemplative vs. unreflective	contemplative vs. unreflective
	deep vs. shallow
5.5 sophisticated vs. unsophisticated	sophisticated vs. unsophisticated
5.6 alert vs. absent-minded	alert vs. unobservant
5.7 open-minded vs. bigoted	unprejudiced vs. prejudiced
5.8 articulate vs. inarticulate	articulate vs. inarticulate
5.9 inquisitive vs. uninquisitive	inquisitive vs. uninquisitive
	knowledgeable vs. ignorant

so far, it appears that a relatively limited number of features characterize this model of the person.

One class of features involves kinds of "feeling" that the person experiences or expresses. Subfactors that directly involve feelings are:

Good feelings
- 1.2 cheerful vs. joyless (generalized expression of positive feelings vs. absence of good feelings)
- 2.1 warm vs. cold (positive feelings toward others vs. no affective response to others)

Not fear inhibited
- 1.1 daring vs. unaggressive (actions not inhibited by fear vs. actions against others not tried)
- 4.1 confident vs. timid (nonfear feelings about self vs. fear of others)
- 4.3 relaxed vs. nervous (not experiencing bodily reactions to fear vs. experiencing such reactions)
- 4.4 courageous vs. cowardly (not afraid vs. fear driven)

Angry feelings
- 1.6 irritable (easily aroused expression of anger)
- 2.5 tolerant vs. quarrelsome (capacity not to get angry even under provocation vs. frequent unprovoked hostility expressed toward others)
- 4.2 imperturbable vs. irritable (not easy to arouse to anger vs. easily aroused to anger)
- 1.7 impulsive (easily moved to act on desire or wish)
- 2.3 extroverted vs. shy (freely expresses impulses and feelings to others vs. inhibited in expressing impulses and feelings to others)

Generally, it appears that three kinds of emotion—happiness or love, anger, and fear—are most explicitly lexicalized. The lack of fear, or the positive experience of nonfear, is also frequently employed in terms such as "courageous," "confident," and "relaxed." Desire and impulse seem to be treated mostly with respect to how easily or how inhibited the person is in the release into action of desire or impulse, rather than with regard to the content of the desire or impulse.

Overall, the model of a person that appears in these terms is of someone who has feelings of love, anger, and fear (or their lack), along with nonspecific impulses and desires, which may—or may not—be easily expressed or aroused. These feelings can be directed explicitly toward other people, or aroused by them, or may be just generally expressed or experienced. In some cases the "self" may be an object of these feelings.

Another class of features that is lexicalized in character terms is a diverse set of "norms." Norms refer to culturally given standards of evaluation by which an action may be judged. Norms not only contain a standard but also involve a complex body of relatively explicit cultural rules that state how something is to be done, and entail positive evaluation if done as stated and negative evaluation if not done as stated. The subfactors directly involving norms are:

Treatment of other people

- 2.2 respectful vs. impolite (follows norms concerning manners and expression of deference in interpersonal behavior vs. acts contrary to these norms)
- 2.4 amiable vs. ungracious (follows norms concerning sociability and hospitality in interpersonal behavior vs. acts contrary to these norms)
- 2.7 generous vs. stingy (follows norms concerning appropriate ways of giving and exchanging goods and services vs. acts contrary to these norms—also the sense that the person "enjoys" or does not "enjoy" conforming to these norms)
- 2.8 modest vs. conceited (follows norms concerning appropriate way to express evaluation of one's self vs. acts contrary to these norms—also includes the sense that the person really has a low/high regard for self)

Task performance

- 3.3 precise vs. sloppy (follows norms concerning appropriate "fit" to some standard of exactitude vs. does not follow these norms)
- 3.4 industrious vs. unambitious (tries to follow norms concerning level and degree of accomplishment vs. does not try to follow these norms)
- 5.2 logical vs. illogical (follows norms for appropriate reasoning vs. acts contrary to these norms)

Duties involving both the expectations of others and task performance

- 2.6 honest vs. dishonest (follows the norms of honesty vs. does not follow these norms)
- 1.5 dependable vs. unreliable (follows norms concerning duties and responsibilities in carrying out tasks vs. does not follow these norms)

The model of person lexicalized in character terms has a special relation to norms, glossed above as "follows" or "does not follow" some set of norms. To say that someone "follows" a set of norms presupposes that the person *knows* the norms, *intends* to abide by the norms, and is *successful* at doing so. Most character terms in English involving norms contain all three parts of the triad of *knowledge, intent,* and *successful accomplishment*. There do not seem to be terms for people who *know* and *intend* to follow a norm but for some reason are not *successful* at doing so. Thus there is no term for someone who wants to be honest but just can't keep on the straight and narrow, or for a person who is extremely knowledgeable about the rules for being "gracious," who strives to be "gracious," but who is overwhelmed by "shyness" and is unable to follow the norms. The major exception to this generalization is the set of terms involving "industriousness," such as "industrious," "ambitious," "purposeful," and "decisive," which have to do more with what the person wants to do, not whether or not the person succeeds in the effort.

The norms of honesty, duty, deference, sociability, generosity, precision, logicality, and industry lexicalized in character terms exemplify the way in which what is "outside" a person can also be seen as "inside" the person. Thus, while norms can be seen as sets of rules external to the individual, in learning to be "guided" by these norms, what is "learned" becomes "intrinsic" to the person who has learned them, and thereby part of the person's character. This inside/outside duality of norms, often mentioned in the social sciences, appears to be part of the folk knowledge system, in that "honesty," "duty," etc. are conceptualized both as sets of rules, laws, or conventions outside the person, and as character traits, or internal aspects of the person. In the case of the characteristics of "generosity" and "modesty" there is the further feature that the person is prototypically defined as "feeling" generous or modest, as well as following the normative rules.

Several other subfactors might also be considered to involve norms. The subfactors "organized" versus "disorganized" and "creative" versus "uncreative" could be argued to involve rule systems concerning "orderliness" and "creativity." While there are at least some normative expectations with regard to both orderliness and creativity, in general it appears that being "organized" and "creative" are considered to be kinds of "abilities": there is no way to become creative or orderly just by learning some set of rules and striving to follow them—both demand that the person bring to the task a capacity beyond conformity. One might consider these subfactors to be a special kind of normative system in which one can't state beforehand how something can be done, but one can tell afterward if it has been done well.

Abilities

5.1 intelligent vs. unintelligent (can and does solve problems, learn things, and understand events in an effective manner vs. does not)

5.3 creative vs. uncreative (can and does integrate ideas in a new and effective way vs. does not)

5.8 articulate vs. inarticulate (can and does state things in a clear and effective way vs. does not)

Related to "abilities" are "strengths." These appear to be things a person is able to do that are in some way difficult. Unlike "abilities," which relate to a production of some kind on which the evaluation is based, "strengths" relate to a capacity to *maintain* performance in spite of some difficulty.

Strengths

4.5 independent vs. prideless (can and does maintain own course of action and self-respect vs. does not)

3.3 organized vs. disorganized (can and does maintain the integration of the subparts of a task vs. does not)

5.6 alert vs. absent-minded (can and does maintain a state of perceptual readiness vs. does not)

5.7 open-minded vs. bigoted (can and does maintain the capacity to take in new information and change vs. tries not to learn new facts and change opinions despite incorrect understandings)

The subfactors "imperturbable vs. irritable" and "courageous vs. cowardly," discussed above as semantic dimensions related to feelings, also involve "strength." That is, "imperturbable" or "courageous" persons are considered to be "strong" in that they do not give in to the external provocations and dangers that would affect the more ordinary person.

Several subfactors remain that cannot be classified as kinds of feelings, internalized norms, abilities, or strengths. "Talkative vs. quiet" appears to refer primarily to "mode" of expression, with some additional supposition that the "talkative" person generally expresses more emotion and impulse than the "quiet" person. "Straightforward vs. meek" also seems to refer to the "way" in which persons express themselves—in this case with respect to how freely and undisguisedly thoughts and feelings about things are expressed. Both these subfactors seem to involve primarily "manner" of expression, secondarily "degree" or "amount" of expression.

Finally, three subfactors concerning cognition remain to be discussed. The first is "contemplative vs. unreflective," which seems to refer to the "degree" to which the person is involved in cognitive activity. The second is "sophisticated vs. unsophisticated," which seems to refer to a specific kind of information or understanding that a person controls. The third is "inquisitive vs. uninquisitive," which seems to refer to a particular kind of "cognitive impulse"—the wish to know, the desire to find out.

In sum, the cultural model of person lexicalized in character terms contains the following elements. First, people have two major kinds of internal process, *feeling* (including "impulses" or "desires") and *thinking*. Feelings are subdivided into something like *happiness, anger,* and *fear*. An additional process of "striving" or "intending" appears to be presumed in the terms involving internalized "norms" and "strengths." Second, "outside" the person there is the world, which contains *other people, tasks,* and a variety of *norms.*

This limited number of "things" is linked to what the person "does" with these things: particular feelings can be *expressed* or *inhibited, directed toward* or *aroused* by other people, *easily* aroused or *not easily* aroused, and *given-in-to* or *not given-in-to*. Other people can be *treated* or *not treated* in the way the norms of honesty, deference, and sociability dictate. Tasks can be done in a way that indicates the person *follows* or does *not follow* the norms of duty, accuracy, and level of effort or accomplishment. Thinking can also be done in a way that indicates the person *follows* or does *not follow* the norms of logic, or has or does not have the *ability* to understand and create new things. And, finally, people vary in the amount of *strength* they have to keep alert, maintain their independence, stay organized, and keep their minds open to new ideas.

Thus the intersection of relatively few "things" with a relatively small number of "doings" can create a fairly rich vocabulary. The word that is created by these combinations has a commonsensical character, consisting of distinctions learned as part of the acquisition of language. Perhaps this world of feeling, thinking, expression, people, norms, tasks, strengths, and abilities is so distinct a part of the human experience that it could not have been conceptualized otherwise. Investigations of character terms in other languages and other cultural traditions would be relevant to this issue (White 1980).

In working through this analysis, I have been struck by the many parallels between the distinctions to be found in the world of character terms and various distinctions made within the academic disciplines of anthropology, sociology, and psychology. Mental "ability," character "strength," and the contrast between affect and cognition are basic concepts in psychology. The distinction between "socioemotional" and "task-oriented" domains of social behavior constitutes an important conceptual framework in sociology. The concept of "internalization" of norms is a central idea in anthropology. Such parallels make apparent the connection between the folk knowledge of a culture contained within the lexicon of the normal speaker and the slowly achieved refinements and elaborations of cultural specialists like psychologists, sociologists, and anthropologists.

Finally, it should be pointed out that only a part of the cultural representation of what makes up a person appears in the lexicon of character terms. Investigation of the implicit representations of the person found in other kinds of material, such as speech act classification systems, verbs of action, emotion terms, excuses, the metaphors used to describe important types of interpersonal relationships, and expressive cultural forms like games and stories, offer further perspectives on a pervasive model in American and European culture.

REFERENCES

Cattell, Raymond B.

1957 *The Scientific Analysis of Personality*. Baltimore: Penguin Books.

D'Andrade, Roy

1965 Trait Psychology and Componential Analysis. *American Anthropologist* 67:215-28.

1974 Memory and the Assessment of Behavior. In T. Blalock, ed., *Measurement in the Social Sciences*. Chicago: Aldine-Atherton.

Goldberg, Lewis R.

1979 Some Ruminations about the Structure of Individual Differences: Developing a Common Lexicon for the Major Characteristics of Human Personality. Paper presented at the Western Psychological Association Meeting, Honolulu.

1981 From Ace to Zombie: Some Explorations in the Language of Personality. In C. D. Spielberger and J. N. Butcher, eds., *Advances in Personality Assessment*, vol. 1. Hillsdale, N.J.: Erlbaum.

Hakel, Milton D.

1974 Normative Personality Factors Recovered from Raters' Descriptors: The Beholder's Eye. *Personal Psychology* 27:409-21.

Kim, Moonja Park, and Seymour Rosenberg

1980 Comparison of Two Structural Models of Implicit Personality Theory. *Journal of Personality and Social Psychology* 38:375-89.

Lenneberg, Eric H., and John M. Roberts

1956 The Language of Experience: A Study in Methodology. *International Journal of American Linguistics*, Memoir 13.

Shweder, Richard A., and Roy D'Andrade

1980 The Systematic Distortion Hypothesis. In R. A. Shweder and D. W. Fiske, eds., *New Directions for Methodology of Behavioral Science: Fallible Judgment in Behavioral Research*. San Francisco: Jossey Bass.

Veldman, Donald J.
1967 *Fortran Programming for the Behavioral Sciences.* New York: Holt, Rinehart and Winston.

White, Geoffrey M.
1980 Conceptual Universals in Interpersonal Language. *American Anthropologist* 82:759-81.

15

"Bad Ways" and "Bad Talk": Interpretations of Interpersonal Conflict in a Melanesian Society

Geoffrey M. White

Interpretations of social behavior are constructed and reconstructed on the basis of cultural knowledge of human action. Because this knowledge usually remains tacit and unspoken in the course of ordinary conversation, the task of rendering an account of others' understandings of behavior is as uncertain as it is difficult. However, there are certain ethnographic clues to the ways a culture organizes its interpretations of social interaction. For example, by paying attention to the recurrent topics and contexts of everyday conversation, one may learn about the kinds of social matters which attract local interest and concern. And language itself may reflect these cultural concerns through the elaboration of words and phrases available for talking about them.

While most social behavior seems to occur without comment or reflection, departures from expected norms of conduct frequently evoke commentary and attempts at explanation. "When action appears to depart from what we consider ordinary, expectable or approvable behavior, we begin to speak about it in certain ways. We become interested in making evaluative judgments about the behavior in question" (Much and Shweder 1978:21). The interest in interpersonal conflict, as a broad area of concern among A'ara speakers of Santa Isabel, Solomon Islands, is evident in the fact that it is a common topic of conversation, whether in gossip or in more formal contexts, as well as in the fact that it is represented in a wide range of linguistic expressions available for talking about it.

The A'ara language includes a rich lexicon of words, metaphors, and other forms used to describe and evaluate interpersonal conflict.

This paper begins with an investigation of the meanings of these linguistic forms as a first step toward understanding the premises which guide folk reasoning about interaction and conflict. The meanings of a corpus of interpersonal verbs describing conflictful actions are explored by asking a small number of informants to define them and give examples of their use, and by asking a larger sample to make judgments about their similarity in meaning. However, as critiques of lexical approaches to meaning have made clear (Fillmore 1975, Tyler 1978), these data, in and of themselves, do not take us very far in understanding natural discourse about social interaction. In the remainder of the paper, then, I seek to relate the findings of the lexical investigation to the semantic and moral content of "social images," and to the nature of social contexts for talking about conflict.

The significant premises of a moral code, those which have evaluative force, are likely to be shared widely and given public expression in prominent symbols of social identity. One of the most common devices for representing behavioral ideals is in culturally constituted notions of identity that are emblematic of desired forms of behavior, such as images of the "good person" or a "good president." In A'ara society, important understandings about persons and action coalesce in the image of a 'Christian person,' which is a highly salient symbol of identity, spanning social categories based on age, sex, kinship, or regional attachments (White 1980b). By setting up a structured task to probe the behavioral entailments of the 'Christian person' notion, it is possible to show that some of the themes evident in the lexicon of interpersonal conflict also contribute to the social meanings of Christian identity.

Each type of enthnographic data contributes to an emerging understanding of cultural interpretations of social action, of an A'ara "ethnopsychology" of interpersonal conflict (White 1985). The conceptual analysis of key words and the investigation of social images give complementary perspectives on social perception. Whereas the lexical model gives an overview of salient themes in the interpretation of interpersonal conflict, examination of the 'Christian person' image reveals which of these themes carry moral force and are evaluated as personally and socially significant. The methodological aim of the paper is to demonstrate the usefulness of an approach to cultural analysis which draws upon diverse methods and looks for convergence in their results as a way of lending greater credibility to the process of ethnographic interpretation.

Setting

Fieldwork for this study was done in the Maringe area of Santa Isabel, one of the major islands in the Solomon Islands. The language of this region is referred to as *cheke holo,* 'bush language,' and specifically as A'ara in the villages where fieldwork was carried out. A'ara is a variety of Austronesian language related to other languages in the western Solomons (White 1978b:44-53). The people engage in subsistence gardening and grow coconuts and other agricultural products as cash crops. Until extensive contact with Westerners in the mid- to late nineteenth century, residential patterns were characterized by small, shifting settlements composed of a few households pursuing swidden gardening in the interior of the island. After a disruptive period of inceased headhunting raids and internecine fighting, most of the island population embraced Christianity, brought by the Anglican Melanesian Mission, and moved into larger villages in coastal areas (White 1979b). Almost the entire population was converted by a single church, which is highly unusual for a Melanesian island as large as Santa Isabel.

Prior to these changes at the turn of the century, A'ara social organization was based on kinship relations and regional alignments in which local leaders (*funei*) of varying prestige and influence would mobilize followers for the purposes of feast giving or raiding. Exogamous matrilineal clans and smaller descent groups were identified with territorial regions focused on ancestral shrines (*phadagi*), which were the site of propitiatory offerings. These social patterns resemble closely descriptions for neighboring peoples in the western Solomons (Oliver 1955, Scheffler 1965).

The traditional pattern of small-scale settlements dispersed throughout the island, interconnected by ties of kinship and shifting political alignments, contrasts sharply with the organization of present-day Isabel society. Current patterns of residence are centered on larger and more permanent villages (generally ranging from 50 to 300 people). Political activity was formerly organized by local leaders whose power was based largely on personal reputation and accomplishments in feasting or warfare. Present-day political leaders continue to derive legitimacy from personal reputation but now operate within wider structures of church and state as well. These changes in sociopolitical organization have been paralleled by the introduction of Christian ceremony and social ideology that provides much of the rhetoric for expressing social and moral ideals. In contrast to the period of heightened raiding a century ago, contemporary Isabel society is remarkable for the absence of overt violence. If acts of sorcery are omitted, there has only been one recorded murder in several decades on the island, and cases of violent assault are practically nonexistent.

The Interpersonal Lexicon

The English language has an extensive vocabulary for describing the behavioral dispositions of individuals in terms of personality traits such as "kind" or "domineering" (see D'Andrade this volume). A considerable number of social-psychological studies have examined the conceptual organization of this vocabulary with an eye to understanding Americans' "implicit theories of personality" (see, e.g., Schneider 1973) as well as the structure of the personality lexicon and the organization of personality itself (Wiggins 1979, Goldberg 1981). Studies that have examined the co-occurrence of trait words in person descriptions have discovered a number of basic and recurring themes in implicit concepts of personality, which have been represented in terms of underlying factors (Norman 1963, Goldberg 1981) or dimensions (Rosenberg et al. 1968). I have used similar methods to explore implicit A'ara concepts of personality. The somewhat unexpected result of this research showed that the A'ara lexicon of person descriptors is primarily about *inter*personal behavior, and only encompasses the inner workings or dispositions of individuals insofar as they impact upon interpersonal processes. The conceptual dimensions that organize A'ara descriptors represent meanings that are essentially interactive in nature. Although similar dimensions are evident in the English lexicon (see below), and may even be universal in social cognition (White 1980a), the absence of intrapsychic or other individuated constructs is suggestive of the essentially *inter*personal orientation of A'ara views of the person and social reality (White 1985).

Analysis of the A'ara corpus of person descriptors shows that most of the terms entail understandings about the degree of solidarity or conflict between interactants. The labels "solidarity" and "conflict" are global indicators of various possible meanings and implications. They signify that the relations, goals, or plans of social actors are frequently perceived to be either consistent, harmonious, and aligned or inconsistent, contradictory, and misaligned. Furthermore, the conceptual opposition of solidarity and conflict represents a fundamental *evaluative* dimension evident in interpersonal vocabulary cross-culturally. Informants typically characterize conflictful actions as "bad" and actions involving harmony or solidarity as "good."

As noted above, conflictful or negative behavior tends to be a more frequent topic of conversation than harmonious interaction. Rule violations and breakdowns of social norms seem to be more noticeable than expected and normative actions. In the A'ara language, this is reflected in a greater number of verbs for describing actions regarded as negative and undesirable than for those seen as moral and rule-following. This observation about the preponderance of verbs for interpersonal conflict was the unforeseen outcome of my efforts at language learning and documentation. During the course of fieldwork I catalogued whatever linguistic expressions were used in conversation and discourse to talk about persons and interpersonal behavior. Words and phrases that could be used in adjective-like ways to describe personal attributes appear to be nearly balanced in terms of evaluative meaning. However, verb forms describing social actions include a disproportionate number of words describing behavior regarded as bad and socially undesirable. The lopsided growth of this interpersonal dictionary suggests that A'ara words for interpersonal conflict represent significant cultural knowledge about departures from the moral code in social interaction. As symbols of this cultural knowledge, verbs describing interpersonal conflict provide an opportunity for exploring the conceptual themes they are capable of expressing.

The corpus of interpersonal verbs was accumulated as part of general work on a dictionary of the A'ara language, for which there is almost no linguistic documentation at the present time.[1] Although it is difficult to say how many words could have been included in the corpus of interpersonal verbs, this study was begun with a set of about 300 words. This differed from the corpus of adjective-like person descriptors in several interesting ways. The verbs included more items, more close synonyms, and more monolexemic forms. These differences suggest a greater degree of lexical "density" in the realm of interpersonal conflict, where the language encodes forms of interaction more readily than qualities of persons as social isolates. The greater lexicalization of interpersonal processes is consistent with the finding noted above that A'ara person descriptors are primarily interactive in meaning and represent conceptions of the person and social reality which are defined less in terms of individual constructs than interpersonal processes.

The study of culture through language in general, and through lexical structures in particular, provides one kind of window through which to examine commonsense understandings of the social world. Ethnosemantic knowledge in the form of word meanings given by native speakers draws extensively from presupposed, taken-for-granted models of reality (Keesing 1979). However, naturalistic definitions, particularly for words as abstract as interpersonal verbs, are typically multiple, ambiguous, and often not easily articulated except on the basis of *examples* of action sequences. Words may express different meanings when placed in different sentences; sentences change their meaning when embedded in discourse; discourse may be interpreted variably depending upon who is speaking to whom on what occasion. Nonetheless, much of the variability in word meanings results from a potential *range* of propositional meanings signified by a lexical item rather than from a lack of definitional clarity. Furthermore, the range of meanings expressed by a lexical item may be internally structured in a highly regular way (see Coleman and Kay 1981). Information about lexical semantics can be used to investigate the interpretive possibilities available to participants in interaction.

Interest in semantic relations among lexical items dates back at least to Leibniz in the seventeeth century and has been pursued and formalized in the structural traditions of field theory (see Lyons 1977:250-61) and ethnoscience (Conklin 1962, Sturtevant 1964). Efforts to specify semantic properties of lexicons as closed systems in isolation from other types of cultural knowledge have produced static and bounded models that have been most successful in domains characterized by discrete features and taxonomic relations, such as ethnobotany. Attempts to represent semantically complex words such as interpersonal verbs on the basis of discrete features have produced results so abstract as to be far removed from actual interpretive processes (e.g. Osgood 1970).

The methodology employed in the present paper utilizes lexical representation as an adjunct to other, complementary forms of ethnographic investigation. A lexical model is used as a heuristic device to direct attention to clusters of words with overlapping or intersecting meanings, rather than as a representation of semantic relations *per se.* In the analysis developed here, a visual model of similarity relations among the set of interpersonal verbs is used to guide discussion of cultural themes of conflict based on analysis of metaphor, exegesis of key words, and discourse.

Similarity judgments and formal models used to represent them do not specify the particular semantic relations or inferences on which they are based. At the same time, however, this nonspecificity makes similarity judgments a highly portable and general type of cognitive operation that may be performed even when the semantic bases of similarity are not easily articulated by informants. Similarity judgments have been elicited in a wide range of psychological and cultural studies of perception and cognitive structure, including attempts to verify models of semantic relations known to the investigator (e.g. Rose and Romney 1979) as well as exploratory studies attempting to discover relevant dimensions in ethnopsychological knowledge (White 1980a, Lutz 1982). Interpretation of visual models of similarity relations requires additional information about what types of inferences could provide a meaningful basis for the structures they represent. As Tyler (1978:300) observes, "This part of the analysis comes from the analyst's catalogue of 'hunches' or is pieced together from clues and hints dropped by informants. In essence, the dimensions are a function of the fertility of the analyst's imagination." It should also be noted, however, that this assessment is a fair characterization of most interpretation in ethnographic research. A model of similarity relations, if constructed well, represents an emergent structure that can be juxtaposed and compared with other types of ethnographic data which are shaped by different constraints on the process of observation and inference.

A Lexical Model of Interpersonal Verbs

Thirty-three representative verbs were selected from among the original corpus of approximately 300 terms by eliminating redundancy (selecting one term from among several judged by informants to be highly similar) and highly specific words such as those describing violent physical contact ('hit,' 'shove') or illegal actions ('kill,' 'commit adultery,' 'steal'). It is not claimed that the corpus of 33 verbs encompasses all the major forms of interpersonal conflict in the A'ara lexicon, only that these words represent a substantial number of those that are important and frequently talked about. These verbs, listed in Table 1, were then used to elicit more extended exegesis from three informants, as well as judgments of similarity in meaning from a sample of 18 middle-aged men.[2]

Because almost everyone middle-aged or younger in Santa Isabel

Table 1. List of Verbs of Interpersonal Conflict

A'ara Term	English Gloss	A'ara Term	English Gloss
1. fasnagru	cheat out of	17. phiephil-ekhuma	deceive both sides
2. gigi	banish	18. ngurungau	grumble
3. cheke faphiephirei	speak deceptively	19. duili	flaunt
4. faheahet'ha	dominate	20. nagho	swear
5. chaichaghi	lie	21. mamagra	quarrel
6. fahaihali	refuse indignantly	22. kukunu	begrudge
		23. keakhegra-hotei	betray both sides
7. faripholai	shout back and forth	24. huhuru	coerce
8. fanuhnughu	mutually refuse	25. gaighani-ghugha	claim falsely
9. fachecheke	tell off		
10. tibri	curse	26. fnaja	berate
11. fafuefunei	make oneself chiefly	27. fat'hogho	make excuses
		28. fat'hoet'hoke	inform on
12. goigoni	spoil	29. fasusughu	intrude upon
13. famahmaghu	threaten	30. fafuafuna	slight
14. tutufu	deny wrongdoing	31. faneinei	hurt
		32. butulaghi	confront
15. suisukhi	goad	33. buiburi	slander
16. saosaklo	talk back		

is literate in their vernacular language (either through schooling or self-instruction), it was possible to use elicitation procedures that relied upon literacy. Each of the 33 terms was written on a 3-by-5-inch index card. The stack of 33 cards was then given to an informant with the instructions that he consider one term at a time, think about its meaning (*gaoghat'ho:* 'thought,' 'idea,' 'meaning'), and select five other terms from the corpus that were the most similar in meaning (see White 1978a:336-38). After the informant had chosen five terms to match the given target word, the cards would be reshuffled and another target word selected at random. This procedure was repeated until each of 33 terms had been judged similar to five other terms in the set. None of the informants expressed any unusual difficulty with the task, although it was quite lengthy and took between one and two hours to complete. The above procedure produces a measure of similarity between any two verbs in the corpus that consists of the frequency with which the 18 informants matched them together in the sorting task. The matrix of similarities between all pairs of verbs in the corpus is the basis for the model of conceptual similarities described below.

The matrix of similarities was analyzed using multidimensional scaling (MDS) (Kruskal et al. 1977) and hierarchical clustering (Johnson 1967) techniques (see also Shepard 1980). The scaling technique represents similarities among a set of items in terms of spatial distances, such that the proximity of any two items in space reflects the measure of similarity for those two items. The degree to which the model of spatial distance departs from the actual similarity measures is indicated by an index of "stress." MDS can be used to produce a model with any number of dimensions. Adding dimensions will decrease the stress between data and model, but also makes interpretation of the model more difficult. The appropriate number of dimensions for representing any given data matrix is chosen to minimize both the number of dimensions and the measure of stress. The first two dimensions produced by multidimensional scaling of the A'ara verb corpus are chosen for analysis here because the greatest reduction in stress is obtained by adding a second dimension. The stress figures indicate that a third dimension could also be considered, but little reduction in stress is gained by adding additional dimensions.

Hierarchical clustering represents the similarities among a set of items in terms of a branching tree-structure that merges the most similar items first and then combines them with less similar items until all the items have been interconnected. Clustering diagrams are complementary to the kind of spatial models described above insofar as the clusters tend to reveal additional information about subsets of items that are more strongly interrelated among themselves. There are now a large number of procedures for carrying out this clustering process in a way that minimizes errors which misrepresent the actual similarity data. The similarity data for the 33 interpersonal verbs were analyzed using a program developed by Johnson (1967), which uses two distinct algorithms to produce two separate clustering diagrams. Although it is advantageous to inspect both diagrams, the tack taken here is to represent the clusters produced by *both* clustering algorithms, while leaving out the discrepancies that occur at higher levels in the hierarchical structures. The resulting hierarchical model is combined with the spatial model by encircling items that were merged by both versions of the clustering process, as shown in Figure 1.

The spatial positioning of the 33 verbs in Figure 1 represents their location on two intersecting axes or dimensions. Visual inspection of Figure 1 shows that the lexical items are distributed evenly throughout

Figure 1. Two-Dimensional Scaling and Clustering Model of 33 A'ara Verbs of Interpersonal Conflict (stress = .232).

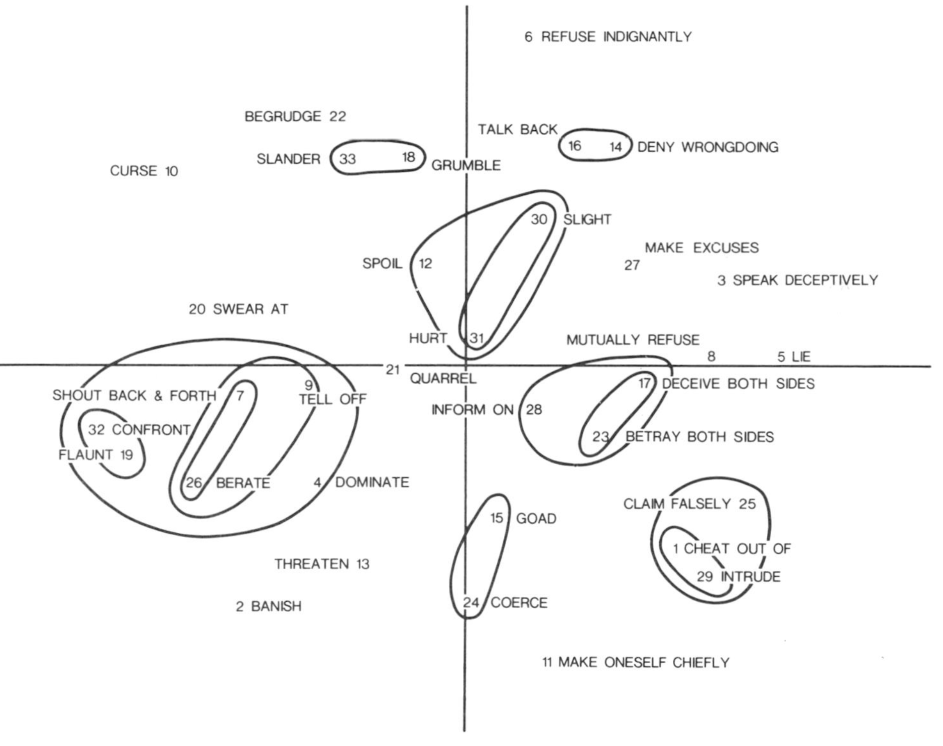

the two-dimensional space, forming several clusters of two, three and, in one case, six items.[3] The clusters represent smaller sets of words that have relatively greater similarity among themselves than with other items in the corpus, suggesting that they overlap more strongly in semantic content. The model shown in Figure 1 is primarily useful as a visual representation of relative proximity among lexical items, such that regions of the dimensional space may be interpreted as indicative of overlapping meanings among subsets of terms. The structural configuration in Figure 1 can be used heuristically to interpret some of the specific aspects of meaning among the interpersonal verbs. The interpretations offered below are based on a combination of informants' exegesis of word meanings (not discussed in detail here because of limitations of space) and ethnographic information concerning cultural understandings about persons and social conflict. Since the diagram depicts only English glosses of the A'ara verbs, a note of caution should be sounded about making any direct interpretations from it.

Ethnopsychology of Interpersonal Conflict

Inspection of the configuration in Figure 1 with attention to the meanings of verbs proximal to one another suggests possible semantic bases for the similarity relations that are represented. For example, the verbs included in the large cluster on the left side of the diagram describe harsh words or agonistic displays of anger that are open forms of aggression and confrontation ('flaunt,' 'confront,' 'berate,' 'shout back and forth,' 'tell off,' and 'dominate'). Other verbs in the left-hand region of Figure 1 also describe expressions of *hostility.* Most of the terms positioned above the large cluster represent covert forms of hostility, such as 'curse,' 'slander,' 'begrude,' or 'grumble.' Verbs located to the right of center generally entail an element of *falsity* or deception rather than directly hostile or aggressive actions. For example, the verb 'lie' is located at the extreme right side of the diagram, and the meanings of many of the other verbs in the right-hand region (such as 'claim falsely,' 'cheat out of,' 'deceive both sides,' 'betray both sides,' 'speak deceptively,' 'make excuses,' and 'deny wrongdoing') presuppose some form of lying or making false claims.

The most clear bi-polar opposition in the dimensional model is represented by the contrast of words located high and low on the vertical axis in the diagram. Verbs found in the lower portion of Figure 1 describe actions that assert power or status in an attempt to *dominate* others (e.g. 'make oneself chiefly,' 'banish,' 'coerce,' 'intrude,' 'cheat out of'), while those in the upper region involve powerlessness or reactions to dominance (e.g. 'refuse indignantly,' 'talk back,' 'deny wrongdoing,' 'grumble,' 'begrudge'). The emergence of a dimension of dominance in the lexicon of interpersonal verbs is consistent with claims that dominance is a universal theme in "interpersonal language" (White 1980a, Osgood 1970). The other major opposition in interpersonal language ("solidarity" versus "conflict") is excluded from these data because only conflict verbs are represented.

Several of the semantic groupings in Figure 1 are interpreted below on the basis of their relation to certain key constructs in A'ara ethnopsychology. After a brief look at folk reasoning about the personal consequences of various forms of conflict, several interrelated conflict themes are discussed: notions of anger and aggression, 'bad talk,' deception and revelation, and dominance.

The Metaphor of Pain

Informants' explications of many of these verbs describe actions that may have *harmful* effects, usually for the object of action. The relevance of harm for the meanings of many of the verbs is evident in the fact that the term glossed here as 'hurt' (*faneinei*) was the word most frequently selected as similar to other verbs in the corpus. This is reflected by its location in the center of the configuration shown in Figure 1. The verb 'spoil' (*goigoni*), which is an elementary expression of 'harm,' 'damage,' or 'ruin' synonymous with *fadidi'a* (literally, 'make bad'), is also clustered together with 'hurt' in the central region.

The harmful consequences of actions such as those shown in Figure 1 are conceptualized in numerous metaphorical expressions that describe personal harm in terms of bodily pain (*khabru*). The term *faneinei* ('hurt') in Figure 1 is nearly synonymous with the term *fakakabru* ('cause pain'). The pain metaphor is an apt way of conceptualizing personal or social harm in concrete images of bodily experience. In addition, harmful actions are usually construed as *deliberately* causing pain. This purposeful aspect is expressed in metaphors of harmful action constructed with verbs that describe 'poking' or 'jabbing' some object with a sharp implement that, if directed at a person, would certainly cause bodily pain. Examples of these metaphors are: *fajiojito* ('poke a fire with an ember'), *fajaija'i* ('plant with a digging stick'), *juijuli* ('pluck fruit from a tree with a long pole'), and *fachacha* ('poke, stab, or stick'). When extended into the domain of social interaction, these verbs become expressions for purposeful efforts at harming someone, similar to the more general form *fakakabru,* 'cause (someone) pain.'

The perception of a threat to personal well-being may take different forms. Verbs that describe aggressive actions (mostly positioned on the left side of Figure 1) take a direct object which is placed in jeopardy, either by an immediate threat of physical force (in the case of open confrontation) or by the power of verbal aggression (e.g. 'curse,' 'slander') to cause illness, misfortune, or death (see below). Those actions involving false claims describe attempts to obtain status or property *at the expense of others.* One person's (unjust) gain is another's loss. Thus the assertion of a false claim is perceived as a threat to the social status (and, hence, personal well-being) of others. Actions that entail some form of deception are seen as attempts to distort information such that it is damaging to others, and not to oneself. Finally, actions regarded as a refusal or lack of cooperation ('talk back,' 'refuse indignantly,' or 'slight') imply a denial of social obligations, which may cause unhappiness or suffering on the part of the other. It is especially interesting to note that the verb 'hurt' clusters most closely with 'slight,' indicating that the *absence* of expected action may be interpreted as intentionally causing harm, as in our clinical notion of passive aggression. Thus, with varying degrees of directness or immediacy, almost all of the verbs describe actions that entail harmful consequences caused by the agent of that action (cf. Schwartz 1973). A more complete understanding of this point requires an account of folk theories of misfortune (White 1985).

'Anger' and Aggression

The description of behavior as intentionally causing pain characterizes it as hostile and aggressive. The notion of harmful action directed at someone is incorporated in the meanings of many of the verbs located on the left side of Figure 1, which describe expressions of hostility. For other verbs in the corpus the element of 'causing (someone) harm' is not encompassed within their basic definition but is associated conceptually through inference. The actions interpreted here as explicitly hostile and aggressive were all described by informants as motivated by the agent's 'anger,' usually directed at a person or group who evoked that anger.

As already noted, actions involving expressions of hostility appear to take two general forms in this corpus: those that entail open, behavioral confrontation (as in the large cluster of verbs including 'berate,' 'shout back and forth,' and 'confront') and those that involve covert forms of hostility (such as 'slander,' 'curse,' and 'begrudge'). Most of the covert forms of expression are verbal in nature. However, verbal aggression is also an important aspect of open confrontations, as indicated by the terms 'berate,' 'tell off,' and 'shout back and forth,' and by the term 'swear at,' which may be either overt or covert. Openly aggressive actions involving public displays of anger and loud talk appear to be extremely infrequent in contemporary Santa Isabel, which by any index is an extraordinarily nonviolent society. Indeed, the Santa Isabel case calls to mind Hallowell's comment (1940:395) that his study of aggression in Salteaux society could be titled "aggression among a patient, placid, peace-loving . . . people." However, the quieter expressions of hostility in the form of conversations that evaluate the behavior of others (and, hence, could be regarded as 'slander'), and suspicions or accusations of ill-intent, are very common.

The notion of 'anger' is not only an important element of meaning in verbs that describe hostile and aggressive actions but also a central organizing concept in reasoning about social interaction. 'Anger' does not just motivate aggressive actions, it is also regarded as a likely *response* of the individual threatened by such actions. So, for example, expressions of hostility are perceived as *provocative* actions that may evoke an angry response from the object of hostility. The concept of 'quarrel' (*mamagra,* which is also located in the central region of Figure 1 between the 'hurt' cluster and the 'confront' cluster) represents the minimal elements of a conflict script in which one antagonist provokes another into an exchange of verbal or physical assaults.

In A'ara understandings about social process, anger is regarded as a likely response to any form of moral breech or rule violation. So, for example, 'breaking a promise,' 'telling a lie,' or 'stealing' may give rise to 'anger' in anyone affected by those actions. However, the moral code also proscribes expressions of anger and aggression. This poses an important cultural dilemma in social interaction: responses to a rule violation ('anger') are also likely to be seen as a rule violation (expressions of hostility and aggression). Many of the actions described by verbs on the left side of Figure 1 represent a kind of metaconflict in which reaction to an instance of moral transgression is itself evaluated negatively as a transgression of behavioral ideals.

Reactions to transgressions or conflictful events that might be expected to cause anger are frequently spoken of as feeling 'knotted up' (*haru*) or 'tangled' (*fifiri*). Just as one may 'tie up' (*haru*) a parcel of almond nuts, one may keep bad feelings inside because of the moral conflict experienced with expressions of anger. This experience of ambivalence is described metaphorically as 'tangled feelings' (*fifiri nagnafa*). The personal dilemma associated with the experience of anger is especially acute in light of folk theories which postulate that suppressed emotions may cause illness or misfortune. A'ara society provides a culturally constituted solution to the dilemmas of anger and conflict in the form of a social activity termed 'disentangling' (*graurut'ha*) (White 1979b, 1983). Given that 'tangled' feelings are those problematic emotions associated with social conflict which are kept inside, 'disentangling' extends the metaphor by providing an occasion for 'speaking out' (*cheke fajifla*) about bad feelings. 'Disentangling' is discussed further below.

'Bad Talk'

A'ara speakers will often refer loosely to two broad types of interpersonal conflict: 'bad ways' (*puhi di'a*) and 'bad talk' (*cheke di'a*). The notion of 'bad ways' refers to any behavior regarded as negative and socially undesirable, and hence would encompass all of the actions included in Figure 1. 'Bad talk,' on the other hand, refers specifically to verbal aggression and expressions of hostility. Verbal expressions of hostility include face-to-face speech (such as 'berate' or 'swear at'), as well as covert forms of verbal aggression (such as 'slander,' 'curse,' and, again, 'swear at').

The moral evaluation of angry speech is a function of social relations between speaker and listener. Although the (post-Christian) moral code ideally proscribes expressions of hostility *in general*, 'anger' and 'bad talk' are traditionally regarded as most inappropriate between persons related through ties of kinship (cf. Read 1955). Violation of proper speech codes between closely related persons is referred to as *jojoghara* ('use of improper or offensive speech'). For example, in a village meeting called to 'disentangle' ill-feelings about past incidents of interpersonal conflict, villagers discussed the behavior of a teenage boy who had stolen some betel nut from a tree belonging to his mother's brother. However, the conversation shifted quickly to the actions of the uncle, who had 'berated' his nephew with 'bad talk' because of the theft. One of the participants said to the uncle, "This kind of talk that you are making is as if you are separate from other people. It is better to speak to your nephew to teach him, like I do with my nephew. . . . That kind of bad talk can be aimed at other people, but to our own nephews, our own children, it is very bad." This passage illustrates the way in which the characterization of a speech act as 'bad talk' carries evaluative force in sanctioning the verbal expression of hostility. However, the evaluation of 'bad talk' is contextualized by the social relations between the interactants, so that 'bad talk' *between kin* is said to be improper rather than 'bad talk' in general.

Covert forms of 'bad talk' or verbal aggression ('slander,' 'curse,' 'swear at') are referred to as 'hidden talk' (*cheke pouporu*). Perhaps the best exemplar of the notion of 'hidden talk' is the verb 'slander,' which, like the verb 'lie,' is potentially applicable to a broad range of speech behavior. Almost any discussion about another person absent from the conversation could be interpreted as an instance of 'slander.'

Notions of "loose talk," 'just talking' (*fiti cheke*) or 'starting talk' (*vuvuhu cheke*), are likely to be regarded as hostile, harmful, and slanderous by the object of such talk. The covert nature of 'hidden speech' seems not to decrease but actually to increase the power of the spoken word in A'ara perceptions. In the local perspective, 'anger' and other strong emotions are potent forces that may cause illness and misfortune (White 1985).

Verbal expressions of hostility may also have potent effects, either on the speaker or on the object of hostility. For example, one old woman did not want to talk with me about historical incidents of raiding or fighting between two regions because discussion of the formal hostilities might cause blisters to form around her mouth. The harmful effect of 'hidden talk' on the object of that talk is most obvious in the concept of 'cursing' (*tibri*), which is closely akin to notions of sorcery. Uttering a curse out of anger toward someone who evoked that anger is believed to cause that person harm or even death. The perceived effects of 'slander' (*buiburi*) are evident in its literal meaning, which builds upon the metaphor of a painful bite by a horsefly (*buri*). According to local belief, seeing a *buri* fly in one's house is a sign that one is being slandered at that moment. The notion of 'hidden talk' relies upon the cultural understanding that any aspect of thought, emotion, or behavior may be kept hidden from others.

Deception and Revelation

While conversation may be hidden from others, speech itself may be used to hide or distort knowledge of events. The potential for systematically or deliberately distorting the propositional content of speech is an important aspect of meaning in most of the verbs located on the right side of Figure 1, many of which involve the premise that the *quality* of information in an assertion or action is flawed in some way. These verbs describe behavior that entails some element of falsity, as indicated by the central location of the verb 'lie' in this region.

Understandings about potential duplicity add an important dimension to social discourse, which allows *interpretations* of behavior, as well as behavior itself, to be evaluated and debated in ordinary conversation. The assertion that some utterance is 'false' (*cheke chaghi:* 'false talk') is very common in village gossip and debate about social events. The accusation of 'lying' may be a moral defense as well as a challenge. For example, in a village meeting called to discuss preparations for an upcoming feast, one brother accused another of not fulfilling his obligations in planting and harvesting sweet potatoes for the occasion. The (angry) response of the accused brother was that his accuser was 'lying,' an assertion which simultaneously implied that he in fact was fulfilling his obligations and that his brother had transgressed normal rules of speech.

Other concepts of speech that in some way distort or hide knowledge of events resemble English concepts of "double talk" or "beating around the bush." Deceptive speech is conceptualized with metaphors such as 'raveled' (*faphiephirei*) as opposed to 'straight' (*doglo*), 'covered' (*fruni*) as opposed to 'uncovered' (*fatakle*), and 'upside down' (*tautagru*, from *t'hagru:* 'backside'). These concepts of deceptive speech represent knowledge about the process by which private understandings are expressed in public meanings—thought of in spatial terms as moving from 'inside' the person to 'outside.' Thoughts and emotions concerning moral quandaries or socially undesirable events may either be kept 'inside' and 'hidden' or be 'spoken out' (*cheke fajifla*) and 'revealed' (*fatakle*). When a previously hidden topic is raised at a meeting, it may be said to 'surface' (*t'hagra*), just as a turtle comes up from underneath the water to breathe.

As is the case in many cultures, the experience of visual perception is used to conceptualize knowledge. To 'see' (*filo*) is also to 'understand' (*filo glani*), as in English. If wrongdoing is not revealed, then it is actively 'concealed' (*tutufu*), a concept similar to the American colloquial expression "stonewalling." The A'ara notion of concealment pertains particularly to verbal denial in the face of social confrontation. It is described not in terms of avoidance or private isolation but rather as public debate and moral negotiation in the arena of face-to-face interaction. The complementary speech act is that of 'goading' someone in order to 'pry out' (*suisukhi*) concealed information, as if it were lodged within a person like a thorn.

Dominance

The fact that the complementary actions of 'goad' (*suisukhi*) and 'conceal' or 'deny wrongdoing' (*tutufu*) are not proximal to one another in Figure 1, but are separated by their positioning on the vertical dimension, illustrates the way in which this dimension represents dominance in verb meanings. Verbs describing actions in which the agent is attempting to influence another or assert power or status are located in the bottom portion of Figure 1. In contrast, verbs located in the upper portion of the diagram represent the actions of an agent who is without power or status and is *responding* to the actions of others, whether attempts to gain cooperation or some implied wrongdoing (which would evoke 'slander,' 'cursing,' or 'begrudging').

This interpretation of the vertical dimension in the spatial model pertains more to knowledge about the *social context* of interaction than to the particular actions described by each verb. While discussing verb meanings, informants made frequent reference to social statuses and relations between interactants. For example, a number of the verbs in the upper portion of the diagram were explained by making the agent of the action a child. In one instance where the action 'refuse indignantly' was illustrated by the actions of a village leader, the leader was described as having been powerless to get villagers to do what he wanted. In contrast, the verbs in the lower portion of Figure 1 either were about illegitimate attempts to claim power and status (e.g. 'make oneself chiefly,' 'claim falsely') or were exemplified by reference to legitimate village leaders or government authorities.

The A'ara concern with dominance emerged clearly in the previous study of adjective-like person descriptors (White 1978a:345) and is also reflected in spatial metaphors used to characterize social relations in terms of physical positioning. In addition to descriptions of size (BIG/SMALL), any descriptive term that plays on UP/DOWN and FRONT/BACK oppositions can also be used to describe relations of dominance between actors. So, for example, an actor whose behavior is regarded as self-aggrandizing (to the detriment of others in the community) is described as 'making oneself high' (*fahaehaghe*) and, by implication, 'making others low' (*fapaipari*); as 'being in front' (*au fa'ulu*) rather than 'being behind' (*au faleghu*); as 'being on top' (*au fakligna*) rather than 'being underneath' (*au fapari*); as 'making oneself bigger' (*fabi-obi'o*) and 'making others smaller' (*fa'ikoi*).

The relational structure of these oppositions makes them a good vehicle for characterizing social relations between actors. The use of complementary oppositions such as HIGH/LOW is also effective in describing the A'ara perception of interdependence among actors, such that one cannot 'make oneself high' without 'making others low.' The framing of interaction in terms of its implications for dominance relations between interactants appears to cut across the entire corpus of verbs represented in Figure 1.

Social Symbols and Moral Judgments

Conversational accounts of social conflict derive their moral force from behavioral ideals that are frequently symbolized by important social personae or images. In order to explore the mutual relevance of semantic knowledge of verbs of interpersonal conflict and moral judgments about their evaluative weight, I used the same 33 verbs discussed above to ask informants which types of undesirable behavior are the most inappropriate for a 'Christian person'—a highly valued and widely shared aspect of social identity in Santa Isabel. The results of this investigation can best be interpreted after a brief sketch of the cultural and historical significance of Christian identity among A'ara speakers.

The nineteenth century was a highly turbulent era that witnessed extensive disintegration of society in Santa Isabel. The island was the target of repeated large-scale headhunting raids from islands in the western Solomons capable of devastating entire villages. These external pressures contributed to massive migration, depopulation, and increased fighting among Isabel groups (White 1979b). It was in this context of disruption and failure of traditional religious and political institutions that the Anglican Melanesian Mission gained a strong foothold on the island, and ultimately achieved a dramatically rapid conversion to Christianity among the entire island population. The process of conversion involved the adoption not simply of a new syncretic religious creed but of a new social identity ('being Christian') with accompanying social and moral ideals. The Christian ideology of peace and nonviolence gave symbolic expression to the cessation of raiding at the turn of the century. The 'new way' (*puhi majaghani*) of Christianity was viewed as a holistic transformation of society, which replaced 'fighting' with 'peace,' 'darkness' with 'light.' These images are perpetuated in oral legend and present-day ceremonial events that symbolically reconstruct the process of conversion (White 1980b).

Many of the social ideals expresssed in the moral rhetoric of the mission were consistent with traditional behavioral norms of cooperation and nonaggression among kin relations. The mission, however, introduced a universalistic ethic that extended these norms ideally to all social relations, thus not only proscribing aggression between kin but proscribing expressions of hostility *in general* (see Leenhardt 1979, Read 1955, and Hogbin 1958 for similar observations about differences in Melanesian and Christian moral reasoning). Although it is difficult to reconstruct history, it appears as if this attempt to shift behavioral ideals was accompanied by a marked change in the ethos of social life on the island, which saw the virtual elimination of institutionalized violence and sanctioned displays of aggression. The adoption of Christianity was associated not only with the cessation of raiding but with attempts to control and defend against the other major threats to personal and community well-being: sorcery and malevolent spirits. Traditionally, the fear of possible raids by enemies was matched by comparable fears of sorcery and 'spirits' (*na'itu*), which could cause sickness and death. Christian belief and ritual were immediately taken up to provide people with spiritual power (mana, *nolaghi*) and protection against threats from powerful spirit forces. Suspected sorcerers were made to confess in church ceremonies conducted by local catechists in order to neutralize their powers; dangerous ancestral spirits and malevolent 'bush spirits' were exorcised by ceremonial processions led into the bush for prayer and hymn singing aimed at dispelling their power (White 1978b:188-90).

Becoming a Christian on Santa Isabel, then, entailed the adoption of a posture toward the social and spiritual world represented by cultural notions of the 'new way' and the 'Christian person.' The 'new way' provided knowledge and ritual that were *used* to protect against potential dangers in the "behavioral environment" (Hallowell 1967). In addition, Christian socio-moral ideals contributed symbolic and pragmatic means for dealing with forces inherent in social conflict and ill-feeling, especially 'anger,' which might cause sickness and misfortune just as surely as a 'spirit attack.'

In a related study I explored the social meanings of Christian identity by asking a sample of informants to characterize their image of a 'Christian person' using a set of descriptive terms. The results showed that the notion of the 'Christian person' consists of traits such as 'kind,' 'sympathetic,' 'humble,' 'willing,' and 'peaceful' (White 1980b:361). Analysis of the cultural significance of these person descriptors in a lexical model indicates that they represent social behavior which is essentially harmonious and submissive. As a symbol of the ideals of social harmony, the 'Christian person' image is frequently used rhetorically in speeches to publicly express social ideals and direct social action.

I further investigated the behavioral implications of the 'Christian person' image by asking informants to make judgments about which of the 33 forms of conflictful interaction were the most inappropriate for a 'Christian person.' Twenty-nine middle-aged men were asked to examine the 33 verbs, presented on cards in random order, and select ten of them judged to be the most inappropriate (*t'he'ome naba gna:* 'don't fit') for the 'way' (*puhi*) of a 'Christian person' (*naikno Khilo'au*). This task produced 290 judgments of 'inappropriateness' distributed across the 33 verbs. The results are shown in Table 2, which lists the verbs ranked according to the frequency with which they were selected as inappropriate.

Inspection of the frequencies listed in Table 2 shows that the judgments about inappropriate behavior are not distributed evenly across the 33 types of interpersonal conflict. There is a definite gap between the five most frequently selected items and the remainder. The four highest-ranking verbs all describe forms of verbal hostility: 'slander,' 'swear at,' 'lie,' and 'curse.' The fifth verb, 'quarrel,' is a more general, blanket term for social conflict. Furthermore, it is particularly the various forms of *covert* 'bad talk' or 'hidden talk' that are the most negatively evaluated forms of interpersonal conflict. The strictly overt

Table 2. Ranking of Behaviors Judged Inappropriate for a 'Christian Person' (N = 29)

Rank Term	Frequency	Rank Term	Frequency
1. slander	24	18. claim falsely	7
2. swear	23	19. refuse indignantly	6
3. lie	22	20. shout back and forth	5
4. curse	21	21. tell off	5
5. quarrel	20	22. deny wrongdoing	5
6. banish	15	23. dominate	5
7. begrudge	13	24. berate	5
8. talk back	13	25. threaten	3
9. spoil	13	26. confront	3
10. inform on	12	27. mutually refuse	2
11. deceive both sides	10	28. goad	2
12. betray both sides	10	29. make excuses	2
13. grumble	9	30. cheat out of	1
14. hurt	8	31. speak deceptively	1
15. slight	8	32. flaunt	1
16. make oneself chiefly	8	33. intrude upon	1
17. coerce	7		

types of 'bad talk,' such as 'berate' and 'tell off,' were selected as inappropriate less than one-fourth as often as the forms that may be covert. Although the verb 'lie' does not necessarily describe a form of hostility, its high ranking with the other forms of 'bad talk' suggests that informants may have selected this word on the basis of its sense 'to lie about *someone,*' which is similar to the verb 'slander.'

Table 2 gives some insight into the *kind* of interpersonal conflict that is regarded as the most antithetical to contemporary social ideals. Just as Christian belief and ritual are used to protect oneself and one's community from hostile forces in the spirit world, so Christian moral premises proscribe expressions of hostility in the interpersonal world, which are also covert and not easily seen. In the case of 'curse' (*tibri*), there may also be a supernatural aspect of cursing that invokes a spirit attack, referred to as 'spirit curse' (*na'itu t'hibri*). Causal reasoning about the power of 'slander' or 'swearing' to harm the target of such 'bad talk' is analogous to that of 'cursing,' insofar as both may cause pain or illness.

The high ranking of 'hidden talk' in Table 2 is an indication of ethnopsychological understandings about the power of speech to affect people, whether directly as in 'cursing,' or through the engendering of 'bad feelings' and a social reality perceived as harmful. Speech is the vehicle by which inner thoughts and emotions affect others. However, negative emotions, especially 'anger,' also have the power to harm others or oneself if left unexpressed. If not worked out, feelings kept 'inside' become 'knotted up' and may cause sickness or misfortune. The moral dilemma of 'anger' lies in the fact that it is regarded as personally dangerous if left to fester, but as socially fractious if expressed publicly. In particular, public expressions of anger may have social repercussions which can neither be contained nor controlled. This is the problem of *meta*conflict referred to earlier in which responses to conflictful events can themselves become the object of moral evaluation and conflict.

As mentioned above, the traditional solution to the twin dangers of 'anger' suppressed and 'anger' expressed consists of a ritualized forum for conversational exchange about interpersonal conflict and bad feelings called 'disentangling.' Disentangling sessions constitute a special context that suspends normal strictures about 'bad talk,' thus creating an occasion within which talk about conflict or bad feelings is acceptable and even encouraged (although in a referential mode rather than as an immediate expression of emotion) (White 1979a, 1983). In light of folk theories about conflict and pent-up emotion as a cause of misfortune, disentangling meetings are frequently held before major cooperative endeavors such as hunting for turtle or pig in order to 'talk out' any personal grievances that could cause injury or failure (*braku*). The framing of the 'disentangling' context as an occasion for 'bad talk' was stated quite explicitly by a local priest who initiated a meeting to disentangle disagreements about a marriage by calling for the revelation of any 'anger,' 'slandering,' or 'grumbling': "I want all of us to sit here and talk this out. Everyone must talk together to straighten things out. That's the good and correct way in custom and in the Church . . . so if you all have any anger, slandering or grumbling, you should talk about it now, because today is the time for disentangling. There won't be any fines, just disentangling and straightening. . . ."

It is not coincidental that local priests frequently play a mediating role in 'disentangling' meetings, even though they are not church functions. More than one informant compared 'disentangling' meetings with Holy Communion ceremonies, which have from the earliest days of conversion been embraced enthusiastically as a ritual that places one within the power (mana) and protection of the Christian God, just as earlier rites of propitiation gained a person the assistance of ancestral spirits. In order to take Holy Communion, one must prepare oneself by confession and silent prayer at a prior church service. The vernacular term (*tarabana,* from *bana*: 'build') for this process of 'preparation' suggests that it is analogous to the process of protecting oneself from sorcery by carrying ginger or other talismans perceived to have protective power. It is regarded as dangerous to take Holy Communion if one has internal conflicts that have not been 'revealed,' 'spoken out,' or "confessed" (cf. Levy 1973:181). One informant suggested that the introduction of Christian priests on the island was an important innovation that allowed for revealing moral transgressions in a private rather than public forum. By confessing to a priest one could defuse the potential danger of moral transgressions, which could harm oneself and others if kept inside, without creating the turmoil likely to be evoked by public discussion and debate.

These brief observations about A'ara views of 'disentangling' and Holy Communion indicate that both of these events obtain their meaning on the basis of folk theories of misfortune which explain personal and community harm in terms of interpersonal conflict, moral transgression, and suppressed emotion, particularly 'anger' (see White 1985). Similar beliefs about the severe personal and social consequences of various Pacific analogues of anger have been reported for other ethnopsychologies in the region (e.g. Strathern 1968, Levy 1973, Lutz 1982). In symbolizing social ideals of harmony and proscribing the most damaging forms of hostility (e.g. 'hidden talk'), the image of a 'Christian person' takes on cultural and pragmatic significance in maintaining personal well-being and community harmony. Linking discussion of the meanings of verbs of interpersonal conflict to this broader context of ethnopsychological reasoning gives a fuller description of cultural notions of 'bad ways' and 'bad talk.'

Conclusion

In cultural interpretations of social action it is interpersonal *conflict,* departures from the moral order, that most engender explanation and evaluation. Perhaps because they represent problems in the reconciliation of the public and private self, of cultural ideals and personal experience, conflict, disagreement, and transgression are frequent topics of everday conversation. The cultural emphasis on problematic or negatively evaluated behavior is reflected in the linguistic resources (words and metaphors) available for talking about conflict. An analysis of the lexicon of interpersonal conflict indicates that verbs describing various types of 'bad ways' include concepts of overt aggression, hostility, covert verbal aggression ('hidden talk'), deception, and dominance. In each case ethnographic investigation of these various interpretive forms is aided by the convergence of lexical data, analysis of related metaphors, and insight into the contexts and concerns that evoke ordinary thinking and talking about conflict.

The symbolic structures that emerge from this type of analysis represent more than interpretive schemata used to assign meaning to instances of social conflict; they are moral premises that have evaluative force in sanctioning social conduct and in regulating threatening or harmful forces in both the self and others. In particular, this investigation has produced a picture of the moral dilemma of 'anger' for A'ara speakers. Moral judgments about behaviors most appropriate for a 'Christian person' show that Christian identity ideally proscribes various kinds of covert verbal aggression or 'hidden talk,' which are associated with suppressed or 'tangled' anger, perceived as a threat to self and other. The implicit logic of these understandings becomes apparent in the analogy between traditional 'disentangling' sessions and Holy Communion ceremonies, both of which are culturally constituted activities for attempting to deal with the problems of unresolved conflict and hostility. These findings suggest that the image of a 'Christian person' embodies symbolic and pragmatic attempts to "exorcise" negative emotions and harmful actions, just as Christian belief and ritual are used to protect self and community from dangerous spirits. The course of the analysis followed in this paper, then, illustrates the close interdependence of symbol and praxis in ethnopsychology, such that the meanings of key symbols are shaped by contexts of pragmatic action, in turn constituted only through those processes of interpretation that give them social significance.

NOTES

This paper is based on fieldwork carried out during 16 months in 1975 and 1976. Support for that work by the Social Science Research Council and the Wenner-Gren Foundation is gratefully acknowledged. I would also like to thank Richard Ashmore, Ronald Casson, Janet Dougherty, John Kirkpatrick, and Catherine Lutz for helpful comments on an earlier version of this paper.

1. A xerox copy of the author's card-file dictionary of A'ara is lodged in the Pacific Collection, Hamilton Library, University of Hawaii.

2. Collection of similarity data was limited to male informants because of pragmatic difficulties with administering the tasks to women. Instructions for performing the sorting task were given in the A'ara language by the author with the assistance of Nancy Montgomery.

3. The structural interrelation of the items in Figure 1 is markedly different from the configuration of similarity relations obtained using similar procedures with the set of person descriptors mentioned previously (White 1978a, 1980a). The contrast in the shape of the two similarity models pro-

vides an instructive example of some of the semantic considerations that bear on the interpretation of dimensional models. The model of person descriptors depicts a nearly uniform distribution of items in a smooth and symmetric circular pattern around the point of intersection of two dimensions (White 1980a:763). The structural regularity of the circular configuration reflects certain properties of adjective-like terms, which tend to form bi-polar oppositions. Also, the evaluative opposition of good ("solidarity") and bad ("conflict") traits that forms the primary axis in the model of person descriptors is absent from the corpus of verbs, which pertain solely to conflict.

REFERENCES

Coleman, L., and P. Kay
1981 Prototype Semantics: The English Verb *Lie. Language* 57:26-44.
Conklin, H.
1969 Lexicographical Treatment of Folk Taxonomies. In S. Tyler, ed., *Cognitive Anthropology.* New York: Holt, Rinehart and Winston (first published in 1962).
D'Andrade, R.
1984 Cultural Meaning Systems. In R. Shweder and R. LeVine, eds., *Culture Theory: Essays on Mind, Self, and Emotion.* New York: Cambridge University Press.
Fillmore, C.
1975 An Alternative to Checklist Theories of Meaning. In C. Cogan, H. Thompson, and J. Wright, eds., *Proceedings of the First Annual Meeting of the Berkeley Linguistic Society.* Berkeley: University of California Press.
Goldberg, L. R.
1981 Language and Individual Differences: The Search for Universals in Personality Lexicons. In L. Wheeler, ed., *Review of Personality and Social Psychology.* Beverly Hills, Calif.: Sage Publications.
Hallowell, A. I.
1940 Aggression in Saulteux Society. *Psychiatry* 3:395-407.
1967 The Self and Its Behavioral Environment. In *Culture and Experience.* New York: Schocken Books (originally published in 1955).
Hogbin, H. I.
1958 *Social Change.* London: Watts.
Johnson, S. C.
1967 Hierarchical Clustering Schemes. *Psychometrika* 32:241-54.
Keesing, R.
1979 Linguistic Knowledge and Cultural Knowledge: Some Doubts and Speculations. *American Anthropologist* 81:14-36.
Kruskal, J. B., F. W. Young, and J. B. Seery
1977 *How to Use KYST-2, a Very Flexible Program to Do Multidimensional Scaling and Unfolding.* Murray Hill, N.J.: Bell Laboratories.

Lakoff, G., and M. Johnson
1980 *Metaphors We Live By.* Chicago: University of Chicago Press.
Leenhardt, M.
1979 *Do Kamo: Person and Myth in the Melanesian World.* Chicago: University of Chicago Press (original French ed. published in 1947).
Levy, R. I.
1973 *Tahitians: Mind and Experience in the Society Islands.* Chicago: University of Chicago Press.
Lutz, C.
1982 The Domain of Emotion Words on Ifaluk. *American Ethnologist* 9:113-28.
Lyons, J.
1977 *Semantics.* Vol. 1. Cambridge: Cambridge University Press.
Much, N., and R. Shweder
1978 Speaking of Rules: The Analysis of Culture in Breach. *New Directions for Child Development* 2:19-39.
Norman, W. T.
1963 Toward an Adequate Taxonomy of Personality Attributes: Replicated Factor Structure in Peer Nomination Personality Ratings. *Journal of Abnormal and Social Psychology* 66:574-83.
Oliver, D. L.
1955 *A Solomon Islands Society: Kinship and Leadership among the Siuai of Bougainville.* Boston: Beacon Press.
Osgood, C. E.
1970 Interpersonal Verbs and Interpersonal Behavior. In J. L. Cowan, ed., *Studies in Thought and Language.* Tucson: University of Arizona Press.
Read, K. E.
1955 Morality and the Concept of the Person among the Gahuku-Gama. *Oceania* 25:233-82.
Rose, M. D., and A. K. Romney
1979 Cognitive Pluralism or Individual Differences: A Comparison of Alternative Models of American English Kin Terms. *American Ethnologist* 6:752-62.
Rosenberg, S., C. Nelson, and P. Vivekenanthan
1968 A Multi-Dimensional Approach to the Structure of Personality Impressions. *Journal of Personality and Social Psychology* 9:283-94.
Scheffler, H. W.
1965 *Choiseul Island Social Structure.* Berkeley: University of California Press.
Schneider, D. J.
1973 Implicit Personality Theory: A Review. *Psychological Bulletin* 79:294-309.
Schwartz, T.
1973 Cult and Context: The Paranoid Ethos in Melanesia. *Ethos* 1:153-74.

Shepard, R. N.
1980 Multidimensional Scaling, Tree-Fitting and Clustering. *Science* 210:390-98.

Strathern, M.
1968 Popokl: The Question of Morality. *Mankind* 6:553-62.

Sturtevant, W. C.
1964 Studies in Ethnoscience. In A. K. Romney and R. D'Andrade, eds., *Transcultural Studies in Cognition.* Special publication of *American Anthropologist*, vol. 66.

Tyler, S. A.
1978 *The Said and the Unsaid: Mind, Meaning and Culture.* New York: Academic Press.

White, G. M.
1978a Ambiguity and Ambivalence in A'ara Personality Descriptors. *American Ethnologist* 5:334-60.
1978b Big Men and Church Men: Social Images in Santa Isabel, Solomon Islands. Ph.D. dissertation, University of California, San Diego.
1979a Some Social Uses of Emotion Language. Paper read at the 78th Annual Meeting of the American Anthropological Association, Cincinnati, Ohio.
1979b War, Peace and Piety in Santa Isabel, Solomon Islands. In M. Rodman and M. Cooper, eds., *The Pacification of Melanesia.* Ann Arbor: University of Michigan Press.
1980a Conceptual Universals in Interpersonal Language. *American Anthropologist* 82:759-81.
1980b Social Images and Social Change in a Melanesian Society. *American Ethnologist* 7:352-70.
1983 'Disentangling': Talk about Conflict and Emotion in Santa Isabel. Paper read at the Conference on Talk and Social Inference: "Straightening Out" Contexts in Pacific Cultures, Pitzer College, Claremont, Calif.
1985 Premises and Purposes in a Solomon Islands Ethnopsychology. In G. White and J. Kirkpatrick, eds., *Person, Self, and Experience: Exploring Pacific Ethnopsychologies.* Berkeley: University of California Press.

Wiggins, J. S.
1979 A Psychological Taxonomy of Trait-Descriptive Terms: The Interpersonal Domain. *Journal of Personality and Social Psychology* 37:395-412.

B. EMERGENCE OF UNDERSTANDING: The Mutually Constitutive Relationship of Knowledge and Experience

These chapters emphasize the relationship between prior knowledge and ongoing experience in the achievement of understanding.

16

Individual Experience, Dreams, and the Identification of Magical Stones in an Amazonian Society

Michael F. Brown

Knowledge is always accompanied with accessories of emotion and purpose.

Alfred North Whitehead,
Adventures of Ideas

Over the past 15 years or so there has been an astonishing increase in research related to non-Western systems of classification, especially in the domain of folk biology. Using an increasingly sophisticated methodology and enlisting the collaboration of natural scientists, cognitive anthropologists have relentlessly plotted the lexical grids of informants from London to Lhasa, Terre Haute to Tierra del Fuego, in search of universals in human classificatory behavior. This effort has produced monographs of unparalleled ethnographic detail (e.g. Berlin, Breedlove, and Raven 1974, Hunn 1977, to name but two) and generated an appreciation for the skill with which native people organize their perception of the natural world. Still, I suspect that I am not alone in wondering whether taxonomic trees and Venn diagrams will ultimately tell us much about how classification fits into the texture of daily life or how it is informed by the "accessories of emotion and purpose" to which Whitehead alludes. There is evidence, for instance, that the concept of the omniscient informant, a cornerstone of many ethnoscience studies, has finally been discredited (Gardner 1976, Ellen 1979b), and that there is a growing understanding of the role of intracultural variability in cognition. An equally serious misconception—the notion that one can analyze semantic domains in isolation from broader cultural concerns—has also come under challenge. James Fox (1971) and Michelle Z. Rosaldo (1972), for example, argue convincingly that one must consider the connotative as well as the denotative qualities of classificatory terms to understand how people assign things to categories. This suggests that metaphor, and symbolism in general, should be as important to cognitive anthropologists as more strictly lexical matters.

In this essay I describe the processes by which the Aguaruna Indians of Peru identify and employ certain stones whose use can be considered "magical" in Western terms. Although these stones are natural objects, physically unmodified by human beings, the principles by which they are assigned identities have little to do with the observation of objective discontinuities in nature. Indeed, the stones are identified on the basis of the finder's experimentation with them, as well as through the interpretation of dreams and omens that reveal aspects of the stones' true nature. These procedures are meaningful only within the context of abstract, culture-specific propositions about the means by which human beings obtain knowledge of the spirit world, the reality that lies behind or within the events of ordinary life.

This case merits scrutiny for several reasons. First, it concerns classificatory behavior in a nonbiological domain, magic, that has received little attention from cognitive anthropologists. Second, it illustrates how natural objects can be identified according to arbitrary, culture-specific criteria rather than observed or "real" discontinuities in nature. Finally, it provides further evidence that a classificatory field can support a considerable degree of intracultural variation—variation based on the kind of private insight that Goodenough (1981:98) has called "propriospect"—and still convey information that is meaningful to others. Although the Aguaruna are in general agreement about the criteria used to identify magical stones, people weigh the criteria differently according to the circumstances of each case. The resulting variability creates no insuperable obstacles to communication or understanding.

Before beginning, a brief note on terminology: I have tried to use the terms *identification* and *classification* in a more precise manner than is usually the case. Following a definition proposed by Roy Ellen (1979b:341), I understand identification to mean the initial assignment of names to things. Classification, in contrast, is the allocation of named things to more inclusive categories. In actual practice, of course, the two processes often go hand in hand; once a thing is identified, its classification usually follows from it by convention. Nevertheless, each presents slightly different problems to the person doing the identifying and classifying. Here I am primarily concerned with how the Aguaruna identify, rather than classify, stones.

Ethnographic Background

The Aguaruna, a Jivaroan people living in the eastern foothills of the Andes, are one of the largest native societies of the Peruvian Amazon. The research on which this paper is based was conducted in several villages located along tributaries of the Alto Rio Mayo in the Department of San Martín. Like other Aguaruna populations, the people of the Alto Mayo support themselves by a mixture of root-crop horticulture, hunting, fishing, and gathering. They are also increasingly involved in such commercial activities as animal husbandry, timber extraction, and the sale of agricultural commodities.

The traditional Aguaruna worldview bears a strong resemblance to that of the Shuar or Jívaro proper (Harner 1972) and the closely related Canelos Quichua (Whitten 1976). The rapidly changing social milieu, which now includes missionaries, teachers, non-Indian colonists, bureaucrats, and, for that matter, curious anthropologists, has had a substantial impact on Aguaruna thought, yet it is fair to say that the Aguaruna view of the world is still quite different from that of the surrounding non-native society.

The Aguaruna continue to think of the world as a place permeated by consciousness or thought, which takes its concrete form in anthropomorphic beings whose presence most people perceive only sporadically. These beings include a powerful but distant creator called Apajuí (literally "Our Father"),[1] spirits of the earth and water (Nugkui and Tsugki respectively), and many other souls or spirits of lesser importance. Such beings are at once forces to be reckoned with and cognitive reference points around which people organize their experience. The degree to which people perceive the influence of these spirits is directly proportional to their individual knowledge. For the Aguaruna, as for the Quichua of Ecuador (Whitten 1978:845), knowledge is a combination of practical skills and visionary insight, that is, understanding obtained through dreams and trance states induced by the consumption of psychotropic plants. When the Aguaruna were engaged in hostilities, including intertribal warfare, they regularly sought fruitful contacts with spirits who could help them prevail over their enemies. The people of the Alto Mayo are less concerned with these things today, but the value they place on spiritual knowledge is revealed in their continued patronage of shamans and the resilience of certain forms of magic.

Magic, I hasten to add, is not thought of as a kind of behavior categorically different from, say, practical work, nor do the Aguaruna mark it by a specific term. From their point of view, there exist certain techniques that one uses to increase the prospects of success in important activities. These techniques include the singing of special songs and the use of a large inventory of charms, as well as the observation of taboos or avoidances. I call such techniques "magical" because they do not fall within the accepted limits of technology, nor are they informed by theories of cause and effect that are acceptable in Western terms.

Among the magical objects used by the Aguaruna are several kinds of stones that aid people as they hunt, fish, cultivate gardens, pursue enemies, or seek lovers. To understand the significance of these stones, however, we must first consider the technological and symbolic importance of all lithic materials in the Amazonian context.

The Amazon rain forest is remarkable for the rate at which it recycles organic matter; in the words of Alejandro Camino (1980:525), it is characterized by an accelerated "decomposition and recomposition" of its raw materials. In this context stone is the only enduring substance known to man. Before the introduction of steel tools, stone (in the form of polished stone axes) was vital to native technology, since it allowed human beings to transform forest into garden, natural things into cultural things. Even today whetstones remain essential to the maintenance of steel machetes and axes. Moreover, stone is hard to find in those vast portions of the Amazon that consist of ancient alluvial soils. The people of the Alto Mayo do not have to purchase whetstones from traders, as do native groups located downriver, but the residents of some Alto Mayo communities are obliged to collect sharpening stones from rocky areas located several kilometers from their houses and then carry them home. Stone is thus an essential but frequently scarce commodity.

The significance of stone transcends the purely technological and economic, however. Rocks of all sizes may house powerful beings. Vision-seekers traditionally consume hallucinogens next to rocky waterfalls deep in the forest in the hope of making contact with the souls of ancient warriors (Harner 1972:136). Escarpments and large boulders are the homes of "souls," "demons," or "rock mothers" who possess shamanic powers that they use to kidnap unwary travelers. For the Aguaruna, stone embodies external stasis concealing internal activity. It is a paradoxical substance that simultaneously resists change and enables humans to effect change by means of its physical properties and the spiritual forces contained within it.

Despite the technological and symbolic importance of lithic materials, the Aguaruna mineral lexicon is rather impoverished, especially when compared to their highly developed lexicon of plants and animals (Berlin and Berlin 1977). The word *kaya,* "stone," is used as a general term for all mineral substances as well as to refer to specific stones; numerous adjectives can be used with *kaya* to specify size, shape, color, or texture.[2] Within the general category *kaya,* there are also a few commonly used primary lexemes denoting specific minerals: *kuji,* "gold"; *jiju,* "iron"; and *jiinchag,* an unidentified white mineral. Some informants also include within the category *kaya* certain substances used in pottery manufacture, including *duwe,* "clay," and *bukáu* and *majánk,* two mineral dyes.

Three terms denote the categories of stones used in magic: *yuka, nantag,* and *namúg.* The relationship of these terms to the general taxonomy of stones is less than straightforward. For example, if one asks an Aguaruna informant "What kinds of stones are there?" the three terms for magical stones are rarely, if ever, elicited. If, however, one asks "What is a *yuka* (or a *nantag* or a *namúg*)?" people invariably reply, "It is a stone." Two factors may account for this. Since information about magical charms is considered valuable personal property, people sometimes hesitate to mention them unless pressed. More important, *yuka, nantag,* and *namúg* are primarily associated with the domains in which they are used (hunting, courtship, horticulture, etc.) and only secondarily with stone as a class of material.

Identification and Use of Magical Stones

Since the qualities of the three principal kinds of magical stones show significant differences, I shall first treat each category separately. Nevertheless, the qualities that the three categories have in common will become apparent as the analysis proceeds.

Yuka

The term *yuka* denotes a category of stones that possess an unusual power of attraction. Some *yuka* attract game animals, birds, and fish; others attract human beings of the opposite sex. When people wish to clarify exactly which sort of *yuka* they are talking about, they use terms like "game grabber" (*kuntin achitai*), "woman grabber" (*nuwa achitai*), and so on.

Descriptions of the external appearance of *yuka* vary widely. Most informants describe them as small, shiny pebbles that are white, black, red, or brown in color.[3] Some *yuka* are said to consist of a soft, almost claylike material, while others are hard and crystalline. *Yuka* may also have an unusual shape or surface texture (cf. Karsten 1935:164-65). I could discover no clear correlation between the shape, color, or texture of a stone and its supposed powers.

The kinds of *yuka* that attract birds and mammals are used by hunters to bring game in their direction and, in conjunction with magical hunting songs, to render the creatures passive so that they can be easily killed. To exploit the attracting powers of his *yuka*, a man seals the stones in a container full of red face paint and then applies the paint to his body and weapon (either blowgun or shotgun) before he hunts.

Yuka for fishing reportedly attract fish and increase a man's ability to grab them when fishing by hand for species that adhere to rocks in the river. People were less certain about whether these stones are helpful when a man fishes with a net, a hook and linc, or fish poison.

Yuka that attract human beings are part of an elaborate set of love charms and songs used by the Aguaruna to conduct amorous affairs (Brown 1981:171-213). In principle, either men or women can use *yuka* for this purpose, but people vehemently deny that a woman would want or need to use a love charm.[4] Even the use of charms by men is considered reprehensible, since the charms' power is so deranging and uncontrollable that their mere possession threatens the social order. Privately, though, men confide that they are anxious to obtain "woman grabber" *yuka* and other kinds of love charms so that they can enjoy the sexual favors of women.

A man who succeeds in finding a "woman grabber" *yuka* immerses it in face paint, which he then applies before going on a social visit to another house. He contrives to bring a bit of the paint into direct contact with the woman he desires, either when they are dancing or as she serves him a bowl of manioc beer. Once she touches the paint, the woman "goes crazy" with desire for the stone's owner. The power of a strong *yuka* is said to be so unhinging that a woman may commit suicide by throwing herself in a river if her passion cannot be immediately satisfied.

Thus far I have explained how people use *yuka*, but not how they get them in the first place. Most *yuka* are found in the stomach or crop of an animal as it is being cleaned. More rarely, the stone may appear in the animal's mouth or in some other part of its body. One elderly man told me that the stones are often found "wrapped in a white cloth," by which he apparently meant that they are surrounded by a thin film of tissue.

The Aguaruna tend to identify the attractive power of the stone with the species (or at least the life-form) from which it is obtained. A stone found in a peccary has the power to attract other peccary and, to a lesser extent, other edible mammals. Stones found in a curassow attract curassow and other birds, and so on. As one man said, "Each animal has its own stone." The obvious exception to this pattern is the "woman grabber" *yuka*, which is commonly found in the entrails of aquatic mammals, among them the dolphin and the nutria. These creatures are linked symbolically to the water spirit Tsugki, the ultimate source of all love magic (cf. Whitten 1976:61).

It is important to note that the circumstances surrounding the discovery of a stone are suggestive but not definitive clues as to its true identity. After finding a stone, say, in the stomach of an armadillo, a man seals it in a container and begins a rigorous fast that includes sexual abstinence and avoidance of desirable foods, including meat, palm grubs, and salt. If during the fast the man dreams of armadillos or other game animals, he may come to the preliminary conclusion that the stone is indeed a *yuka* and that it attracts armadillo. On the other hand, dreams about women suggest that the stone is a love charm. A definitive identification is achieved only after experimentation, however. Potential love charms can be tested by bringing them into contact with a neighbor's dog. If the dog suddenly becomes affectionate, the charm will undoubtedly produce the same effect in women. Likewise, when acquisition of a new stone is followed by several successful hunting trips, a man can be confident that this stone attracts game.

The identity of a stone is thus determined by a complex process of observation, attention to dreams and omens, and experimentation. Sometimes a man who finds a stone in an animal experiences dreams suggesting that the stone encourages the growth of manioc. In this case he concludes that the stone is not a *yuka* at all, but a *nantag* or gardening stone. He will then give it to his wife. A stone that produces no noticeable effect is unceremoniously discarded. This testing and observation take place in the utmost privacy, for fear that someone else might either steal one's stone or inadvertently destroy its power by touching it without observing the proper ritual precautions.

Aside from the chance encounters with *yuka* I have just described, the Aguaruna also know of complex procedures by which *yuka* can be obtained in a more purposeful manner. The following narrative, which explains how a man can acquire a stone that attracts women, is typical of this kind of procedure. I cannot say whether this technique is really used, but the narrative certainly illustrates some of the concepts underlying notions of magical attraction:

> A man who wants a strong *yuka* should kill a snake [species not identified] and bury it in the forest. After a while, another snake will come to the place because it is attracted to the dead snake. The man must kill this one too and bury it in the same spot. Later another snake will come, an enormous snake with a glowing stone in its mouth. The man quickly pins the snake's head to the ground

with a forked stick, then pries the stone out of its mouth. He runs away. He does not kill the snake, because when it dies the stone is ruined. This stone is called *yuka*. It attracts women.[5]

This account, which I heard repeated in many variations, offers several avenues of interpretation. The obvious Freudian gloss—that snakes represent male sexuality and are thus an appropriate provider of male sexual magic—has undoubted merits, although it oversimplifies the multiple associations surrounding snakes in Aguaruna thought. More germane, perhaps, is the belief that snakes possess an uncanny power of detection, i.e. reverse attraction. Victims of snakebite invariably isolate themselves in a forest shelter surrounded by four small fires, the purpose of which is to frighten off the many poisonous snakes that are drawn to a person who has been bitten by one of their kind. The snake's stone is a palpable representation of the reptile's ability to find its prey. By reversing the usual predator/prey relationship through the theft of the stone, a man converts the snake's power of detection into a human power of attraction.

Nantag

Each Aguaruna woman owns one or more stones called *nantag* that she uses in a planting ritual intended to increase the productivity of her garden. Alto Mayo women almost invariably describe *nantag* as small, shiny, red stones. The *nantag* that I have actually seen, however, as well as those seen by my colleague Margaret Van Bolt, were small, smooth pebbles of various colors. (See Brown and Van Bolt 1980 for details of *nantag* beliefs and rituals.)[6]

Women believe that *nantag* exert a favorable effect on the growth of root crops such as manioc, taro, cocoyam, and arrowroot. To bring this power to bear on her crops, a woman places the stones in a bowl, adds water, achiote (*Bixa orellana*, a red dye), and several other plant substances, then pours the liquid over the cuttings of the plants before they are inserted into the ground. After planting is completed, a gardener hides her *nantag* in a covered bowl buried in some protected part of the garden.

Alto Mayo women explain the origin of *nantag* in several ways. Some insist that human beings first obtained the stones from Nugkui, the feminine earth spirit who taught women how to cultivate manioc and other crops. A different though not necessarily contradictory account is as follows: "Our ancestors in the Alto Marañón had *nantag* just after the earth was made, but they threw them away. The bird *sukuyá* [*Nyctidromus albicollis*] collected the best ones and has them now. The bird *waga* [*Tinamus major*] also has them. So do the crab and the honey bee."

Today women obtain *nantag* either by inheriting them from older kinswomen (in which case the stones are said to be especially powerful owing to their antiquity) or by finding them in the course of their daily labors. The circumstances under which women find *nantag* vary greatly. Some encounter them in the soil of their gardens while cultivating or weeding. Others claim to have discovered a stone in the claw of a freshwater crab or in the shell of an aquatic snail. One woman explained that she obtained a *nantag* after her husband was led to it by a person who appeared to him in a dream (Brown and Van Bolt 1980:180). Both ancient *nantag,* which a woman has inherited, and newer stones, which she has acquired in her own lifetime, are hidden from the sight of other women, since they might envy the owner's beautiful gardens and thus be tempted to steal the stones. Indeed, women handle the stones only when they can be assured of privacy, usually in some little-traveled portion of their manioc gardens.

As with *yuka,* the discovery of a suspected *nantag* is only the first step in an extended process by which a woman establishes the stone's identity and then consolidates its power. After finding a stone, she pays increased attention to dreams, omens, and other signs that might clarify the stone's nature. True *nantag* speak to a woman in dreams. Typically, a young girl or woman appears to the stones' finder and warns her that the stones are "thirsty" and need to be fed a mixture of achiote and water that is likened to blood. *Nantag* tend to "run away," that is, disappear from their storage place only to reappear in another location. They may also attract objects such as leaves, insects, or strands of human hair to the bowl in which they are stored. A stone that shows one or more of these traits can be classified as a *nantag* with some certainty. The ultimate test, of course, is whether the stone produces a noticeable improvement in a garden's productivity. Some women report that newly acquired stones are tested experimentally by bringing them into contact with specific plants and then observing the plant's growth,[7] but I could not verify the extent to which this experimentation actually takes place. Stones that show no promise are simply thrown away.

Namúg

The Aguaruna recognize a third kind of stone, called *namúg,* that has a quasi-legendary status. A myth describes *namúg* as a set of stones that the vulture used to detect carrion in various stages of putrefaction (Chumap and García-Rendueles 1979:549-53). A source on the Shuar of Ecuador mentions a stone called *namúr* ("a rock similar to pyrite") that is used by shamans to manipulate their bewitching darts (Pellizzaro 1978:34). Informants in the Alto Mayo, however, primarily associate the term *namúg* with a stone used by warriors to ensure their success in battle. These stones are said to be like *yuka* in that they helped legendary warriors attract and kill enemies just as *yuka* help hunters attract and kill game animals.

Like *yuka* and *nantag, namúg* are attributed no fixed appearance: some people describe them as dark colored, others as light; some say that the stones are shiny and attractive, others that they are nondescript. It is the circumstances of their discovery, as well as their magical powers, that define them as *namúg:*

> There was once a young man who had never touched a woman. Again and again he drank *datém* and *baikuá* [hallucinogenic plants of the genera *Banisteriopsis* and *Brugmansia* respectively]. . . . He went to fight his enemies. He and the others killed several men and cut off their heads. They peeled the skin off the heads. Where they had piled the heads, the man found a stone, a *namúg*.
>
> After he found this, he killed many people. It was impossible to defend oneself from his attack. . . .

Another narrative about *namúg* explains that the stone was obtained by a man who had embarked on a vision quest. He was visited by an *ajútap,* or ancient warrior spirit, in the form of a small feline. In the mouth of the animal was a glowing stone, a *namúg,* which the man pried loose and concealed in his house. With this stone he turned attacking warriors into peccaries, which he and his family easily killed and ate.

Alto Mayo people say that it is still theoretically possible to obtain a *namúg,* but highly unlikely because young men are no longer willing to dedicate themselves to a life of sexual purity and the constant consumption of hallucinogenic plants. Today, they lament, everyone is too tainted by sexual pollution and the taste of sweet foods to be granted the power of a *namúg.*

Discussion

In a preliminary presentation of their exhaustive analysis of Aguaruna ethnobiology, Brent and Elois Ann Berlin (1977:4-6) argue that Aguaruna classification of living things is "based fundamentally on the recognition of groupings or organisms in terms of their gross similarities and differences in overall appearance and behavior." They further contend that this system of classification "capitalizes on the objectively real discontinuities in the biological world." Their conclusions seem appropriate for the biological domains that they analyze, but it should be clear that something quite different is taking place when the Aguaruna identify stones as *nantag, yuka,* and *namúg.* Let me summarize the factors that bear on the identification process in this domain.

Appearance. The external features of a stone provide clues as to its ultimate identity, yet these clues are perhaps the least important of the qualities that people take into account during the identification process. With the possible exception of *nantag,* which are consistently described as red (although they are, in fact, often of other colors), there is no clear pattern of external features associated with each taxon. (The color associations of magical stones are so open-ended that Alto Mayo women now reportedly use as *nantag* cat's eye marbles purchased from non-Indian merchants.) Strangeness of appearance—be it in color, shape, or surface texture—is suggestive of magical power, but by no means firm proof. Ordinary stones may prove just as efficacious as exotic ones.

Circumstances of discovery. The fact that a stone turns up in an unusual place or that it behaves in an odd way ("moving by itself," "making noises," etc.) is more indicative of special powers than is its external appearance. More important, the circumstances of discovery may advance the identification process by suggesting connections to the broader cosmological system. A stone discovered in the soil of the garden, for example, sets off a series of associations in the mind of the finder: the stone may possess special powers, since stones are not ordinarily found in the soil; these powers are connected to Nugkui, the feminine earth spirit who inhabits the soil; hence the stone may have the ability to bring some of Nugkui's fecundating power to the plants in the finder's garden. Similarly, a stone that appears in the entrails of a nutria, a mammal symbolically linked to the water spirit Tsugki, is likely to be thought of as a potential love charm (i.e. a *yuka*), since Tsugki is the mythical source of all love magic. These inferences are logical only within the confines of an arbitrary set of symbolic equations whose significance extends far beyond the limits of the semantic domain "mineral substances."

Personal experience. The most important criteria employed in the identification of magical stones are private and—from the Western point of view, at least—largely subjective experiences: dreams, omens, judgments of the degree to which the possession of a stone has increased one's success in a specific endeavor. These experiences are perceptually based (cf. Berlin and Berlin 1977:4), of course, but here perception is organized by a set of cultural conventions rather than by an objective order existing in nature. Prominent among these conventions is the idea that dreams constitute as important a source of information about the world as the observations of ordinary waking life.

The contrast between the results of the Berlins' study of Aguaruna classification of the biological world and my own observations on the identification of magical stones raises an obvious question: why do the same people fix on nonarbitrary criteria (e.g. objective discontinuities in form and behavior) in some cases and more arbitrary, culture-specific criteria in another?

Before addressing this question, let me say that I believe the contrast as stated is more apparent than real. Although it is true that the criteria used by the Aguaruna to assign an identity to a given plant or animal are usually quite concrete, involving such things as color, morphology, size, and habitat, they are not invariably so. Elsewhere (Brown 1978) I have argued that the identification of hallucinogens of the solanaceous genus *Brugmansia* is based as much on the type of vision that the plant induces as on any visible morphological traits, and analogous criteria may apply to the identification of some medicinal plants as well.

Assuming that the contrast has some degree of legitimacy, however, I think that two factors can be held accountable. First, there are undoubtedly strong selection forces favoring consistency in the identification of species that are necessary, or in some cases inimical, to survival (cf. M. Z. Rosaldo 1972:87). Hunters must communicate information about animals, herbalists about herbs, and so on, and in these contexts communicative errors could have an immediate impact on the well-being of the communicators. Thus consistency follows from exigency.

A second variable is the degree to which communication takes place in a public setting, where it will presumably be more subject to what Goodenough (1981:105) has called "normative selection." The identification of plants and animals is carried out on a daily basis in the presence of other people and often with the object of the identification process available for immediate inspection. The magical domain, on the other hand, is intensely private. To my knowledge, adults rarely, if ever, show one another their magical stones; indeed, they go to great lengths to keep their stones' very existence a secret. The infrequent public discussions of magical charms are conducted at a high level of generality, with few attempts to reconcile divergent opinions. The impact of this social variable—that is, the extent to which the classificatory process is open to public inspection—on the choice of classificatory criteria lends support to the view of Ellen (1979a:4) and others that research on folk taxonomies should not be divorced from more conventional sociological analysis.

I am well aware that this discussion raises as many questions as it has answered. One would like to know more about the ways in which parents teach their children about magical stones, or the extent to which the magical knowledge of shamans differs from that of laymen. Even more instructive would be an analysis of a larger inventory of case studies, based on firsthand observation, describing how individuals evaluate the efficacy of magical stones during the course of the testing process. In lieu of such information—which may, in any case, be impossible to acquire, given the intensely private nature of the activity—we can at least appreciate how the flexibility inherent in the identification process enables people to assign names to a specific class of objects while simultaneously imposing order on a broad array of complex experiences. What might be seen mistakenly as a lack of precision is in fact a remarkable sensitivity to context.

NOTES

The research on which this paper is based was supported by grants from the Doherty Foundation, the Wenner-Gren Foundation for Anthropological Research, and the Centro Amazónico de Antropología y Aplicación Práctica, Lima. A grant from Williams College enabled me to make a follow-up visit to the Alto Mayo in 1981. I am grateful for comments provided by Gillian Feeley-Harnik, Janet Dougherty, and William Merrill in response to an earlier draft of this paper.

1. The spelling of Aguaruna words follows the system developed by the Summer Institute of Linguistics (Larson 1966) and now used by the Aguaruna themselves. Most letters are pronounced more or less as in Spanish, with the exception of *e* (the high central vowel ɨ), *g* (pronounced like *ng* as in *ring*), and *b* and *d* (pronounced like *mb* and *nd*, respectively). Nasalizations have been deleted, and all accents fall on the first syllable unless otherwise noted.

2. Larson (1966:164) lists the phrases *ashí jiju* (literally, "all iron") and *ashí kaya aidau* ("all stones those-that-are") as generic terms for "mineral."

3. The color terms here translated as black, red, white, or brown do not cover exactly the same chromatic range as their English equivalents.

4. In part this reflects the prevailing double standard with respect to the legitimacy of extramarital affairs. The Aguaruna believe that love charms are useful only for brief extramarital liaisons; between spouses, their effects are ultimately destructive. Since women have no license to philander under any circumstances, people deny that a woman would want a *yuka*.

5. An informant whose close kinsman had reportedly obtained a *yuka* in this manner told me that the man put the stone in a small gourd, which he then sealed in a clay vessel containing balls of cotton thread. Before he could test the stone's power, however, it escaped its hiding place by "eating the lid of the pot." He never succeeded in recovering it.

6. Both Karsten (1935:127) and Harner (1972:72) state that the stones used by Shuar women are red. Harner describes them as "chips of unworked jasper." Perhaps the absence of this mineral in the Alto Mayo has led Aguaruna women to substitute other kinds of stone.

7. The stones are brought into contact with the plants indirectly, by immersing them in a mixture of achiote and water and then pouring the liquid over the plant cuttings.

REFERENCES

Berlin, Brent, and Elois Ann Berlin

1977 *Ethnobiology, Subsistence, and Nutrition in a Tropical Forest Society: The Aguaruna Jívaro.* Studies in Aguaruna Jívaro Ethnobiology, Report no. 2. Berkeley: Language Behavior Research Laboratory, University of California.

Berlin, Brent, D. E. Breedlove, and P. H. Raven

1974 *Principles of Tzeltal Plant Classification.* New York: Academic Press.

Brown, Michael F.

1978 From the Hero's Bones: Three Aguaruna Hallucinogens and Their Uses. In Richard I. Ford, ed., *The Nature and Status of Ethnobotany,* pp. 119-36. Anthropological Papers no. 67, Ann Arbor: Museum of Anthropology, University of Michigan.

1981 Magic and Meaning in the World of the Aguaruna Jívaro of Peru. Ph.D. dissertation. Ann Arbor, Mich.: University Microfilms.

Brown, Michael F., and Margaret L. Van Bolt

1980 Aguaruna Jívaro Gardening Magic in the Alto Rio Mayo, Peru. *Ethnology* 19:169-90.

Camino, Alejandro

1980 Ecología e ideología en la cultura nativa del bosque tropical. *Shupihui* 5:523-30.

Chumap, Aurelio, and Manuel García-Rendueles

1979 *Duik Muun: Universo mítico de los Aguaruna.* Lima: Centro Amazónico de Antropologiá y Aplicación Práctica.

Ellen, Roy F.

1979a Introductory Essay. In Roy F. Ellen and David Reason, eds., *Classifications in Their Social Context,* pp. 1-32. New York: Academic Press.

1979b Omniscience and Ignorance: Variation in Nuaulu Knowledge, Identification and Classification of Animals. *Language in Society* 8:337-64.

Fox, James J.

1971 Sister's Child as Plant: Metaphors in an Idiom of Consanguinity. In R. Needham, ed., *Rethinking Kinship and Marriage,* pp. 219-42. London: Tavistock.

Gardner, Peter M.

1976 Birds, Words, and a Requiem for the Omniscient Informant. *American Ethnologist* 3:446-68.

Goodenough, Ward H.
1981 *Culture, Language, and Society.* 2d ed. Menlo Park, Calif.: Benjamin Cummings.

Harner, Michael J.
1972 The Jívaro: People of the Sacred Waterfalls. Garden City, N.Y.: Anchor/Doubleday.

Hunn, Eugene S.
1977 *Tzeltal Folk Zoology: The Classification of Discontinuities in Nature.* New York: Academic Press.

Karsten, Rafael
1935 *The Head-Hunters of Western Amazonas.* Societas Scientiarum Fennica, Commentationes Humanarum Litterarum, vol. 7, no. 1. Helsingfors.

Larson, Mildred L.
1966 *Vocabulario Aguaruna de Amazonas.* Serie Lingüística Peruana, No. 3. Yarinacocha, Peru: Summer Institute of Linguistics.

Pellizzaro, Siro
1978 *El Uwishin.* Mundo Shuar, ser. F., no. 3. Sucua, Ecuador.

Rosaldo, Michelle Z.
1972 Metaphors and Folk Classification. *Southwestern Journal of Anthropology* 28:83-99.

Whitten, Norman E., Jr.
1976 *Sacha Runa: Ethnicity and Adaptation of Ecuadorian Jungle Quichua.* Urbana: University of Illinois Press.
1978 Ecological Imagery and Cultural Adaptability: The Canelos Quichua of Eastern Ecuador. *American Anthropologist* 80:836-59.

Whitehead, Alfred North
1933 *Adventures of Ideas.* New York: Macmillan.

17

From Situation to Impression: How Americans Get to Know Themselves and One Another

Dorothy C. Holland

In describing her weekend visit to her friend, an informant, Rachel, made it clear that Robert regarded her as a romantic partner while she regarded him as a good friend but nothing more. She told of a conversation between herself and Robert in which she let him know that she was dating other men:

> I've talked to Robert before about how I felt in . . . romantic situations [with other men], and I kind of did it as an experiment Saturday night. I was talking about dating situations . . . and he told me that it made him really feel funny to hear me talk about that. . . . I kind of did it as an experiment, you know, like: "See, I like other people."

Her "kind of experiment"—treating him as though he were a confidante to whom one reveals one's romances—was an attempt to tactfully refuse his romantic overtures.

This story of Rachel's, like many of the others collected in the study described here, exhibits the complex reasoning that Americans engage in about one another as well as the vast amount of cultural (learned, conventional) knowledge about the social world—about friends, love, individual psychology, crazy people, and the rest—which they apply to interpersonal problems. In this paper these stories are analyzed for what they reveal about the application of cultural knowledge to actual social situations. Stimulated by current expanded horizons of cognitive anthropology, the analysis is directed to identifying patterns and content in Americans' social reasoning about themselves and others, particulary the patterns that are evident in the process of getting to know someone.

Expanded Horizons in the Study of Cultural Knowledge of the Social World

In the 1950s the study of cultural knowledge was influenced by an orienting paradigm rooted in descriptive linguistics (Goodenough 1956, 1957). Despite this influence, practitioners of the newly emergent field of cognitive anthropology failed to embrace the antimentalist, behaviorist stance of the descriptive linguistics of the day and, in fact, quickly began to pose questions about the cognition of cultural knowledge. This trend is especially clear with regard to the study of social knowledge. Initial research in cognitive anthropology concerned social categories such as kin terms, focusing on their referential meaning (e.g. Lounsbury 1956, Tyler 1969). By the early 1960s, however, these descriptions began to be accompanied by discussions of the cognitive processing of these classificatory systems (e.g. Romney and D'Andrade 1964). Today the cognitivist emphasis is even more pronounced as anthropologists join with linguists, social psychologists, and others involved in the interdisciplinary effort of cognitive science to study the mental processes and units that humans use not only to understand words and their meanings (e.g. Keesing 1979, Coleman and Kay 1981, Sweetser in press, Quinn this volume) but also to construct and understand stories and other discourse sequences (e.g. Agar 1980, Hutchins 1980, Colby and Colby 1981). This paper reflects the expanded cognitivist approach to the study of cultural knowledge of the social world. The remainder of this section is devoted to elaborating three aspects of this expanded perspective that are relevant to the design of the research to be reported and to the interpretation of the findings.

Knowledge Structures

The first aspect to be elaborated concerns units of cognitively organized knowledge. Instead of focusing upon verbalized categories, the cognitivist perspective shifts attention to the structure of implicit or tacit cognitive understandings. The basic concepts for describing this structure—"knowledge structure," "schemata," and "frame"—derive from the tradition of cognitive science.

In 1977 Roger Schank, a computer scientist specializing in artificial intelligence, and Robert Abelson, a social psychologist, published a now well-known book about tacit cognitive understandings. They posited a set of knowledge structures to account for the fact that humans are able to make sense of such sketchy descriptions of human action as the following: "Harry sat down at his favorite table and happily ordered. He wasn't so happy, however, when the waitperson spilled water on his tie. As he paid the cashier, he grumbled that his tie had been ruined." In this story only a few sketchy details are provided. Nonetheless, the reader can understand the sequence of events by relying upon tacit knowledge that he or she has about the way American restaurants operate. Few readers, for example, could be expected to have any difficulty answering questions such as: "What was Harry paying for?" or "Who took Harry's order?" What Schank and Abelson do is posit that omitted portions of event descriptions are filled in by tacit knowledge which is organized into various types of knowledge structures such as "scripts" and "plans." In interpreting what happened in the story of Harry, we rely, supposedly, on a script about the conventional "stereotyped sequence of actions that defines [the] well-known situation" (1977:41) of dining at a restaurant, which we have inferred from our many experiences in restaurants.

The concept of knowledge structure is very similar in meaning to two other concepts: "schema" and "frame." These concepts were developed to handle issues in modeling human problem solving. Such models must contend with the fact that humans apply old knowledge to new situations and the fact that humans do not apply all their vast amount of knowledge about the world to any one situation. Clearly, there must be some organizational structure or procedure that permits only a subset of knowledge to be brought to bear in a given situation. It has been proposed that knowledge is organized into "schemata" and "frames." In a given situation these schemata and frames orient a person's attention to a particular set of objects and relationships, thereby restricting what is likely to be noticed in the situation (Abelson 1975, Neisser 1976, Minsky 1975). In listening to folktales, for example, we orient to certain structural components and tend to ignore and forget "alien" components that do not fit our cultural schemata for stories (Rice 1980).

Although "knowledge structure" and "schema" have only recently begun to appear in the vocabulary of cognitive anthropology, in fact, cognitive anthropologists have either stimulated or directly contributed to progress in the description of a number of knowledge structures. Notions about a very basic knowledge structure, that of concepts or categories, for example, have been revised in light of cognitive data provided by anthropologists as well as cognitive psychologists and linguists (Rosch 1975, Coleman and Kay 1981, Sweetser in press). Studies of the "dimensions of meaning" of role terms and character trait terms such as those described in Burton and Romney (1975) and Harding and Clement (1980) were precursors to notions of "conceptual schema" (White 1980:776) and "cultural schema" (D'Andrade this volume).[1] In addition, cognitive anthropologists have previously described a number of other types of what the more recent articles refer to as schemata or knowledge structures, including beliefs and propositions (Frake 1964, Stefflre et al. 1971, Metzger 1973, Clement 1982, D'Andrade 1976), recipes, grammar, or scripts (Metzger and Williams 1963, Gladwin 1970, Agar 1973), and story schemata (Rice 1980). Basically, the new concepts of "knowledge structure" and "schema" provide generic categories that subsume these various structures that have been described and underscore the point that they are cognitive entities.

Knowledge Systems

Although cognitive anthropologists have made significant contributions to the study of knowledge structures and schemata, they have tended to focus on only one or two of these structures at a time. Part of the importance of Schank and Abelson's (1977) book is that it describes not just one knowledge structure but a set of four knowledge structures and their interrelationships. In their conceptualization, for example, the knowledge structure of "goals" is linked to that of "theme." "Role theme," to give a specific example, "is a bundle of knowledge containing the following: . . . a role member with one or more role member goals . . ." (1977:137).

Although no one else has presented such an extensively developed approach for the domain of social knowledge as that of Schank and Abelson, other types of knowledge systems—or sets of interrelated knowledge structures—have been proposed. These include "propositional networks" (sets of tacit cognitive propositions at least one of which logically entails another—see D'Andrade 1976 and Hutchins 1980, for example), "games" (which include such things as victory conditions, rules, and moves—see Meehan et al. 1979), and "folk theories" (sets of tacit cognitive schemata at least one of which is linked to another as causal—see Quinn this volume for a portion of her research on American folk theories of marriage, Holland 1981, Coleman and Kay 1981, and Sweetser in press). In this paper two macro knowledge systems and their interrelationships are discussed. These macro knowledge systems are extensive compendia of knowledge structures and knowledge systems related to two broad categories: person and situation.

Knowledge and Behavior

In the language of artificial intelligence a given cognitive schema or system is "instantiated"—activated—by certain conditions. Although the label itself may conjure up visions of computers, the concept of instantiation might prove to have some utility in cognitive anthropology, since research indicates that it is sometimes difficult to specify the conditions under which a given set of knowledge will be activated or instantiated. The cultural schemata that are inferred by cognitive anthropologists as guiding individuals' behavior do not always seem to be consistently applied in action. They are acted upon in some situations but not in others. The study of the semantic rules for using social terminology, for example, has yielded cases in which naming behavior does not reflect the knowledge that would seem to be relevant. Instead some other knowledge is applied. A case of this unexpected application of other knowledge in American culture concerns what anthropologists call "fictive kin." In order to indicate unusual closeness in a friendship, for example, a Southerner might say someone is a cousin even though the person is not a cousin according to genealogical criteria (see also Lave et al. 1977, Frake 1977, Hutchins 1980, Clement 1982).

Another seemingly unexpected application of cultural knowledge has been uncovered by the research of D'Andrade (1965, 1973, 1974) and Shweder (1977), which shows that cultural knowledge is used to construct "inaccurate" memories of the personalities of others. Working with personality trait lists, the researchers found that personality ratings of brief acquaintances made at the time of meeting do not correlate well with personality ratings made at a later date. In other words, the traits attributed to a person at the time of meeting him or her tend not to be the traits that are attributed to a person a week or so after the meeting. The ratings that are made from memory, however, do correlate with ratings that are made on the basis of judgments of which terms have shared meanings (e.g. "aggressive" and "hostile" are more similar in meaning than "aggressive" and "docile"). Evidently, parts of the initial impression of the person are replaced by trait terms which are similar in meaning to the few traits that are remembered. Other examples of this type of faulty recollection come from studies of stereotypes which show that the biographical details of others' lives and living styles tend to be misremembered in ways that fit stereotypes (e.g., see research described in the NSF publication *Mosaic* 1979). Both of these examples suggest that recollections of individuals may not be assembled as might be expected from the actual information to which one has been exposed but rather may be, at least in part, constructed from cultural knowledge of types of people.

Although some cultural schemata do seem to be consistently applied to naturally occurring tasks (see Johnson 1974, for example), the inconsistencies that have been uncovered suggest that more attention should be paid to analyzing and describing the everyday tasks in which cultural knowledge is used (see Clement 1976, 1982, for development of this point; see also Dougherty and Keller this volume). Appreciation of the importance of task or situation is reflected in the design of the research reported upon in this paper.

Methodology of the Study

The data reported in this paper were collected in the course of research on everyday cognitive tasks that involve the use of social knowledge. An inductive strategy was pursued for two reasons. First, tasks demanding the use of social knowledge have not been well described; one purpose of the research was to identify some naturally occurring tasks that could be productively studied. Second, most of cognitive anthropology's standardized research techniques are useful only for the study of a limited, though important, set of knowledge structures (i.e. linguistically labeled concepts, propositions, and the type of cultural schema D'Andrade describes in this volume). Since there was no reason to presume that these knowledge structures exhaust the range that is important in social tasks, an inductive strategy was pursued using open-ended ethnographic interviews.

Eight informants—all women between the ages of 19 and 45—were interviewed six times for one to two hours per interview. The data for this paper consist primarily of the portions of the interviews that had to do with "person recollections" and "encounter descriptions."

The data from the study were analyzed for what they reveal about how Americans use their cultural knowledge in the process of "getting to know" someone. "Getting to know X (where X is a specific person)" is a phrase that the informants used primarily to describe the situation of interacting with the person before the awareness of assessing and being assessed by the other person has passed away. Later, when something unexpected is discovered about the person, the informants would be likely to say they had "gotten to know X better." Here the former term, "getting to know X," is used loosely to refer to both situations.

In the "person recollection" interviews the informant was asked to choose someone she had met who was important to her or stood out in her mind and to then describe her first recollection of that person, her next recollection, and so on up to the present. Strict and precise chronological order was not required and informants were asked at the end of the interview if they had any other recollections of the person. In providing each recollection, the informants were first encouraged to describe whatever they remembered. After the description the interviewer probed for recollections of the feelings and thoughts of the informant about the other person during and after the episode or period of time that the informant had described. The "encounter descriptions" proceeded in roughly the same manner except that the informants were first asked to describe a recent incident or interaction involving at least one other person.

For the purposes of describing the length of each set of recollections and the frequencies of different types of recollections, a subset of the data was tallied. This subset consisted of 216 transcribed pages of person recollections collected from five informants—all of whom were young (19-20 years old) women attending a North Carolina university. All were North Carolina residents; one was black, the rest white.[2] In all, these five informants supplied recollections of 13 individuals. They had known the subjects of their recollections an average of two and a half years.

The first task in coding the recollections was to identify distinctive recollections—distinctive, that is, in terms of time and topic. After identification each of the approximately 160 distinctive recollections was coded as to whether it focused on a specific episode or was a generalized description of repeated episodes. It was also coded as to whether it involved a change in the informants' feelings or thoughts about the person. The frequencies of the different types of recollection are referred to in the body of the paper.

Getting to Know Someone

Informants, when they were asked to describe their recollections of a person they know, often recalled particular encounters or interactions that occurred between themselves and the other person. These episodes, some of which are described below, include a high frequency of what Clement et al. (1979:33) have referred to as "symbolic encounters." Symbolic encounters involve actions that are unexpected: "The term *symbolic encounter* . . . is used here to draw attention to those encounters which are distinctive by their impact. A symbolic encounter causes an emotional response because it implies a redefinition of at least one participant's view of the relationship, the 'self,' or 'the other.'" In other words, these encounters are surprising, and they often result in a change in what the informants call their "impression" of the other person. Anne, for example, in describing her relationship with her friend Dave, explained that her first impression of Dave was negative but that it changed once they actually met and talked.[3] The interviewer asked Anne for an explanation of why she did not like Dave before she met him.

ANNE: . . . because, you know, he was . . . Okay, he's a baseball player and the image of being a jock was there, you know. . . .

INTERVIEWER: Was it just because he was a jock or did he say anything or do anything that made you feel that way?

ANNE: No, it was just because he was a jock. You know, you form first impressions, and that was my first impression, but it changed.

INTERVIEWER: Can I ask what your image of a jock would be?

ANNE: Okay, someone that makes . . . kind of stuck on themselves, maybc that they play a sport here so they feel like that gives them the right to do things that other people couldn't do, just things like that.

Further comments from Anne made it clear that she expected Dave the jock to be unkind and inconsiderate. When instead he, in their first meeting, was nice to her, she revised her impression of him. She decided that he was "a really friendly person and really outgoing" and someone worth being around.

An examination of further examples of symbolic encounters reveals types of knowledge that are used by the informants in drawing inferences about themselves and others. The next recollection is based upon an encounter—a very brief encounter—between Arlene and a guy on a bicycle.

ARLENE: And this guy on this bicycle came flying down this hill out into the street in front of us and I—it was really inconsiderate because I know for a fact from looking at him that he did not look to see if anybody was coming, so he could have gotten himself killed or someone seriously hurt anyway. And so, when we were riding past, I rolled down the window and I said, "You can really get hit that way," and he looks at me like, "Well, thanks a lot.". . .

INTERVIEWER: How do you think he took it [what you said]?

ARLENE: He didn't like it. Because, well, it was like he, I don't know, he said something, but by that time I had rolled the window back up, but I know he didn't like it because you know he was trying to make it seem like it was all my fault. . . .

INTERVIEWER: He was saying it was your fault? You could tell that by the way he was saying something?

ARLENE: The way he looked it was like, "What are talking about? I didn't do anything wrong." You know, and by the simple fact that he didn't look he did do something wrong. But it was like whatever he said was the way it was and there was no other alternative. But he was really the one that was in the wrong.

INTERVIEWER: Do you think he knows that?

ARLENE: Probably, but . . . if you had said something to him that he was in the wrong, he would have said . . . he would have denied it flatly.

INTERVIEWER: Why do you think he would have?
ARLENE: It's just a feeling that he seemed like an arrogant-type person that no matter what you say, whatever he says is right. It's just an air about the way he acted. It was a quick instant but still you could see all these little different things about how his personality was that he would have denied being wrong. Unless you had like taken a picture of him not looking, he wouldn't have believed you anyway. . . .

Despite the brevity of the encounter, Arlene drew some far-reaching conclusions about the cyclist. She remembered him not simply as someone who'd made an error in traffic but as an "arrogant-type person that no matter what you say, whatever he says is right." At a later point she responds as follows to the interviewer's question about the clues she noticed in deciding what the guy was like.

> Mostly it was the way he looked, like, "What are you talking about?" Or, "What did I do?" He was just acting innocent, like he didn't do anything . . . it was like he didn't care about anything else you know, just so long as he got wherever he was going on his bicycle. He didn't care what happened along the way. It reminded me of the—I guess you call it—similar situation where they say this old woman, she's a very careful driver and everything, but all behind her is a fifty-mile pile up, all these cars that have been behind her and everything and that to me would picture in my mind how he would be on that bicycle. You know, he's just flying through all these cars and everything, and causing all these wrecks behind him but he doesn't care as long as he gets where he's going.

The guy on the bicycle acted in a way that, to Arlene, was divergent from the way a normal bicyclist would act. He did not appear to care that he'd almost caused and been in an accident. This behavior symbolized to Arlene that he was a certain type of person and she was reminded of a stereotype—the old lady who drives intently, but slowly, down the road, seemingly oblivious to the traffic backed up behind her.

In describing the following encounter, another informant, Rachel, comments on the unexpected nature of Catherine's behavior.

RACHEL: . . . I first heard of her [Catherine] through my sister who met her before I did . . . my sister told me that she was going to be in my English class and that she seemed to be real nice and I remember meeting her outside of the English class one day and I thought she was sort of weird.
INTERVIEWER: What made you feel that way . . . have that impression?

RACHEL: I went up to her and said, "Hi," and "We live near each other," and she just kind of brushed me off and walked off and she wasn't wearing any shoes and she just looked real strange.

INTERVIEWER: What was she wearing . . . ?

RACHEL: She had on shorts and was carrying an old notebook and she just had a real strange look in her eye.

INTERVIEWER: When your sister first mentioned her to you, did you have an impression then about her from what your sister said?

RACHEL: I just thought that she must be real friendly if my sister liked her right off the bat. I pictured more of your classic friendly Carolina person, you know, so I was kind of, you know, surprised by her.

INTERVIEWER: Then she was different from what you expected?

RACHEL: Right. Do you want me to go on to the second time?

INTERVIEWER: Um-hum.

RACHEL: Okay, the second time I remember talking to her we were in the bathroom and I heard that it was her birthday—this was a few days later—and I said, "Today's sort of a special day isn't it?" And, she said, "Yeah, how'd you know?" and then just sort of let it drop at that. And, you know, I felt like I was the one trying to be friendly and she wasn't responding to that at all. . . .

INTERVIEWER: The second time when you met her and mentioned her birthday to her, what impression did you have of her that time?

RACHEL: Still thought she was rude. She just .. she seemed real self-centered. Just really blunt, that's the first impression and it scared me because I had never really been around any really honest females, I don't think.

Rachel, in these passages, goes through a process similar to that which Arlene did in the bicyclist incident. But Rachel's description is more explicit in showing that she is using two types of world knowledge to understand Catherine. First, Rachel has an expectation of what will happen in the two situations she describes. She knows how a "classic, friendly Carolina person" would act when meeting someone new or when someone pays special attention to them by mentioning their birthday. When Catherine does not respond as expected, Rachel draws conclusions about Catherine as a person, turning to her knowledge of types of people to interpret Catherine and how Catherine makes her feel. Rachel says that her knowledge of the type of person she believes Catherine to be—a "really honest female"—is limited, and she fears Catherine.

Another informant, Karla, supplies an even more explicit case of applying two systems of knowledge in an encounter with her boyfriend. She describes her third meeting with him—a date. At the end of the date Christopher makes a pass at her. In deciphering the meaning of his behavior, Karla reasons first from her knowledge of what usually occurs in such a situation.

KARLA: . . . He took me to a concert that was given by a pianist . . . and I had a pretty good impression of him that night, too. It just went down a little bit because we went to the concert and that was fun and then he took me to the coffee shop and we had a late-night dessert and then he took me home and I think that before we, before I went back into my room, and . . . [I] got the distinct impression that he was pushing for a little more out of me (laughs) than I thought that our—well, the duration of our friendship really—he kind of wanted to hit the hay. . . .

INTERVIEWER: How did you feel about that?

KARLA: Well it didn't make me nervous or anything or it didn't make me want to stop seeing him, it just sort of, it seemed to me a really macho mentality thing to say . . . a lot of guys say, oooh, well like the girl expects it of me. I don't think that's true at all. I just don't think that's true. I think that's an excuse.

But, I wondered, where did he come off thinking that I'm going to agree to this? What, have I given him this sort of impression or not? I thought: did he think he's that irresistible that on the second date that I am going to say yes to a proposition? Because I thought that talking to me the way he had, he would realize that I was not really that kind of girl, that would just—well. But here I was thinking that I was dazzling him with my witty repartee and quick wit and he's thinking he's going to get me into the sack (laughs). It was just that sort of situation. . . . I . . . have been used to that [turning people on with my personality] from guys that I perceived as being intelligent and worthwhile. I have been hassled by men, but that was guys I considered beneath notice (laughs). Here was this guy who was extremely intelligent and had this tremendous talent and obviously very well brought up and then outwardly appearing to be a real gentleman. I just didn't expect that sort of question on the second date. You can understand that?

Later the interviewer asks: "How did you feel about him then? Did your feelings change towards him?"

With this question, Karla moves to reasoning about Christopher from her knowledge of people and their characteristics.

KARLA: Yes, . . . I guess for about two weeks there, I was looking around for a surrogate for my old boyfriend. And [after this incident] I started looking on him [Christopher] as somebody who would be more of a challenge, someone who'd be kind of fun to play with because I realized this attitude which would lead him to ask me that sort of question on the second date would also make him rather interesting to deal with, and so I was not put off from dating him at all, I just realized that I'd have to be rather clever about it.

INTERVIEWER: Could you explain your reasoning a little more on that?

KARLA: I'll try. I think that guys like Christopher who have an extremely strong sex drive and feel sort of a need sometimes to prove themselves can be interesting because this strong sex drive often goes hand in hand with a very strong personality and character. I have always . . . all the guys that I've enjoyed dating have had an extremely strong character, personality, and mind of their own. . . .

Karla, in this situation, is clearly employing at least two types of her knowledge of the world to make sense of the encounter with Christopher. From one knowledge system she views the situation as bounded by familiar roles that she and Christopher adopt and act out. In this perspective Christopher is Christopher the date, whose acts may be explained by his role in the situation. From the other knowledge system she considers what Christopher's unexpected acts or perhaps choice of styles of enacting the role of date mean about Christopher the person. Again, as Rachel did with Catherine, Karla reasons as to what type of person Christopher is and how she feels about him in general.

Situation and Person Knowledge

At this point some commonalities might be noted between some of the processes that have been identified in the informants' recollections of others and the patterns that have been uncovered by "attribution research." A large number of attribution studies of the perceived causes of behavior have been conducted primarily by social psychologists.[4] The basic process uncovered by attribution research is also evident in the present study. Attribution researchers have found in general that behavior is explained in terms of either some aspect of the situation or some characteristic of the actor as a person. A point that has been studied in fine detail concerns when situation is evoked versus when person is evoked to explain behavior; the results are that "situation-indicated behavior tends to be attributed to the situation and contraindicated behavior to the person" (Kelley and Michela 1980:470). In other words, behavior in keeping with the social demands and/or contingencies of the situation is attributed to the situation. If a mailman delivers mail, we account for his behavior by reference to his role in the situation—delivering mail is what a mailman is hired to do. Behavior not in keeping with the demands and contingencies of the situation we account for by referring to a disposition of the person. If a mailman dumps his bag of mail into a trash can, we tend to attribute his behavior to a disposition he has as a person—perhaps he is lazy, perhaps irresponsible.

Attribution research, in short, can be construed as supporting a central point suggested by the present data, namely that Americans use two distinctive knowledge systems in the process of interpreting behavior. As derived from the research described here, one knowledge system has to do with situation, that is, with the routinized or institutionalized aspects of life in the society of people with whom one associates. The other has to do with person, that is, with the knowledge that one has about the characteristics of specific individuals, of types of individuals, and of humans in general, that transcend situation.

From the present study it is possible to discern the broad outlines of situation and person knowledge. Fleshing out the content and structure of these two macro knowledge systems, however, is a more difficult task. As alluded to above, attribution research is relevant to the question of how people interpret behavior. However, it has concentrated primarily upon the cognitive processes of attribution and thus ceases to be directly useful when the topic shifts to elucidating the structure and cultural content of either the situation or person knowledge systems. More relevant for these purposes is the work of Schank and Abelson (1977) and Schank (1980). Their work is useful here, although it is limited, as will be discussed in more detail below, in the area of person knowledge. With these resources, filling in the content and structure of these knowledge systems becomes a matter of piecing suggestive data from the present study together with concepts and findings from previous work. Fortunately, for present purposes, it is necessary to describe only a few aspects of these systems. For this paper the most relevant part of the situation knowledge system is the set of generalizations that people have about routinized activities. For Americans, routinized activities that might be the subjects of such generalizations include parties, board meetings, Sunday school, getting drunk with the boys, running for office, visiting the family, parent-teacher conferences, going to the dentist, dates, arguments, meeting a friend's parents, and going to the store. From the present data, Agar's (1973) work on what he calls "event cognition," and Schank and Abelson's (1977) ideas particularly about "scripts," it can be hypothesized that schemata for these generalized episodes have the following associated with them: parts or roles (e.g. parties have hosts, hostesses, and guests) with rights and obligations and potential rewards and risks; permissible and/or likely (sequences of) activities (e.g. parties may include dancing, talking, eating, drinking); and obligatory (sequences of) activities (e.g. leave taking). Besides roles, some situations also have what may be called "role-identities" associated with them (see Clement 1979). That is, there are recognized variations on the usual or unmarked styles of enacting the roles that are associated with a situation. Names for remarkable ways of enacting the guest role at a party, for example, include "life of the party," "wet blanket," "good mixer," and "shrinking violet." All of this situation knowledge is relevant to understanding others, since behavior can be understood, at least in part, as a function of the individual's role or role-identity in the situation.

"Person knowledge" is information about persons as entities with a history and a continuity that transcend day-to-day activities. Knowledge of the person is the set of information one has about specific individuals, types of persons, and humans in general including general makeup and character, characteristic role-identities, appearance, interests and talents, current and past social positions, likely background, disposition toward others including oneself, values and attitudes, moral and societal value, and the disposition they engender in oneself. As reflected in the recollections of informants in this study, person knowledge is used in tandem with situation knowledge to interpret behavior in that (1) person knowledge may be used initially to "cast" the other in a role-identity for the situation, and (2) person knowledge is used to account for unexpected behavior in a situation. With regard to the initial ascription of role identities to others, Karla, for example, began her date with Christopher with the idea that he was a certain type of date. She derived her expectation from a notion that there is a relationship between the kind of date one is and how one was brought up. In Arlene's and Rachel's cases they began the described episodes with the ideas that the other person was a normal, reasonable bicyclist and Carolina co-ed respectively.[5] These notions, however, could not account for the ways the other people acted. Christopher did not act like the kind of date Karla thought he was; the bicyclist's actions could not be accommodated by Arlene's ideas about how a normal bicyclist would act; Catherine's behavior could not be interpreted by Rachel as that of the usual Carolina co-ed. In interpreting cases of unexpected behavior, informants moved from knowledge of the situation to knowledge of the person, "getting to know" the other person in the process. The interpretation of the unexpected behavior led to impressions about Christopher's character and personality, the personality traits of the bicyclist, and Catherine's nature as a certain type of female.[6]

A Continuing Process

An argument can be made that this process of going from situation to impression is continued even after two individuals have become well acquainted. In the three cases discussed above, the people involved were relative strangers who had had only brief contact with one another. Perhaps, one might suppose, knowledge of the situation becomes irrelevant in learning about the other once the other person is known. It does seem to be the case that once two people have routinized their joint activities, the activities cease to be a source of new information about the other. However, new, unresolved, and forgotten situations still arise. Some examples indicate that interpretations of behavior in new situations may be applied even to those individuals informants know well, including themselves. Anne, for example, described the time that she found out that her high school friend Sheila was accepting dates from Anne's boyfriend. Despite the fact that Anne had known and trusted Sheila's friendship for two and a half years, she took Sheila's action in the matter as indication of a serious lack of regard for her feelings and therefore as indication that Sheila after all was not disposed toward her as a friend would be.

Rachel, in describing recent encounters with Chloe and another woman, Susan, provides an example of an interpretation of her own behavior:

> . . . they [Chloe and Susan] talked about art and acting and old movies all the time and stuff that I was really out of touch with. I felt left out a lot and I felt like, "Come on y'all, let's get back to reality." And, you know, by feeling like that I thought, "Oh no, have I turned into a bureaucrat or something?"

Lila, an informant in another study,[7] says about her own sexual behavior:

> . . . it also tied into how I felt about myself before we got married, sexually before we got married. Which was that ah . . . I'd often got into situations where I felt like I had no control of it but I didn't understand how it was I would all of a sudden end up in bed with someone and I had sort of formed this concept of myself as . . . a loose woman and yet I really wasn't. I knew I didn't believe in that.

For Rachel and Lila, their behavior in the situations they described symbolized something about themselves as persons. Despite their extensive knowledge of themselves, they, at least for a time, entertained or were tortured by inferences about themselves that derived from the meanings an observer might attach to their behavior.[8]

Rediscovery also occurs. In the following, Rachel talks about how she failed to remember some distinctive characteristics of her friend Chloe. The interviewer asked Rachel what impressed her most about Chloe when she saw her again after a few months' separation. Rachel responded:

> I had forgotten . . . how different she was socially. . . . I'd been back

> in my small-talk chit-chat polite environment and I'd forgotten that she wasn't like this at all and that she would just do what she felt and gosh, I mean, you know, that she would walk out, walk into another room or something when, without any explanation . . . just little things. I'd forgotten about that and it was just more of a remembering because through the letters I think I'd, you know, I'd kind of perceived her a little more the way, a little more like me. All the differences didn't come in through the letters. It wasn't negative to see her as she really was, but, I'd forgotten and I'd kind of created a little different thing. But it wasn't negative seeing her again, it was just an "oh yeah" type thing.

Rachel did not recall that Chloe's style tended to differ from that which her other friends exhibited in their "small-talk chit-chat polite environment [situations]." As when she was initially getting to know Chloe, Rachel was surprised by Chloe's unorthodox manner of interacting and was reminded of her former sense of Chloe as a person.

These cases suggest that situation knowledge continues to play a role in knowing someone even after two individuals are well acquainted. Situation knowledge continues to provide notions of standard or unmarked behavior—the backdrop—against which new impressions of individuals are formed and old impressions, in some cases, are reconstructed or reinforced.

Other Recollections

Symbolic encounters constituted the subject of approximately 60 of the 130 recollections described by the informants in the subset of the data that was tallied. Most of the remaining 70 recollections concerned routinized activities in which the informant and the other person jointly participated, such as dates, going out on weekends, class, and skipping class. These activity recollections as described by informants were usually generalized episodes, although one or two particular episodes of the activity might be recalled if they were special in some fashion. Although the informants were not systematically queried on this point, they seemed to recall joint activities that were somehow distinctively associated with the subject of their recollections. Joint activities that they also did with others or did in a commonplace way figured less prominently in their recollections.

It is interesting that two of the 13 tallied descriptions of others were aberrant in that they lacked recollections of symbolic encounters. Unlike the other 11 cases, where roughly half of the recollections were of symbolic encounters, these two cases contained only one or two recollections of such encounters. In these two cases the women retained their original impression of the subject pretty much intact.

Perhaps it is significant that in these two cases the subjects were not peers as in the other 11 cases but, instead, were older males in authority positions relative to the informants. In both cases the situations in which the informant and the other person participated were very circumscribed (e.g. class, discussions in the hallway, office visits).

Summary and Conclusions

Getting to know oneself and others is an everyday cognitive task in American society that involves social knowledge and social reasoning. In this paper I have presented an aspect of this process that is reflected in informants' recollections of others, namely the drawing of inferences about an individual as a person from his performance as an actor in a situation. On the basis of these reports, it has been argued that two macro knowledge systems are important in the process of understanding others: situation knowledge and person knowledge. Cultural knowledge of the routinized and institutionalized aspects of group life—knowledge of situation—is used to understand the behavior of others in the first place. If the behavior of a person cannot be made sense of by knowledge of the roles (and role-identities) he or she is assumed to have in a given event or situation, then the person's behavior is taken as symbolic of whatever she or he is like as a person. That is, the behavior is then interpreted in terms of person knowledge. Inferences are drawn about aspect of the person, perhaps about character, personality, values, disposition toward oneself, or perhaps about his or her potential place in one's future plans.

Beyond pointing out the relevance of person and situation knowledge systems to the task of getting to know someone, there are further implications of the study for characterizing American cultural knowledge of the social world. It is fruitful, first of all, to set the findings about the importance and complexity of person knowledge alongside Schank and Abelson's (1977) model of how we humans understand behavior. In their model humans see goals as the driving force behind, and therefore the key to, explaining the behavior of their fellows. Schank and Abelson's hypothesized cognitive structures—"script," "plan," "goal," and "theme"—presuppose a world in which each individual sees himself and everyone else as busily trying to achieve a set of goals either by enacting conventional routines or by carrying out plans devised because no suitable routine for achieving the goal exists. While some of the stories I collected from informants did describe the behavior of others in terms of attributed goals and plans, most of them accounted for the other's unexpected behavior in terms of such things as personality and character traits (e.g. hyper-arrogance, strong personality), stereotypes (e.g. loose woman, honest woman, bureaucrat), and disposition toward others (e.g. prejudiced). The folk theory of goal-driven behavior that Schank and Abelson emphasize, in other words, does not seem to be the primary folk theory that informed the accounts of the women in my sample.[9] They seemed, in contrast, to rely upon a variety of folk theories of behavior, including theories of trait-driven behavior, emotion-driven behavior, and pathology-driven behavior as well as goal-driven behavior. At the least, it may be said that, for the present sample, attributed goals do not seem to be the central focus of person knowledge.

A second and more speculative implication of the study concerns the importance of person knowledge in American explanations of behavior. Although it cannot be fully argued here, a suggestion can be made that person knowledge is of a different status than situation knowledge. To employ a spatial metaphor, person knowledge seems deeper than situation knowledge. A foreigner who learns the situation knowledge that is commonplace among Americans has not penetrated the culture as far as someone who has also acquired the symbol system that allows interpretation of behavior according to its meaning about the type of person the actor is. Another way of making the point is to argue that situation knowledge can be learned through socialization, whereas person knowledge is more likely to be acquired through enculturation. Although the distinction between socialization and enculturation is drawn in different ways by different anthropologists, a typical feature of the differentiation is that socialization has to do with learning behavioral routines whereas enculturation has to do with learning what behavior and action mean in the larger context of cultural values and goals. I am encouraged to see person knowledge as the more difficult type of knowledge to acquire across subcultural boundaries, not only as a result of this study but also as a result of a two-and-a-half-year ethnographic study of a desegregated school. While students and teachers, both black and white, had a shared situation knowledge of school events and school roles, they had difficulty informing black-white friendships, that is, in getting to know and like one another. In that study we (Clement et al. 1979) found that subcultural differences in knowledge of styles of self-presentation caused miscommunication and barriers to relationship formation between blacks and whites in the school. The study also indicated that this person knowledge of the other subcultural group was hard, if not impossible, to fathom from a distance. Fluency with the alternate group's system of person knowledge depended upon extensive exposure to the expression of this knowledge in interpersonal ritual and conversation (see also Clement 1979).

That person knowledge should constitute a deep layer of meaning in American culture also seems fully consistent with the structure of American society in which individuals are frequently in positions of social agency. In other societies, such as that of the Oriya of India, person knowledge may not, in contrast to the case for American society, constitute a very important system for interpreting the meaning of behavior (Shweder and Bourne 1981). In those societies some other "actor" or "agent" category—that is, some other societal or supernatural unit, such as couples, families, lineages, spirits, or, as for the Oriya, the group as a whole—might well be the subject of inferences when situation knowledge fails to account for behavior.

In sum, study of how Americans get to know one another has led into two important realms of American cultural knowledge—situation and person knowledge—both of which seem important in Americans' interpretation of behavior. Situation knowledge is necessary for the understanding of behavior, but it is not always sufficient. In American culture, apparently in contrast to some other cultures, person knowledge is a highly elaborated system of knowledge, perhaps encompassing a number of folk theories, which is employed when situation knowledge proves inadequate.

NOTES

This research was supported by a Kenan Leave from the University of North Carolina at Chapel Hill and by a postdoctoral grant (1-F32-MH08385-01) sponsored by Duke University from the National Institute of Mental Health. The women who shared their stories and my research associate, Isabel Terry, deserve most of the credit for the rich data collected in the study. The paper has also profited from the helpful comments made on earlier drafts by Michael Agar, Janet Dougherty, Jean Lave, Michael Livesay, Naomi Quinn, and Geoffrey White.

1. Holland's pre-1981 publications are listed under the name of Clement.
2. Obviously, this is a very restricted sample. As a study of "American" patterns, these data can be considered suggestive only.
3. In order to ensure the anonymity of the informants, all names are pseudonyms.
4. See Kelley and Michela's (1980) extensive review of the last decade of attribution research.
5. Role-identity assignment has been studied under the rubric of "defining the situation" (see Heise 1979:3-8 for a review of some of the relevant concepts) and "altercasting" (see McCall and Simmons 1978:135-37, for example).
6. Unexpected behavior may also lead to the development and elaboration of generalized person knowledge. The data include cases in which an informant treated the other person as a representative of a type of person

and drew inferences about the class as well as the specific person. Kim had met a man at a costume party, for example, whom she considered to be "outspoken" because he made suggestive remarks to other women in her presence and because he would yell across the room to people he didn't know. She pointed out that she had never dated a Northerner before she began to wonder if he was "the way Northern guys are."

7. I also reviewed a subset of interviews from Quinn's study (this volume). This excerpt is from one of those interviews.

8. This process of seeing oneself as one might appear in the eyes of others is, of course, the subject of a great deal of theorizing and research initially stimulated by George Herbert Mead (1934).

9. In partial corroboration of this conclusion, Schank and Abelson (1977) point out (see, e.g., pp. 62-64, 148-49) that their model does not incorporate the kind of knowledge that is used to understand behavior when goal-oriented notions prove inadequate.

REFERENCES

Abelson, Robert

1975 Concepts for Representing Mundane Reality in Plans. In D. Bobrow and A. Collins, eds., *Representation and Understanding: Studies in Cognitive Science,* pp. 273-311. New York: Academic Press.

Agar, Michael

1973 *Ripping and Running: A Formal Ethnography of Urban Heroin Addicts.* New York: Academic Press.

1980 Stories, Background Knowledge and Themes: Problems in the Analysis of Life History Narrative. *American Ethnologist* 7:223-40.

Burton, Michael L., and A. Kimball Romney

1975 A Multidimensional Representation of Role Terms. *American Ethnologist* 2:397-407.

Clement, Dorothy C.

1976 Cognitive Anthropology and Applied Problems in Education. In Michael Angrosino, ed., *Do Applied Anthropologists Apply Anthropology?* pp. 53-71. Athens: University of Georgia Press.

1979 Role and Role-Identity Knowledge in Social Cognition. Paper prepared for a Social Science Research Council workshop on "Representation of Cultural Knowledge," 10-12 Aug., San Diego, Calif.

1982 Samoan Folk Knowledge of Mental Disorders. In Anthony Marsella and Geoffrey White, eds., *Cultural Conceptions of Mental Health and Therapy,* pp. 193-213. Boston: D. Reidel Publishing Co.

Clement, Dorothy C., Margaret Eisenhart, and Joe Harding

1979 The Veneer of Harmony: Social Race Relations in a Desegregated School. In Ray C. Rist, ed., *Desegregated Schools: Appraisals of an American Experiment,* pp. 15-64. New York: Academic Press.

Colby, Benjamin N., and Lore M. Colby

1981 *The Daykeeper: The Life and Discourse of an Ixil Diviner.* Cambridge, Mass.: Harvard University Press.

Coleman, Linda, and Paul Kay
1981 Prototype Semantics: The English Word Lie. *Language* 57:26-45.
D'Andrade, Roy G.
1965 Trait Psychology and Componential Analysis. *American Anthropologist* 67:215-28.
1973 Cultural Constructions of Reality. In L. Nader and T. W. Maretzki, eds., *Cultural Illness and Health,* pp. 115-28. Washington, D.C.: American Anthropological Association.
1974 Memory and the Assessment of Behavior. In H. M. Blalock, ed., *Measurement in the Social Sciences,* pp. 187-211. Chicago: Aldine-Atherton.
1976 A Propositional Analysis of U.S. American Beliefs about Illness. In Keith H. Basso and Henry A. Selby, eds., *Meaning in Anthropology,* pp. 155-81. Albuquerque: University of New Mexico Press.
Frake, Charles O.
1964 Notes on Queries in Ethnography. *American Anthropologist* 66:132-45.
1977 Plying Frames Can Be Dangerous: Some Reflections on Methodology in Cognitive Anthropology. *Quarterly Newsletter of the Institute for Comparative Human Development* 1:1-7.
Gladwin, Thomas
1970 *East Is a Big Bird: Navigation and Logic on Puluwat Atoll.* Cambridge, Mass.: Harvard University Press.
Goodenough, Ward H.
1956 Componential Analysis and the Study of Meaning. *Language* 32:195-216.
1957 Cultural Anthropology and Linguistics. In Paul Gavin, ed., *Report of the Seventh Annual Round Table Meeting on Linguistics and Language Study.* Monograph Series on Language and Linguistics no. 9. Washington, D.C.: Georgetown University.
Harding, Joe R., and Dorothy C. Clement
1980 Regularities in the Continuity and Change of Role Structures: The Ixil Maya. In Susan Abbott and John van Willigen, eds., *Predicting Sociocultural Change,* pp. 5-26. Athens: University of Georgia Press.
Heise, David R.
1979 *Understanding Events: Affect and the Construction of Social Action.* Cambridge: Cambridge University Press.
Holland, Dorothy C.
1981 American Folk Theories of the Person and Reasoning about Insults. Unpublished MS., University of North Carolina, Chapel Hill.
Hutchins, Edwin
1980 *Culture and Inference: A Trobriand Case Study.* Cambridge, Mass.: Harvard University Press.
Johnson, Allen
1974 Ethnoecology and Planting Practices in a Swidden Agricultural System. *American Ethnologist* 1:87-103.

Keesing, Roger
1979 Linguistic Knowledge and Cultural Knowledge: Some Doubts and Speculations. *American Anthropologist* 81:14-37.

Kelley, Harold H., and John L. Michela
1980 Attribution Theory and Research. *Annual Review of Psychology* 31:457-501.

Lave, Jean, Alex Stepick, and Lee Sailer
1977 Extending the Scope of Formal Analysis: A Technique for Integrating Analysis of Kinship Relations with Analysis of Other Dyadic Relations. *American Ethnologist* 4:321-39.

Lounsbury, Floyd G.
1956 A Semantic Analysis of the Pawnee Kinship Usage. *Language* 32:158-94.

McCall, George J., and J. L. Simmons
1978 *Identities and Interactions.* Rev. ed. New York: Free Press.

Mead, George Herbert
1934 *Mind, Self, and Society.* Chicago: University of Chicago Press.

Meehan, James R., et al.
1979 Understanding Social Interaction in Terms of Games: An AI Model. Unpublished MS., University of California, Irvine.

Metzger, Duane
1973 Semantic Procedures of the Study of Belief Systems. In Henning Siverts, ed., *Drinking Patterns in Highland Chiapas,* pp. 37-48. Bergen: Universitetsforlaget.

Metzger, Duane, and Gerald E. Williams
1963 A Formal Ethnographic Analysis of Tenejapa Ladino Weddings. *American Anthropologist* 65:1076-1101.

Minsky, M.
1975 A Framework for Representing Knowledge. In Paul Winston, ed., *The Psychology of Computer Vision,* pp. 211-77. New York: McGraw-Hill.

National Science Foundation
1979 The World as You Think It Is. *Mosaic* 10:9-16.

Neisser, Ulric
1976 *Cognition and Reality.* San Francisco: W. H. Freeman.

Rice, G. Elizabeth
1980 On Cultural Schemata. *American Ethnologist* 7:152-72.

Romney, A. Kimball, and Roy G. D'Andrade
1964 Cognitive Aspects of English Kin Terms. *American Anthropologist* 66 (no. 3, pt. 2, special pub.):146-70.

Rosch, Eleanor
1975 Universals and Cultural Specifics in Human Categorization. In Richard E. Brislin, Stephen Bochner, and Walter J. Lonner, eds., *Cross-Cultural Perspectives on Learning,* pp. 177-206. New York: John Wiley.

Schank, Roger C.
1980 Language and Memory. *Cognitive Science* 4:243-84.
Schank, Roger C., and Robert Abelson
1977 *Scripts, Plans, Goals and Understanding: An Inquiry into Human Knowledge Structures.* Hillsdale, N.J.: Lawrence Erlbaum Associates.
Shweder, Richard A.
1977 Likeness and Likelihood in Everyday Thought: Magical Thinking and Everyday Judgments about Personality. *Current Anthropology* 18:637-59.
Shweder, Richard A., and Edmund J. Bourne
1982 Do Conceptions of the Person Vary Cross-Culturally? In Anthony Marsella and Geoffrey White, eds., *Cultural Conceptions of Mental Health and Therapy.* Boston: D. Reidel Publishing Co.
Stefflre, V. J., P. Reich, and M. McClaran-Stefflre
1971 Some Eliciting and Computational Procedures for Descriptive Semantics. In Paul Kay, ed., *Explorations in Mathematical Anthropology,* pp. 79-117. Cambridge: M.I.T. Press.
Sweetser, Eve
in press The Definition of *Lie:* An Examination of the Folk Theories Underlying a Semantic Prototype. In Naomi Quinn and Dorothy Holland, eds., *Cultural Models in Language and Thought.* New York: Cambridge University Press.
Tyler, Stephen, ed.
1969 *Cognitive Anthropology.* New York: Holt, Rinehart and Winston.
White, Geoffrey M.
1980 Conceptual Universals in Interpersonal Language. *American Anthropologist* 82:759-82.

18

How to Grow Schemata out of Interviews

Michael H. Agar and Jerry R. Hobbs

A core problem for ethnographic research is the management of large amounts of qualitative data whose form and content are primarily under informant control. A particular tension in the analysis of this type of material lies in the desire to attend to detail while at the same time offering more global statements about group life (Geertz 1976). In research over the last year on an extensive anthropological life history, we have tried different ways to resolve this tension. We would like to report on and demonstrate part of a proposed solution.

The approach draws on recent work in both cognitive anthropology and natural language processing in artificial intelligence, and therefore participates in the new interdisciplinary field of cognitive science. At the same time, it also emphasizes the emergent nature of text interpretation by researchers who bring their own background understandings to the task. Because of this, some peculiar things happen to the term "cognitive." However, this and other issues are deferred until later.

The life history analyzed here was conducted over an 18-month period with an older career heroin addict whom we call "Jack." At the time of the interviews in the early 1970s, Jack was about 60 years old, enrolled in a methadone program in New York City. The specific interview used for this discussion centers around Jack's story of how he became a burglar. In other papers we have looked at portions of this interview to develop our approach. Now we would like to consider the interview as a whole to show the interaction between detailed microanalysis of a portion of text and the validation and enrichment of that analysis across the text as a whole. Eventually, we hope to use the approach to treat the entire life history.

Methodology

Our goal is to relate schemata developed in the analysis of a small fragment of text to the interview as a whole. Although the broad outline of our approach was given in an earlier article (Agar and Hobbs 1981), we would like to specify the more detailed application of it that we have used in our recent work. As described elsewhere (Agar and Hobbs 1983), we begin with an effort to get a sense of the overall organization of the interview. Our assumption is that the interview, analyzed as a completed act, can be understood as the expression of an informant's plan. We make no assumption that the plan is a representation of what the informant "really" thought, nor do we assume that a plan was consciously worked out in detail before the interview. On the contrary, our earlier paper shows that viewing the completed interview as an expression of a plan forces on us assumptions that highlight the creative emergence of Jack's story.

At the same time, the planning view gives us a sense of the global coherence of the interview, an understanding of how different pieces of the interview hang together to produce a coherent whole. To get a sense of these "pieces," we first do a high-level segmentation of the interview that makes cuts using major shifts in content as the guideline. Though this process is hardly foolproof (as discussed in Hobbs and Agar 1981b), most of the spots for cuts seem intuitively obvious. Although we have not tested it out, it is likely that members of Jack's subculture would mark major segment boundaries in similar ways. Further, segmenting is made easier still by the fact that we are working with data produced by another speaker of American English.

Once the segments are marked, the problem is to infer the plan of which they are interrelated expressions. As will be shown in the next section, some of the high-level goals for an interview are in fact explicitly negotiated in the segments themselves. Where such explicit discussion is not available, we are forced to infer goals and subgoals whose interrelationships provide a coherent account of the interview as a whole. Like most students of phenomena—natural or human—we assume there is an implicit order that it is our task to bring to light.

The results of this part of the analysis leave us with a sense of the major segments of the interview together with the goals and subgoals that show them to be coherently linked. The next step is to pick a segment and look for coherence at a lower level—what we call local coherence. This "microanalysis" begins by specifying what it is that each utterance has to do with the ones that immediately precede and follow it. The analysis presupposes that we have a sense of utterance content, a presupposition that is again facilitated by the fact that we are working with another speaker of American English. The microanalysis in terms of local coherence requires us to specify the relations between utterances such that they are seen as parts of a connected discourse.

The local coherence relationships lead us to the next step in the analysis. If two utterances are related because one "elaborates" on another, we must now make explicit the propositions that justify our claim. If two sequences of utterances in a segment are said to "contrast," we must show the knowledge in terms of which that contrast can be seen. The local coherence analysis of a segment forces us to develop explicit inferences that make sensible those relations. As will be seen shortly, some of these inferences bunch together through their interlinked predicates and arguments. This "bunching" of inferences, so characteristic of human knowledge, was the reason for the development of the notion of "schema" in AI and psychology. "Schema" is simply a convenient term to characterize some related inferences.

Schemata are of particular interest to ethnographers because they are potentially useful in understanding not just the segment that motivated their construction but other segments as well. High-level schemata that offer such understanding of a variety of acts have been a traditional goal of cultural anthropology, whether called "patterns," "themes," or "value orientations." However, ethnographers typically construct the high-level schemata and demonstrate the resulting understanding anecdotally. It is this gap that the more detailed local coherence analysis can help fill.

At the same time, a local coherence analysis of every segment to which the schema is applied would be too time-consuming and leave us buried in a mass of detail. To solve this problem in the sample analysis of one interview presented here, we have developed the following strategy. We picked a particularly interesting schema from the microanalyzed segment and specified some conditions under which it should apply to other segments. In the analysis done here, we were interested in an "arrest" schema, so we decided that any segment that concerned itself with illegal acts would qualify.

The "concern" might be reflected in a single utterance, or it might be the focus of an entire segment. It might be semantically encoded in the utterance, or it might be understood only through inferences connected to that surface semantic content. Any segment that satisfied these conditions was then examined for its schematic relevance. As will be seen shortly, this process led to a generalization of the schema, a richer understanding of its details, a better sense of its relation to other schemata, and validation through its use in understanding other segments of the interview.

However, the examination of the range of application of the schema will not contain the detail of the microanalysis that produced it. We will stop the discussion at the point where we feel that the connection is obvious. At the same time, there is an assumption that such a detailed analysis is possible for each segment; in principle an analysis of local coherence could be done that would explicitly show the connections. In other words, we will trade off detail for breadth of coverage, without abandoning the obligation to fill in the detail should it be required.

This careful use of different levels of description in different analytical contexts will, we hope, resolve the tension between detailed analysis and breadth of coverage. The strategy is hardly unique to our approach. Learning often works like that—the beginner attends to low-level detail, gradually builds higher-level knowledge of what he is doing, and eventually develops a global sense of whatever he is learning and forgets the details unless some problem forces him to return to that level to solve it. We are simply trying to learn to understand an interview in a way that points to strategies for learning to understand even broader ranges of human action.

Our approach is not "objective" in the traditional positivist sense. We agree with the common wisdom that text understanding involves active inferencing and schema construction on the part of the understander, where those schemata emerge in a dialectic way in interaction with the text. As Hutchins (1980) argues, the schemata are not necessarily contained in the text; rather, an ethnographer draws on his/her sense of group life to construct understandings of a bit of material. The emphasis shifts from "discovery procedures" to a concern with explicit representation and validation (see also Quinn this volume).

However, the approach is "cognitive," though in a different sort of way than indicated by the traditional use of the term in cognitive anthropology. The schemata that we construct are cognitive in the sense that they are knowledge structures to enable understanding of the interview. It is unproductive to argue over whether they are resident in Jack's head or in ours. They serve as an interpretive bridge between partially distinct traditions. It is not necessary to claim that they are models of anyone's mind.

In the next section we will begin the analysis by developing the global plan of the burglary interview. Following that, we will microanalyze a segment to show the construction of some schemata related to arrest. Then we will look at the schema as it recurs thematically in other segments of the interview to modify and enrich it. Finally, we will conclude with some thoughts on the approach in the context of broader issues of anthropological interest.

The Interview Plan

The interview dealt with here, taken as completed act, has a reconstructed plan shown in Figure 1. As often happens in the interviews, the first segment (marked "S" in the figure) contains an explicit negotiation of the interview goal between the ethnographer (Agar) and Jack. The interview is to be about "how I became a burglar." In Figure 1 this is represented by the arrow from the first segment upward to the interview goal. This part of the interview is organized into three major subgoals—describe the setting, explain how Johnny (the person who teaches Jack burglary) was first encountered, and then describe the burglary.

The structure of this part of the interview is further detailed by interview segments as shown in Figure 1. Jack describes the setting for the story in segment (2). (Numbers in parentheses refer to segment numbers shown in Figure 1.) He talks about the time at which the story took place, his social isolation, and the general kind of life he was leading. Since he is confused about both the time and the reasons for his isolation, he slides around all three topics at the same time, making it impossible to divide any of that discussion clearly into individual segments. Finally he remembers the details, and then begins an account of how he met Johnny, the young man who eventually teaches him burglary.

First we learn about the network of subway tunnels and train stations that Jack was using to move around the city and keep warm at the same time (3). A young kid leaves his luggage with Jack while

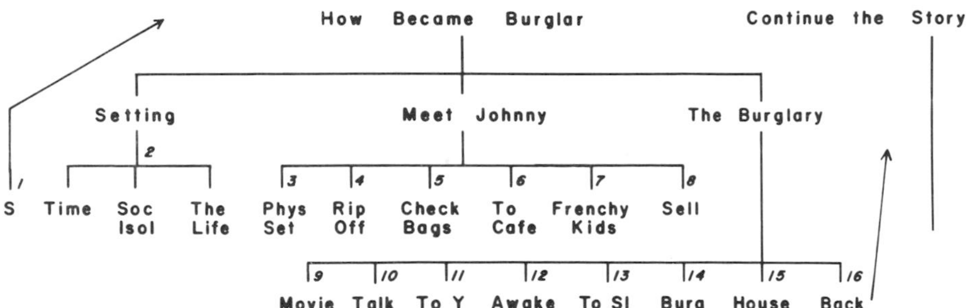

Figure 1. The Interview Plan

he is sitting in a train station, and he steals it (4). He goes through the bags and, though there is little of value, he does find some things that he can sell to a fence (5). He describes his walk to a cafeteria (6) where he finds a fence talking with two young kids, one of whom is Johnny (7). The kids are noisily discussing a mugging they did, so Jack tells them to be cool, sells his goods, and leaves (8).

Now that Johnny has been introduced, Jack tells the story of how their relationship was established and how that eventually led to the burglary. He goes to a movie to get out of the cold and Johnny follows him there (9). They talk in the movie, and Johnny convinces Jack to be his partner (10). He gives Jack some money for heroin, and they then go to a YMCA, get a room, and sleep for some time (11). They get up and Johnny gives Jack some clothes to wear (12), and after eating breakfast they go to Staten Island (13). Johnny suddenly announces that they are going to break into a house, and after a discussion he goes in and Jack follows (14). Jack describes the burglary as they work their way through the house (15), and then describes the trip back to the YMCA (16).

Now, as often happens in the interviews, there is a problem: the original goal is satisfied—Jack has described how he became a burglar—but the interview isn't over. The lower time limit on an acceptable interview hasn't yet been reached. Jack has to keep talking. Since the chronological ordering of events is a theme of the life history, it is not surprising that the rest of the interview can be seen as a description of what happened next, a description that continues until Jack can explain how the relationship with Johnny ended. The structure of this segment of the interview is indicated as a continuation of the story in Figure 1.

Now, this account doesn't give the richness of detail in the interview; the purpose is to give a sense of the global coherence. Though some of the segmentations and groupings under subgoals may be arguable, the overall structure gives a sense of how the story was organized. To begin to probe into the details, we selected segment (8) for a more careful microanalysis of local coherence, utterance by utterance. In the preceding segment (7) Jack introduces the fence, named "Frenchy," and describes the kids, one of whom is Johnny. We now turn to the microanalysis.

Local Coherence

The segment is presented in its entirety in Figure 2. Notice that it is divided into utterances. The division was made using both linguistic and paralinguistic cues, although the process is far from a

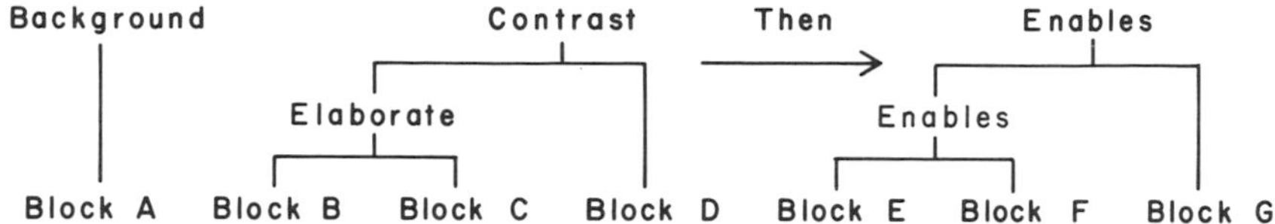

Figure 2. Microanalysis of Segment 8

BLOCK A

1. meanwhile Frenchy's called me to come over and sit at the table with him
2a. so you know I looked at these two kids
2b. and I—I sat down at the table
2c. and I was just in no mood to listen to a lot of bullshit

BLOCK B

3. so I turned to the kids
4. I said hey look you guys why don't you just soft peddle it
5a. I said I don't know what your story is
5b. and I care less
6. but you're making a general display of yourself
7. this place is loaded with rats
8. it's only going to be a matter of time until a cop comes in here and busts the whole table.

BLOCK C

9. I told Frenchy I said Frenchy what the fuck is the matter with you you know
10. I says why don't you tell these dudes to—to shut up
11. but Jack they've got blah blah blah you know
12. and I want to get this stuff

BLOCK D

13a. I said well look I said you guys may not care if you go to jail
13b. but I do
14. I said I spend 75 percent of my time trying to stay out of jail
15. and I don't want anybody to come up here and bother us

BLOCK E

16a. meanwhile I flashed the—the gloves
16b. and I don't know—
17. I—I wish I could remember what—
18. I guess it was a cheap watch

BLOCK F

19. and I said Frenchy I said give me anything at all

20a. give me enough to get to the movies
20b. and get out of the scene
21. well I can't give you very much
22. they're not worth anything
23. and he tried the gloves on
24. the gloves fit him
25. alright he said I'll give you a couple of dollars for the works
26. I said ok
27a. just give it to me
27b. and let me get out of here

BLOCK G
28a. so I took the two dollars
28b. and I didn't even say goodbye to these guys
29. and I split

determinate one (Labov and Fanshel 1977, Coulthardt 1981). Some of the utterances contain more than one proposition. Where that is the case, they are further divided in the figure. For example, "2a, 2b, and 2c" in the figure are three propositions that were grouped together given the cues of language and intonation, while "3" was both a single proposition and a single utterance according to the cues. The only exception to this procedure in the segment are the utterances with conjoined verbs that encode change in location followed by an act which the change occasions. Examples are no. 1, "come over and sit," or no. 8, "comes in here and busts."

The microanalysis leads to a consideration of the following question: given our intuitions that this is coherent discourse rather than a list of unrelated utterances, how can we make explicit our sense of its texture? At the lowest level we look for relationships between any two contiguous utterances. However, there will also be relations between blocks of utterances as well. For convenience of presentation, we begin with a more global view of the segment and then move into the detailed utterance-by-utterance account. In Figure 2 this high-level coherence is represented. We will introduce the specific coherence relations as we go along, drawing from Hobbs's (1978) work.

Hobbs, in the spirit of work in discourse analysis by Longacre (1976) and Grimes (1975), developed and formally defined a small number of relations to show the logical connection between any two utterances or larger pieces of discourse. We will not fully recapitulate those definitions here, though some informal comments will be offered in the discussion to come. At this point in our work we are still developing guidelines for the use of the relations in analyzing the text. Fortunately, most of the applications to follow are straightforward.

As will soon become apparent, the relations do not apply in some mechanical way to the text. Their use presupposes both an understanding of the utterances' semantic content as well as intuitions about the relationship between those utterances. The coherence relations help give those intuitions more precise form, so that they can be examined against subsequent portions of the text in a way that makes the interpretation explicit and grounded enough to be vulnerable to criticism.

The first block of utterances, Block A, marks the beginning of the segment in one of the typical ways—a change in location is specified which introduces an account of the activities to occur in that location. It serves as BACKGROUND for the segment, since it describes people and acts who will be involved in it. In Block B Jack lectures the kids about their attention-getting behavior, and then in Block C he ELABORATES on the issue by asking Frenchy why he would allow such a situation to come about. (The two segments are related by elaboration because they are both about the same thing—the kids' noisy display.) Block D CONTRASTS with the contents of B and C as Jack explains why, unlike the group at the table, he worries about going to jail. (Two segments contrast when they imply contradictory predications about similar entities.)

This part of the segment introduces Johnny and portrays him in an uncomplimentary way from a street point of view. The next part of the segment takes care of Jack's official reason for being there—fencing stolen goods. In Block E he reminds us of the stolen goods, and this ENABLES him to deal with Frenchy and sell them, as reported in Block F. (One segment enables another when it sets up preconditions for the actions in the second.) The activities in these blocks, in turn, ENABLE him to leave the cafeteria, which he does in Block G, and with this the segment ends. In short, on a global level the segment does two jobs. Jack wants to introduce Johnny and show him to be a certain type of person, while at the same time giving an account of the activities in which the meeting occurs. Now we can push into the different blocks and do an utterance-by-utterance analysis along the same lines.

In Block A in Figure 2 there is a straightforward action sequence, indicated by the THEN link in Figure 3. (In this and the following figures the local coherence structure is coded with the proposition numbers from Figure 2, together with a mnemonic word from that proposition.) This act sequence serves as background for two utter-

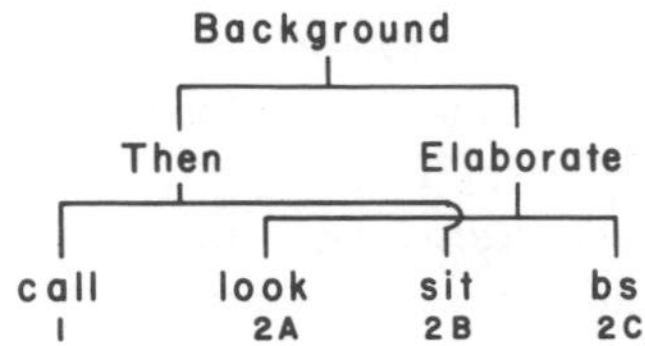

Figure 3. Block A

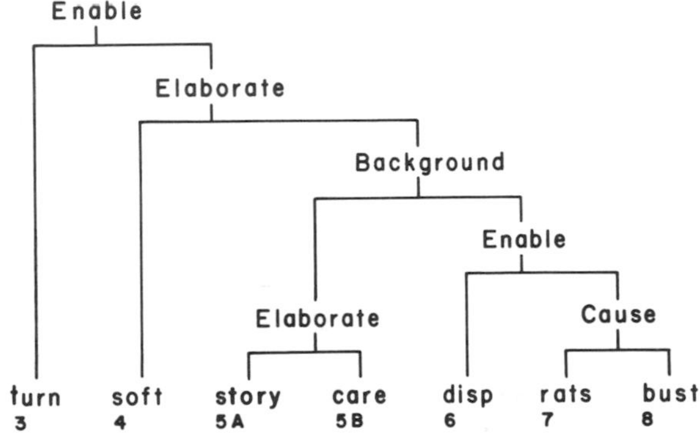

Figure 4. Block B

ances that ELABORATE Jack's attitude toward the kids. Now examine the analysis of the last segment, G, and notice that it has a similar structure—an act sequence that is BACKGROUND for a comment on the kids. The first and last blocks both combine an account of the acts that are the context with a comment on the actor—Johnny—who is being introduced. In fact, the organization of these two blocks mirrors the segment as a whole.

In Block B, shown in Figure 4, Jack lectures the kids. He turns to them, which ENABLES him to tell them to "soft peddle" it. (We say ENABLE rather than CAUSE, since the turning doesn't cause the telling but, rather, establishes a missing precondition.) This is ELABORATED by first giving as BACKGROUND the comment that he doesn't know their story, ELABORATED by noting that he could care less what it might be. This in turn is BACKGROUND for the next utterances, where he explicitly states that making a "display" of themselves ENABLES a "rat" to CAUSE a "bust" to occur.

In Block C, shown in Figure 5, Jack ELABORATES on this state of affairs by holding Frenchy accountable for it. Jack first addresses Frenchy, then SPECIFIES his accusation by noting that Frenchy should

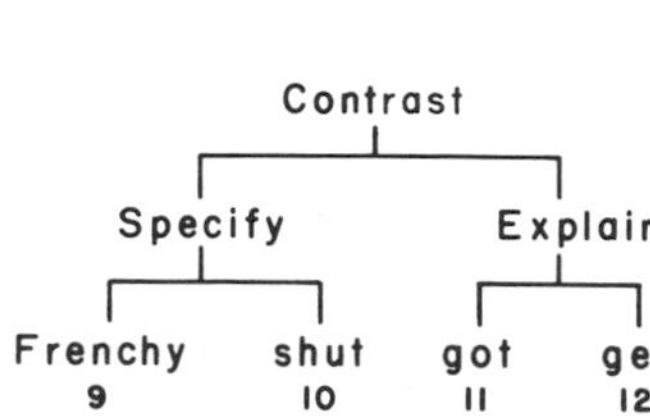

Figure 5. Block C

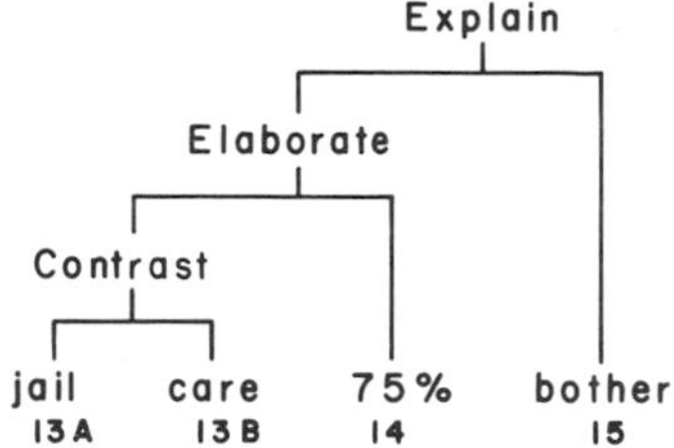

Figure 6. Block D

tell the kids to "shut up." (SPECIFY indicates that the right branch further specifies the more general left branch.) Frenchy disagrees with this (the CONTRAST relation) by saying that the kids have some stolen goods, which EXPLAINS why he tolerates them. In Block D (Figure 6) Jack tells them all that, in CONTRAST to them, he wants to stay out of jail. He ELABORATES by saying that he spends "75 percent" of his time worrying about it, which EXPLAINS why he doesn't want anyone to "bother" them.

In Block E Jack lists the items he has for sale. (These utterances exemplify the PARALLEL relation, since they make the same predication about similar entities.) In this segment he also notes that he can't remember exactly what they were, which is ELABORATED by saying that he wishes he could remember better. This may be interpreted as an EXPLANATION of "I guess it was a cheap watch." Another way to treat the "remember" utterances might be to argue that they are on another level—a metalevel where Jack comments on the story rather than tells it. However, we are more interested for the moment in a view of the text that emphasizes the interrelationships of utterances rather than a partitioning of them to reflect different levels.

The penultimate Block F describes the dealing between Frenchy and Jack. Jack asks for "anything," which he SPECIFIES by asking for enough to get him into the movies and ENABLE him to get out of the scene. In CONTRAST, Frenchy says he can't give him much, SPECIFICALLY because the goods aren't worth much. In CONTRAST, Frenchy tries on the gloves, BACKGROUND for the statement that they fit him, which EXPLAINS why he offers Jack a "couple of dollars." This ENABLES Jack to agree, which he SPECIFIES by requesting the money so that he can (ENABLES again) get out. Then comes the closing block, which was discussed earlier.

The local coherence analysis is not an end in itself. It makes explicit our intuitions as a first step toward constructing an understanding of the world expressed in the segment. As argued elsewhere (Hobbs and Agar 1981a, Polanyi 1978), stories are constructed so that parts of that world are highlighted. In Hobbs's terms the "strong temporal" relations (THEN, ENABLE, CAUSE) set out the structure of the world within which the story takes place. "Linkage" relations (BACKGROUND, EXPLANATION) bring out those aspects of the world where a "reason" for something in the story is called for. The "expansion" relations (ELABORATION, SPECIFICATION, CONTRAST, PARALLEL) repeat the key propositions that are significant parts of that world for the story. The coherence relations, in short, lay out some of the texture of the world that the schemata must account for.

From the previous segment (see Agar 1980 for a transcript of a larger segment of the interview), we know that the kids are making a lot of noise, talking about a mugging, and flashing stolen goods above the table, and we also know that there's something improper about this from the comments in Jack's description. From the initial and final blocks we learn that in this context the kids are doing something wrong. This is a case of what Holland (this volume) calls a "symbolic encounter"—one learns about a person through his/her violation of expectations in a conventional context.

In Block B Jack lays out the problem by lecturing the kids. They are making a display of themselves, which can attract an informant's attention and lead to arrest. The importance of this schema is indicated in several ways. In 5a and 5b Jack says there is no situation that justifies ignoring the schema; in Block C Frenchy is held accountable for ignoring it and explains this through his goal of getting the stolen goods; in Block D Jack shows why the schema is important—arrest, in turn, can lead to jail, something Jack spends "75 percent" of his time avoiding. Through the account of the kids and Frenchy, then, we see a link between this "arrest schema" and street competence. The kids are not competent because their actions in the fencing situation set up the preconditions for arrest. Frenchy's action is questionable because he allows the "display" to occur.

The patterning of the relations in the microanalysis leads us to posit a more general schema—illegal acts ENABLE arrest ENABLE jail. One way for illegal acts to lead to arrest is for a "rat" or informant to get some information about them and pass it on to the police. Action that is bound to this schema is cause for strong negative evaluation and an indication of street incompetence. The arrest schema plays a central role in articulating some higher-level knowledge that is pointed to by, and in turn justifies, the microanalysis.

The ethnographic question of interest is whether or not the schema, so plausibly central in understanding this segment, plays a role in understanding other segments as well. Such recurrently useful schemata have often been the quest of American cultural anthropology. Though they have been characterized under a variety of labels, we prefer Opler's term "themes" (1959). In some earlier work (1979, 1980) Agar used the notion of "theme" to guide a search for pattern in interviews much like the one discussed here. The problem in that work was that themes were not adequately grounded in the text. The microanalysis in terms of coherence relations helps fill in that gap, though as noted earlier some problems in their application remain to be worked out. However, the coherence analysis so far analytically reduces the text into its parts and shows their interrelations, but it does not capture the cross-cutting themes that give one a sense of its unity. In order to maintain the parallel with the global and local coherence analysis, we call this patterning "thematic" coherence. The schema that we grew out of the local coherence analysis looks like a possible candidate for a theme. In the next section we set out to explore this possibility.

Thematic Analysis

In order to explore the thematic status of the schema, we first draw on our knowledge of junkie life and note that "illegal acts" or "hustles" connect it with those situations where it is relevant. Therefore, we decided to go through the interview and lift out portions of text where illegal acts were mentioned. Fifteen portions were identified and abstracted for examination. In some cases the portions are parts of segments, in some they are an entire segment, and in one case a portion spans three segments. The process allows us to preserve the relationship between abstracted portion and interview context, a feature lacking in Agar's earlier work with themes. We get two major enrichments through the analysis of these portions. First, we learn the intricate relationship between competence at a particular illegal act and avoiding the attention that might lead to arrest. Second, we learn some of the details of what goes into competence for a house burglar. Let's deal with the first issue first.

Two portions mention two hustles—buying heroin and breaking into cars—that are routine for Jack at the time of the story. In fact, he explicitly mentions his familarity with breaking into cars. These hustles, in short, are practiced skills. The arrest schema is noteworthy by its absence. We begin to get a sense that the arrest schema is less salient when one knows what he is doing.

This point is made more obvious by considering the different accounts Jack gives of burglaries. Jack reports the first burglary that

Johnny led him into. He describes much personal anxiety, giving as explanations his lack of knowledge on how to do burglary and his fear of attracting attention. As in the microanalysis, we again infer a relationship between competence and risk of arrest. The kids didn't know how to sell stolen goods in a public setting, and this came with concern for arrest. Jack doesn't know how to burgle, and this occasions the same concern. The schema generalizes to cover both instances.

As the interview progresses, Jack gives examples of other burglaries. The tone changes dramatically from the first description. Though he again mentions anxiety about attracting attention, we also see an account of some of the details of a burglary schema (to be discussed shortly). Another burglary story further shows competence in the details, and ends with a matter-of-fact account of how Jack and Johnny left through one door while the occupants came in another. In contrast to the first burglary, anxiety about arrest is striking by its absence. In yet another burglary story details are again described, but the story ends with Jack and Johnny running out through the returning occupants. What in the first burglary would have led Jack to panic is now seen as the climax to a "funny" story.

The comments on scoring heroin and breaking into cars, together with the decline in anxiety about arrest in the different descriptions of burglaries, further support the schema developed in the microanalysis. Now let's focus more on the "attention" issue. Recall that the kids' making a "display" of themselves was a concern in the microanalysis. Now we see attention explicitly remarked on in a number of portions.

Jack comments on how much less attentive people are than he expected; he talks about how proper use of the car helps avoid attention, as does dressing in a way so that one does not stand out. So we learn that first of all Jack was overconcerned, but also we see that there are particular things to do to help minimize it. Now we get into an interesting link between risk of arrest through attention and the details of the burglary schema as Jack reports them.

Jack lays out more details in other parts of the interview. It is noted that one picks a house because it is isolated (on top of a hill, surrounded by trees). One also works at certain times, when people are unlikely to return home and one can expect neighbors to be busy. Finally, one breaks in using proper techniques that are quiet. One must learn what the best things are to take—easily portable, high-value items. We learn of the importance of a good partner, somebody who will help keep an eye out for the police. And we also learn of the importance of a "second exit" to use in an emergency. In the description of another burglary the importance of house selection is again mentioned (isolated, surrounded by trees, vacant lot next door). Proper appearance and a good car are brought up again. Since they now have a woman working with them, she goes up to the house and rings the doorbell to check if anybody is home. We again learn the importance of knowing what to take and of having two exists.

In short, in these portions Jack lays out some of the details of the burglary schema. The interesting issue for the moment is the number of those details that in fact specify how to avoid attention or how to set up strategies to deal with it if it should arise. This further supports our original schema link between arrest and competence. As we see Jack's growing competence as a burglar, reflected in his articulation of the details of different instances, we also see that part of that competence is in fact knowledge about avoiding attention or about strategies to avoid arrest if it should occur.

The schema is related to the other portions as well, in a variety of ways. For example, fences are evaluated negatively just because they profit from the illegal acts of others without the risk of arrest that they endured to obtain the stolen goods. The use of a room at the Y by two people when only one paid motivates a "then/now" comment, as Jack explains that in those days this involved no risk of getting caught.

More interesting is the elaborate (three-segment) account of Jack's eventual arrest. The story first of all justifies the core concern represented in the schema because the story shows in detail the difficulties that ensue on arrest and conviction. Second, the story shows how there is one problem that the schema does not represent—Johnny is busted after his return to Detroit, and under police pressure he tells the whole story. This leads to Jack's arrest for burglary when he is picked up in connection with another illegal act in which, in fact, he was not directly involved. Plea bargaining with arrested people in return for information that leads to other arrests is a well-known police strategy, and the story in this interview begins to show how it relates to the schema developed in the microanalysis. However, the relationships are not developed fully for the present.

By iterating through the interview and applying the schema to all mentions of illegal acts, we at the same time validate and enrich it. We wind up with a simple core to the schema—illegal activities ("hustles") ENABLE arrest ENABLES conviction and incarceration. However, arrest has as a precondition information and/or evidence of some sort, obtained either by the police directly, through an informer ("rat" or "snitch"), or from the victim, like the occupant of a burgled house. Therefore, a major problem for the hustler is to block the precondition by preventing information from reaching the police, or, as we have been saying in this discussion, by avoiding attention. We see in Jack's story that failure to do so is occasion for comment, argument, and lecture. From a street point of view, one who violates the expectations represented in these schematic relationships is not competent.

Even more interesting, the schema points to some important details that are likely to be found in the schema for any hustle. Not only does one minimize attention by knowing the hustle and carrying it out smoothly. In addition, a schema for any hustle will contain within it knowledge about ways to avoid attention that are specific to the activities it represents. Further, we expect that the schemata will also contain strategies to use should the hustle in fact attract attention from people who may serve as information conduits to the police.

We can summarize the schema so far. Suppose *x* is a hustle and *a*, *b* are persons. Then:

Let (Do(*a*,*x*) or Talk-about(*a*,*x*) be chunked as Draw-Attention-to(*a*,*x*).

Draw-Attention-to(*a*,*x*) and Observe(*b*,*a*) and Inform(*b*,police,*a*) causes Arrest(police,*a*).

If *b* is the police, then the schema shortens to:

Draw-Attention-to(*a*,*x*) and Observe(*b*,*a*) cause Arrest(*b*,*a*).

The schema then suggests that to maintain his goal of avoiding arrest, a hustler can avoid talking about or doing hustles. If he hustles or talks about it, then he can try to avoid observation. If he is observed, he can try to prevent the information from reaching the police.

We also expect a more general schema link between the arrest schema and any hustle. It will contain a number of actions one can take to avoid attention and a number of ways to fix things up if one does. To summarize, we can say that for any hustle *H* for some actor *x*, it will contain plausible inferences of the following form:

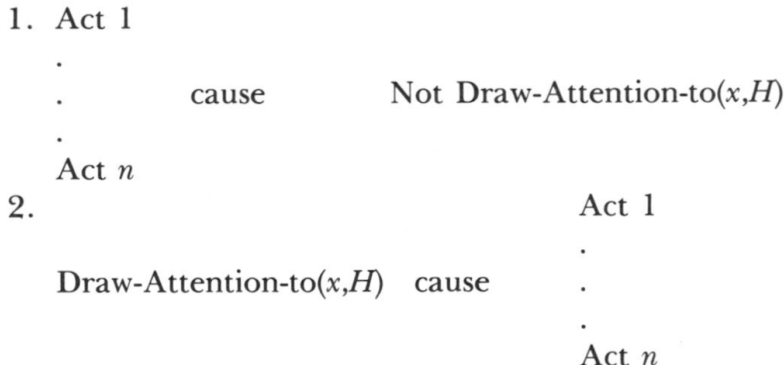

In this interview we learned how this schema was in part filled out for one kind of hustle—burglary of private residences. We also saw how it worked for selling stolen goods to a fence in a public place.

Other hustles, of which there are many in junkie life, will carry different strategies, but we expect this general arrest schema to be relevant to any hustle.

Conclusion

In this analysis we have illustrated how a general schema can be constructed through detailed microanalysis of an interview segment and then applied to other segments to validate and enrich it. Though we have restricted ourselves to a limited schema and have done the iterative application in only one interview, we hope we have shown that the strategy of combining detailed analysis with more global coverage is a reasonable one.

In the context of general ethnographic work, the schemata could be applied over a much wider range than just a single interview. The same schema might guide observations as an ethnographer moved through situations that constituted daily life for a group. Alternately, he/she might design systematic questions based on the inferences encoded in it, and ask a sample of group members to respond to them. Our analysis was drawn from our ongoing work with Jack's life history, but our intention is to come up with a perspective that applies to whatever combinations of talk and action ethnographers choose to regard as data.

Our work fits into a recent trend in cognitive anthropology that blends in with the interdisciplinary field of cognitive science. As described elsewhere (Agar 1982), the trend is characterized by concerns with schemata and discourse rather than categories and lexemes. It is less focused on mechanical discovery procedures and more on explicit representation of knowledge. Finally, when compared to earlier cognitive work, it is more concerned with broader cultural patterns and relations between group conventions and intentional action.

Besides this general fit, however, there are some other aspects of the approach that should be mentioned. First, it is interpretive, in the sense that the understandings of the analyst and the semantic content of the text mutually inform each other in an emergent, dialectic way. We actively "grow" the schemata, rather than claiming to shake the text and watch them fall out. The various kinds of coherence analysis serve to clarify and refine intuitions through iteration in a way that puts the argument "on the streets" for inspection.

Second, the approach is cognitive, in the sense that we are concerned with the representation of knowledge needed to understand the expression of one tradition through the eyes of another. However, we do not claim that it is "psychologically real" or that we have arrived inside Jack's head. Whatever the internal cognitive and affective processes were that constituted Jack's "lived experience" of the interview, the coherence analysis only sets out to understand the results of those processes from a particular point of view.

The point of our analysis is not just to develop higher-level schemata out of detailed analyses; it is also to demonstrate the power of the schemata through their recurrent use in making sense of a variety of situations and through the richness of their links with other, equally central schemata. The differences between street and straight life are not primarily in abstract schema content but more in such elusive areas as pervasiveness, salience, and frequency of use. The only way to document those differences is to demonstrate the relevance of the schemata in a variety of expressions of group life, showing their repeated value in understanding them. The schemata alone are inadequate to the ethnographic goal.

The difference between straights and junkies is not that junkies know about hustles, attention, and arrest and straights don't. The difference is in the centrality and elaboration of such knowledge for a junkie, as shown by a tour through numerous situations with which he/she routinely contends. An outsider gets a sense of the schema through its repeated application to junkie life, not through an appreciation of a statement of it in isolation. The proper ethnographic bridge doesn't just show that junkies worry about arrest; rather, it shows what it is like to worry about it most of the time. Jack said he spent 75 percent of his time trying to stay out of jail. The analysis shows that he meant it.

NOTE

The support of a Research Career Development Award (DA-00055) is gratefully acknowledged.

REFRENCES

Agar, M.

1979 Themes Revisited: Some Problems in Cognitive Anthropology. *Discourse Processes* 2:11-31.

1980 Stories, Background Knowledge and Themes: Problems in the Analysis of a Life History Narrative. *American Ethnologist* 7:223-39.

1982 Whatever Happened to Cognitive Anthropology: A Partial Review. *Human Organization,* forthcoming.

Agar, M., and J. R. Hobbs

1981 Interpreting Discourse: Coherence and the Analysis of Ethnographic Interviews. *Discourse Processes* 5:1-32.

1983 Natural Plans. *Ethos* 11:33-48.
Coulthard, M.
1981 The Place of Intonation in the Description of Interaction. Paper presented to 32d Annual Georgetown University Round Table on Language and Linguistics.
Geertz, C.
1976 "From the Native's Point of View": On the Nature of Anthropological Understanding. In K. H. Basso and H. A. Selby, eds., *Meaning in Anthropology.* Albuquerque: University of New Mexico Press.
Grimes, J.
1975 *The Thread of Discourse.* The Hague: Mouton.
Hobbs, J. R.
1978 *Why Is Discourse Coherent?* SRI Technical Note no. 176. Menlo Park, Calif.: SRI International.
Hobbs, J. R., and M. Agar
1981a Topic in the Analysis of Discourse. Unpublished MS.
1981b Text Plans and World Plans in Natural Discourse. *Proceedings* of the International Joint Conference on Artificial Intelligence Research, Vancouver.
Hutchins, E.
1980 *Culture and Inference.* Cambridge, Mass.: Harvard University Press.
Labov, W., and D. Fanshel
1977 *Therapeutic Discourse: Psychotherapy as Conversation.* New York: Academic Press.
Longacre, R.
1976 *An Anatomy of Speech Notions.* Ghent: Peter de Ridder Press.
Opler, M.
1959 Component, Assemblage and Theme in Cultural Integration and Differentiation. *American Anthropologist* 61:955-64.
Polanyi, L.
1978 The American Story: Cultural Constraints on the Meaning and Structure of Stories in Conversation. Ph.D. dissertation, University of Michigan, Ann Arbor.

Notes on Contributors

MICHAEL H. AGAR received his Ph.D. in anthropology from the University of California, Berkeley. He has taught at Hawaii, Berkeley, and Houston, and worked in clinical applied settings in Lexington, Ky., and New York City. Currently he is on the faculty of the University of Maryland, College Park, working on the development of an applied graduate program. His reseach interests include ethnographic theory and method and American cultures.

JAMES D. ARMSTRONG is assistant professor of anthropology at SUNY Plattsburgh, specializing in complex societies, cognitive anthropology, and social organization. He received his Ph.D. from the University of California, Riverside, in 1982. He did field research in Israel in 1977-78, 1980, and 1983, and has also worked with Vietnamese refugees in California and recovering alcoholics in an alcoholism treatment program. Armstrong recently co-authored an article entitled "Circannual Changes in Immune Function" which appeared in *Life Sciences.* His current research involves the study of friendship and response decisions.

JAMES SHILTS BOSTER is a cognitive anthropologist concerned with how people understand their natural environment and the consequences of that understanding for their adaptation. His research has been directed toward demonstrating simple ideas: that cultural concerns determine how closely people pay attention to natural things while natural structure determines what will be seen, that the degree of correspondence between folk and scientific systems of biological classification reflects the evolutionary history of the organisms classified, that cultivators select cultivars for their perceptual distinctiveness and thereby change the world in the process of understanding it, and that the limitations of human reason may have adaptive significance.

MICHAEL F. BROWN is assistant professor of anthropology at Williams College in Williamstown, Mass. He is the author of *Una Paz Incierta,* an ethnographic study of the Aguaruna of the Alto Rio Mayo, Peru, as well as several articles on ethnobotany and magic.

DON BURGESS received his B.A. and M.A. in history at Texas Western College (now the University of Texas, El Paso). He undertook graduate studies in linguistics at the University of Oklahoma and has taught Tarahumara ethnology and field linguistics at the University of Texas, El Paso. His interest in the Tarahumara area began about twenty-six years ago when he visited the area with his father, who was writing feature articles for several U.S. newspapers on the construction of the Chihuahua al Pacifico Railroad, which passes through the Tarahumara homeland. Two years later he spent a summer working on the construction, helping to build tunnels and bridges for the railroad. His study of the Tarahumara language and culture began about twenty years ago, and it has been his major concern since then. He has worked with the Tarahumaras in helping them prepare for themselves books concerning their foods, sports, and folklore. He has also translated parts of the Bible.

BENJAMIN N. COLBY is professor of anthropology in the Social Relations Group of the School of Social Sciences, University of California, Irvine. He has done fieldwork with the Ixil Maya of Guatemala and is currently doing an ethnographic study in Japan.

ROY G. D'ANDRADE is professor of anthropology at the University of California, San Diego. He received a B.A. from the University of Connecticut in 1953 and a Ph.D. in social relations from Harvard University in 1957. He has previously taught at Stanford University and Rutgers University, and has been a Fellow of the Center for Advanced Study in the Behavioral Sciences. His principal research interests concern American culture and cognitive anthropology.

JANET W. D. DOUGHERTY is associate professor of anthropology at the University of Illinois, Urbana-Champaign, and was an associate editor (1979-84) for the *American Ethnologist.* She completed her Ph.D. at the University of California, Berkeley, with a thesis in cognitive anthropology which resulted from field research on West Futuna, Vanuatu (Oceania). Before coming to the University of Illinois, Dougherty was a postdoctoral fellow in linguistics at the Massachusetts Institute of Technology. In 1981 Dougherty organized a symposium for the national meeting of the American Anthropological Association entitled "Renewing the New Ethnography." The present volume grew out of this session.

JOHN B. GATEWOOD received his Ph.D. in social anthropology from the University of Illinois, Urbana-Champaign, in 1978. He is currently assistant professor of anthropology in the Department of Social Relations at Lehigh University. The paper included in this volume is based upon his doctoral research, which included working for three seasons as a paid crew member on Alaskan salmon seine boats.

JERRY R. HOBBS received his Ph.D. degree in computer science from New York University in 1974. He has taught at Yale University and the City University of New York, and has been a researcher at SRI International since 1977. He has done research in a wide variety of areas in natural language processing and discourse analysis, especially on the coherence of texts, co-reference resolution, planning models for conversation, metaphor interpretation, and methods for the analysis of ethnographic interviews.

DOROTHY C. HOLLAND, who received her Ph.D. from the University of California, Irvine, in 1974, is associate professor of anthropology at the University of North Carolina, Chapel Hill. Her primary areas of interest are culture and social cognition, cultural transmission, and the anthropology of knowledge. She is currently conducting research on gender stereotypes, insults, and American folk models of "face." She plans to do similar research in Scandinavia, and is presently editing a volume with Naomi Quinn entitled *Cultural Models in Language and Thought.* Her other recent publications include "Samoan Folk Knowledge of Mental Disorders" and "Learning Gender from Peers."

EUGENE HUNN is professor of anthropology at the University of Washington, where he has taught since 1972. He has conducted ethnobiological research since 1976, and is currently involved as researcher and consultant for the Pinelands Folklife Project in the Pinelands Reserve, N.J. His interest in ethnobiology represents a fortuitous coincidence of professional interest in culture-as-knowledge and avocational obsession with natural history. Major publications include *Tzeltal Folk Zoology: The Classification of Discontinuities in Nature, Resource*

Managers: North American and Australian Hunter-Gatherers, edited with N. M. Williams, and *Birding in Seattle and King County*.

CHARLES M. KELLER is associate professor of anthropology at the University of Illinois, Urbana-Champaign. He received his Ph.D. from the University of California, Berkeley, in 1966, with a thesis resulting from archaeological fieldwork at Mantagu Cave, South Africa, a late Acheulian site. His current research focuses on folk technology and the organization of technological knowledge. He is a skilled blacksmith, and his current research approaches this activity from a phenomenological perspective.

WILLETT KEMPTON is a cognitive anthropologist with interests in category structure, folk theory, and cognitive variations. He is now applying these interests to American conceptions of home energy use. He received a B.A. in sociology and anthropology from the University of Virginia, and a Ph.D. in anthropology from the University of Texas, Austin. He has taught at Michigan State University and at the University of California, both Berkeley and Irvine campuses. He is currently research associate on the Family Energy Project at Michigan State University. Kempton has also worked as a commissioned automobile mechanic, and has written and maintained large software systems.

DAVID B. KRONENFELD received his Ph.D. in anthropology from Stanford in 1970. His dissertation on Fanti kinship was based on fieldwork in Ghana. He has conducted fieldwork in Oaxaca and parts of the United States as well. His current position is professor and chairman of the Department of Anthropology at the University of California, Riverside. His long-term research interests concern the nature of culturally shared cognitive systems, perhaps with special emphasis on the semantics of natural language.

F. K. LEHMAN (U Chit Hlaing) grew up in India and Burma, took a B.A. in mathematics in 1950, and a Ph.D. in anthropology and linguistics at Columbia University in 1959, with a dissertation on Indian culture history and the theory of cultural evolution. Since 1957 he has done extensive ethnographic research in Burma among Chin, Kayah, Shan, and Burmese, and in Thailand among Shan and Red Karen, as well as linguistic research in both countries on a variety of Tibeto-Burman and Tai languages. He is the author of monographs on both Chin and Red Karen societies, and numerous papers on the societies, cultures, languages, and histories of mainland Southeast Asia and on theory in sociocultural anthropology. He is professor of anthropology and of linguistics at the University of Illinois, Urbana-Champaign, where he also teaches Thai and Burmese languages. He has for some years been permanent chairman of the Burma Studies Group of the Southeast Asia Council, Association for Asian Studies. He studied Southeast Asian anthropology under Heine-Geldern in the late 1940s, in New York, and Burmese history and philology under the tutelage of Gordon Luce, in Rangoon.

ROBERT E. MACLAURY is a doctoral candidate in anthropology at the University of California, Berkeley. He is completing his dissertation on the color categorization of Mesoamerican Indians, the result of a three-year survey that he administered with the aid of 80 collaborators among 120 indigenous languages and dialects of Mexico and Central America. He conducted earlier fieldwork in the linguistics and semantics of Zapotec toward his M.A. degree at the University of the Americas in Mexico City. His dissertation title is "Color Categorization in Mesoamerica."

NAOMI QUINN received her Ph.D. in anthropology from Stanford University in 1971. She is now associate professor of anthropology at Duke University. She studies the role of culture in the ongoing understanding of experience. Her paper in this volume is part of a larger project on the American cultural model of marriage, investigated through the analysis of metaphor, reasoning, and other features of discourse about marriage. This research will be fully reported in a forthcoming book, *American Marriage: A Cultural Analysis.*

ROBERT A. RANDALL is assistant professor of anthropology at the University of Houston, University Park. His primary academic interests include economic language and cognition, ethnographic methods, Southeast Asia, and comparative social organization. He holds a B.S. in mathematics from Bucknell University, an M.A. in anthropology from SUNY Binghamton, and a Ph.D. in anthropology from the University of California, Berkeley. His most recent publications focus on bilingualism, blast fishing, address terminology, and folk biology.

JAMES STANLAW is a Ph.D. candidate in anthropological linguistics at the University of Illinois, Urbana-Champaign. He has conducted fieldwork in Japan and Indonesia, most recently focusing on the use of English in Japan. His research interests include cognitive anthropology, symbolism, and sociolinguistics.

PENNY VAN ESTERIK, currently on the anthropology faculty at York University, Ontario, received her degrees in anthropology from the University of Toronto and the University of Illinois, Urbana-Champaign. Her Ban Chiang research was published by Ohio University Press in 1981 as a monograph in the Southeast Asia Series. In addition to past fieldwork on Thai symbolism and religion, she has recently worked on an interdisciplinary team studying infant feeding practices in developing countries (Thailand, Indonesia, Kenya, and Colombia). Current research interests include nutritional anthropology and advocacy research.

OSWALD WERNER received his Ph.D. in anthropology in 1963, and is currently a professor at Northwestern University with a joint appointment in anthropology and linguistics. He has been a major contributor in the field of cognitive anthropology for the past fifteen years. In 1969 he published a paper outlining "The Basic Assumptions of Ethnoscience," which appeared in *Semiotica* 1:329-38. One of his most recent publications, co-authored with A. Manning, is entitled "Tough Luck Ethnography versus God's Truth Ethnography in Ethnoscience," which appears in *Essays in Humanistic Anthropology: A Festschrift in Honor of David Bidney* (University Press of America, 1979). His continuing interests include ethnoscience, linguistic anthropology, medical communication, and Native American Indians with particular emphasis on the Navajo.

STAN WILMOTH, a doctoral candidate in anthropology at the University of California, Riverside, is currently completing his fieldwork in Montana among the Blackfoot people. His research interests at the moment focus on social processes, including conflict and conflict resolution.

GEOFFREY M. WHITE is a research associate on the staff of the East-West Center and an affiliate member of the Department of Anthropology at the University of Hawaii. He received his Ph.D. in anthropology from the University of California, San Diego, in 1978. His research interests focus upon cultural understandings of persons, social experience, and interaction. He has done field research in the Solomon Islands on the cultural construction of social identity and change. More recently he has been doing research on social perception and interaction in clinical or therapeutic settings. In addition to numerous articles based on his work in the Solomon Islands and other projects at the East-West Center, White has edited two recent books: *Cultural Conceptions of Mental Health and Therapy* with Anthony Marsella (Reidel, 1982) and *Person, Self, and Experience: Exploring Pacific Ethnopsychologies* with John Kirkpatrick (University of California Press, 1984).

BENCHA YODDUMNERN is research associate and assistant professor at the Institute for Population and Social Research, Mahidol University, Bangkok, Thailand. Specializing in medical anthropology, she has published on the role of Thai traditional doctors, beliefs and food habits of northern Thai people, Thai primary health care, and the premarital use of family planning in a Thai-Lao village, central Thailand. She currently is completing her doctoral dissertation in anthropology at the University of Illinois, Urbana-Champaign. Her doctoral fieldwork, conducted in northern Thailand, focuses on the effects of northern Thai social and family structure on the fertility behavior of women. Playing a key role in her analysis is the function of matrilineality and associated spirit cults in determining residence, inheritance, and the sex preference of children by northern Thai parents.

Index